Frederick G. Whelan was educated at
Harvard and Cambridge. He is associate
professor of political science at the
University of Pittsburgh and author of
*Order and Artifice in Hume's Political
Philosophy* and of numerous articles in
political theory and the history of
political thought.

EDMUND BURKE
AND INDIA

PITT SERIES IN
POLICY AND INSTITUTIONAL
STUDIES

Edmund Burke
and India

POLITICAL MORALITY
AND EMPIRE

Frederick G. Whelan

University of Pittsburgh Press

Frontispiece: "The Right Hon. Edmund Burke," by John Jones, after George Romney, 1790. By permission of the Yale Center for British Art, Paul Mellon Collection.

Published by the University of Pittsburgh Press, Pittsburgh, Pa., 15260
Copyright © 1996, University of Pittsburgh Press

Library of Congress Cataloging-in-Publication Data
Whelan, Frederick G., 1947–
Edmund Burke and India : Political morality and empire / Frederick G. Whelan.
p. cm.
Includes bibliographical references and index.
ISBN 0-8229-3927-4 (cloth : alk. paper)
1. India—Politics and government—1765–1947.   2. Political ethics—India.
3. Burke, Edmund, 1729–1797—Views on India.   4. Burke, Edmund, 1729–1797—
Views on political ethics.   5. Great Britain—Colonies—South Asia—Administration—
History.   I. Title.
JQ224.W48   1996
325'.3141'095409033—dc20   95-45590

A CIP catalogue record for this book is available from
the British Library.

Eurospan, London

CONTENTS

CONTENTS

ILLUSTRATIONS

PREFACE

This book was written in Pittsburgh, Pennsylvania, during the years 1990–1995. It is intended primarily to be a contribution to the interpretation of the political thought of Edmund Burke, and hence to the field of political theory, which it has been my vocation to study and teach for the past two decades.

I have focused primarily on the analysis of the ideas and arguments expressed in Burke's texts, as is appropriate in the study of a major political thinker. Making sense of the hitherto neglected Indian component of Burke's writings and speeches, however, requires some familiarity with the development of the British Empire in India during Burke's lifetime, and I have tried to sketch the necessary background, bearing in mind that many of the basic facts and their construction—not to mention a moral assessment of them—were matters of great controversy even at the time. Burke's engagement in these controversies, both as a responsible statesman and as a profound thinker, provided the occasions for the texts and ideas that are analyzed here.

Contemplating events in eighteenth-century India, and the judgments made upon them by a politician in London, from the vantage point of a university in Pittsburgh is not quite as disconnected as it may seem. A few miles from where I write, on November 25, 1758, a small British army under General John Forbes and Colonel George Washington took Fort Duquesne from the French, reconstructed it as Fort Pitt in honor of the British prime minister, and thus not only founded Pittsburgh but—in conjunction with the British victory in Canada—assured English control of the Ohio region. A little over a year earlier, on June 23, 1757, another small British military force under Colonel Robert Clive had defeated the army of Siraj al-Daula, the nawab of Bengal, who was assisted by the French, at Plassey, thus giving the English East India Company effective control of Bengal and a dominant position in India. Both these momentous events were distant repercussions of the Seven Years' War in Europe, in which Great Britain joined Frederick the Great of Prussia against France, and of the long-standing Anglo-French commercial and colonial rivalry. Pittsburgh and Bengal marked two far-flung possessions of the first great British Empire, which was soon to pose serious problems of governance to British statesmen. Prominent among those who took an active and conscientious interest in these problems was Edmund Burke, who entered Parliament in 1765. Ten years later Pennsylvania and the other American colonies were in rebellion, and Warren Hastings was governor-general of Bengal, energetically consolidating and expanding British rule in India. Burke unsuccessfully urged conciliation with the Americans; even more insistently, he condemned oppression and corruption and urged just rule in India. It is this latter campaign, in relation to Burke's general political thought, that this book addresses.

Research for this book was carried out entirely through the facilities provided by the department of political science and Hillman Library of the University of Pittsburgh. A brief visit to Madras in 1990 as a participant in the university's Semester at Sea program provided a glimpse of Fort St. George, where Warren Hastings once served, and inspiration for the project. A portion of chapter 1 was presented at the 1992 meeting of the American Political Science Association. Wendy Mann created the map of eighteenth-century India. I am grateful to Elsie Fried, Michael Mosher, Bill Scheuerman, Jeff Spinner, Richard Tobias, and Andrew Valls for reading and commenting on all or part of the manuscript, to David Whelan for assistance in proofreading, and to Barry Shields for good questions and encouragement.

I regret that my parents did not live to see the appearance of this book, and thus that its dedication to them must take the form of a memorial.

NOTE ON SPELLING

Both eighteenth-century and modern systems of spelling or trans-
literating Indian names are variable. When quoting Burke and Hastings I
have retained their orthography; in my own text I have followed the modern
(and relatively familiar) system used by the editors of *The Writings and
Speeches of Edmund Burke* (Oxford: Oxford University Press, 1981–). Thus, I
prefer "Mogul" to "Mughal," "Oudh" to "Awadh," "Benares" to "Varanasi,"
and "Poona" to "Pune," for example.

Most alternative spellings are readily recognizable as such. A few common examples:

Burke	*Modern*
nabob	nawab
vizier	wazir
banyan	banian
Mahrattas	Marathas
Oude	Oudh
Fyzabad	Faizabad
Surajah Dowlah	Siraj al-Daula
Sujah Dowlah	Shuja al-Daula
Cheyt Sing	Chait Singh
Hyder Ali	Haidar Ali
Asoph ul Dowlah	Asaf al-Daula
Munny Begum	Munni Begam
Nundcomar	Nandakumar

xiii

Kabul

AFGHANS

Ganges River

ROHILKHAND

Delhi

OUDH

Kora ■Lucknow
Faizabad

Gwalior BIHAR

SINDHIA Allahabad Benares Buxar

Murshidabad
BENGAL

MARATHA CONFEDERACY
BERAR Plassey

Calcutta

ASSAM

BAY OF
BENGAL

NIZAM

Bombay ■Poona
Hyderabad

MYSORE CARNATIC
Madras

Arcot

INDIA IN THE
1770s–1780s

TANJORE

EDMUND BURKE
AND INDIA

Introduction

At the end of Edmund Burke's *Reflections on the Revolution in France*, the work for which he is best known, he asserted that his opinions on the Revolution should be seen as coming from someone "almost the whole of whose public exertion has been a struggle for the liberty of others," from someone whose anger was aroused by "what he considered as tyranny," and who had snatched a few hours from his endeavors to "discredit opulent oppression" (*Reflections*, 376).[1] Any contemporary reader familiar with Burke or British politics would have recognized in these comments an allusion to the major political cause in which Burke had been engaged for some years: the impeachment of Warren Hastings, former governor-general of Bengal, and more broadly, the campaign to expose corruption and oppression in Great Britain's recently acquired Indian empire. Similarly, in a valedictory defense of his career, Burke said that if he deserved any reward, it was for his fourteen years' labor on the affairs of India: "They are those on which I value myself the most; most for the importance; most for the labour; most for the judgment; most for the constancy and perseverance in the pursuit" (*Noble Lord*, 295).

It is odd, in light of his own assessment, that Burke's ideas concerning India have been relatively ignored by students of his political thought. This book aims to redress that neglect, to present as systematically as possible the Indian component of his thought, and so contribute to a more balanced and complete interpretation of his political theory as a whole. The subject of India led Burke to analyze and reflect on a large number of topics, including the nature and purposes of empire; the history, culture, and society of India;

the workings of corruption and corrupt political organizations; the pernicious influence of imperial power and wealth on British domestic politics and the constitution; the nature of despotic or arbitrary methods of rule; and the claim that government in Asia was traditionally and inescapably despotic. India provided occasions for Burke to reassert principles that he upheld in other contexts as well: the rule of law, the desirability of constitutional checks on power, the conception of government as a trust for the welfare of the governed, and the need for rulers and officials who were properly motivated by an appreciation of their duties under this conception. Burke's arguments about India offer important evidence bearing on large themes in his political theory, such as his claim to seek an appropriate balance between "reformation" and "conservation," his respect for tradition, and his adherence to natural law or natural justice. Above all, Burke appears in his Indian writings as a political moralist, a practicing politician and political thinker, who, like his contemporary Kant, insisted on the requirement of moral standards and constraints in public affairs in the face of empire, revolution, power politics, and Machiavellianism.[2] Although Burke's thought is the subject of this book, the views of Hastings, his principal opponent, will be given their due: Hastings was an empire builder and a successful practitioner of *raison d'état*, and in the dramatic antagonism between these two men we may see and appraise a confrontation between the principles of political moralism and those of political realism.

As a member of the House of Commons from 1765 to 1794, Burke was a strategist and leading parliamentary orator of the Whig party, under the leadership first of the marquess of Rockingham and later of Charles James Fox. Burke's party was usually in opposition to the ministries of the day and in an adversarial relation to King George III. Burke was a party politician who espoused a larger conception of public-spirited statesmanship. As such he was directly involved with many of the great public issues of the period and commented influentially on them in speeches and pamphlets. He defended party government and ministerial responsibility to Parliament, while decrying undue royal influence, all within the framework of Britain's balanced constitution. He upheld the traditional structure of the House of Commons and its deliberative function against demands for a more extensive franchise and more equal and direct representation, and he supported the established position of the Church of England against the complaints of Dissenters. At the same time, he pleaded for the removal of the civil disabilities imposed by the Protestant elite on the Roman Catholic majority in Ireland, while endorsing the imperial connection between Great Britain and his native country. As discontents developed in the American colonies, Burke argued eloquently for a policy of conciliation and local self-government within a remodeled empire, opposing the doctrinaire intransigence of Lord North's administration. From 1790 onward, Burke was a conspicuously early and vociferous opponent of the French Revolution, with its ideology of popular sovereignty and the "rights of man," and he supported militant measures to prevent its spread.

Among all his various public commitments, however, it was to India that Burke devoted the greatest time and effort. Through the East India Company, the British had moved beyond mere commerce and had acquired the beginnings of a territorial empire in India just before Burke began his political career, and thereafter, questions about the administration of this new dominion were recurrently on the parliamentary agenda. Burke's deep engagement with India began with his service on a parliamentary select committee in 1781–1782. The investigations of that committee convinced him of the existence of grave abuses. In 1783, with his party briefly in office, Burke supported a major Indian reform bill offered by Fox; the defeat of this measure, followed by Pitt's victory in a general election, pointed to the corrupt influence of ill-gotten Indian wealth and hence to a threat posed by the empire to politics and the sense of justice in England. From 1786 until 1794 Burke's major effort was the prosecution of Hastings, whom Burke believed to be personally guilty of serious offenses, and the personification of the general corruption of the East India Company's regime. Contrary to expectations, Burke and his colleagues carried the impeachment of Hastings in the House of Commons. The opening of his trial before the House of Lords in 1788, immortalized in T. B. Macaulay's description, was a highly dramatic event that surely focused public attention on the problems of governing an Indian empire in a just manner, even though Hastings was ultimately acquitted seven years later.

The political wisdom of the long prosecution of Hastings has been questioned. Other leading Whigs no doubt undertook it in a partisan spirit, as an attempt to embarrass the Pitt government, and were willing to abandon it when it ceased to serve this purpose. Since Burke is a favorite subject for psychological speculation, some have seen his determination to carry it through to the bitter end as obsessive.

While we do not deny that Burke became preoccupied and even emotionally involved with this cause—as, simultaneously, with the danger posed by the French Revolution—to a greater degree than his colleagues, it does not seem necessary to impute subconscious motives. In the first place, it was not unreasonable for Burke to believe that the prosecution would serve useful purposes—airing abuses, influencing public opinion, deterring future misconduct by imperial officials—quite apart from the prospects of an actual conviction of Hastings. Second, the protracted prosecution of this cause can be taken as an example of Burke's fundamental political moralism. "The punishment of real tyrants," he proclaimed, "is a noble and awful act of justice; and it has with truth been said to be consolatory to the human mind" (*Reflections*, 178). In writing these words Burke was trying to exonerate the falsely accused Louis XVI, but at the same time he remained persuaded that Hastings was a real tyrant, and that his crimes demanded an appropriate response on the part of those with final responsibility for British affairs. "Justice is grave and decorous, and in its punishments rather seems to submit to a necessity, than to make a choice" (*Reflections*, 178). Finally and more generally, Burke saw his involvement with India as a matter of discharging the duty that all rulers have toward those under their authority, colonial subjects as well as fellow countrymen. "What but some irresistible Sense of Duty," he asked, could have induced him to pursue so "unthankful" a task (*Corr.* 7:116)? Parliament's duty toward the Indian empire, moreover, was of an especially challenging nature. "My Lords," Burke told Hastings's judges, "to obtain empire is common; to govern it well has been rare indeed. To chastise the guilt of those who have been instruments of imperial sway over other nations by the high superintending justice of the sovereign state has not many striking examples among any people" ("Speech in Opening," 9:398).

Burke insisted repeatedly that just and beneficial rule for Indians had to be the standard for Britain's empire; he was also determined that British rule should offer an exception to the familiar historical pattern by which imperial states were corrupted into tyrannies by their power and greed. "We have been confounded with the herd of conquerors. Our dominion has been a vulgar thing. But we begin to emerge; and I hope that a severe inspection of ourselves . . . is a glory reserved to this time, to this nation, and to this august tribunal" ("Speech in Opening," 9:398). Ireland was not an encouraging example for Burke's hopes, nor was Britain's policy toward its American colonies, and the first ventures of Englishmen governing India presaged even worse. Imperial success and imperial justice went together in the long run, in Burke's view, and he worked hard to overturn opposing attitudes in all three cases, but especially with respect to India. Largely as a result of his efforts, India consumed more parliamentary time (and certainly more of his own) than any other issue in the 1780s;[3] his speeches and writings on India make up about a third of Burke's total works (apart from his letters). At the very end of his long campaign, expecting failure (acquittal) in the immediate sense, Burke nevertheless affirmed in characteristic fashion the historical significance of such a quest for justice and the meaning it would have for "a recording, retrospective, civilized posterity" ("Speech in Reply," 12:395).

The general significance of the fact that such a distinguished political thinker as Burke took up the cause of India may be assessed from three different angles. First, Burke was one of the first major European thinkers, and one of the few writers in the traditional canon of Western political theory, to have made a serious effort to understand a non-Western civilization and to incorporate his findings into his general political thought. Montesquieu preceded him in this, but Montesquieu concluded that despotic government was standard for all major Asian nations, an influential thesis that Burke sought to refute. After laborious study of the imperfect materials available to him, and assisted no doubt by his well-known historical imagination, Burke arrived at a view of India as a venerable and well-ordered society, with distinctive religions and customs, which was worthy of respect, even admiration, not to mention just and lawful rule. "This multitude of men does not consist of an abject and barbarous populace; much less gangs of savages . . . but a people for ages civilized and cultivated; cultivated by all the arts of polished life, whilst we were yet in the woods" (*Fox's Bill*, 389). While acknowledging the reality (and legitimacy) of certain obvious cultural differences from Europe, Burke was more concerned to argue that, at a deeper level, Indians possessed conceptions of law, justice, honor, property, religion, and familial virtue that were perfectly comprehensible and essentially similar to those accepted in the West, and that were entitled to respectful treatment by the English rulers of India.

In taking India seriously, Burke was at the same time one of the first major Western thinkers to grapple with the moral and political problems of European empire over non-Western nations. In considering his views on empire, we need to avoid anachronistic considerations, or at any rate to appraise Burke's outlook with sensitivity to its historical context. The concept or ideology of global "imperialism" as a political program bound up with the rivalry among the great powers in Europe had not been very clearly articulated in Burke's time, though the commercial and colonial contention between Great Britain and France that produced the British Indian empire anticipated later attitudes. If the idea of imperialism was not current, neither was a general critique of imperialism resting on the idea of a right of self-determination for all nations. The related democratic doctrine of popular sovereignty, to be sure, was being asserted by English radicals and the French revolutionaries, but Burke rejected this idea as a general principle of legitimate government, even in Europe, or as a natural right. Burke regarded political liberty in the sense of representative institutions as a valuable part of the political traditions of some countries, such as England, but he did not insist on it universally, and he did not fundamentally call into question the propriety of rule by foreigners—the rule of Englishmen over Indians—so long as their title was sound and their government just and beneficial.

Furthermore, the profound conviction of European cultural superiority to India and the rest of the non-Western world, sometimes grounded in racial distinctions, took root among European thinkers and colonial officials only in the nineteenth century, when it led to an idea of the imperial mission as deliberately modernizing or civilizing backward societies.[4] East India Company officials in the eighteenth century knew that the power they had acquired was based on their superiority to Indian rulers in some respects, especially their military discipline, technology, and organizational efficiency; but they seem to have had a certain respect for the existing Indian states and in some cases, genuine appreciation for Asian culture. Neither Burke nor his opponents, including Hastings, ever imagined—as the generations of Macaulay and John Stuart Mill were later to do—that British policy should systematically aim to transform Indian customs and society in a progressive direction.[5] Rather, Burke and Hastings agreed that India had to be governed in accordance with its own cultural norms and political practices, though they disagreed on what these were. Imperial rule, like all rule, was properly understood as a trust for the welfare of the governed, bound to observe the principles of political morality and justice and to apply them prudentially to particular local circumstances; the central theme of Burke's famous speech on Fox's East India Bill, as in many of his works, was "the awful duty which attaches to all power."[6]

Burke's insistence on the quality of imperial rule, however, still leaves a lingering question: why empire at all? If Indian civilization was sound, its traditions admirable and stable, what justified the entry of the British as rulers? What was their role to be? To modern ears, these very questions imply that foreign rule is prima facie illegitimate and therefore in need of special justification. Since Burke did not accept the doctrine of national sovereignty that underlies this assumption, he did not address these questions directly, but he did suggest some answers. The British had stumbled into a position of authority over parts of India, he implied, by chance or fate, through an unplanned sequence of remarkable events, and they were usually replacing previous regimes of recent and violent origin. Sometimes he suggested, without elaborating the point, that these events simply had to be accepted as providential. Although many people in England questioned the wisdom of acquiring territorial sovereignty in India, and most leading political figures in the 1770s and 1780s opposed any expansion of British rule there, it seemed to Burke and others that there was no preferable alternative to the position they had attained; withdrawal would simply open the way to renewed French incursions, or to political disorder that would jeopardize legitimate British commercial interests and the welfare of ordinary Indians. The best course of action had to be worked out within the constraints of the given circumstances. Besides, although the East India Company's regime had quickly become corrupt and abusive, its title to rule in Bengal was sound, arising as it did from a combination of conquest in justifiable wars and formal grants of authority from the Mogul emperor, the nominal suzerain. Burke referred to the series of tumultuous events that created the empire as "revolutions," but he saw them as acceptable, given the background of turmoil and political disintegration in Indian government. The very fact that a small number of British, from their commercial outposts, had been able to acquire such power over large parts of the subcontinent indicated defects in the local systems of government. We shall suggest that, although Burke admired the traditional social and moral life of India, he was willing to concede that Indian political institutions exhibited serious shortcomings, at least in recent times, and that British rule—suitably reformed— offered the possibility of a more securely institutionalized system of lawful government.

Second, Burke is usually portrayed as a conservative social and political theorist, a view that derives primarily from his attack on the French Revolution, and the Indian component of his thought has a dual bearing on this interpretation. On the one hand, Burke's favorable construction of Indian customs and history seems to confirm the normative traditionalism that is apparent elsewhere in his work, especially in the *Reflections*, and his approving account of the traditional Indian social structure, with its stable system of ranks and property, seems to correspond to his defense of the existing European social order. He condemned Hastings and other avaricious company personnel for wantonly violating Indian customs and destroying the established order, much as he condemned the Jacobins for their reckless assault on the religious, political, and legal traditions of Europe; and he condemned them in the name of values and principles that were themselves, in his view, part of the received moral heritage. On the other hand, Burke's stance toward India and the East India Company from the time he became deeply involved in Indian affairs was consistently that of a reformer—if, as seems plausible, his prosecution of Hastings was partly motivated by a desire to perpetuate reform by deterring future abuses in the imperial administration. This reminds us that Burke sought to distinguish reform from revolution, that he proposed a model of appropriate and prudential reform that was consistent with preserving what was valuable in tradition, and indeed, that he did not always oppose even revolution, or relatively radical reforms, when he concluded that they were necessitated by circumstances. Burke's willingness to override the "chartered rights" and vested interests of the East India Company, and his support for transferring authority over India from the company to Parliament, were not conservative positions. This fact further reminds us that on many issues in his political career—including the affairs of Ireland and America as well as India—Burke was known as an outspoken proponent of reform in the name of justice or policy. Giving India its due weight in the interpretation of Burke's political thought contributes to the development of a more balanced view, which at any rate avoids overly simplistic notions of conservatism.

Finally, Burke is often portrayed as an outsider of humble origin who identified himself with the British aristocracy, made his political career under the patronage of Whig notables, and spoke eloquently on behalf of a constitution and social order in which the landed gentry played a prominent role. It was this Burke, it is said, who reacted against the revolutionary challenge to the privileged orders, and, one might add, who came to the defense of the traditional landed aristocracies of Bengal and Oudh against the depredation of East India Company fortune seekers.[7] It would be difficult to dismiss this view completely, but Burke was a complex individual, and it is quite possible to see the guiding threads of his career and thought in a completely different light. Conor Cruise O'Brien, for example, presents Burke as a defender of the oppressed and an opponent of power when wielded arbitrarily and selfishly, especially by ambitious or corrupt elites in a position to exploit subordinate and vulnerable groups.[8] If Burke upheld the position of the great political families of England, it was because he believed that this class, or its better representatives, possessed the characteristics of a true aristocracy, providing statesmanlike governance—at least for the people of Great Britain. In America, in Ireland, and above all in India, matters were different, and Burke was consistently opposed to established regimes and policies (and these three cases comprise by far the greater part of his work). This is the Burke who solemnly swore in the House of Commons, just before launching the impeachment, "that the wrongs done to humanity in the eastern world, shall be avenged on those who have inflicted them. . . . The wrath of Heaven would sooner or later fall upon a nation, that suffers, with impunity, its rulers thus to oppress the weak and innocent" ("Almas Ali Khan," 477). Regarding France as well, Burke's early opposition to the Revolution appears to have been precipitated less by solicitude for the monarchy and nobility than by horror at the attack on the Church in the autumn of 1789, including the confiscation—or as he saw it, the pillage—of Church property by the unscrupulous and self-serving group that had seized power in Paris. Central to his critique of the Revolution was his perception that the claim of the revolutionaries to rule by the will of the people—like any claim to rule willfully, and hence unrestrained by reason or justice—was a prescription for tyranny over those outside the dominant faction.

This interpretation of Burke corresponds to his own view of his career as he reflected on it toward the end, when it seemed to him he had continually been fighting, and with only limited success, against powerful oppressors and oppressive interests. Among his opponents were George III, whose intrigues had threatened British liberty, and Lord North, whose dogmatism had led to the disastrous American policy. As villains, however, these figures paled in comparison to three more insidious and more persistent enemies: the Anglo-Irish Ascendancy, which used the commanding position it had captured in the previous century to monopolize power and privilege and, under pretext of a religious danger, to suppress and impoverish the majority of the Irish population; the East Indian oppressors, who wielded their arbitrary power to extort wealth from the natives of India, which they then used to buy political influence in Great Britain so as to perpetuate the whole corrupt system; and the Jacobins, a strange coalition of militantly irreligious intellectuals and unprincipled adventurers who were prepared to exert power ruthlessly in pursuit of their objectives.

O'Brien argues in particular that the causes of the oppressed in Ireland and India came to be fused in Burke's mind.[9] Regina Janes has explored parallels in Burke's treatment of India and France and has argued that Burke's previous involvement with India explains his quick denunciation of what struck him as similar patterns in the French Revolution.[10] Burke himself explicitly associated all three campaigns. To an Irish correspondent he wrote, just after Hastings's acquittal, that he could "hardly over-rate the malignity of the principles of Protest and ascendancy, as they affect Ireland; or of Indianism, as they affect these Countries, and as they affect Asia; or of Jacobinism, as they affect all Europe, and the state of human society itself" ("Second Letter to Langrishe," 667). Of these, he said, Jacobinism was the worst, presumably because of the extent, persistence, and strength of its threat. In subsequent letters, he continued to condemn Indianism and Jacobinism as related evils until the end of his career (*Corr.* 7:553). Once (after Hastings was granted a pension by the company) he even ranked Indian corruption as the paramount evil—"the worst by far, and the hardest to deal with" (*Corr.* 8:432).

Several similarities led Burke to associate these three enemies. First, all three involved the blatant use, by narrow interests, of political power for personal enrichment through the victimization of powerless or defeated groups. Nothing could be further removed from Burke's normative conception of government as a trust to be exercised on behalf of the governed and of the public good. Ireland's distress was due not to the imperial connection with England, but to the local Protestant political elite's control of all "places" in the country;[11] in India a company of merchants, having fortuitously acquired political sovereignty over Bengal, simply continued its quest for profits by the new means at its disposal; and the French Revolution financed itself and enriched its supporters by confiscating the wealth of its opponents. Second, Burke analyzed all three targets, especially the Indian empire and revolutionary France, as corrupt political machines, that is, as organized conspiracies that converted some of their extorted wealth into continued political power so as to be self-perpetuating. Indianism as it affected Great Britain meant the growing influence of East Indian wealth in British elections and of the East Indian interest in Parliament itself; the French revolutionaries had ensured the complicity of many in the Revolution by distributing nobles' estates and basing a new paper currency on the confiscated Church lands. All three of Burke's opponents threatened the principles of constitutional government that Burke thought had been achieved in Great Britain, the Ascendancy and Indianism through habits of corruption, Jacobinism through the spread of its ideology to English radicals, all three through their willingness to employ arbitrary power. Just as Burke alluded several times in his *Reflections* to the concurrent prosecution of Hastings, so he concluded the trial with a reference to the ongoing "moral earthquake" in France and the threat it posed both to stable government in England and to traditional ideas of justice ("Speech in Reply," 12:395). Third, Burke detected enthusiasm for the French Revolution among the returned East Indian "nabobs" and their friends, which led him to postulate a common motivational basis for Indianism and Jacobinism: not only had the Indian officials acquired sudden fortunes by questionable means; they then, like the "monied people" and "speculators" in France, could not "bear to find that their present [social and political] importance does not bear a proportion to their wealth" ("French Affairs," 212). Burke's famous characterization of Jacobinism as "the revolt of the enterprising talents of a country against it's property" (*Regicide Peace 1*, 241) would seem in part to capture his view of Indianism as well—capable adventurers plundering the property of India and then trying to displace the established propertied class of England.

One important dissimilarity between Burke's analyses of the French Revolution and East Indian oppression, however, concerns the role of theory or ideology in politics. Burke is sometimes said to have been drawn to conspiracy theories of political disorder,[12] and he certainly saw the East Indian interest, both in India and in England, as an organized group intent on maintaining its lucrative prerogatives. The conspiracy or "cabal" that Burke held responsible for the French Revolution, however, notoriously included "political Men of Letters," radical intellectuals or ideologues whose outlook combined militant atheism or anticlericalism, a distorted doctrine of natural rights, and a determination to remodel French society and government according to an abstract or "geometrical" plan (*Reflections*, 211, 262). No such tendencies were apparent in the case of Hastings and the other villains of India, however, in keeping with Burke's statement that he knew of no such party in England (*Reflections*, 185): they were merchants, not intellectuals, political pragmatists or realists, not ideologues, and they exhibited no particular hostility toward religion. Their disruptions of India were motivated by simple avarice rather than any abstract or revolutionary plan to transform native society. Even the imperial designs transcending avarice that could be attributed to Hastings seemed to flow from a straightforward and atheoretical love of power and conquest. Like the revolutionaries-to-be in France, East Indian servants sometimes aspired to join their nation's political elite on the basis of their ability and new wealth; unlike them, they could not be said to have nourished unrealistically radical ideas as a result of their lack of experience of practical affairs. If, for Burke, Jacobinism meant a fanatical tyranny, Indianism meant merely a corrupt tyranny. Hence one important and well-known theme in Burke's political thought, his critique of political rationalism and his analysis of the threat posed to traditional social orders by the intelligentsia, is largely absent from the Indian component of his theory.[13]

As we consider the many charges Burke brought against the rulers of the British Empire in India, readers may well wonder whether he was right in his assessment of the situation and of his opponents, and, conversely, whether Hastings and his East India Company colleagues were guilty as charged. This is a very complex question, and a judicious answer would have to be measured and qualified in many ways. This book is a study of Burke's political thought, and it offers no original research on the actual history of the British in India; its assumption is that Burke's political analysis of the empire, and the reasoning that led to his normative judgments, given the facts as he understood them, are of great interest from the point of view of political theory, whether or not he was always correct about the facts—

which he probably was not, despite his conscientious efforts to learn. A sketch of the subsequent historiography of the issues, and of the reputations of the main antagonists, may be helpful here.

Although Burke failed to achieve a conviction, he succeeded in disgracing Hastings and the company's regime in the eyes of many of the British public. Although Hastings was briefly and partially rehabilitated before he died, the Burkean view of the episode steadily gained ground. The first publication of Burke's collected works, including the impeachment speeches, coincided with the growth of a moralistic sense of imperial mission in the early nineteenth century. James Mill, for reformist reasons of his own, presented a Burke-like denunciation of the abuses and corruption of the Hastings era in his influential *History of British India*. More important, Macaulay offered a somewhat balanced but largely unfavorable picture of the governor-general in his 1841 essay "Warren Hastings," which elevated a largely Burkean view of India and Hastings into a high point of English literature—a status Victorian readers also accorded to Burke's speech on Fox's East India Bill. Burke's general reputation remained high among mid-nineteenth-century English liberals, who therefore tended to accept his verdict on Hastings and to assume that on the whole he had had a major positive impact on the quality of the empire.[14]

A revisionist view, however, was expressed by a series of writers (Fitzjames Stephen, John Strachey, Sophia Weitzman, M. E. Monckton Jones, Holden Furber, C. C. Davies, Lucy S. Sutherland, and Keith Feiling) in the late nineteenth and early twentieth centuries—not fortuitously, one assumes, the era of the most confident and assertive British imperialism, and a time when Burke's general reputation was in abeyance. Hastings was appreciated as a founder of the Indian empire, even a great imperial statesman, who had merely done what was necessary to negotiate successfully through a very dangerous period: that he had saved the Indian empire—while America was being lost—had been his own ultimate defense against his accusers. Fitzjames Stephen, writing in 1885, called him "the ablest Englishman of the eighteenth century."[15] Scholars of this school dismissed the idea that Hastings had been personally corrupt, and held that his occasional arbitrariness served honorable intentions pursuant to the responsibilities of his office. More important, detailed scholarly research into the historical record tended to vindicate Hastings's account of the difficulties and emergencies he had faced, and suggested that Burke had frequently presented an erroneous or distorted interpretation of many facts. Contemporary scholars, epitomized by P. J. Marshall, attuned both to the complexity of the situation and the changing standards of imperial conduct over time, offer a more balanced assessment, which on the whole is not unfavorable to Hastings.[16] A common view is that Burke was moved to action by "pure and noble motives"—a commitment to justice and sympathy for the oppressed—but was misinformed by Hastings's enemies; that his emotional involvement in his cause led him to exaggerate; and that he was unfair in holding Hastings personally responsible for the abuses that undoubtedly took place in India.[17]

It seems pointless to pass judgment on a simplistic "Burke vs. Hastings" question (as the House of Lords had to do in 1795, and as some writers have been inclined to do ever since). Their conflict was of epic proportions, grounded in fundamentally different moral stances toward political life that it seems best to exhibit for ongoing debate and reflection. As a study of Burke, this book naturally reflects the belief that there is much merit and much historical and analytical interest in Burke's views. However, to take Burke's political thought seriously, one must also take Hastings seriously as a worthy opponent. If Hastings had been simply a petty-minded, corrupt scoundrel—as Burke sometimes portrayed him—the entire episode and the issues of political theory that arise from it would be much less important.[18] Hastings was not a theorist, but he sufficiently indicated his views of events and justifications for his policies in letters, reports, and defense speeches. There is certainly something to Hastings's account of his governorship as "a most important and weighty Administration of Thirteen Years, comprehending perhaps a greater Variety of interesting Events than have fallen to the Lot of any Man now living."[19] Although Burke did not always acknowledge Hastings's positions, much less treat them as adding up to a compelling (if objectionable) political argument, we shall attempt to do so. Hastings followed the conventional opinion, reinforced by his own professional experience, that Asian societies and governments were traditionally despotic, and that an empire in Asia must therefore be ruled despotically; notwithstanding the prestige of Montesquieu, Burke attempted to refute this thesis and the practical conclusion Hastings drew from it. More generally, Hastings was a political realist who believed that the maintenance of an empire in adverse circumstances—threatened as it was by Britain's rivalry with France, hostile Indian powers, unreliable allies, recurrent wars, and inadequate finances—required concentrated and arbitrary authority and a willingness to use it as necessary. Although Burke supported the empire as potentially beneficial for all concerned, he held that imperial politics, like all politics, had to be constrained by principles of justice; he therefore openly proclaimed that if Great Britain could not "contrive some method of governing India *well*," a separation of the two countries—renunciation of empire—was in order (*Fox's Bill*, 383). This opposition between political morality and imperial realism is the central theme of this study.

In conclusion, let me say a few words about the approach I have taken in reading Burke. This study is undertaken with the conviction that Burke is a major political theorist, and that the significance and interest of his ideas transcend the role they played in their immediate historical setting. The desirability of airing his arguments about the Indian empire follows from the belief that Burke's political thought as a whole is worth ongoing study. It must be admitted, however, that Burke's place in the canon of political theory is controversial. His standing as a political thinker of the first rank has been challenged on three grounds, which will be briefly considered (and rejected) here.

One common charge is that Burke was inconsistent in the basic normative standards that underlie his particular arguments and judgments, sometimes invoking expediency and beneficial consequences, sometimes the sanctity of tradition and prescriptive rights, sometimes natural law, without ever systematically addressing potential conflicts among them. It seems arbitrary, however, to demote or dismiss an otherwise challenging thinker for this reason. One of the tasks of interpretative scholarship is to identify, clarify, and perhaps reconcile apparent contradictions in important bodies of writing; and indeed, when this task has been done we may be left with tensions, sometimes fruitful ones, even in the work of major figures. Throughout this book I compare arguments made by Burke with respect to Indian affairs to passages taken from his writings on other subjects; the assumption, which I hope is borne out in the execution, is that certain themes recur throughout many of Burke's writings, and that there are no major changes or inconsistencies of orientation between his thought on India and his thought on other matters. In particular, Burke's Indian and French involvements were temporally intertwined, since the Revolution occurred in the midst of the protracted impeachment proceedings against Hastings; this fact invites not only a comparison of his views on the two issues, but an inquiry into how his reactions to each event may have influenced his thinking on the other. On the deeper question of underlying values, an effort is made in the final chapter to show, not uncritically, how Burke's various standards might converge or be combined in practical judgments about complex political matters, in keeping with his own notion of political prudence. Although questions remain, a case is made that the supposed normative inconsistencies are not as deep or as damaging as some have held.

The charge of inconsistency, however, often merges with the two other lines of criticism. A second charge holds that Burke was not a philosopher, with the implication that his thought is neither systematic enough nor sufficiently grounded in first principles to count as political philosophy.[20] The premise may be granted; Burke not only criticized "metaphysical" or overly abstract reasoning in political life, but he himself showed little interest in formal philosophical doctrine.[21] This study, however, addresses Burke's political thought or political theory, and political theory can draw and has historically drawn upon a variety of disciplines other than formal philosophy, such as historiography, theology, law, and, as in Burke's case, active political practice and statesmanship. Furthermore, political theory can be expressed in a number of literary genres other than the philosophical treatise, including, for Burke, speeches, letters, polemical pamphlets, even legislative committee reports. Burke's political theory, it is often said, is ad hoc, expressed in reaction to particular political issues that arose in the course of his parliamentary career, and partisan, in that he was always arguing for one position or another on controversial matters.[22] His thoughts on India certainly exemplify this point, since they were expressed entirely pursuant to parliamentary business and especially the highly contentious prosecution of Hastings. Burke, however, is hardly unique in this. The major historical works of political theory were generated as often as not through the theorists' involvement with the political issues of their time, rather than in philosophical detachment. Political theory of lasting value is distinguished from more ephemeral opinion in that it rises above its immediate concerns to give particularly cogent expression to ideas and insights of continuing interest in the study of politics. Sophisticated analyses and substantial normative doctrines that involve fundamental principles can dignify occasional pieces. The exposition of Burke's thought in this book may help the reader decide whether Burke meets this test.

Finally, Burke is often viewed as a master rhetorician. His speeches and other texts, it might follow, should be interpreted as rhetorical performances in the service of advocacy, designed to elicit desired responses from his audiences on particular occasions, rather than as vehicles for the expression of any stable "thought" or "theory." Alternatively, some commentators have held that it is difficult or impossible to give a persuasive account of Burke's political theory because its substantive statements cannot be separated with assurance from the rhetorical flourishes, and attempts to do so are arbitrary (was Burke a utilitarian who invoked natural law for dramatic effect, or a natural law theorist who sometimes chose to speak in terms of expediency to an audience of practical politicians?).[23] These objections call attention to an unquestionable feature of Burke's writings—their persuasive and eloquent quality—but they do not negate or seriously obstruct the study of him as a political theorist.

Admirers of Burke have long commented on his "magnificent speeches,"[24] not intending such praise to be double-edged. More recently, however, Burke's rhetoric, imagery, and related topics have attracted the attention of numerous literary scholars less favorably disposed toward Burke as a political figure or thinker. Their studies have the merit of focusing close attention on certain features of the texts, though in a highly selective fashion; the general effect, however, is to deconstruct or undermine the claim that Burke's works present a coherent theory grounded in perceptions of political reality, rather than merely in his fertile imagination or, frequently, his alleged unconscious mind. Sometimes the results are distinctly unhelpful: when Ronald Paulson states that Burke treats the French Revolution as "a series of isolated outrages," in which he reveals an "obsession with sexuality," one can only wonder if he has read Burke's *Reflections* all the way through, or indeed has looked closely at any of it other than the passage on Marie Antoinette.[25] If some have held that Burke's French Revolution was an imaginative or rhetorical construction, others have—with greater plausibility—explored the ways in which he sought, given his limited information, to imagine India as an attractive civilization, skillfully idealizing it so as to evoke the "nostalgia" of his European audience.[26] Another promising approach attempts to relate both Burke's political theory and his rhetoric to his aesthetic categories of the "sublime" and the "beautiful."[27] Burke, an emotional man himself, consciously used rhetorical devices to arouse desired emotions in his audiences, or to link his feelings with theirs.[28] Sara Suleri uses this approach to the Indian material to explore the "locutions of astonishment and horror" (sublime sentiments) that are said to pervade Burke's speeches as a semiconscious reflection of the realities of imperialism.[29] Her argument that Burke's rhetorical excesses and exaggerations contributed to Hastings's acquittal, however, overlooks the possibility that Burke's actual target was public opinion; it also misses the ways in which Burke strove to avoid portraying Hastings as a sublime figure—terrifying but awe inspiring—for example, by concentrating on his rather commonplace avarice.

An influential modern approach to the study of historical political theory emphasizes the necessity of recognizing and grasping the meaning, for contemporaries in a particular historical setting, of a variety of political "languages" or discursive traditions—conceptual frameworks marked by distinctive vocabularies—that thinkers and writers have employed. The focus here may be on languages or discourses as objects of study, rather than on the individual thinkers who participated in them; but a more accurate grasp of languages and their resonances can also illuminate the work of a given thinker. Burke has not escaped interpretation by this method, and some of the results will be discussed below. The problem is that Burke appears to have drawn upon a great variety of competing languages, adeptly switching among them and deploying them to suit his polemical purposes. He could argue in terms of utility and expediency, or then again invoke either natural rights or a more traditional version of natural law;[30] he sometimes alternated between the argument of imperial self-interest and the language of humanitarianism;[31] he could use the traditional common law idiom of prescription and the "ancient constitution," as well as notions drawn from modern political economy;[32] he eloquently expressed the outlook of eighteenth-century Anglican "political theology,"[33] and just as readily invoked eighteenth-century concepts of sympathy and the moral sentiments; he could speak or write in the legalistic mode of a lawyer presenting a brief or an indictment;[34] he could slip into the "Gothic romance" genre of popular fiction to enhance Hastings's villainy;[35] when he believed his cause was popular, as in his campaign for "economical reform," he could even argue in a democratic or populist idiom.[36] Such versatility, testimony to the richness of Burke's texts, reinforces the idea that he was fundamentally a rhetorician and creates confusion in understanding his political theory.

There is no question that there is a rhetorical dimension to Burke's texts, most of which were generated in response to specific political issues and addressed to definite audiences. Burke was a noted parliamentary orator, usually (until his break with Fox over the French Revolution) on behalf of his party.[37] He was also a careful student of classical rhetoric and a conscious practitioner of that art.[38] A follower (in this respect) of Aristotle rather than Plato, Burke valued rhetoric and made a place for it—more by example than explicit doctrine—in his political theory, as a respectable and desirable element of political practice. Burke distrusted abstract theory in political life, arguing that general principles had to be adapted to particular circumstances; an important component of his ideal of statesmanship was the practical wisdom, based on experience, needed to guide this enterprise, a wisdom that understood how to combine necessary reforms with the preservation of what was of value in traditional practices. Burke, however, eschewed authoritarian methods of rule, even for good ends or in settings, such as India, where others argued that despotism was necessary; his unequivocal rejection of the permissibility of arbitrary power stands out as a fundamental commitment in his Indian speeches against Hastings. Politics was properly a matter of discourse and argumentation, preferably within the framework of a constitutional and representative system such as that of

Great Britain, and issuing in the rule of law, not sheer force. This applied to imperial as well as domestic politics, and to the affairs of India as well as those of America. To achieve their objectives, then, politicians and states-men had to rely on persuasion in the public forum, and hence employ rhetoric, the art of persuasion, as the medium for effecting the transition from general principle to beneficial practice.

On this view of the status of rhetoric, it is incorrect to assume the disjuncture between rhetoric and political philosophy suggested by some of Burke's critics; rather, the study of Burke's rhetoric—a perfectly legitimate inquiry, though not the focus of this book—should seek to link his manner of expression to his political aims and the substantive ideals of his political theory. Nor is the difficulty in distinguishing between the mode of expres-sion and these aims or ideals insurmountable, even if Burke's style, indepen-dent of the substance of his writings, has attracted more attention than that of other political theorists. If rhetoric is the art of persuading listeners or readers to accept a certain argument, then the text is the vehicle for convey-ing an argument. This implies that the argument is something distinct from the manner of its presentation;[39] all we need reject is the seemingly absurd notion that a political speech or pamphlet is nothing but rhetoric, or per-haps, nothing but a text and what it may happen to evoke in readers. This book proceeds on the assumption that one can plausibly extract and sum-marize Burke's arguments and teachings on many topics, and the general elements of his political theory, using his texts as evidence. There are no doubt obvious rhetorical flourishes, exaggerations, even excesses, in Burke's Indian speeches that are discounted or disregarded here, but no pattern of substantive claims has deliberately been ignored on the ground that it is merely rhetorical. The only effective response to the criticisms indicated here will consist in analyzing Burke's arguments and making the case for the cogency of his political thought. Doubtful readers are also invited to con-sider the recantation of one distinguished historian, who began by seeing in Burke only a "supreme rhetorician," but who later came to appreciate the consistent defense of political wisdom and virtue that underlies the eloquence.[40]

Chapter One

"Opulent Oppression"

EMPIRE, INDIA, AND
REFORM

Burke's View of the British Empire

During Burke's lifetime the first great British Empire took shape. During his parliamentary career a major part of that empire (America) was lost, despite his efforts; another part (India) was consolidated and its government reformed, in part as a result of his efforts. No one doubted that overseas trade, the original basis for most of the empire, was central to British prosperity, but in the eighteenth century many Englishmen had doubts about the political wisdom, and the economic benefits, of actual imperial rule over foreign lands;[1] the almost unquestioningly positive imperialist spirit we associate with the Victorian empire was a thing of the future. Englishmen traditionally prided themselves on their liberty and self-government: "Skill in ruling subject nations was not prized by those brought up in this tradition. It was associated with more degenerate societies and more despotic constitutions."[2]

It is noteworthy, then, that Burke endorsed both the legitimacy and the beneficial nature of an appropriately organized and governed empire. He indeed feared political degeneracy and despotism as potential dangers of imperial misrule. "Our Empire in India," he said, "is an awful thing." Empire meant power, and imperial rule unleashed the ambitions of enterprising and sometimes unscrupulous men. Burke was always concerned to emphasize his conviction that duty and responsibility accompanied power. "I dread our own ambition—I dread our being too much dreaded" (*Policy of Allies*, 490). Nevertheless, just as Burke sought fair terms that would allow America to remain part of the British Empire, and opposed measures he feared would dissolve the connection between Ireland and Great Britain,[3] so also his extremely severe criticisms of British rule in India concerned the particular quality of that rule and did not rest on a more general opposition to empire as such.

Burke said: "My idea of an empire . . . is that [it] is the aggregate of many states under one common head, whether this head be a monarch or a presiding republic" ("Conciliation," 136). Since Burke was here speaking of America, he pointed out that the "subordinate parts" of an empire may have various "local privileges and immunities," and that the problem of imperial rule lay in reconciling the legitimate claims of the colonists with the central authority. More generally, however, he was claiming that an empire was a collection of diverse parts, with diverse histories and customs, and that therefore a variety of laws and government arrangements may be appropriate. This surely applied to India, whether or not that part of the empire was in his mind when he gave this famous speech in 1775: knowledge of local conditions and sensitivities and a statesmanlike prudence in accommodating them within a system of effective rule were as necessary in dealing with India as with the troublesome thirteen colonies. Returning to this theme a few years later, Burke wrote: "It was our duty, in all soberness, to conform our government to the character and circumstances of the several people who composed this mighty and strangely diversified mass . . . the natives of Hindostan and those of Virginia" (*Sheriffs of Bristol*, 227). Different institutions should promote the same end, the happiness of the people, throughout the vast empire.

Still speaking of America, Burke affirmed that an Englishman might well "[gaze] with admiration" on "the rising glories of his country," not only its obvious "commercial grandeur" but also the whole "progressive increase of improvement, brought in by varieties of people, by succession of civilizing conquests and civilizing settlements" throughout its history. This improvement had recently been accelerating with the growth of the colonies ("Conciliation," 114–15). India, unlike the American wilderness, was already a highly civilized country; but otherwise both Burke's claim to glory and his conviction that the empire was a mission of improvement were applicable to India as well as to America. Burke's charge against Hastings was that, instead of "augmenting the territory, honor, and power of Great Britain, and bringing the acquisition under the dominion of law and liberty"—which would have been praiseworthy—he had subjected the previously prosperous countries of Bengal and Oudh to "arbitrary power, misrule, anarchy, and ruin" ("Speech in Reply," 11:303). Were the pattern of misrule to be corrected in the East as well as in the West, one might perhaps say of both halves of the empire:

> We balance inconveniences; we give and take; we remit some rights, that we may enjoy others. . . . As we must give away some natural liberty, to enjoy civil advantages, so we must sacrifice some civil liberties, for the advantages to be derived from the communion and fellowship of a great empire. ("Conciliation," 169)

Burke's message of conciliation and accommodation was primarily directed at his fellow Britons; if this message were heeded, he believed, both East Indians and Americans might have reason to value their membership in a great empire.

Burke's view of empire was not only favorable on the whole; it was also providential. As is often the case in his speeches and writings, references to the divine are associated both with a sense of awe in the face of a given situation, and with a sense of the moral duty appropriate to it.

> Magnanimity in politics is not seldom the truest wisdom; and a great empire and little minds go ill together. If we are conscious of our situation, and glow with zeal to fill our place as becomes our station and ourselves, . . . we ought to elevate our minds to the greatness of that trust to which the order of Providence has called us. ("Conciliation," 181; cf. *Sheriffs of Bristol*, 227)

This plea for America was echoed a few years later in a famous Indian speech. After acknowledging the difficulties facing the would-be reformers, Burke said, "All these circumstances are not, I confess, very favourable to the idea of our attempting to govern India at all. But there we are; there we are placed by the Sovereign Disposer; and we must do the best we can in our situation. The situation of man is the preceptor of his duty" (*Fox's Bill*, 404). And finally, toward the end of his life, Burke reflected again on the "glorious Empire given by an incomprehensible dispensation of the Divine providence into our hands," and the responsibilities this presented (*Corr.* 9:62–63).

Burke's moral doctrine generally, and especially the large part of it that was addressed to public actors and statesmen, emphasized a practical wisdom sensitive to context and circumstance as well as certain more abstract principles. We find ourselves in a situation given by history or providence, and not of our own making, and we do the best we can. Fundamental moral obligations, such as those to parents and country, arise from a person's having been born in a particular community, with the benefits that such relations bring, "without their choice" ("Appeal," 160–62). Great Britain found itself with an Indian empire, and Burke, finding himself a member of Parliament with responsibilities in this area, sought (as he did with America) to make it work to the advantage of all concerned. Commenting on the subject of duty in an earlier speech to his constituents, Burke explicitly included the empire in the larger perspective that he, as a member of Parliament, was bound to consider:

> We are now members for a rich commercial *city*; this city, however, is but a part of a rich commercial *nation*. . . . We are members for that great nation, which however is itself but part of a great *empire*, extended by our virtue and our fortune to the farthest limits of the east and of the west. All these wide-spread interests must be considered;—must be compared;—must be reconciled, if possible. ("Electors of Bristol," 97)

The larger public interest, imperial as well as national, which, Burke believed, a member of Parliament was obliged to pursue, was soon to embrace the affairs of India as well as the affairs of America that preoccupied him in 1774.

The remark that the British had been passively "placed" in India by providence exemplifies an approach to political life that was characteristic of Burke; but it also suggests, if not a fatalistic outlook, at any rate the belief, which Burke presumably shared with most of his countrymen, that Great Britain had not deliberately sought or conquered its empire in India but had inadvertently stumbled into it. The East India Company, seeking only to pursue its legitimate trade and to secure its bases in an unstable political environment, had gradually acquired influence over the native authorities in several parts of India; and by 1772, through a sequence of events that was unplanned and only retroactively accepted by the British government, it had achieved what amounted to sovereignty over Bengal from the declining Mogul Empire.[4] Since the likely consequences of withdrawal (continuing political disorder in India and the loss of mutually beneficial trade) would have been worse for all concerned, and since British rule properly administered held the prospect of definite improvements for the people of Bengal, the outcome, whatever its immediate difficulties, could be viewed as providential: "There we are placed."[5]

Would the judgment have been different if the English had deliberately gone forth and conquered the empire? Perhaps not, though Burke's comments on the subject of conquest are mixed. The Revolution of 1688, for example, which secured liberty in England, was a liberty-destroying conquest in Ireland, "which is not to say a great deal in its favor" (*Letter*

22

to Langrishe, 614). In North America, on the other hand, where the English had conquered not only a "savage wilderness" but also a previously French empire, Burke referred approvingly to "the only honorable conquests, not . . . destroying, but . . . promoting the wealth, the number, the happiness of the human race" ("Conciliation," 181–82). He used the term "conquest" more than once in reference to India as well, without apparent misgivings. For one thing, most of the native governments of India had originated in relatively recent Muslim conquests or in violent usurpations attending the decline of the Mogul Empire. In this situation, "it was our business to respect *possession* as the only title that can be valid, where a great empire is broken up; and the more so, as it is the title on which we ourselves stand" (*Conquests,* 113). Among the steps leading to empire, after all, had been two momentous victories of British military forces over the armies of the nawabs of Bengal (Plassey in 1757, Buxar in 1764). Both these battles, however, were seen by the British, and evidently by Burke as well, as justifiable responses to previous surprise attacks on the East India Company's outposts, with massacres of civilians, by the notorious nawabs Siraj al-Daula and Mir Kasim. Such military conquest as there had been, therefore, had consisted of just wars undertaken not in pursuit of an imperial design, but as legitimate defense; in accordance with the eighteenth-century law of nations, Burke recognized the legitimacy of sovereignty acquired through victory in a just war, or through formal cessions accompanying the terminations of wars.[6] The empire, as the ultimate and largely unforeseen result of the Indian victories, could thus also be seen as providential.

More important in Burke's eyes than the origins of the empire was the quality of rule over it, and the results for everyone affected by it, including the imperial subjects. Having been placed by the Sovereign Disposer in India, the British had a duty to rule well. Burke sometimes cited a legalistic reason: British rule in Bengal rested formally not on right of conquest, but on authority ceded to Great Britain by the Mogul emperor, the weak but nominal "ancient sovereign Power of that Country," in a compact supposed to have granted limited, not arbitrary, powers, to be exercised "in Favour of the Natives" (*First Report,* 172). Regardless of such details, however, central tenets of Burke's political philosophy were that all power (whatever its origin) was a trust, that holders of power had a moral duty (to God) to use it justly and beneficently, and that they were accountable for abuses.

Burke's trusteeship conception of government was common currency among eighteenth-century Whigs, with roots in Locke's political philosophy; like Burke's theory of prescription, it involved the application of a legal concept to the political sphere. According to Locke, the government established within civil society occupies the position of a trustee, strictly bound to exercise the powers it has been granted to further limited and specified purposes; the people are both the trustors, or source of the delegated powers, and the beneficiaries of the arrangement. The accountability of trustees for the proper discharge of their trust is central to the idea: in a legal system, procedures should be available through which both the trustors and the beneficiaries can compel performance by the trustees, seek remedies for dereliction of duty, or even revoke the trust altogether. For Locke, revolution is a right and the ultimate recourse of the people.[7]

In proclaiming that empire in India was a trust, Burke too invoked the familiar notion of accountability: "Every species of political dominion . . . [is] in the strictest sense a *trust*; and it is of the very essence of every trust to be rendered *accountable*; and even totally to *cease*, when it substantially varies from the purposes for which alone it could have a lawful existence" (*Fox's Bill*, 385). For Burke, the East India Company had forfeited the "derivative trust" it held from Parliament through its misgovernment in India, and authority over the empire should be assumed by Parliament, the principal trustee. But to whom was Parliament accountable, and how? It was difficult to regard the people of India as the formal trustors of the British Empire (or, less formally, to see them as having any reason to trust their new rulers). The concept of a trust implies they had rights as beneficiaries, but there were no procedures—except rebellion—through which they could press such rights.[8] Although Burke sympathized with certain cases of Indian resistance to Hastings's oppression, he was reluctant to define a right of revolution or other procedures for expressing a popular will. Indeed, Burke's trusteeship theory generally emphasizes or insists upon the accountability of governors not to the governed, but rather to God. "All persons possessing any portion of power ought to be strongly and awefully impressed with an idea that they act in trust; and that they are to account for their conduct in that trust to the one great master, author and founder of society" (*Reflections*, 190). Thus, Burke's idea of a government trust seems looser and further removed from its legal prototype than Locke's; although he took the idea of a trust very seriously, it is usually equivalent to an assertion of the moral duty or responsibility of rulers to promote the well-being of their subjects.[9] In this sense, it unquestionably applied to India and motivated Burke's concern with abuses there.[10]

Good rule is not only morally required; it is also expedient. In the long run, it brings better results than severity or tyranny in governing an empire: "I am sure the natural effect of fidelity, clemency, kindness in governors, is peace, good-will, order, and esteem, on the part of the governed" (*American Taxation*, 426). By 1777 Burke preferred independence for the Americans to their suppression by war and terror, which would create a situation from which no one could benefit: "Bodies tied together by so unnatural a bond of union as mutual hatred are only connected to their ruin" (*Sheriffs of Bristol*, 236). For the same reason, it was Britain's interest, as well as its duty, to provide better government for its Indian empire than it evidently had for its American.

Such convictions underlay Burke's campaign to establish control by Parliament, the ultimate trustee of any imperial power exercised by British subjects, over Indian affairs; but these ideas also surely applied directly to the East India Company officials themselves (and most notably Hastings), who were vested with immediate power over Indians. The outrage that is conspicuous in so much of what Burke had to say about India seems to have arisen from his belief that an important trust had been violated by unscrupulous men in power. This necessitated an assertion of parliamentary oversight, remedial action, and perhaps punishment of the offenders. But Burke's reaction suggests an even deeper concern, for the very fact that such abuses could have occurred presented a challenge to the theory of trusteeship government that constitutes such an important—one may say aristocratic—element in Burke's thought. Such government depends on the honor and conscientiousness of the rulers rather than on direct accountability to the governed. If trustees could not be trusted, then Burke's opponents, the radicals who called for democratic representation in Great Britain, might have been right.

India as a Special Case

Burke occasionally made general statements about empire, just as he put forward general claims about morality and duty; at the same time, his political thought was characteristically oriented toward particularistic circumstances, and most of its statements were provoked by specific events. As he emphasized in his most important single work, it is actual circumstances that give practical meaning to abstract principles, and "render every civil and political scheme beneficial or noxious to mankind" (*Reflections*, 90). Burke devoted a great deal of his attention to definite problems that arose in the two major components of the eighteenth-century British Empire—in America (primarily in the 1770s) and India (in the 1780s). The Indian case had a few similarities to the American, but for the most part it was quite different; comprehending these differences and coming to terms with them was one of the major problems facing Burke and other British politicians as they contemplated their new possessions in Asia.[11]

Two features that India shared with America—size and distance from England—were obvious and noted by all, yet they did not lead Burke to the same conclusions in the two cases. In his famous "Speech on Conciliation," Burke denounced the doctrinaire intransigence of Lord North's government toward the American colonies and argued instead that a sensible and successful policy had to be adapted to the actual circumstances of the case. It was therefore important for statesmen to study the relevant facts, and the first and most basic fact that Burke adduced was the large and rapidly growing population of America, which called for both caution and a loosening of direct control from the mother country. Burke was also at pains—more so than most of his peers—to get the facts straight about India, as evidenced in his committee reports (esp. *Ninth Report*, 194–333), and to educate his audiences about them, for example in the long impeachment speeches. Bengal too was obviously densely populated—the actual numbers were unknown, but by all contemporary estimates the region's population was much larger than that of Great Britain itself at the end of the eighteenth century.[12] Large numbers of human beings have moral significance, and one of Burke's comments on America surely was applicable to India as well:

> Some degree of care and caution is required in the handling such an object [as a large subject population]; it will show that you ought not, in reason, to trifle with so large a mass of the interests and feelings of the human race. You could at no time do so without guilt; and be assured you will not be able to do it long with impunity. ("Conciliation," 110)

Whereas the sheer number of Americans strengthened Burke's argument for allowing local self-government, however, the even greater number of Indians under British rule merely strengthened his case for just and beneficent government. Burke upheld not only the empire in India, but also the desirability of more direct supervision of its government from London; he did not entertain the notion that the East Indians, like the Americans, were entitled to self-government. The reasons for this will emerge when we turn to the theme of liberty in relation to the empire, and to a more detailed account of Indian history and society.

A second relevant circumstance was the distance—in space and thus in time—between the American colonies and London. "Seas roll, and months pass, between the order and the execution; and the want of a speedy explanation of a single point is enough to defeat an whole system" ("Conciliation," 126). Calcutta, of course, was much farther away—an average four months' voyage in favorable seasons, hence eight months between a request for and the receipt of instructions. As Hastings remarked, "The dominion exercised by the British Empire in India is fraught with many radical and incurable defects, beyond those to which all human institutions are liable, arising from the distance of its scene of operations."[13] On other occasions Hastings expressed frustration, when requesting approval for a sensitive diplomatic initiative, at not being able to know who the chairman of the company would be (a friend or an opponent?) when his letter arrived in England. He learned only in July 1778 that war between Great Britain and France had been declared the previous March.[14]

Burke was surprisingly unsympathetic toward these difficulties. In the case of America, distance, like population, added force to his argument for provincial autonomy: since "abuses of subordinate authority increase, and all means of redress lessen, as the distance of the subject removes him from the seat of the supreme power" ("Address to the King," 166), local representative government was all the more necessary. Similarly, distance, compounded by ignorance in England of the Indian scene, contributed to Hastings's argument that the governor-general needed undivided authority and a large measure of discretion.[15] Burke's position on India differed from Hastings's, and from Burke's own position on America. To deal with "abuses of subordinate authority" in India, he called for increased parliamentary control of the East India Company's personnel and policies, notwithstanding the communications problem. The difference was that, in the absence of representative self-government in India (as in America), the opportunity—and the historical reality—of abuses by company officials was only enhanced by their distance and autonomy: "A Great Empire [is] liable to abuse of Subordinate Authority—more especially if it is distant—most of all if the people have no distinct priviledges secured by constitutions of their own and able to check the abuse of the subordinate Authority" ("Rohilla Speech," 93).

A third feature was the distinctiveness of the Indian empire—rule by British officials, and ultimately by Great Britain, over a distant country fully inhabited by an alien people. By late in the nineteenth century this was the usual connotation of "empire," at least in the case of Europe's overseas empires, but in the eighteenth century this circumstance was unusual and problematic. The North American empire consisted of colonies in the sense most familiar to classically educated Europeans: citizens of the mother country had emigrated to lands that were to all intents and purposes vacant, and had established new civil societies there, societies that were in most respects replicas of the old. Such an origin carried implications for their mode of government and ultimate destiny, which did not necessarily apply to a country such as Bengal and its people, now clearly ruled by a small group of foreigners.

One can see Burke striving to work out what this might mean. Foreign dominion as such was nothing new, nor was it intrinsically reprehensible. Most of India had long been ruled by a succession of conquering invaders, from the current Moguls back to the Tartars and Arabs: "All the Mahomedans in India are strangers, and for many Generations past every distinguished person of that Country has been an Adventurer from Tartary or Persia" ("Rohilla Speech," 99). The rule of these peoples, whom Burke compares to the Goths who invaded Europe in a similar manner and to the Normans in England, had at first been violent and rapacious, but these ill effects had subsided as the conquerors settled down as a ruling class and acquired an interest in the prosperity of the country.[16] The English had something of the appearance of a new wave of foreign conquerors; but although their intentions may have been more benign than those of their predecessors, the results were not always so. The crucial difference was that they did not come as permanent settlers, and in that respect they differed not only from the Muslim rulers of India but from the ancient Romans and the modern Iberian empire builders as well. They were merely a "succession of Officers," a "Nation of placemen," "a State made up wholly of magistrates." As a tiny minority lacking knowledge of or sympathy with the population around them, they developed a strong "esprit de corps" with special interests of their own. They were, so to speak, a "Commonwealth without a people," with the unnatural result that there were no controls or checks on the ruling group, which are normally provided by the presence of a well-defined and acknowledged people, "to control, to watch, to balance against the power of office" ("Speech on Opening," 285–86). What was worse, power lay in the hands of men who until recently had been primarily merchants, men whose first thoughts continued to be of profits, primarily young men whose hope in coming to India was to make a fortune as quickly as possible and then return home. Combining the "avarice of age, and all the impetuosity of youth, they roll in one after another; wave after wave; and there is nothing before the eyes of the natives but an endless, hopeless prospect of new flights of birds of prey and passage" (*Fox's Bill*, 402). Hence, Burke concluded, Great Britain's "friendship" with India might in the end prove more detrimental to India than the violence of the Tartars, unless decisive steps were taken to correct the abuses that would seem, at least in part, to be intrinsic to this new kind of empire. In disposing of matters in this fashion, providence conferred responsibility as well as empire upon the British.

Finally, there was the question of liberty in the colonies, and in particular, liberty in the familiar old Whig sense of the right of the people not to be governed or taxed without being able to register their consent through a representative assembly. In Europe, such a right was medieval in origin, and Burke frequently defended it as part of the political heritage of Englishmen. Speaking of a still-British America (and perhaps thinking also of Ireland), Burke put forward "[his] idea of the constitution of the British Empire" (*American Taxation*, 460): The Parliament of Great Britain should function both as a local legislature for Great Britain and as an imperial legislature with power over specifically imperial matters, but coordinate provincial legislatures should enjoy broad powers (or privileges) with respect to ordinary local legislation and taxation. The following year, in a final effort to salvage the empire, Burke argued even more strongly that the colonial assemblies in America should be granted the exclusive power to tax themselves and make voluntary contributions for imperial purposes ("Conciliation"). In this way, the "imperial rights of Great Britain" could be reconciled with the privileges upon which the colonists were understandably insisting. At one point, Burke upheld these privileges in terms of a general principle of "political equity" as it applied to empire—"by which equity we are bound, as much as possible to extend the spirit and benefit of the British constitution to every part of the British dominions" (*American Taxation*, 439).

I shall argue that Burke sought to realize the "spirit and benefit" of just and lawful rule in India, which he certainly believed was a British constitutional principle, but at no point did he suggest that the practice of representative government should be implemented there. The principal reason for this difference was that the Americans, as Englishmen or as British subjects, had a prescriptive entitlement to representative institutions; and more practically, they knew they had such rights and were prepared to assert them. A major theme of Burke's "Speech on Conciliation" is the powerful love of liberty (including the peculiarly English sensitivity about being taxed without consent) that was brought from England by the colonists and was deeply ingrained in their political culture and education. This too was one of the facts that British imperial statesmen had to face, even if it made the problem of imperial finance more difficult. The history of English rule had been successfully distinguished, Burke noted, by the steady expansion of English law, liberties, and representation (either in Westminster or in parliaments of their own) to outlying countries such as Wales and Ireland—so why not to America? ("Conciliation," 120, 127, 152).

But the Indians, in contrast to the English, appeared to have no tradition of liberty in this sense, and made no claims to it. In fact, given the ambiguity surrounding the formal status of British rule there, it was not even clear whether Bengalis counted as British subjects: in 1773 Parliament established a Supreme Court for Bengal with jurisdiction over "British subjects" there, but it was questionable what if any classes of natives were meant to be included. Disputed questions about the constitution of the Indian empire in the late eighteenth century concerned the respective claims of the East India Company, the Crown, and Parliament; relations between British officials, native rulers, and the Mogul Empire; the powers of the governor-general and his council; the balance between local discretion and oversight from London; and of course the eventual extent of British dominion. A question about representative government, or a claim by India to take part in an imperial system of provincial legislatures, did not arise for Burke, or for anyone else at that time.[17] Burke rejected the claim that participation in government was a natural right, and he did not hold such general participation to be conducive to, much less a condition of, good government. The total exclusion of the Roman Catholics of Ireland from the franchise meant they were in "a lower and degraded state of citizenship," though not "absolute slavery," as Jacobin theory would have had it (*Letter to Langrishe*, 599). Presumably, he would have agreed that the Indian subjects of the empire had a similarly subordinate political status, but he did not say so.

The absence of any Indian claim to enjoy representative institutions made the problem of taxation in India easier. Burke did not challenge the legitimacy of the Mogul emperor's formal granting of authority over taxation in Bengal to the British in 1765; he insisted only that this power be executed equitably and lawfully. It follows that Burke must have regarded the right not to have one's property taken by government without the consent of one's representatives—which Locke considered a natural right—as, in truth, only a right guaranteed by particular national traditions and systems of civil law, such as the English.[18] Government requires public revenue. Burke often insisted that the power to raise revenue must be balanced against respect for property, in India and elsewhere, but for him the restraining standard appears to have been nonarbitrariness and nonoppression.

Lack of liberty in India also meant government by foreigners—government by the British—rather than local or native self-government. This may seem to be the defining feature of what we think of as "empire," yet the case was not quite so clear to Burke. Empire in America need not have meant this, according to Burke's proposals. Furthermore, empire in the sense of foreign rule was nothing new for much of India: it was by now the custom of the country, institutionalized in the prevailing dual system of Hindu and Muslim law, for example. More generally, it does not seem that Burke objected in principle to rule by foreigners as something fundamentally illegitimate as such, though on occasion he suggested it might be prima facie undesirable. Condemning the British-supported conquest of Tanjore and the deposition of its (Hindu) raja by the (Muslim) nawab of the Carnatic, Burke noted that the Hindu people of Tanjore detested "Mahometan government," and remarked:

> It will hardly be believed, that all men do not infinitely prefer a subjection to Princes of their own blood, manners, and religion, to any other; that they will not be more obedient to such Princes; and that such Princes will not be reciprocally more tender of them. This natural and reciprocal partiality, is matter of great consideration in all governments; but it is peculiarly so among those nations where there is no settled law or constitution, either to fix allegiance, or to restrain power. (*Conquests*, 113)

Indeed, in this passage Burke was nearly implying that the people of Tanjore had a right to a prince who was one of their own. Such a ruler might be expected—or perceived—to have the interests of his subjects at heart, and therefore to enjoy his people's "unsuspecting confidence" in his good intentions and "parental affection" toward them—the happy outlook of the Americans at one time toward their "mother-country" (*Sheriffs of Bristol*, 234–35). Similarly, Burke criticized Hastings not only for deposing Chait Singh, the raja of Benares, but for replacing him with a Muslim administrator; this was something previous Muslim conquerors had refrained from doing, out of deference to the sacred Hindu city, and it made the people of Benares "feel their servitude in all its degradation" (*Fox's Bill*, 417). The desirability of native rule, however, was a point which, if generalized, would have undermined British rule in India (and Quebec and Ireland) altogether, since England could scarcely appear as the "mother country" there. Despite these remarks on Tanjore and Benares, therefore, Burke did not insist on the point, and in the end he was more concerned about the quality of the rule exercised than its formal characteristics.

The fact was that rule by foreign princes was not uncommon in Europe, even in England itself, for instance in the persons of William III and the early Hanoverians. (If we count George II, Burke himself—even leaving aside his Irishness—had been the subject of a "foreign prince.") In adopting the Hanoverian succession, Burke pointed out, Parliament had reaffirmed the value of hereditary monarchy even though "they had a due sense of the evils which might happen from such foreign rule . . . all the dangers and all the inconveniences of its being a foreign line" (*Reflections*, 110). Burke also praised Catherine the Great, who, though a foreigner, "made herself a Russian" and ruled in the spirit of the country (*Regicide Peace 3*, 325).[19] The occasional rule of foreigners could not be rejected in principle without a repudiation of hereditary monarchy and its adjunct, the practice of dynastic marriages among European royalty. These institutions were indeed to be repudiated by some in the near future in the name of "national" self-governance, an idea associated with the democratic principles of Burke's radical opponents in Britain and in France—but not of course by Burke himself.[20] A foreign prince was no doubt more palatable in Great Britain because Britain possessed what Tanjore lacked—a "settled law [and] constitution" by which the prince would be restrained, mitigating the potential dangers.

With respect to India, Burke urged the reinstatement of the raja of Tanjore as a quasi-independent state, but he did not reject Great Britain's rule over Bengal. Rather, he seems to have believed that by cultivating sympathy with the manners and laws of the Indians, British governors of integrity might exhibit the "tenderness" toward the governed that came more naturally to compatriot rulers. Responsible rule need not be made accountable through representative institutions, or through any concept of representative government. At one point, Burke did say that "the House of Commons, who are virtually the representatives of Lucknow [in Oudh], . . . will not suffer the natives first to be robbed of their property, and then the titles, which by the laws of their own country they have to the goods they possess" ("Speech in Reply," 12:41); but on a more considered view the grounds on which Burke dismissed the claim that the Americans were "virtually represented" in Parliament would surely have applied to the Indians as well. His convictions regarding the duty to deliver moderate and beneficent government, especially in the absence of representative accountability and the control on power it provides, was what motivated Burke's extensive efforts on behalf of India.

A Merchant Empire

Burke and others during the period, including the loyal company servant Hastings, often referred to the "British Empire" in India, but one of the most important and peculiar features of this empire was that it was originally acquired and administered not by the British state but by the East India Company. The general perception in Britain of the detrimental consequences of this circumstance led to the assertion of parliamentary control over the company's regime in the 1770s and 1780s, and formed the background for Burke's own attacks on company rule in India. Let us precede the analysis of the problem as Burke and others saw it by a brief historical sketch.

The Honourable United Company of Merchants of England Trading to the East Indies (as it was officially known from 1709) was a commercial corporation with a periodically renewed parliamentary charter dating back to the reign of Elizabeth I—"a period," Burke commented in reviewing the history, "of projects, when all sorts of commercial adventures, companies, and monopolies were in fashion" ("Speech in Opening," 348). The East India Company was granted a monopoly, so far as England and Englishmen were concerned, on overseas trade with Asia east of the Cape of Good Hope. (It was in competition, of course, with other European companies.) In the seventeenth century, as a result of negotiations and treaties with the Mogul government, it established three major fortified settlements, with rights of internal self-administration and defense, at what became the burgeoning commercial cities of Calcutta in Bengal, Madras in the Carnatic, and Bombay on the western coast. It also established a network of factories or trading outposts in the interior and received exemption from tariffs on overseas trade, which was profitable for Indian rulers and merchants as well as for the English. In the seventeenth and eighteenth centuries, there was a net flow of Indian exports, especially spices and textiles, to England; Indian goods (including opium) were also shipped to China to be exchanged for tea, to supply the British and American markets.

As its trade and its operations in Indian territory became more extensive, the company received various powers from Parliament, which Burke reviewed without complaint: to administer naval discipline on its ships, to exercise civil and criminal jurisdiction and martial law in its settlements and over its employees, to maintain armed forces under British officers, and to make peace and war. This represented, as Burke noted, an almost unprecedented transfer of "high prerogatives of Sovereignty" to private British subjects; at some point in this process the East India Company ceased to be "merely a Company formed for the extension of the British commerce, but in reality a delegation of the whole power and sovereignty of this kingdom sent into the East" ("Speech on Opening," 282–83).

Insofar as the company's operations remained a commercial enterprise,

Burke made no objections to them. Like most of his contemporaries, he approved (if on political or strategic more than economic grounds) of the policy of mercantilism in foreign trade.[21] For example, he defended the restrictive commercial laws applicable in America against the colonists' complaints ("Conciliation," 143–44); and he noted as an established fact the commercial interconnections throughout the empire as a whole—especially the tea trade—which provided a rationale for the otherwise burdensome "East India conquests" (*American Taxation*, 416). Different issues arose, however, when commercial networks evolved into imperial rule. Early modern states, it has been argued, were willing to entrust extraterritorial violence to quasi-official, nonstate entities such as the East India Company because such arrangements offered advantages to the state with minimal responsibilities. Burke's whole Indian campaign, of course, rested on the premise that British rulers had to accept rather than evade responsibility for the authority they possessed.[22]

The East India Company became established in India when the power of the Mogul Empire was at its peak, with the emperor in Delhi exerting effective control over governors and local rulers throughout most of the subcontinent. In the eighteenth century, however, following the death of the last effective emperor, Aurangzeb, in 1707, the empire began to disintegrate. Invaders from Persia and Afghanistan repeatedly overran northern India; a confederacy of warlike Hindu chiefs called the Marathas continued a revolt against Mogul rule that had begun in the previous century, expanded their control over central India, and continually attacked Mogul territories; most important, Mogul provincial governors established their de facto independence of Delhi and attempted to found hereditary dynasties in states such as Bengal, Oudh, and the Carnatic.[23] "It is true that the Mogul continued to grant sanads [charters] but his authority was merely traditional and nominal [by 1750], though it was freely used as a screen under which all parties found it convenient to hide their advancing pretensions"[24]—a familiar situation in traditional, quasi-feudal empires in decline. With or without the formal legitimacy Mogul titles conferred, Indian princes of various descriptions maneuvered for power and wealth; the result was great political instability, with wars, assassinations, coups d'état, and succession struggles becoming frequent occurrences among and within the Indian states.

The Europeans soon discovered they could exploit this situation. Their determination to do so was furthered by the natural competition for trade and influence among the several European nationalities present in India, especially the English and the French, and it was particularly intensified by the periodic outbreak of war between the European powers, in which India became a theater and company possessions and trade privileges became stakes in global contests.

In southern India in the 1740s, the French first discovered the ease with which, through the use of a few well-disciplined European troops, they could intervene decisively in the internal disputes of Indian states, extract new privileges and concessions from the winning party, now dependent on them, and thus strengthen their position vis-à-vis the English. For the English, survival on the subcontinent dictated retaliation by the same methods, and, under the emerging leadership of Robert Clive, they proved themselves even more adept at this. By the end of the war of 1740–1748, the English controlled most of the Carnatic through the nominal government of a dependent and pliable nawab.

Even more momentous were subsequent developments in Bengal, which was to become the principal holding of the early British Indian empire.[25] In 1756, war again broke out between Britain and France, and there began a series of what Burke called "revolutions," which ended in outright British rule there. The nawab of Bengal, Siraj al-Daula, annoyed at commercial abuses and evidently receiving French encouragement, launched an attack that briefly succeeded in driving the British from their settlements;[26] but the following year, after the recapture of Calcutta and some fruitless negotiations, Clive decisively defeated the nawab's army at Plassey, and (by prearrangement) placed a more friendly pretender, Mir Jafar, on the throne of Bengal.

Burke does not appear to have questioned the justifiability of these critical events. Hastings argued at his trial that India was not "an empire wrested in blood from those people to whom God and nature had given it," but rather an empire won in a just war of self-defense "against extirpation and destruction" on the part of a notoriously cruel and treacherous tyrant.[27] Although Burke agreed with this characterization of Siraj al-Daula, his comment on the events surrounding his overthrow, by the "daring and commanding genius of Clive," was more philosophical:

> There is a secret veil to be drawn over the beginnings of all governments. They had their origin, as the beginning of all such things have had, in some matters that had as good be covered by obscurity. Time in the origin of most governments has thrown this mysterious veil over them. Prudence and discretion make it necessary to throw something of that veil over a business in which otherwise the fortune, the genius, the talents and military virtue of this Nation never shone more conspicuously. ("Speech on Opening," 316–17)[28]

Siraj al-Daula, nawab of Bengal (1756–1757), whose defeat by
Clive at Plassey led to British rule over Bengal.
From J. H. Tull Walsh, *A History of Murshidabad District*.

This passage anticipates Burke's approving account, a few years later, of how the English leaders of 1688 "threw a politic, well-wrought veil" over the illegality of the Revolution (*Reflections*, 103), and the point is similar. The origins of government are rarely or never pristine; violence and irregularities are the norm. What matters is the quality of rule thereafter: "The first step to empire is revolution, by which power is conferred; the next is good laws, good order, good institutions, to give that power stability" ("Speech in Opening," 402). The company laid itself open to criticism by the way they used the power that the Sovereign Disposer had thus thrown into their hands.

One problem was the irresistible temptation of the large private fortunes the British found they could acquire by applying their new political influence. Clive and his associates set the precedent, returning to England with great wealth gained in the form of "presents" from Mir Jafar, and their successors followed their example by arranging several more changes in the nawabship in the hope of similar payoffs. Burke remarked: "By the vast sums of money acquired by individuals upon this occasion, the immense, sudden, prodigious fortunes, it was discovered that a revolution in Bengal was a mine much more easily worked and infinitely more productive than the mines of Potosi and Mexico. . . . Accordingly, [the first] revolution that ought to have precluded other revolutions unfortunately became fruitful of them" ("Speech on Opening," 317). Burke acknowledged the necessity of the original coup, but he denounced the subsequent instability as having been provoked for purely mercenary reasons. He thus drew a clear distinction between the constitutional "revolutions" that brought sovereignty to the British, and the ensuing "revolutions" against Indian property and the social order perpetrated by unscrupulous British officials (*Fox's Bill*, 427–29). Burke also seems to have recognized that these abuses were partly rooted in the decadent Mogul system that was still nominally in place, with its history of usurpations and its lack of clear rules of succession; his charge was that the company officials exploited these defects rather than reformed them.

A further problem had to do with the indirect nature of British rule from 1757 to 1772, which facilitated both extended trade privileges and various forms of extortion from native officials by Englishmen who, behind the scenes, were clearly dominant. After several chaotic years, Clive, back as governor, negotiated the Treaty of Allahabad with the Mogul emperor in 1765. This treaty granted the East India Company the *diwani* of Bengal, which included the right to collect taxes and the responsibility for civil justice; the company, that is, assumed an official role within the constitution of the Mogul Empire and acquired formal, semisovereign powers in Bengal.

Burke expressed approval for Clive's management of "the great grand period of the constitutional entrance of the Company into the affairs of India," his acquisition of "a legal right, acknowledged and recognized now for the first time by all the Princes of the Country." He approved of attaining a position from which the English could provide legal government and "[quiet] the minds of the people" ("Speech on Opening," 341). He also praised, apparently on grounds of political expedience, the policy of maintaining the nawab in a subordinate role and of ruling primarily through native officials, since this "prevented that vast Kingdom from wearing the dangerous Appearance, and still more, from sinking into the terrible State, of a Country of Conquest" (*Ninth Report*, 321). The particular "veil" represented by Clive's so-called system of indirect rule was soon judged not to have corrected the abuses, however; and in 1772, although a ceremonial nawab was retained, the new governor, Hastings, was charged with fashioning a more direct and more centralized administration for Bengal from Calcutta.

Why were abuses of power, especially those related to pecuniary corruption, so great and so persistent during this first period of the Indian empire, as Burke and others who studied the record soon concluded? Burke later held Hastings personally responsible for abuses that continued after he attained the governorship, but in fact, according to a growing opinion, the problem lay with rule being entrusted to the East India Company in the first place. A band of merchants, whose long-standing corporate ethos and personal attitudes were focused on making profits, had suddenly come to occupy a position of political power over a large country and its wealth. As a result of this enhanced position, moreover, the number of company "servants" or professional employees in Bengal rapidly increased, from about 50 early in the century to about 250 in the 1760s.[29] In historical retrospect, the entire period between the battle of Plassey and Hastings's replacement by Cornwallis, when a more effective system of British government control was implemented, may be viewed as a transitional phase characterized by the anomaly of sovereign powers almost wholly in the hands of a private commercial company. The dangers or pathologies of rule that were likely in this situation were not lost on contemporaries.

The enterprising spirit of the great overseas merchant companies of early modern Europe was not in doubt, given their contributions to geographical discovery, their pioneering of trade routes, and their success both in commerce and in incipient colonial ventures around the world. No less a commentator than Montesquieu celebrated these achievements and the historically unprecedented power of Europe that it signified. Writing before Britain's acquisition of Bengal in 1757, Montesquieu praised commercial empires with limited colonial outposts over large-scale territorial conquests. He also endorsed the (historically unusual) way the early colonies were governed: "Many [European] nations acted so wisely that they granted sovereignty to trading companies who, governing these distant states only for trade, made a great secondary power without encumbering the principal state." Montesquieu implied that such delegation of authority was politically convenient; and it made sense, given that "the goal of the establishment was [commercial monopoly, and] the extension of commerce, not the founding of a city or a new empire."[30] The emergence of the hybrid commercial-territorial empire in India after 1757 might have led to a different conclusion. In any case, others doubted the wisdom of this policy of entrusting rule to merchants; and Burke certainly came to regard East India Company rule as an "encumbrance" as well as an embarrassment to Great Britain, once such rule had indeed passed beyond mere commerce to territorial sovereignty.

The opposing view was put forward in no uncertain terms by Adam Smith in *The Wealth of Nations*, which appeared in 1776, in the midst of growing public discussion of alleged abuses in India (even though the imperial problems of America were more pressing at that moment). Smith argued that the natural impulse of an "exclusive" trading company as such was to protect and enlarge its monopoly and then to restrict the supply of its commodities so as to maximize the profit it realized from its export trade. This policy, however, was "directly contrary to the real interest of those companies, considered as the sovereigns of the countries they have conquered." The interest of a sovereign is to maximize the capacity of the country to generate revenue, a capacity that depends on its general prosperity; and this prosperity in turn is promoted by a policy of opening markets, abolishing monopolies, and instituting "the most perfect freedom of commerce." Merchants, however, seem

> incapable of considering themselves as sovereigns, even after they have become such. . . . Their mercantile habits draw them in this manner, almost necessarily, though perhaps insensibly, to prefer upon all ordinary occasions the little and transitory profit of the monopolist to the great and permanent revenue of the sovereign.

This divergence between short- and long-term interest was exacerbated by a further conflict between the immediate interest of company personnel in the colony, namely, to realize quick private fortunes, and the somewhat larger perspective of the company directors and stockholders in England. It was, moreover, the local personnel who directly exercised political power over the colonized country: sovereignty was effectively conferred upon a "council of merchants, a profession no doubt extremely respectable, but which in no country in the world carries along with it that sort of authority which naturally over-awes the people, and without force commands their willing obedience." The rule of merchants thus tended to become the rule of force, "military and despotical," the more so since this power was applied in ways that obviously served the interests of the rulers to the detriment of the people. In Smith's opinion, "the English company have not yet had time to establish in Bengal so perfectly destructive a system" as the Dutch had done in their East Indian possessions; but the pattern and its logic were perfectly clear within the analytical framework provided by the increasingly persuasive science of political economy.[31]

Burke, himself a student of political economy, agreed with this analysis. In his speech in support of Fox's East India Bill, which would have transferred sovereign power from the company to Parliament, Burke remarked that he would not condemn those who, like Smith, "argue *a priori* against the propriety of leaving such extensive political power in the hands of a company of merchants." At the same time, foreshadowing his famous attacks on the political rationalism of the French Revolution, he expressed "an insuperable reluctance in giving my hand to destroy any established institution of government, upon a theory, however plausible it may be" (*Fox's Bill*, 386–87). In his well-known later words: "I reprobate no form of government merely upon abstract principles" (*Reflections*, 228)—even Smithian principles. An abstract or theoretical critique had to be confirmed by actual evidence of great abuses. In the case of India, to be sure, the necessary evidence was available and could be summed up in Burke's overall assessment of company rule a few years after it attained power: "Commerce, which enriches every Country in the World, was bringing that Country [Bengal] to total ruin" ("Speech on Opening," 334). Smith's argument that merchants should not exercise sovereign powers was correct in the case of the British Indian empire.[32]

At times, however, it appears that Burke, despite his antitheoretical reputation, was attracted to a view that saw dangerous incongruities or ambiguities in the rule of merchants as such, and was prepared to pronounce such rule defective for this reason. In a parliamentary committee report on abuses arising from company practices in the 1760s, Burke argued:

> The Company's Servants, armed with Authorities delegated from the nominal [the nawab's] Government, or attended with what was a stronger Guard, the Fame of their own Power, appeared as Magis-

trates in the Markets in which they dealt as Traders. It was impossible for the Natives in general to distinguish, in the Proceedings of the same Persons, what was transacted on the Company's Account, from what was done on their own; and it will ever be so difficult to draw this Line of Distinction . . . as long as the Company [and its servants] . . . aim at any Advantage to itself in the purchase of any Commodity [while at the same time exercising political power]. (*Ninth Report*, 245)

A regime of law and legal justice requires, among other things, that "lines of distinction" be carefully drawn and maintained, among them the distinction between public power and private interest, between governing official and merchant. Later, in a somber reflection on the history of the empire—on the "improvement in Europe coinciding with the general decay of Asia, (for the proud day of Asia is passed)"—Burke remarked that, in becoming "a great empire, carrying on, subordinately, a great commerce," the East India Company had in practice become "that thing which was supposed by the Roman law irreconcilable to reason and propriety,—*eundem negotiatorem et dominum*," the same agency both trader and lord ("Speech in Opening," 9:350).[33]

The Movement for Reform

A growing sense in England that all was not well in the Indian empire led to a series of efforts at reform in the 1770s and 1780s. Burke eventually took a leading role in this movement, joined by other prominent members of his parliamentary party, the Whig group under the leadership of Charles James Fox, the successors to the Rockingham Whigs with whom Burke had earlier been associated. The attention given to India coincided with Great Britain's preoccupation with the American crisis, and was interrupted by that crisis to a certain extent. Hence, during these decades, the problems of empire and their constitutional implications for Great Britain itself figured prominently in the deliberations of Parliament.

Indian reform was provoked by a growing belief among the British political public that the East India Company was abusing its newly acquired power and dominion. It was believed that Bengal, and later, the neighboring country of Oudh, were being ruined economically, not so much by the company's long-standing monopoly on export trade, but by the extension of trade privileges and monopolistic practices to internal commerce, to the detriment of native merchants, manufacturers, and producers. This was exactly the kind of abuse to be expected in light of Smith's argument. Burke, who generally looked favorably upon the "great wheel of circulation," or free markets, in economic life (*Reflections*, 271), reviewed the damaging consequences of internal monopolies in the Ninth Report of the select committee charged with investigating the Indian situation (Burke served on this committee in 1781–1783). At one point, Burke went so far as to assert that the company's opium monopoly not only created hardships for the peasant cultivators, but "deprived [them] of their natural right of dealing with many competitors" ("Articles of Charge," 63).[34] In 1770 there had been a devastating famine in Bengal, which many in England believed had been exacerbated by company mismanagement, and worse, by speculation in rice by its servants and native protégés in the interior. Finally, Burke developed an influential argument that the company's practice of partly financing the goods it purchased for export out of the revenues it collected amounted to an "annual plunder" that was systematically draining away the wealth of Bengal (*Ninth Report*, 226).

These damning conclusions—which were reflected in a generally negative popular impression of the situation—were the result of heroic efforts on the part of Burke and a few others to comprehend an extremely complex state of affairs in a remote and exotic place, based on information with varying degrees of reliability, some of it certainly hostile and biased against Hastings. The truth is unclear. There were clearly numerous abuses, especially in the fifteen years after Plassey, when many fortunes were made by disreputable methods; nevertheless, the verdict of a leading modern historian is that, overall, Bengal was probably more prosperous—it certainly enjoyed more peace—throughout this period than most other parts of India.[35] The beliefs about the famine were probably inaccurate or exaggerated.[36] Such beliefs are nonetheless important in that they reflected a predisposition among influential sectors of the English public to assume the worst about the company's regime. Horace Walpole, for example, remarked to a correspondent: "We have outdone the Spaniards in Peru. They were at least butchers on a religious principle, however diabolical their zeal. We have murdered, deposed, plundered, usurped—nay, what think you of the famine in Bengal in which three millions perished being caused by a monopoly of the servants of the East India Company?"[37] Adam Smith, too, commenting on deaths from famine in a fertile country, referred to "the mercantile company which oppresses and domineers in the East Indies."[38] If these sentiments were representative, it is understandable that political leaders found themselves under pressure to act.

In addition to scruples about the supposed effects of company misrule on its native subjects, some critics in Britain may have been motivated by other concerns. Bengal (like India generally) was traditionally thought by Europeans to be a wealthy country, an impression furthered by the conspicuously large private fortunes being made there. As Burke remarked, Oudh was also supposed to have been the equal of England itself in size, fertility, population, and culture until its spoliation under Hastings (*Eleventh Report*, 352; "Articles of Charge," 95). Many people in England accordingly entertained the prospect of an influx of wealth, both public and private, as the natural fruit of empire. It was hoped that the acquisition of the *diwani* of Bengal in 1765 would alleviate the problem of imperial finance, which was such a pressing issue in Great Britain following the Seven Years' War. At the same time, the price of East India Company stock rose as many, including many well-connected people (and Burke himself), sought to share in the profits. Hence the shock was great when in 1772 the company, near bankruptcy, was unable to pay dividends and appealed to the government for a loan.[39] Gradually, it became apparent that the cost of maintaining the company's regime in Bengal exceeded the revenues it was able to extract from the country or, as Burke commented, that there was paradoxically an inverse relation between the "Power and Dominion" of the company and its profits (*Ninth Report*, 243). In conjunction with reports of misrule in India and resentment at the personal fortunes somehow acquired by company servants, this disappointment precipitated the reform movement to which Burke was to be converted.

The first, relatively minor parliamentary inquiry into company affairs took place in 1767, shortly after Burke first entered the House of Commons. The Rockingham group to which Burke belonged opposed interference with the company in the name of the inviolability of its charter; its partisan opposition to Lord North's government and its fear of growing court influence also led it to take this position.[40] In 1772, when the company directors were under pressure to set their house in order, Burke himself received an offer to chair a committee of supervisors that would go out to Calcutta and set things straight. This offer was an indication not only of Burke's recognized capability but also of the fact that at this point he was seen as a friend of the company (*Corr.* 2:319).[41] Burke declined, and instead, the experienced company man Hastings was transferred from Madras to Bengal to carry out reforms as governor—thus removing the intriguing possibility that Burke himself might have played the role of the man whose career he was later to condemn so violently.

In 1773, despite continuing opposition from the Rockingham Whigs, the first major piece of Indian legislation was passed: as the price of the loan required to relieve the company's financial distress, Lord North's Regulating

Act established a limited form of parliamentary control over the Indian empire. Power was conferred on a governor-general of Bengal (Hastings was retained in this position), balanced by a council whose members were named by the government, and by an independent Supreme Court; various restrictions were imposed, including prohibitions on further territorial acquisitions, offensive wars, and the taking of presents from Indians. Symbolically, the Regulating Act for the first time clearly asserted the right of the British Crown or state to exercise supervision as necessary, and to have ultimate control over British territories abroad, and hence, over the East India Company as the imperial intermediary. As unfavorable reports and allegations of persisting oppressive rule by Hastings continued to filter back over the next decade, this precedent was to be acted upon.

By the early 1780s, partly as a result of information forwarded by Hastings's opponents on the Bengal council and widely publicized in England, many became convinced that North's Regulating Act had not sufficed to solve the problems. Burke and others in his party were converted to this opinion. In 1781–1783 Burke studied Indian affairs extensively while serving on the parliamentary select committee charged with investigating the matter, and he wrote several of its reports, which severely condemned both company rule in general and Hastings's policies in particular. This committee work marked a decisive change in Burke's view of India. "Now, in absolute contradiction of his former beliefs, but in harmony with his new knowledge of Indian affairs, he was a clamant advocate of close governmental supervision of company affairs."[42] His chance soon came: in November–December 1783, when Burke and his group were briefly in office as part of the precarious Fox-North coalition government, Burke helped formulate what is known as Fox's East India Bill and delivered his best-known Indian speech in its favor. Against a background of wide agreement that something needed to be done to bring the company to account, the Burke-Fox bill stands out as a relatively radical legislative proposal, which would have effectively transferred authority over British India, both political and commercial, from the company to commissioners who were members of Parliament and directly responsible to that legislative body.

Caught up in partisan politics, Fox's bill failed to pass, and the coalition fell. Pitt came into office, won a general election, and successfully offered a more moderate alternative, which left the company in charge of its commercial affairs while reserving political oversight of the empire to a government board of control. Pitt's East India Act of 1784 seemed to contemporaries to work well and provided a fairly stable basis for Indian government until 1858.[43] Although Burke perfunctorily opposed this legislation in the House,

"Edmund Burke in Conversation with His Friend Charles James Fox,"
by Thomas Hickey. Fox was the leader of the major
Whig party in the House of Commons.
Courtesy of the National Gallery of Ireland, Dublin.

he did not criticize it in operation thereafter; with reform of the system accomplished, Burke's Indian efforts from the mid-1780s onward were concentrated on the prosecution of the returned Hastings and the detailed scrutiny of his actions that this involved.

Two Obstacles to Reform

Several problems for Burke's political thought emerge from this brief historical sketch of the Indian reform movement. In changing his mind on the position of the East India Company, Burke became a reformer on this issue (something he often claimed to be throughout his career) and, moreover, embraced a radical position, an exception to his generally conservative approach to political innovation. The justification of radical reform will be addressed in the following section; meanwhile we might ask: If there was a general sense in Britain that India was being misgoverned, why were reform measures not more readily adopted? Why was Fox's bill defeated—apart from the general political weakness of the coalition, the king's disfavor, the opposition of the company and its friends, and other factors not germane to the substantive issue?[44] Why did the Rockingham Whigs and Burke himself at first oppose reform (North's Regulating Act), and only gradually become convinced of its necessity? We may note two important stumbling blocks that mark principled reservations.

In the first place, the position that the East India Company had attained in India, especially since 1765, amounted to a constitutional problem for Great Britain. Sovereignty—powers of rule over persons and over "British" territory—had fallen into the hands of a private corporation that appeared inadequately motivated to exercise such a public trust. This power had to be made accountable in the same way that sovereign power in Great Britain itself was held to be accountable, that is, through the existing system of legal and constitutional government; this in turn would require some form of government or parliamentary control over the company. The problem facing even well-meaning British politicians was how to establish this control without dangerously upsetting the constitutional balance within Great Britain itself and without advantaging certain parties in the British political system at the expense of others. As Burke remarked in launching his famous speech, it was difficult for Parliament to consider how to correct Indian abuses without at the same time noticing how any proposed reform might "[tend] to set this man a little higher, or that a little lower in situation and power" (Fox's Bill, 381). Ideally, the system or machinery of government itself should be neutral vis-à-vis the various interests and parties that contend within it, but this ideal is notoriously difficult to achieve, and any proposal for systemic change is likely to be contentious in light of it.[45]

The traditional objection to any political tampering with the East India Company was that doing so might increase the power of the Crown within the delicate constitutional balance. Efforts to restrict the royal prerogative and the Crown's influence in Parliament were a century-old preoccupation of the Whigs, and the desirability of an appropriate balance was a widely shared conviction. Burke himself had carried on this tradition on behalf of his (opposition) party in 1770, analyzing the resources available to the king and his private advisers by means of which they could corrupt members of the House of Commons and circumvent the will of Parliament (*Present Discontents*, 299). When it was thought that possession of Bengal would generate public wealth, it was feared that the Crown might secure a source of revenue independent of Parliament. More realistically, it was feared that the Crown (or ministries responsive to the king) might capture the extensive and valuable patronage of positions in the Indian service hitherto in the hands of the company directors; this, like other forms of eighteenth-century patronage, could then be converted into executive influence over the House of Commons, a familiar concern of the period.[46]

These fears were expressed by the elder Pitt as early as 1759, when Clive first broached the idea that the Crown might assume the dominion of Bengal,[47] and they were still being expressed as late as 1784. By then, however, a different issue had arisen: Fox's bill sought to transfer control over the company not to the Crown but to Parliament, that is, to a ministry not favored by the king and that acknowledged its accountability to Parliament. Fears that the widely mistrusted coalition would be able to perpetuate itself in office through the deployment of Indian patronage, or that this patronage could be used by any future government for partisan advantage to bolster and protect its base of support in the House, figured significantly in the defeat of the bill.[48] Burke was a leading contemporary theorist of party government and of ministerial responsibility to an organized and disciplined parliamentary party. Ironically, any approximation of reality to this model would increase the danger that governments would feel compelled to manipulate whatever patronage was at their disposal for clear-cut partisan objectives, since party support would be the condition of office. The Fox-North coalition scarcely fit this picture, but fears that control of India would enable it to become a solid party government helped defeat the Indian bill Burke favored.

Burke, on the defensive, alluded to these problems in his speech on Fox's bill. True to his reputation as an opponent of royal influence, Burke denied that the bill would tend to increase such influence; at the same time, he attempted to deflect attention away from the procedural problem to the all-important substantive purpose of the bill:

> If I am not able to correct a system of oppression and tyranny, that goes to the utter ruin of thirty millions of my fellow-creatures and fellow-subjects, but by some increase in the influence of the Crown, I am ready here to declare, that I, who have been active to reduce it, shall be at least as active and strenuous to restore it again. I am no lover of names; I contend for the substance of good and protecting government, let it come from what quarter it will.

He expressed a hope that Indian reform need not depend on the Crown, but could proceed from "the uncorrupt public virtue of the representatives of the people of England" (*Fox's Bill*, 442).

Burke, however, was too astute a practical politician not to understand the political (even constitutional) implications inherent in any particular method of implementing reform; moreover, he was unwilling to trust too far in public virtue alone. Turning to the more important charge, that the bill would transfer power from the Crown or, more plausibly, the company, "to the use of a party" and the present ministry, Burke adopted a more realistic approach. For one thing, he argued, such influence as the government gained would merely serve to counteract the influence that the company already had through its friends, including former Indian servants, in the House of Commons: parliamentary politics was, in fact, less often an exercise in "uncorrupt public virtue" than a contention among various interests. As Burke had remarked a moment earlier, rejecting any suggestion that the company could be made to reform itself, "It is not easy to choose men to act in conformity to a public interest against their private: but a sure dependence may be had on those who are chosen to forward their private interest, at the expense of the public" (*Fox's Bill*, 441). Any effective reform, carried out against vested private interests, would of necessity involve conferring power on some agency, and some shift in the present balance of power or influence was indeed inescapable. "This objection against party is a party objection. . . . The minister will name his friends, and persons of his own party.—Who should he name? Should he name his adversaries?" The claim that a reform would necessitate an increase in the power of government, and hence in the power of the party currently in office, was not a good argument against the reform, especially if it was urgently needed; in fact, that argument would rule out all reform. The proper response to this problem was that, in a parliamentary system, the ministry would be accountable to the

House of Commons—an "independent" and "virtuous" House, one would hope—and would thus be subject to removal from office upon misuse of its powers (*Fox's Bill*, 445). The fear that Indian patronage could confer immunity from such accountability was overstated. At the beginning of his speech, Burke asserted that "if we are not able to contrive some method of governing India well, which will not of necessity become the means of governing Great Britain ill," then the empire should be given up; his efforts rested on a belief that no such "incompatibility of interest" existed, and that the removal of oppression in India could be accomplished consistently with the maintenance of the "freedom and integrity" of the British constitution (*Fox's Bill*, 383).

The second obstacle to reform lay in the fact that an assertion of government control over the East India Company would involve a major revision—in essence, a violation—of the company's charter and thus its chartered rights. Such action was widely viewed and denounced as despotic in an age when the privileges embodied in corporate charters (and for that matter, the merely customary prerogatives of corporate bodies) were regarded both as a principal expression of the "liberties of the subject" and as a form of property, in Britain and throughout western Europe. The sanctity of charters, moreover, was a traditional Whig cause, since defending charters (especially those conferring representation on parliamentary boroughs) had been part of the resistance to the absolutist tendencies of James II a century earlier. Finally, the violation of any charter (even for the purpose of reforming abuses) seemed to represent a threat to all chartered rights, and hence to the constitution itself, a consideration that had to be weighed against the value of the proposed reform.

These concerns figured in Rockingham's and Burke's opposition to North's act in 1773, which Burke himself had argued was repugnant to "the laws, liberties, and the constitution of this country" ("North's Resolutions," 391). They led other important corporate interests, including the Bank of England and the City of London, to rally behind the East India Company's resistance to change; and they were invoked by the opposition, notably by Pitt and Grenville, in the debate on Fox's bill.[49] As Burke noted at the beginning of his speech, the fact that many members of the House regarded the whole issue more "as a point of law on a question of private property, and corporate franchise . . . [than as] concerning the interest and well-being of the people of India, and concerning the interest which this nation has in the commerce and revenues of that country, is a strong indication of the value which they set upon these objects" (*Fox's Bill*, 381). Again, this was a problem that aroused the concern not only of those with interests directly at stake but also of members of the educated public: Edward Gibbon, for example, remarked to a correspondent in the wake of the defeat of Fox's bill: "The vices of the Company, both in their persons and their constitution were manifold and manifest, the danger was imminent and such an Empire with thirty millions of Subjects was not to be lost for trifles. Yet on the other hand the faith of Charters, the rights of property! I hesitate and tremble."[50]

It is readily apparent from Burke's general political thought that this matter would have been of concern to him as well. Condemning certain abstract theories, Burke argued that society was not a collection of un-differentiated individuals but a complex fabric in which corporate entities of many kinds had a legitimate and useful place. In his *Reflections*, Burke attacked the revolutionaries who, motivated by an atomistic and egalitarian vision of the nation, destroyed social orders—such as the nobility—and numerous venerable corporations, most prominently ecclesiastical ones. Re-jecting an "arithmetical constitution," he associated the liberty of England with a complex of established institutions, including the "antient corpora-tions of the kingdom" as well as its monarchy, its courts, its House of Lords, and its episcopacy (*Reflections*, 144). By the fundamental "engagement and pact of society, which generally goes by the name of the constitution," he argued, "the constituent parts of the state are obliged to hold their public faith with each other, and with all those who derive any serious interest under their engagements." If this public faith—including respect for the interests embodied in the corporations—were not kept, government would be reduced to the arbitrary will of the sovereign: "No law [would] be left but the will of a prevailing force" (*Reflections*, 105). In 1772, consistently with this later view, Burke had argued on behalf of the East India Company that "the *Charter* ought to be held inviolable," and that this was a matter in which the "*faith* of Parliament" was implicated ("East India Select Committee," 372).

It was true that corporations were artificial creations of law (the East India Company's charter was originally granted by the monarch, and since 1698 had been confirmed by Parliament), and no one doubted that formally the government had the authority to revoke or modify what it had created. On the other hand, according to Burke, liberties become secure only when they are declared and stabilized in charters. Moreover, rights or practices of whatever origin acquire the additional and independent force of prescriptive right through long exercise, and to override prescription is in itself destruc-tive of liberty, which is most valuable when it is expressed in legally pro-tected practices grounded in the network of traditional institutions. Hence Burke announced his support for the Americans over the "invasion" of their colonial charters: "Because the charters comprehend the essential forms by which you enjoy your liberties, we regard them as most sacred, and by no means to be taken away or altered without process, without examination, and without hearing, as they have lately been" ("Address to the Colonists," 188). Finally, Burke held that injustice always attends the arbitrary violation of legitimate interests and expectations, that is, those acquired and pursued in accordance with the previously prevailing state of the law.

> When men are encouraged to go into a certain mode of life by the existing laws, and protected in that mode as in a lawful occupation— when they have accommodated all their ideas, and all their habits to it— . . . I am sure it is unjust in legislature, by an arbitrary act, to offer a sudden violence to their minds and their feelings; forcibly to degrade them from their state and condition, and to stigmatize with shame and infamy that character and those customs. (*Reflections*, 265–66).

Burke made this assertion in reference to the revolutionary attacks on the French Church, but as a general principle it seems applicable to individuals engaged in other ways of life and other corporations, and hence to those who had invested or made careers in the East India Company.

These doctrines are extremely conservative: prescriptive right justifies whatever state of affairs exists, the more so the older it is; a refusal ever to defeat anyone's reasonable expectations would rule out virtually any change in the law.[51] Burke was a reformer, however, and he was not a theoretical absolutist; hence these doctrines must be understood to provide only prima facie arguments against reform, and perhaps only against "violent" or "arbitrary" change. "Bodies corporate," Burke noted, enjoy a "perennial existence," which is appropriate for long-term social purposes—for "designs that require time in fashioning . . . [and] duration when they are accomplished." Their immortality, however, also sometimes causes corporations to outlive their original purposes, whereupon their privileges may come to appear dysfunctional, undeserved, or even corrupt. When this happens, Burke suggested, a corporate body should not be "rashly destroyed"; rather, it was the task of anyone who aspired "to be mentioned in the order of great statesmen" to discover the middle course, to find a way of "converting it to the great and lasting benefit of his country" (*Reflections*, 266–68). Corporate goals can be redefined, their internal governance and their relation to the state rearranged. This is precisely what Burke, Fox, and others determined had to be done with respect to the East India Company in the early 1780s; they differed from opposing statesmen such as Pitt primarily over exactly how to do it. In fact, Burke said, "in a question of reformation, I always consider corporate bodies . . . to be much more susceptible of a public direction by the power of the state, in the use of their property, and in the regulation of modes and habits of life in their members, than private citizens ever can be" (*Reflections*, 273). Whether this is because the habits of private individuals are more intractable, or because corporations are legal artifacts in the first place, this statement reflects Burke's conversion from his initial hesitation to his subsequent campaign to reform the East India Company and indeed to bring it firmly under the direction of the state.

Convinced, then, as he came to be of the necessity of reform, Burke confronted the chartered rights objection straightforwardly; in the course of his argument he enunciated some of the central tenets of his political philosophy. The genuine "natural rights of mankind," he said, "are indeed sacred things," and "if these natural rights are clearly defined and secured against chicane, against power, and authority, by written instruments and positive engagements, they are in a still better condition." The great charters, such as the Magna Carta, insofar as they secured the "chartered rights of men," were sacrosanct. Fox's East India Bill itself, he affirmed, was "intended to form the Magna Charta of Hindostan," establishing effective constitutional government and thus assuring legal protection of rights in India for the first time, thereby initiating a tradition such as that marked by the great constitutional documents of European history.

A charter such as that of the East India Company, on the other hand, however venerable and important in its objects, differed from a great charter in two crucial respects. First, whereas the Magna Carta was "a charter to restrain power, and to destroy monopoly," the company's charter did the opposite: it conferred a commercial monopoly, fiscal authority, and political and military power on a select group of men. Far from declaring or enlarging the natural rights of people in general, it suspended them and constituted "a derogation from the natural equality of mankind at large." The creation of such special powers and privileges—like government itself—may be perfectly justifiable, but all power is attended with responsibilities and is to be evaluated by its consequences for the general well-being, and not by the "private benefit of the holders." All political power and commercial privilege is "in the strictest sense a trust; and it is of the very essence of every trust to be rendered accountable; and even totally to cease, when it substantially varies from the purposes for which alone it could have a lawful existence." The chartered rights of the East India Company were therefore not the kind of rights that limit the legitimate power of government, but were rather subject to continuing oversight by the government and to the requirement of accountability. Second, the company itself, and hence its charter and its rights, were "wholly artificial." They were created by or derived from the authority of Parliament; it was therefore to Parliament that the company was accountable for the exercise—or the abuse—of its privileges. Parliament indeed had a duty, arising from the larger trust on which its own authority was based, to correct abuses perpetrated under its warrant, by agencies licensed or subordinate to it (*Fox's Bill*, 383–86). Convinced that abuses had taken place, Burke held that the company needed to be called to account, and its charter superseded.

The Problem of Radical Reform

Burke thus embraced the cause of reform in India, as in other areas, notwithstanding the political difficulties and scruples about vested interests that he himself shared. More problematically, however, the course he adopted (Fox's bill) was relatively radical; Pitt's eventually successful alternative bill represented a more moderate compromise with the company, preserving its rights (and thus assuaging the general worry about charters and arbitrary power) as far as seemed consistent with the imposition of ultimate government control of the empire.[52] Burke's uncompromising attitude, by contrast, was expressed in his defiant response, toward the end of his speech, to those at the Bank of England and in the City who were concerned about their own charters. In a like case, Burke said, they would have no security at all. If the bank were guilty of mismanagement, or "if the city of London had the means and will of destroying an empire, and of cruelly oppressing and tyrannizing over millions of men as good as themselves, [their charters] should prove no sanction to such tyranny and such oppression" (*Fox's Bill*, 448). Such a virtually revolutionary sentiment raises the question of when radical change, with its attendant violence to traditional arrangements, is permissible and desirable according to Burkean political theory.

Burke's usual opposition to revolutionary change—the "dislike I feel to revolutions," as he candidly put it, especially when they reflected contempt for "antient institutions" in favor of present convenience or inclination (*Reflections*, 110)—is perhaps the best-known aspect of his political thought. What is a revolution? In one sense, it is political change by extraordinary methods, that is, change in violation of existing constitutional or legal norms. The "revolutions in Bengal" of 1757–1765, which Burke accepted, would fit this definition. So would the American Revolution, with which he sympathized, and the English Revolution of 1688, which he explicitly defended in terms of its limited scope, the extraordinary or emergency situation, and the intention and effect of preserving the legal and political traditions of the country against a present threat. In another sense, however, revolution is political change that is both comprehensive and sudden, reflecting a deliberate attempt to replace existing or traditional institutions with new ones that are thought to correspond either to nontraditional normative conceptions or to a putatively superior systematic design or theory. It was primarily revolution in this second sense that Burke opposed, for familiar reasons: the complexity of the social fabric makes rational change on a broad scale impossible; detrimental side effects are unforeseen or inappropriately discounted; valuable elements in old institutions, less apparent than their defects, are overlooked; and the moral costs that always attend disruptions in social continuity are neglected. The French Revolution fit both definitions, but Burke's vociferous antagonism toward it arose not from the legal irregularities involved but from his conviction that it embodied the fundamentally misguided attitudes characteristic of the latter conception of revolution.

Yet Burke defended the propriety of deliberate political reform as the normal business of statesmen, and his career, during which he embraced numerous reformist causes, bears this out. Where is the line to be drawn between permissible reform and impermissible revolution? Or, since this seems to be a matter of degree and not a qualitative distinction, how much change is too much, and when does change come too fast? Burke's answer to these questions was that definitive rules cannot be stated:

> Nothing universal can be rationally affirmed on any moral, or any political subject. The lines of morality are not like the ideal lines of mathematics. . . . They admit of exceptions; they demand modifications. These exceptions and modifications are not made by the process of logic, but by the rules of prudence. ("Appeal," 91)

Prudence is the principal political virtue, and in what may be interpreted as a development of this concept, Burke offered several practical guidelines on reform. First, a "true politician always considers how he shall make the most of the existing materials of his country" (*Reflections*, 267). Preservation and improvement could go together when reformers worked as much as possible with old institutions, modifying or adapting them as changing circumstances demanded. Second, Burke several times suggested that moderation consists in discovering the middle ground or middle course between revolution and stasis, between "absolute destruction, or unreformed existence"; it is the revolutionary's tactic to pretend that there is "no third option" between his own program and an old regime that is thoroughly corrupt or tyrannical (*Reflections*, 266, 227). Finally, Burke offered a clear account of what would now be called incremental reform, in which changes are introduced gradually, with "circumspection and caution," in a spirit of experimentation, and with constant monitoring of "the effect of each step" so that "we are conducted with safety through the whole series" (*Reflections*, 281).

Did Burke's approach to Indian reform accord with these maxims? Fox's bill was a relatively radical—if not exactly "revolutionary"—proposal under the circumstances. If we compare the proposals of Burke and his colleagues to the alternatives (ranging from allowing the company to reform itself, as Hastings was ostensibly trying to do, to Pitt's bill), we find that Burke was less willing to compromise with or adapt existing arrangements, and more willing to repudiate past practice altogether in favor of a newly designed system. This episode thus reveals, in keeping with Burke's rejection of doctrinaire stances, that he was on occasion prepared to countenance radical change when circumstances warranted, to support radical solutions to problems when more moderate approaches appeared futile. Although, as he said, "I have in general no very exalted opinion of the virtue of paper government," that is, plans of governments disconnected from experience, nevertheless, as the American crisis deepened, his "caution gave way" and he cast about (without success) for some new scheme of imperial relations that might salvage the situation ("Conciliation," 105). When an existing situation was bad enough, as for example in Poland, Burke recommended not incrementalism but "bold enterprize and desperate experiment" ("Appeal," 185). Burke did not even rule out revolution, even violent revolution (also in the Polish case), though he did argue that revolutionaries must bear a heavy "burthen of proof" ("Appeal," 90) and that "to make a revolution is a measure which, prima fronte, requires an apology [i.e., a defense]," one invoking "no common reasons," in view of the violence and the affront to tradition (*Reflections*, 276).

What, then, justifies radical political action? Burke suggested several criteria. First, "the subversion of a government, to deserve any praise, must be considered as a step preparatory to the formation of something better, either in the scheme of the government itself, or in the persons who administer in it, or both" ("Appeal," 90). Such a clear-sighted constructive program was present, in Burke's opinion, both in England in 1688 and in his party's proposals for Indian government in 1783. More stringently, Burke approved of revolution (or radical change) only if it could be maintained "that a sore and pressing evil is to be removed, and that a good, great in its amount, and unequivocal in its nature, must be probable almost to certainty" ("Appeal," 91). Given Burke's view of the complexity of society and the often obscure interrelations among social practices and institutions, such a clear showing of the net benefits to be expected from a radical political intervention would be difficult and infrequent. This is why the revolutionary spirit should not be expressed in a frivolous fashion, but should be reserved for "great occasions," or perhaps, as in 1688, for "cases of extreme emergency" (*Reflections*, 154, 105). Having documented great abuses in the East India Company's regime, and convinced that piecemeal or internal reform was impossible, Burke clearly believed that Parliament was confronted with one of those "great occasions" when drastic measures were required. Brushing aside the worries about patronage raised by Fox's bill, Burke pointed to

> the habitual despotism and oppression, . . . the monopolies, the peculations, the universal destruction of all the legal authority of this kingdom . . . combined with the distance of the scene, the boldness and artifice of delinquents, their combination, their excessive wealth, and the faction they have made in England.

He asserted that strong measures were "required by the necessities of India" (*Fox's Bill*, 446). The imposition of a "new experimental government," in violation of the usual norms of prescription and continuity, was acceptable, he affirmed, "as a necessary substitute for an expelled tyranny" (*Reflections*, 276). The company's government, he was convinced, was "one of the most corrupt and destructive tyrannies, that probably ever existed in the world" and was "utterly incorrigible" (*Fox's Bill*, 440–41, 433).

Burke generally accorded a presumption of value and usefulness to old and functioning institutions, and he held that institutions that survive and adapt over time, by a process of unplanned growth, are normally sound on balance, and probably superior to theoretical alternatives. Satisfactory outcomes usually result, as they had until recently in America, "from the natural operation of things which, left to themselves, generally fall into their proper order" (*Sheriffs of Bristol*, 233). He did not, however, put forward these claims as universally true. He insisted that changing circumstances made it necessary on occasion to reformulate purposes and refashion evolved institutions, such as the imperial relations between Parliament and America. He admitted, even while opposing the French Revolution, that anachronisms and abuses in old institutions such as the French nobility and the Church called for ongoing but cautious reform. More surprisingly, Burke even acknowledged that the opposite of his usual presumption in favor of old institutions could sometimes be true: a thoroughly bad system might survive indefinitely, precisely because it lacked the internal capacity for improvement, until (presumably) it was altered or destroyed by an external force. Burke illustrated this possibility by referring to two contemporary Muslim regimes, ones which he must have regarded as aberrant in light of the generally more favorable view of Asian government that he had formulated by the time of Hastings's trial.

> It is not to be imagined because a political system is, under certain aspects, very unwise in it's contrivance, and very mischievous in it's effects, that it therefore can have no long duration. It's very defects may tend to it's stability, because they are agreeable to it's nature. . . . What can be conceived so monstrous as the Republick of Algiers? and that no less strange Republick of the Mammalukes in Egypt? They are of the worst form imaginable, and exercised in the worst manner, yet they have existed as a nuisance on the earth for several hundred years. ("French Affairs," 236)

The case of the East India Company did not quite match any of these, but it may have resembled them to some degree. Here was a venerable institution, at one time perfectly respectable, that in Burke's view had become thoroughly corrupt and so abusive of its privileges as to necessitate a transfer of its power to an entirely new government body. How could this have happened? In the following chapters we shall examine Burke's charges in detail. Here two general points may be suggested. First, the company's moral decline began when it started to operate in radically new circumstances for which all its previous experience had not prepared it. Ironically, as a result of its own successes in dealing with local and immediate challenges, the company in short order added sovereign responsibilities to its mercantile interests and was unable to negotiate this transition smoothly. Such abrupt alterations in environment or in the structures of constraints and opportunities within which institutions operate set limits on the validity of Burke's usual assumption in favor of continuity; they create nonstandard cases that require extraordinary political responses.

Second, when the British East India Company became the ruler of parts of India, the resulting clash between different sets of traditional interests posed a special problem for Burkean theory. Burke came to believe that the traditional values and institutions of Indian society were being seriously and wantonly disrupted by company policies. In this situation he had to make a choice, and his choice was unambiguous: the rights of the Indians were to be defended, even though this meant dismantling the established legal and customary prerogatives of the company and remodeling imperial government. In his Indian speeches Burke often appeared in his familiar role as a defender of tradition, though at the same time his attacks on Hastings and the company lacked the caution and moderation he usually recommended.

Impeachment

With the passage of Pitt's East India Act in 1784, the decisive step in the reform of the Indian empire had been taken; parliamentary control was established, and with it the principle that the empire was essentially a public or state enterprise rather than a commercial one. During the next ten years—the final decade of Burke's career—important events continued to unfold in India, including further wars and imperial expansion, the growth of a more professionalized administration, and legal reforms respecting landed property along the lines that Burke advocated. The fact that his party was out of office no doubt precluded his taking an active part, but it is striking that Burke scarcely even commented on new developments in India after 1785, the year of Hastings's resignation.[53] Rather, Burke devoted much of his final decade to the relentless prosecution of Hastings, with its retrospective preoccupation with past misdeeds, through the lengthy process of impeachment. Burke firmly believed that Hastings was guilty of criminal misconduct, and part of his motivation was doubtless a desire to see retributive justice done through appropriate punishment.[54] Part of the explanation—probably more for his colleagues than for Burke himself—concerns partisan politics: attacking Hastings, whose friends had contributed to Pitt's electoral victory, was a way of annoying the government and vindicating the Whigs' previous position on abuses in India (*Corr.* 5:243).[55] Beyond these points, the decision to impeach Hastings and the conduct of the prosecution raise several issues for the interpretation of Burke, viewed both as a political theorist and as a politician.

First, the impeachment of Hastings was the first such proceeding in Great Britain in half a century and, as it turned out, it was to be one of the last.[56] Burke appears to have admired the institution of impeachment, which had been employed more frequently in earlier centuries, both as an ancient and venerable element of the English constitution and as a useful device for controlling high executive officials in the name of law and liberty.[57] As early as 1770 Burke expressed regret that impeachment had gone out of fashion (*Present Discontents*, 294). Later, in his *Appeal from the New to the Old Whigs*, composed when he was a manager of the Hastings impeachment, Burke identified himself with the Old Whig managers of the Sacheverell impeachment in 1710, who were asserting—as he too claimed to be doing—"the true grounds and principles of the Revolution" (*Appeal*, 122). Impeachment itself, as a vehicle for parliamentary rule, was part of the Old Whig system. Opening the trial before the lords, Burke praised impeachment as an essential constitutional "security for good governors," and expressed concern that its disuse might reflect "apathy" regarding "public justice" ("Speech in Opening," 9:333). Hence, one of Burke's objectives in impeaching Hastings appears to have been the revitalization of impeachment itself as a weapon against official injustice and oppression. In this he failed, and it is ironic that the great length of Hastings's trial, and the eventual acquittal, contributed to a growing sense that impeachment was too cumbersome a procedure for modern parliamentary bodies to undertake. A further irony is that Burke himself, through his championing of the House of Commons and of party government as a means of rendering ministries regularly accountable to the House, promoted the development of practices that made impeachment obsolete.[58]

Second, Burke did not have high expectations that the impeachment would succeed in the House of Commons (as it presumably would not have done had the government treated it as a partisan challenge, since Burke's party was in a minority), and he subsequently and correctly doubted that a conviction could be won from the lords. Why did Burke instigate the impeachment and persist in it if eventual defeat was likely? Writers critical of Burke have persistently regarded his dogged pursuit of Hastings as irrational—either a blind quest to avenge crimes magnified by his own fertile imagination, or a disproportionate effort to vindicate the position he had taken in connection with Fox's East India Bill (which led to his party's defeat), or the product of a personal obsession with Hastings. Psychological conjectures such as these are difficult to disprove, but it may be that a calculated and forward-looking political purpose lay behind Burke's campaign and that the Burke of the impeachment was still the Burke who proclaimed: "I reserve my activity for rational endeavors" (*Sheriffs of Bristol*, 201), not useless or merely expressive causes.

In the first place, the failure to achieve an actual conviction can be discounted as a technicality. Hastings was surely—and predictably—punished both through the costs of defending himself and through the disgrace that attended the extensive airing of his record; Burke made his points to wide acclaim, and was pronounced the moral victor not only by many contemporaries but also by later generations of British writers on India.[59] This outcome accords with what we may suppose to have been Burke's primary intention throughout the affair: to arouse public opinion in Great Britain against abuses in the Indian empire and thereby perpetuate the spirit of reform and deter future abuses by later imperial officials. Parliament had taken charge of Indian affairs, but to whom was Parliament likely to be responsive on this matter? The East Indian interest remained well organized and well represented, Indians themselves were unrepresented, and ordinary people in Britain knew and therefore cared little about so distant a scene. Ministers were aware of the problems, but they had no incentive to act in the absence of pressure from their constituents, and the public so far had not been moved (*Corr.* 5:150–51). In this situation, Burke the politician grasped the problem of the superior force likely to be wielded in a legislative assembly by a special interest, or the concentrated beneficiaries of corruption, in the face of merely diffuse, though potentially more numerous, opposition. The only way out of this vicious circle was to educate public opinion through a dramatic presentation of the case and thus—presupposing a reliable moral sense in a largely disinterested electorate—to stir up an effective public interest in imperial justice.

This reasoning is reflected in various comments and details of the record. At stake in the impeachment was not simply a particular judgment to be passed on the defendant, but "the whole character of your future government in that distant empire" ("Speech in Opening," 9:331). The question was "whether millions of mankind shall be made miserable or happy." Achieving the desired outcome required not only a forceful case in Parliament, but success in rendering "the East" more generally "intelligible," thus overcoming people's inclination "not to know or to care any thing about it" (*Corr.* 5:281). To this end Burke's "Articles of Charge" against Hastings contained lengthy narratives of events; they were apparently composed more with an eye to their educative and political effect than to their legal efficacy.[60] In addition, Burke urged that the trial be held in the large and imposing Westminster Hall, where it could be a public spectacle, not only in England but before all Europe (*Corr.* 5:341; 356–57). Furthermore, he deliberately dwelt on sensational episodes that would "work upon the popular Sense" (*Corr.* 5:372). Burke's willingness, as he put it, to be "mobbish" in his attacks on Hastings (*Corr.* 6:197–99), and, more generally, to go beyond Parliament and appeal to public opinion, were clearly out of character— testimony to his belief in the exceptional quality of the circumstances. The rhetoric of his speeches—and what many have regarded as occasional rhetorical extravagances—should be interpreted in this light.[61] Behind all this lay a determination that the oppression characteristic of Hastings's tenure in India not be repeated. As he opened the proceedings in the House of Commons, Burke remarked that a new governor-general was about to be appointed ("Notice of Motion," 46), and in his first speech he asserted that the prosecution aimed not so much at Hastings as at "a matter of much higher import"—the establishment of principles to guide "future Governors in India" ("Rohilla Speech," 105). The fate of a humiliated Hastings was to serve as a warning, and as a deterrent to future imperial misrule.[62]

This interpretation of Burke's motives raises two problems. There is, first, the question of his fairness toward Hastings. Some historians who are sympathetic to Hastings or who admire his achievements outright have maintained he was made a scapegoat for offenses that were widespread in the company, and that his personal standards of conduct were higher, or at least not lower, than the average during that period. To prosecute an individual as the representative of an offending class, or as an exemplary figure, raises questions both of fairness and of legal justice; Burke himself maintained (simultaneously with the trial) that it was unjust to punish men for the offenses of their ancestors or corporate predecessors, as the French revolutionaries were doing to the nobles and to the Church in France (*Reflections*, 246). And yet Hastings seemed to be suffering in part for the sins of his predecessors in India. Although scapegoating as such is indefensible,[63] it is another matter when the accused individual is in fact personally guilty, as Burke certainly believed Hastings to be. Furthermore, Hastings's position as governor-general exposed him to special accountability and, if guilty, to extraordinary treatment. As Burke said at the outset, this was not a case of crimes committed by "persons unknown," or of a corrupt system without a corrupt agent ("Motion for Papers," 57).

The intensity of Burke's focus on Hastings was of course connected to the decision to impeach, a proceeding that requires a particular defendant, and it served the purpose of publicizing Indian misrule generally. Burke's personalization of this cause remains intriguing, however, because it was not typical of his various campaigns. In his early attack on George III's double cabinet, for example, he refrained from attacking Lord Bute personally, blaming the system rather than the person putatively behind it (*Present Discontents*, 276).[64] No notable individual villains appear in Burke's critiques of British policies in America and Ireland, and though he attributed the French Revolution to disreputable personal actors, it was a "cabal" and not any one individual he denounced.[65] Of course, as Hume argued, foreign affairs depend much more than domestic politics on the "caprices of a few persons," and many of Hastings's questionable exploits occurred in the international arena.[66] Alternatively, the unusually personal animosity that Burke expressed toward Hastings has given rise to a number of psychological explanations, plausible but in their nature bound to remain speculative constructions: that Burke in one part of his personality actually identified with

Hastings, an adventurer in an aristocratic world, but sought to repress this psychic tie;[67] that he sought subconsciously to compensate for not having opposed Irish oppression more forcefully, and for having earlier (in the 1770s) defended the East India Company;[68] and that by blaming Hastings personally he avoided having to confront the systemic injustices of imperialism or the "colonial project" as such.[69] Whatever the explanation, the figure of Warren Hastings as a personal antagonist is unquestionably a major presence in many (though not all) of Burke's writings and speeches on India, and gives a unique quality to this part of his work.

A second troubling matter is that the impeachment of Hastings has clear features of a political trial, in the sense of an attack on a political opponent and his policies carried out in the form of a judicial proceeding respecting his legal guilt or innocence. This problem may be inherent in impeachment itself, whose political-legal character had always been ambiguous—perhaps inevitably so, given its form as a judicial indictment and trial enacted by legislative bodies. Participation in such a proceeding seems questionable for Burke, who was a strong defender of the rule of law and a critic of the political abuse of judicial forms in India and—simultaneously with Hastings's trial—in revolutionary France.[70] Of course, Burke could have defended the propriety of impeachment as an established constitutional practice in English law, the proper forms of which were followed in Hastings's case.[71]

Hastings naturally regarded the impeachment as a political attack. Facing the House of Commons he commented, "It hurts me, I own, to be tried by judges who vote with their party in a judicial, as they do in a political question,"[72] and to the lords he complained about the managers' oratorical excesses.[73] His own partisans responded by agitating and distributing pamphlets in his support, which Burke denounced as "a heinous offence, to endeavour to prejudice, by extraneous discussion, the people, against the Legal Course of proceeding carried on by Legal Magistrates" (*Corr.* 8:381). This complaint was disingenuous, however, if Burke's presentation of the case also aimed to influence public opinion. More often than not, it was Hastings's counsel who sought a narrowly legalistic interpretation of the charges and evidence, and Burke who appealed to broadly moral and political considerations. One of the ambiguities of impeachment was that the precise scope of impeachable offenses ("high crimes and misdemeanors") was undefined; it was unclear whether these could include offenses against moral as well as positive law.[74] With respect to France, Burke condemned prosecutions for "undefined crimes of state, not ascertained by any previous rule, statute, or course of precedent" ("Letter to Depont," 11). Concerning

Hastings, however, Burke set out to demonstrate *"a general evil intention,* manifested through a long series and a great variety of acts," rather than a few discrete offenses, since the former would carry "greater weight with a *publick political* tribunal" (*Corr.* 5:242–43). In an impeachment such as Hastings's, Burke claimed, "our national character" and the "interests of our Constitution itself" were at stake, and in such a tribunal "statesmen who abuse their power are accused by statesmen and tried by statesmen, not upon the niceties of a narrow jurisprudence, but upon the enlarged and solid principles of state morality" ("Speech in Opening," 9:332–33).

In fairness, then, we may conclude by noting Hastings's ultimately successful political defense against what were essentially political charges of general misconduct in office and oppressive rule in India. Most centrally, he argued that he had been successful in saving and strengthening the empire— conspicuously successful, just at the time when, on the other side of the world, another major part of the empire was being lost. This was no doubt why Hastings retained his office for so long: from the mid-1770s he had been hearing from correspondents that the North ministry could not possibly risk the loss of Bengal, and that the government "look[ed] upon the East as an indemnification for the loss we are likely to suffer in the West."[75] India was to be held by whatever means necessary: Hastings took this as his mandate, and on his return to England he confidently proclaimed, "I have never yet planned or authorised any military operation . . . which has not been attended with complete success."[76] Impeachment was a severe disappointment, but in the end he continued to assert defiantly to the lords:

> In this long period of thirteen years . . . while Great Britain lost one half of its empire and doubled its public debt, that government over which I presided was not only preserved entire, but increased . . . [and] the British name and character never stood higher or were more respected in India than when I left it.[77]

If Burke appealed to the "principles of state morality" and demanded justice, Hastings often spoke the language of political realism and invoked success. The following chapters will explore further dimensions of this fundamental tension between political morality and empire building.

Chapter Two

The Charges

CORRUPTION

Burke fervently believed that the East India Company's servants in India, and most prominently Warren Hastings, were guilty of numerous and persistent offenses against both their native subjects and the laws of Great Britain. Burke thought that in Hastings's case, many of these offenses could be specified as "crimes and misdemeanors" that justified impeachment proceedings. In 1786 Burke launched the prosecution by presenting twenty-two "Articles of Charge" against Hastings to the House of Commons, of which only one was actually defeated.[1] In the end, however, because of a lack of parliamentary time, Hastings was impeached on twenty-one charges, which covered only eight of the original ones. Burke drew up these formal "Articles of Impeachment," which were forwarded to the House of Lords in 1787. In view of the numerous delays attending the proceedings, however, Burke and the other managers decided to restrict themselves to what they regarded as the four strongest charges, and on this basis they finally concluded their case in May 1791.[2] The trial then continued, through Hastings's defense and Burke's "Reply," until the final verdict was handed down in 1795.

Of the four charges on which Hastings was finally tried, two ("Presents" and "Contracts") were accusations of "pecuniary corruption." The others (the "Benares" and the "Begams of Oudh" charges) focused on instances of "open violence and injustice" ("Speech in Reply," 11:163), or oppression. Other attacks Burke made against Hastings and the company on different occasions also fall under these two headings: they include formal charges that were either not passed or were dropped, accusations regarding the conquest of Tanjore and the "Nabob of Arcot's Debts," the Nandakumar case, and Burke's general criticisms of company policies as reflected, for example, in his committee reports. Accordingly, in this chapter we will consider Burke's analysis and denunciations of the various forms of corruption he considered rampant in the Indian administration; in the following chapter, we will examine the charges of oppression, including despotism and arbitrary government.

Although the distinction between corruption and oppression is useful, it is not always clear-cut. In some of the specific episodes, Burke saw both kinds of misconduct, and the two general charges were related in several important ways. Most obviously, oppressive government practices could be motivated by the desire for personal enrichment on the part of a public official, that is, by "corruption" in the common sense of the word. Burke held that despotic power in the hands of East India Company officials was systematically used to extort bribes (euphemistically called "presents") from Indians, and that some of Hastings's most outrageous acts of oppression (for example, against the raja of Benares and the begams of Oudh) were motivated by his desire for money. "I will venture to say there is no one [act] in which tyranny, malice, cruelty and oppression can be charged, that does not at the same time carry evident marks of pecuniary corruption" ("Speech on Opening," 374).

Second, Burke accused Hastings of operating a despotic system of government, or a system of "arbitrary power"; and as Montesquieu had taught, corruption was likely to be pervasive in such systems.[3] Corruption of rulers or officials followed as a natural result of arbitrary power, regardless of whether extraction of wealth was the original intention of the regime; power, if not suitably restrained, corrupts. In Burke's words, "An Arbitrary system must always be a corrupt one. My Lords, there never was a man who thought he had no law but his own will, who did not soon find that he had no end but his own profit" ("Speech on Opening," 375).

Finally, Burke was disturbed not only by pecuniary corruption as such (the application of public power for private profit), but also about political corruption in Great Britain, and these two phenomena were linked in his analysis in a manner that reflected a familiar theme of eighteenth-century British politics. Briefly, Burke worried that illegitimately obtained Indian money could purchase parliamentary influence and use it to prevent reform and perpetuate the system of abuses. Corruption in India supported this form of political injustice, if not oppression, and posed a threat to free government at home.

Corruption and Human Nature

Burke himself made the charge of corruption central to his case against Hastings. All the governor's crimes, he asserted, "had their root in that which is the origin of all evil, avarice and rapacity. . . . Though there is undoubtedly oppression, breach of faith, cruelty, perfidy charged upon him, yet the great ruling principle of the whole, and that from which you can never have an act free, is money" ("Speech on Opening," 374–77). Even the Rohilla War, an unjust and brutal conquest, arose, he thought, from Hastings's "ruling principle," his *Spirit of Avarice* and pecuniary Corruption, the Receipt of Bribes, and the Extortion of Money" ("Rohilla Speech," 96).

Apparently this was not true of Hastings's predecessors, the first founders of the Indian empire, whatever moral questions might surround their actions:

> The Government of India undoubtedly originated first in ideas of safety and necessity. Its next step was a step of ambition. That ambition, as generally happens in conquest, was followed by gains of money. But afterwards there was no mixture at all; it was during Mr. Hastings' time, altogether a business of money. ("Speech on Opening," 377)

Neither in his impeachment speeches nor elsewhere did Burke challenge the "necessity" or the rightfulness of the diplomacy, battles, tricks, treaties, and other undertakings—notably those of Clive—that created the empire, or the undoubted political ambition involved. In an early speech, before he had studied India closely or become aware of abuses, Burke praised the conquests and ambition of Clive in tones of enthusiastic imperialism ("East India Settlement," 220). Burke may have also sensed that there is a kind of perverse or "sublime" grandeur attached to unjust actions on a large scale, when they are an aspect of successful conquest and empire building; later he deplored the fact that the desire to punish political offenders soon fades when great crimes produce successful revolutions and establish new regimes (*Policy of Allies*, 496–97). On the other hand, pecuniary corruption was a sordid vice, one that "never is, nor ever looks to the prejudices of mankind, to be any thing like a virtue" ("Speech on Opening," 377). The charge of corruption was central because it decisively tainted Hastings's apparent achievements as a successful imperial ruler.

It was not Hastings alone whom Burke regarded as corrupt; the same charge applied to many of the company's personnel in India. Hastings, however, was not an obscure offender, "misled perhaps by the example of those who ought to have kept him in awe." He was rather "the head, the chief, the captain-general in iniquity; one in whom all the frauds, all the peculations, all the violence, all the tyranny in India are embodied, disciplined, and arrayed" ("Speech on Opening," 275–76). Hastings deserved exemplary punishment because he set an example that his subordinates followed. Two further factors exacerbated his offense. As this passage suggests, Burke accused Hastings of directing a more or less organized conspiracy of company servants in the business of bribery and extortion—a "system of iniquity" ("Speech in Reply," 11:416); Burke believed a corrupt faction of returned company men conspired to acquire political influence in Britain itself. Furthermore, in taking this course, Hastings had betrayed a specific trust, since he had been appointed governor with a clear mandate from the company directors to reform recognized abuses of the kind Burke cited.[4] Far from attempting reform, Hastings simply carried on (and worsened) "a systematic, premeditated corruption of the whole service, from the time when he was appointed, [in] 1772, down to the year 1785," taking advantage of growing opportunities for acquiring wealth as the company's rule was consolidated in Bengal and its influence spread into Oudh and Benares ("Speech in Reply," 12:294).

In attributing such conscious and pervasive corruption to Hastings, Burke may have erred both substantively and tactically. Modern historians exonerate Hastings of the charge, by and large, notwithstanding some questionable transactions and sloppy record keeping. Moreover, Burke may have weakened his own case against Hastings, since this charge seems to have strained the credulity of contemporaries. Not only was the evidence complex and murky, but Hastings did not return from India an especially rich man, given the position he had held for so long.[5] The suggestion that there was something fundamentally wrong with a pervasive concern for money among Indian personnel may have seemed a bit odd, since the East India Company had always been, and remained, a commercial company seeking profits; personal bribes and extortionate methods aside, the mercenary interest was a systemic problem of imperial rule by the company rather than a personal defect in its employees. And while Burke was no doubt correct that there were many cases of personal corruption and abusive methods throughout the Indian service, as well as mutual cover-ups of these activities, his allegations regarding a consciously organized conspiracy under Hastings's management were not proven. Burke undoubtedly believed, on reading the available evidence, that Hastings was corrupt in the ways he publicly charged; one wonders, however, if Burke was not reasoning here in a manner that he elsewhere condemned (in political life) as "metaphysical," striving to identify a "ruling principle" that would allow him to make sense of a large body of disorderly facts, and then drawing conclusions for which the actual evidence was sometimes weak.

Did Hastings and the company arouse such antagonism on Burke's part because he regarded them as extraordinary examples of corruption, or did his view of human nature predispose him to expect such behavior? For Burke there was no question that vicious tendencies existed in human nature, and he sometimes expressed a generally pessimistic view of the political and historical manifestations of the basic vices: "History consists, for the greater part, of the miseries brought upon the world by pride, ambition, avarice, revenge, lust, sedition, hypocrisy, ungoverned zeal, and all the train of disorderly appetites, which shake the public" (*Reflections*, 247). On a more mundane level, there were many in preromantic eighteenth-century Britain who took a worldly, cynical view of the usual motives of human affairs, assuming or arguing that selfishness underlay all actions, however much people tried to disguise it, especially when acting in the public realm, by pretending to embrace noble principles. Applied as a means of explaining eighteenth-century politics, and indeed Burke himself, by Namier and his followers, this view held that the politics of private interest, place seeking, and faction were universal; from this perspective, the operations of the East Indian interest (interpreted along Burkean lines as "corrupt") were nothing out of the ordinary. Burke himself occasionally expressed a cynical, "Namierite" view of the gap between real and ostensible motives: "Vices are the *causes* of those [public disorders]. Religion, morals, laws, prerogatives, privileges, liberties, rights of men, are the *pretexts*" (*Reflections*, 248).

More directly relevant to Burke's charges against Hastings was the influence of Philip Francis, who had been Hastings's determined opponent on the Bengal Council in the 1770s, and who subsequently provided Burke with damning evidence against him. Francis's intense hatred of Hastings has been explained in various ways, for example, as a product of his own ambitions or of a theoretical mind that was convinced a priori that merchants were unfit to be rulers.[6] Francis, however, has also been portrayed as sharing the cynical view of universal political corruption, a view no doubt formed during his previous experience in government. On this basis, he is said to have arrived in Bengal with an unshakable preconception that abusive practices were widespread in India, and that Hastings and his patron, company chairman Laurence Sulivan, headed a dominant self-serving faction within the East India Company with which Lord North's government had had to compromise.[7] Francis may have encountered Hastings with self-fulfilling negative expectations, and ironically, he may have attributed political corruption and factional scheming to him on the basis of a generalized view reflecting his own previous experience of such phenomena.

It is generally agreed that Burke followed Francis in his assessment of Hastings, but it would be mistaken to suppose that he shared such a comprehensively pessimistic view of human nature and politics. "It is not soothing news to my ears, that great bodies of men are incurably corrupt," Burke remarked concerning the French revolutionaries, who had leveled such a charge against most of the past and present nobility and clergy of France. Not only was such a charge unpleasant, he claimed, but it should properly be met with skepticism: "I rather suspect that vices are feigned or exaggerated, when profit is looked for in their punishment" (*Reflections*, 246). Thus, if the East India Company regime was incurably corrupt, as Burke concluded (without any expectation of profit from its reform), it was a special case.

Burke was well aware of the cynical view held by some of his contemporaries, but he did not share it. It was "an effect of vulgar and puerile malignity to imagine, that every Statesman is of course corrupt; and that his opinion, upon every constitutional point, is solely formed upon some sinister interest" (*Present Discontents*, 310). He not only repudiated this view but also argued that belief in the doctrine of general corruption was itself a form of corruption, fostered by corrupt men for self-serving reasons:

> I hope there are none of you corrupted with the doctrine taught by wicked men for the worst purposes, and received by the malignant credulity of envy and ignorance, which is that the men who act upon the public stage are all alike, all equally corrupt, all influenced by no other views than the sordid lure of salary and pension.

Here as on other occasions during his career, Burke may have been warding off slanderous imputations against himself, but he appealed to his general experience at the center of British public life to affirm a more optimistic view. Corruption no doubt existed; public virtue was not universal, but it was also not entirely absent:

> Never expecting to find perfection in men, and not looking for divine attributes in created beings, in my commerce with my contemporaries I have found much human virtue. I have seen not a little public spirit, a real subordination of interest to duty, and a decent and regulated sensibility to honest fame and reputation.

Burke's commitment to political reforms of various kinds was founded on such experience, and, he noted, such commitment would have been pointless if the cynical thesis were valid: "For if all men who act in a public situation are equally selfish, corrupt, and venal, what reason can be given for desiring any sort of change?" (*Sheriffs of Bristol*, 240–41).

Burke surely accepted in some form the standard Whig or liberal conviction that legal and constitutional checks on power are essential precisely because public virtue cannot always be counted on, and because power frequently tempts its holders into abuses. From Burke's point of view, however, Hume overstated the case when he argued that it was a "just *political* maxim, *that every man must be supposed a knave.*"[8] Hume knew this was false in fact, but argued that it was a safe assumption when designing institutions. In contrast, Burke, though he appreciated the importance of formal checks and controls, held that even the best designed political institutions had to rely in practice on some degree of virtue; hence the importance for Burke (but not for Hume) of cultivating a true aristocracy. "Men are in public life as in private, some good, some evil. The elevation of the one, and the depression of the other, are the first objects of all true policy" (*Present Discontents*, 278). Since virtue was a possibility, and in fact a reality among at least some of those who held authority in Great Britain and its empire, the corruption of Hastings was exceptional and culpable, and not a given of human nature.

Burke's view of human nature, as indicated in some of the phrases just quoted, is Christian in essence. Human nature is mixed, corruptible to be sure, perhaps always tainted by an underlying tendency to vice, but not irredeemably so. Restrained by religion and by moral principles that are suitably internalized and supported by stable social practices, people have the capacity to create decent societies and governments; but dangers represented by the various vices are always present. In his attacks on Hastings's alleged corruption Burke naturally emphasized the vice (or sin) of avarice, the love of money which, according to the Bible, is the root of all evil. As Burke said in another summary of the background of the empire, Clive had had "astonishing" success in suddenly acquiring for England an immense territory of great wealth, but "from that aera, wealth did what it generally does, it opened a door to corruption. Abuse crept in upon abuse, till all India became one continued scene of peculation, rapine, fraud, injustice, and disgrace" ("Motion for Papers," 54). In making his case in these terms, Burke was resisting the fact that the love of money, which Christian moralists of an earlier age denounced as avarice, was in his own time being revalued to accommodate the requirements of a modern commercial society. Burke too praised commerce in its proper sphere, and hence merchants and their lawful profit motive; in their case, the very term "avarice" seems quaint or archaic. Avarice, however, remained a vice in various contexts, and particularly when practiced by public officials or those in any way responsible for the exercise of public powers. One of the problems facing a commercial society was to maintain the boundary between two different moral systems, one appropriate for private commercial agents, another—oriented toward public virtue—for rulers and officials. As we have seen, a central difficulty with the Indian empire in Hastings's time was that Hastings and his colleagues occupied an ambiguous position with respect to this distinction. Burke was convinced, however, that Hastings's conduct was corrupted by avarice even when he was exercising a clearly public or sovereign function.

In Burke's philosophy, the vices of human nature could be restrained, and the better potentialities developed, only when people lived under a stable set of laws and customs that upheld moral convictions. Indeed, under the influence of special traditions, some individuals—the true aristocrats—could rise to the level of genuine public virtue, while everyone could at least attain a standard of lawfulness and decency. In Christian terms, Burke's theory is more Catholic than Calvinist, insofar as the restraint of vice is attributed less to hard-won personal discipline and to grace unaccountably bestowed upon individuals, than to the moral practices and laws of a community. Outside such restraining influences, the various vices could be expected to flourish in a mutually reinforcing manner. As Burke said of Hastings:

> The man who is a tyrant would, under some other circumstances, be a rebel; and he that is a rebel would become a tyrant. They are things which originally proceed from the same source. They owe their birth to the wild, unbridled lewdness of arbitrary power. They arise from a contempt of public order, and of the laws and institutions which curb mankind. They arise from a harsh, cruel, and ferocious disposition, impatient of the rules of law, order, and morality.

Apparently civilized Englishmen, finding themselves in a position of power in the (for them) lawless environment of India, became both tyrants toward their subjects and rebels toward higher authority (Parliament). But this outcome was not terribly surprising: "We therefore naturally expect that, when he [Hastings] has thrown off the laws of his country, he will throw off all other authority" ("Speech in Reply," 11:306–07). The problem facing British statesmen was therefore to create a system of governance that would ensure the rule of law for their empire, which responsible officials on the scene would not be tempted to transgress.[9] The corruption of the East India Company's personnel reflected the natural corruptibility of men in certain circumstances. It was not an inevitable feature of political regimes; it was an exceptional and culpable occurrence, though explicable in terms of human nature and the disorder of the empire.

Presents

The first and major part of the corruption charge against Hastings was that he frequently took what he referred to as "presents," but which were in reality bribes or extorted payments from Indians in positions vulnerable to the power he wielded. This charge resonated in England as a result of certain notorious background circumstances. Clive had acquired an extraordinary fortune (about £250,000) in the form of presents from Mir Jafar, whom he installed as nawab of Bengal after Plassey, in 1757. His officers and colleagues in this transaction received proportionally large payments, and despite censure and parliamentary criticism at home, his successors followed this precedent (with gradually diminishing returns) over the next decade, benefiting from the prevalent political instability in India. The example thus set at the top was widely imitated by lower-level company servants who found themselves in a position to dictate or influence the appointment of Indians to lucrative administrative posts throughout Bengal or to positions in the management of the company's privileged commercial operations. Opportunities for bribery increased after 1765 when the company acquired the right to collect the public revenues of Bengal, which they exercised through favored native agents. Burke also alleged instances of outright extortion on the part of important English officials from the native merchants with whom the company dealt (*Ninth Report*, 266). Wealthy returned company servants whose fortunes were believed to have been acquired by such unscrupulous means attracted much unfavorable attention during this period in Britain.[10] Concluding his speech on the "Presents" charge, Burke portrayed an extensive "system of bribery . . . of mystery and concealment, and consequently a system of fraud," and alluded to these popular suspicions: "You now see some of the means by which fortunes have been made by certain persons in India" ("Sixth Article," 449).

Clive, and later Hastings, naturally condemned bribery, but defended the taking of presents (at least by senior officials) in a manner that reflected an attitude that was widespread in the company service. A legitimate present was distinguished from a bribe if it was unsolicited, involved no explicit deal, was a reflection of gratitude rather than a response to a threat, and rewarded actions done purely in the line of duty, in the furtherance of the interests of the East India Company or of Britain. Clive of course argued

Warren Hastings, by Tilly Kettle, 1775.
This portrait was painted shortly after Hastings assumed
the governor-generalship of Bengal.
Courtesy of the National Portrait Gallery, London.

that the payoffs following the 1757 revolution met all these conditions.[11] This rationale indicates a perennial dilemma or temptation for individuals in positions of power; moreover, the concept of a bribe, defined as an "improper inducement or influence," and the distinction between bribes and licit gifts to people in power, are "social constructions" that are culturally variable and sometimes ambiguous.[12] The distinction invoked by Clive and Hastings, however, seemed for obvious reasons questionable to contemporaries, and Burke rejected it outright. It was simply not credible "that any native of India had voluntarily and gratuitously given money privately to the said Warren Hastings, that is, without some prospect of a benefit in return, or some dread of his resentment, if he refused" ("Articles of Charge," 37–38). Expectations of future returns on gifts need not have been explicit; furthermore, given the power relations existing between the Indians and the British governor, Indians may have believed they had to protect themselves from perceived threats, even if these too were not made explicit.

Clive's huge reward for the coup of 1757 was a unique occurrence. Similar payments decreased with subsequent turnovers in the government of Bengal, as the nawabs' treasury became exhausted and the position itself declined in value in the eyes of prospective usurpers. By the time Hastings became governor in 1772, the largely ceremonial nawabship was virtually worthless from this point of view.[13] Burke's charge against Hastings, then, did not focus on any one spectacular instance, but cited a large number of lesser offenses, some indeed involving native rulers in Benares and Oudh, but a greater number involving lesser figures. Burke also accused him of developing over time a regular system of bribery of which both he and his friends were the beneficiaries. Hastings's main vices were not those of a great conqueror, or of a great general guilty of "abusing his military powers," but rather those of "a clerk at a bureau," the vices, as he said, of a weasel or a rat rather than a tiger or lion. Cumulatively, however, Burke argued, this mundane but systematic corruption was more damaging than conspicuous but ephemeral violence: "We know that a swarm of locusts, although individually despicable, can render a country more desolate than Genghis Khan or Tamerlane" ("Speech in Reply," II:220–21). Indeed, some of the other charges against Hastings, Burke warned the lords, being "high tragic acts of superior, overbearing tyranny . . . of superior wickedness in eminent station," were naturally more riveting than mere corruption, with its tedious documentation. This circumstance, however, was perilous for the responsible statesman. "The crimes which are the most striking to the imagination are not always the most pernicious in their effects: in these high, eminent acts of domineering tyranny, their very magnitude proves a sort of corrective to their virulence. The occasions on which they can be exercised are rare." In contrast, "when the vices of low, sordid, and illiberal minds infect that high situation . . . the evil is much greater; it may operate daily and hourly; . . . it will be imitated, and will be improved, from the highest to the lowest, through all the gradations of a corrupt government" ("Sixth Article," 162–63).

The taking of presents or bribes in India, beyond its pervasively debilitating effects, had other culpable features. In the first place, in addition to being a form of moral corruption, in Hastings's time it was illegal. Receipt of presents of significant value was first forbidden by an internal order of the company directors in 1764, in recognition, in Burke's words, that this practice was the "fundamental" abuse in their domain, and that, far from being genuine gifts, these presents were "the donations of misery to power . . . and consequently left neither property nor security in permanence to any persons in the Country" ("Speech on Opening," 340). Clive, though himself a previous offender, was sent back as governor to enforce this rule and other reforms, and company servants were required to sign covenants renouncing presents. Notwithstanding Burke's complimentary treatment of Clive's efforts, however, the prohibition was evaded by personnel in the field, who adhered to their established conventions.[14] As a result, the practice was legally forbidden by North's Regulating Act of 1773, presents being "justly reputed by the Legislature not as Marks of Attention and Respect, but as Bribes or Extortions" (*Ninth Report*, 208); this was among the reforms Hastings was charged with implementing when he was appointed governor-general at that time. Thus, during the period of Hastings's rule in Bengal, he and others were prohibited from taking presents (bribes)

> first, by his official situation, next by Covenant, and lastly by Act of Parliament, that is to say by all the things that bind mankind or can bind them: first, moral obligation, inherent in the duty of their office, next the positive injunction of the Legislature of the Country and lastly a man's own private and particular voluntary act and covenant. These three being the great and only obligations that bind mankind, all united in the focus of this single point: that they take no presents. ("Speech on Opening," 379–80)

Hastings sought to defend his record, avowing that instances of "Rapacity" were relatively few in his regime.[15] Burke, reading the record differently, was outraged that Hastings had violated not only every kind of obligation—moral, legal, and contractual—but also the special trust that had been conferred on him as a reformer.[16]

A second aggravating circumstance was that bribery in the case of officials as highly placed as Hastings was inescapably linked to oppressive and arbitrary uses of public authority. In 1780, for example, the governor-general was called upon to adjudicate a succession dispute in the district of Dinajpur in Bengal. In return for a finding in favor of a minor adopted son (rather than a half-brother) of the deceased raja, and for a favorable settlement of the guardianship, Hastings, Burke alleged, acting through his sinister agent Ganga Govind Singh, received a *peshkash* or bribe amounting to £40,000. This payment, having been "corruptly taken by him as a Judge in a litigation respecting an Inheritance between two great parties" in a distinguished Indian family, thus represented a major procedural miscarriage of justice, regardless of the merits of the decision ("Speech on Opening," 405–06).[17]

In his account of the crime of bribery of judges in England, Blackstone had remarked in 1769 that

> in the east it is the custom never to petition any superior for justice, not excepting their kings, without a present. This is calculated for the genius of despotic countries; where the true principles of government are never understood, and it is imagined that there is no obligation from the superior to the inferior.[18]

Burke did not enter into the question of whether the giving and taking of presents in judicial proceedings was standard procedure in India, or whether this practice would have exculpated Hastings. His rejection of the theory of oriental despotism that Blackstone took for granted might have entailed doubts about this claim, but his unequivocal condemnation of Hastings suggests he was applying higher, general standards of justice, and of what governors owe the governed.

In a second kind of case, Burke accused Hastings of taking large bribes from his favored native protégés in exchange for tax-farming rights in extensive districts of Bengal and the attached province of Bihar. Furthermore, Burke reasoned, "No man ever paid a bribe for a power to charge and tax others, but with a view to oppress them. No man ever paid a bribe for the handling of the public money, but to peculate from it." Only the "worst men" made themselves available for this business, and moreover, "they will be restrained by no dread whatsoever in the execution of their worst oppressions": Hastings could not have punished unjust extortion on the part of his subordinates, even if he had been inclined to do so, "without risking the discovery of bribery in himself." His corrupt revenue collectors, then, proceeded to extract their profits, as well as cover the costs of the original bribes, by violent and oppressive methods, without restraint, against the landowners and peasants of their districts. Hence bribery, which first seems to be merely a mean and "sordid practice," can appear

> in a very different light, when you regard the consideration for which the bribe is given,—namely, that a Governor-General . . . delivers up the properties, the liberties, and the lives of an whole people to the arbitrary discretion of any wicked and rapacious person, who will be sure to make good from their blood the purchase he has paid for his power over them. ("Speech in Opening," 10:138–40)

Finally, according to Burke, Hastings's corruption was not sporadic and ad hoc, but amounted to a system, in several senses. Hastings perfected an array of different kinds of bribery, so many that in England, where "bribes are so little known . . . we can hardly get clear and specific technical names to distinguish them" ("Sixth Article," 161). So regular was Hastings's illicit conduct that Burke was prepared to infer a corrupt motive in an inappropriate appointment (that of Munni Begam), and to accept unsupported testimony from a questionable figure (Nandakumar) that a bribe was involved: "Is Mr. Hastings a man against whom a charge of bribery is improbable? Why, he owns it. He is a professor of it. He reduces it into scheme and system" ("Speech in Opening," 10:26).

Implicated in this system were many of Hastings's loyal subordinates, who, having received a share of the spoils, could be counted on to support him in his attempts to deny or obscure these shady transactions:

> By establishing a universal connivance from one end of the service to the other, he has not only corrupted and contaminated it in all its parts, but bound it in a common league of iniquity to support mutually each other against the inquiry that should detect and the justice that should punish their offenses. ("Sixth Article," 161)

A profitable system of corruption could not only perpetuate itself, in Burke's analysis, by financing its own organization and other overhead expenses; in a situation such as that of the Indian empire, where there was a strong esprit de corps among East India Company servants who had spent considerable time in Asia, systemic corruption also benefited from genuine loyalties and ingrained custom:

> Here is a principle of treacherous fidelity, of perfidious honor, of the faith of conspirators against their masters, the faith of robbers against the public, held up against the duty of an officer in a public situation. You see how they are bound to one another . . . to prevent the Directors having a true knowledge of their affairs. ("Sixth Article," 408)

Finally, according to Burke, Hastings's system relied on a network of dependent native officials, and especially on several trusted banians or personal agents, who were of course well rewarded, sometimes with lucrative official posts. These men actually carried out the negotiations and received the presents, kept indecipherable records in a variety of native languages, and were carefully used by Hastings and played off against English subordinates in such a way that no one of them had full knowledge of the larger schemes ("Sixth Article," 409). In a rare comment on race relations in India, Burke argued that only a profit motive could have united this motley group and inspired the apparently close, even affectionate, ties between Hastings and his banians:

I do not suppose that either generosity, friendship, or even communion, can exist in that country between white men and black: no,
their colors are not more adverse than their characters and tempers.
... There are none of those habits of life, nothing, that can bind men
together even in the most ordinary society: ... It is a money-dealing,
and a money-dealing only, which can exist between them. ... When
black men give money to a white man, it is a bribe ... when money is
given to a black man, he is only a sharer with the white man in their
infamous profits. ("Sixth Article," 423–24)

The impression Burke conveys in these passages is that all the notorious
intrigue and complexity of oriental societies had been mastered by Hastings
and were at his disposal for the furtherance of his corrupt projects.

Hastings naturally denied the charges of direct personal bribery, and
some of the evidence against him indeed seems to have been defective or
tainted by hostile motives on the part of his enemies.[19] He did not completely deny that he accepted presents, however, or that this practice continued throughout the service even after it was prohibited. He and his allies
offered several excuses or pleas in mitigation of this state of affairs, pleas
with which Burke was not sympathetic.

In the first place, the possibility of enrichment through presents and
various other perquisites was a long-standing tradition of company service
in India; it was therefore regarded as a legitimate expectation by company
servants, and its abrupt cancellation was resented and resisted.[20] In 1781, for
example, Hastings was offered a huge gift of about £100,000 by Asaf al-
Daula, the nawab of Oudh, who was by that time under the company's
effective power. In the existing climate of reform, Hastings requested permission from the directors to accept it, and was refused, but he clearly
believed he was entitled to it by virtue of his position, his long service, and
precedents.[21] Burke regarded this present, like others, as extortionate, and
Hastings's request as sheer effrontery (*Eleventh Report*, 351–53). Nevertheless, one might have expected Burke to respond favorably to arguments
based on tradition and precedent, and he conceded that an individual might
be (partly) exculpated if he was "only a partaker in a general misconduct, [if]
it was rather *vitium loci et vitium temporis* than *vitium hominis*."[22] This
excuse, however, was not available to Hastings, since he had been appointed
governor for the purpose, among others, of correcting these very vices: his
"peculiar trust, the great specific ground of his appointment, was a confidence that he would eradicate this very evil, of which we are going to prove
that he has been one of the principal promoters" ("Sixth Article," 170).

Obligations arising from a particular trust or engagement override any opposing claims based on precedent or custom.

A second argument was that, in certain circumstances, the giving of presents—and even, to be blunt, bribery—by subordinates to superiors was the universal and time-sanctioned custom of India. As Montesquieu explained, it was the custom of despotic countries, a custom followed by Mogul rulers, that petitions from subjects be accompanied by presents.[23] This custom might have been "part of a system of conventional politeness" that Europeans misunderstood as corrupt,[24] or an expression of power and domination. Either way, it was argued, if Englishmen were going to accept a ruling position within the (admittedly crumbling) framework of the Mogul Empire, it was appropriate that they should, as much as possible, conform their regime to local customs, including this one. Indeed, it might prove difficult to rule otherwise if, as a modern historian has written, gratuities were "the oil without which no part of the native Government machinery in India could be expected to work."[25] This of course has always been (and remains) a familiar excuse offered by Westerners operating in non-Western environments that appear to tolerate practices that are corrupt by Western standards.

Shortly after taking office in 1772, Hastings traveled from Calcutta to the Mogul capital of Bengal at Murshidabad, where he rearranged the nawab's household in accordance with his plan for administrative reform. Subsequently, he admitted accepting a gift of £15,000 from Munni Begam, whom he had appointed guardian of the minor nawab, and openly defended it as an entertainment allowance that was perfectly customary among governors and Indian notables on such official visits.[26] Again, we would expect Burke to be sympathetic to the claim that local customs had to be respected. In the present context, however, he rejected this defense on several grounds.

First, Burke did not doubt that the money was in reality a direct payment (indeed part of a larger bribe) from Munni Begam in exchange for her appointment, and he questioned whether the alleged custom was genuine or proper in this context. Various kinds of "presents," Burke argued, were known in the East, and the Persian as well as the English language could distinguish those that were actually illicit bribes from legitimate gifts and other payments. If indeed clear-cut bribery was widely practiced in India, it was one of those "vicious practices and customs, which it is the business of good laws and good customs to eradicate" ("Sixth Article," 171). Thus, the claim of custom, in and of itself, was not decisive for Burke; there are bad customs and abuses of custom that are to be repudiated.

Even if such presents were not bribes and were really customary among

Indian rulers, however, the nawab from whose treasury the money had come was by that time a sovereign prince only in a ceremonial or fictional sense. In reality, he was in a completely dependent, indeed, in a "hopeless and un-protected" condition. In this case, the custom was to be rejected, since, its basis gone, it was all too open to the abuse of "frequently visiting the princes" merely in order to extract money ("Speech in Reply," 12:340–41). Hastings's cynicism was evident here since, on the very occasion of accept-ing this lavish present, he was, in the name of reform, drastically reducing the stipends of the nawab and his household, thereby ruining "hundreds of the decayed nobility and gentry of a great kingdom," combining corruption with cruelty ("Sixth Article," 236).

Furthermore, acceptance of "entertainment" expenses by appeal to "the mode of the country" was a transparent means of evading the rules against presents simply by calling them something else: a company official would have only to "make a visit" in order to cover or justify any form of bribery ("Sixth Article," 272). And finally, there remained the decisive con-sideration that presents of any kind—"any Usage or Custom to the contrary thereof in any wise notwithstanding"[27]—had been explicitly prohibited both by company regulations and by law.

> Bribery and extortion have been covered by the name of presents, and the authority and practice of the East has been adduced as a palliation of the crime. My Lords, no authority of the East will be a palliation of the breach of laws enacted in the West: and to those laws of the West, and not the vicious customs of the East, we insist upon making Mr. Hastings liable. ("Sixth Article," 171)

Statutory law nullifies contrary customs; and in the British Empire the duly enacted and clear law of Parliament was authoritative, particularly on a Brit-ish subject and governor such as Hastings, local practices notwithstanding.

Hastings's final and major defense was that, though he had accepted several large "presents" from native rulers, he had deposited the money in the company's treasury, thus applying it to public purposes rather than personal enrichment. Hence these payments were not bribes, nor were they corrupt: they were simply an irregular form of public finance that was, again, customary in India. More particularly, Hastings had accepted money when offered, in an opportunistic fashion, in order to meet pressing financial exigencies, usually military, that were not adequately covered by the ordi-nary revenue available to him. Burke responded to these claims with incre-dulity and sarcasm, ridiculing Hastings for suggesting that he was "a great inventive genius, who [had] gone out of all the ordinary roads of finance,

[had] made great discoveries in the unknown regions of that science, and [had] for the first time established the corruption of the Supreme Magistrate as a principle of resource for Government" ("Speech on Opening," 396). As if misapplying the already disreputable teaching of Bernard Mandeville to the function of a public official, Hastings was pursuing the unlikely course of trying to portray corruption as official merit:

> It has been said of an ambassador, that he is a person employed to tell lies for the advantage of the court that sends him. [Hastings's] is patriotic bribery, and public-spirited corruption. He is a peculator for the good of his country. It has been said that private vices are public benefits. He goes the full length of that position, and turns his private peculation into a public good. ("Speech in Opening," 10:46–47)

Such invective, however, presupposed Hastings's guilt; on what basis did Burke reject his claim?

In the first place, Hastings's documentation of these transactions was clearly inadequate, leading even a sympathetic modern historian to speak of the "strange mixture of candour and furtiveness" surrounding them.[28] This, in Burke's view, was highly suspicious, especially in "a public accountant like Mr. Hastings, a man bred up a book-keeper in the Company's service, who ought to be exact." Inadequate documentation made it impossible to verify Hastings's assertions that he had so disposed of the funds in question, or in general to police the rule against presents. In fact, it created a strong presumption of fraud ("Sixth Article," 353, 344). One of the presents that Hastings claimed to have applied to company uses was a payment of £30,000 in 1783 from his agent Nobkissin (Nabakrishna) in exchange for his appointment as tax collector in the Burdwan district of Bengal. But most of this money was apparently then paid back to Hastings as reimbursement for alleged (but suspicious) expenses he had incurred ("Articles of Impeachment," 183).[29] Given transactions of this sort, Burke asserted that the failure of someone in Hastings's position to maintain adequate accounting was "a proof of corruption" ("Sixth Article," 201). Hastings claimed not only that he had applied the funds to company affairs (and he no doubt did so in some cases), but that this had always been his intention from the moment of accepting the presents. The irregular nature of the transactions, however, made it more reasonable to suppose, in Burke's opinion, that Hastings took this course only when he began to fear that his conduct would be closely investigated, especially after his opponent Philip Francis returned to England in 1780: "I dismiss the idea that any man so acting could have had a good intention in his mind: . . . We shall prove that he never made a disclosure without thinking that a discovery had been previously made or was likely to be made" ("Sixth Article," 337).

Hastings's sloppy record keeping not only cast serious doubts on his motives and integrity by wrapping major financial dealings "in Mystery and Obscurity"; it also constituted an important dereliction of duty in itself, both toward the East India Company and toward the British Empire. Being "entrusted with the Care of the Company's Revenues, [he was] bound in Duty to take care that all Things relating thereto . . . should be clear, open, and distinct." Moreover, as a governor-general "in a Service like that of the Company's Service in *India*, more liable than any other to the Suspicion of Bribery and Extortion," he was "bound to candid, fair, and ingenuous Proceedings in all Things, but more especially in Transactions tending to Corruption" ("Articles of Impeachment," 228–29). Burke alluded here to the "Honour . . . of this Kingdom in *India*," which demanded not only the reality but also the appearance of uprightness; but he also expressed in strong terms the importance of so mundane a thing as complete and exact bureaucratic record keeping to maintain both legal government and the possibility of correcting possible abuses through legal procedures.

Second, the possibility that certain monies were eventually applied to public purposes did not lessen the probability that they, like other "presents," had been extorted in the first place. Hastings accepted one such present from the raja of Benares while simultaneously making public demands on him, which the raja protested he was unable to meet; the reasonable assumption was that the present was "bestowed, if not with an Assurance, at least with a rational Hope, of some Mitigation in the oppressive Requisitions that were made by Mr. Hastings" (*Eleventh Report*, 343). The fact that natives were willing to make secret or private payments to Hastings when they were unable or unwilling to meet their public obligations suggested to Burke that Hastings was following a pattern of despotic rule, to which Indians were responding in the traditional fashion. The legal prohibition on presents, Burke argued, had been imposed to protect the natives and their property, which were otherwise at the mercy of extortionate demands. Hastings's construction of the law, in which any presents, "which when they are given were unlawful, can afterwards be legalized, by an Application of them to the Company's Service," would defeat this purpose and remove the possibility of legal redress for victimized Indians (*Eleventh Report*, 356).

Finally, in Burke's view, Hastings's creative efforts in public finance had various detrimental consequences for the company's Indian regime overall. An accounting system in which "the same Sum may become private Property or public, at the Pleasure of the Receiver," was damaging to the company and surely invited fraud, regardless of Hastings's own guilt (*Eleventh Report*, 356). "A system of private bribery for a revenue," discredited in practice as in theory, "must ruin the Country where it prevails, must disgrace the Country that uses it, and finally end in the destruction of the revenue" ("Speech on Opening," 436). And finally, this method of supplementing the public revenue also invited or perpetuated improper attitudes and conduct on the part of the Indian subjects. Even if the presents in question were not extorted by threats, they were presumably understood to be bribes by the donors; otherwise, if the money was indeed destined to cover expenses of government, why was it not contributed by some public procedure? "It is not a thing to be believed, that any native would give large sums privately to a Governor, which he refused to give or lend publicly to government, unless it were to derive some adequate secret advantage from the favor, or to avoid some mischief from the enmity of such Governor" ("Articles of Charge," 38). Since Hastings's alleged transfers of funds to the company treasury were done clandestinely, the donors could have perceived "nothing in it but Money paid to the Supreme Magistrate for his private Emolument." This practice and the attitudes it would naturally foster could only have a corrosive effect on the relations between the company's government and its native subjects:

> It is plain, that the Powers of Government must, in some Way or other, be understood by the Natives to be at Sale. . . . The very Nature of such Transactions has a Tendency to teach the Natives to pay a corrupt Court to the Servants of the Company; and they must thereby be rendered less willing, or less able, or perhaps both, to fulfill their Engagements to the State.

The fact that they would rather give money privately to the governor than lend it openly to the company simply demonstrated "their Opinion of his Power and Corruption; and of the weak and precarious State of the Company's Authority" (*Eleventh Report*, 359).

Contracts

The second part of Burke's general charge of corruption was that Hastings had often awarded lucrative company contracts on a noncompetitive basis to favored individuals. Some of these contracts were for supplies, usually military, such as draft animals and provisions for forts. Others pertained to the administration of the company's internal monopolies, such as those on salt and opium; indeed, the susceptibility of these monopolies to such abuse was a familiar ground of criticism on the part of members of Parliament and writers such as Adam Smith.[30] In either case, favoritism in this matter was a violation of company regulations, under which, according to Burke, contracts were supposed to be publicly advertised and awarded to the "most reasonable" bidder. In some cases, they were also to be of limited duration. In flouting these rules, Hastings and some of his colleagues were "[reducing] the Company's Government . . . to a mere Patronage . . . which is not only despotic with regard to those who are subordinate to it, but, in all its Acts, entirely independent of the legal Power, which is nominally superior" (*Ninth Report*, 327–29).

In addition to being illegal, this kind of corruption was in Burke's eyes, like bribery, a sordid vice that disqualified Hastings not only as a statesman but as a great empire builder as well, even though some of his potential defenders in England were likely to regard him as such and so excuse his faults. Burke ran a risk, when he spoke of the great power that Hastings wielded, of turning his adversary into an impressive figure; according to Burke's own aesthetic doctrine, great power, along with the fear it arouses, can produce the sentiment of the sublime in us when we delight in contemplating it, as we might in the case of a distant conquest (*Sublime and Beautiful*, 66).[31] The emphasis on Hastings's corruption served to counteract this effect. Rather than a sublime figure, Hastings was merely a "fraudulent bullock-contractor" ("Speech in Reply," 11:220–21; cf. *Corr.* 8:413). What was worse in Burke's view—at least according to the conclusion of his case for impeachment before an audience of lords—was that the reasonably well-born Hastings, who had been hoping for a peerage upon his return to England, had "derogate[d] from such a line of nobles by becoming a contractor for bullocks," not even an "honest bullock-contractor," but a corrupt one, who "carried with him the spirit of a fraudulent bullock-contractor through the whole of the Company's service" ("Speech in Reply," 12:286). This favorite epithet in the Hastings trial found an echo in Burke's contemporaneous *Reflections*: arguing that certain lowly occupations, though by no means disgraceful, are not honorable or suitable for those who rule in a state, Burke quoted from *Ecclesiasticus*: "How can he get wisdom . . . that driveth oxen; and is occupied in their labours; and whose talk is of bullocks?" (*Reflections*, 138n.). Part of a governor's job was to oversee the awarding of contracts: however, excessive preoccupation with army supplies was inconsistent with the wisdom requisite in a ruler, and a corrupt preoccupation in this area was utterly at variance with Burke's idea of high public position.

For the most part, Hastings's plea to the "contracts" charge was in essence "no contest." On the bullocks business (and an elephant contract too) he admitted he broke the rules but pleaded special circumstances.[32] With respect to the most notorious instance—the awarding of a contract for the supply of opium carrying an immediate profit of £40,000 to Stephen Sulivan, the son of the chairman of the East India Company (and Hastings's sponsor)—Hastings rather feebly said he knew of "no law, either moral or municipal, that should preclude my friends from taking upon themselves the charge of an engagement, the profits of which were to arise from their skill, industry, and exactness in the performance of it." He quickly added, however, that this was a "single instance."[33] Elsewhere, he privately acknowledged that he had taken care of some trusted aides' financial embarrassments with lucrative appointments, while at the same time denouncing the excessive "rapacity" of others.[34]

In extenuation it might be said that such practices were commonplace among all factions in the Indian service, and indeed in Great Britain itself, where in the eighteenth century, notwithstanding Burke's suggestion that India was exceptional, the awarding of government contracts and sinecures was more or less accepted as a legitimate or inevitable form of political patronage.[35] In England, military contracts were generally dispensed in this manner rather than through competitive bidding, until reforms in the 1780s.[36] A Namierite perspective on the maneuverings of the East India Company in England emphasizes the pervasively mercenary quality of the political scene in which it operated:

> The crucial weakness of the eighteenth-century standard of political morality, as seen through the eyes of its successors, was that the private and public interests of those taking part in political life were insufficiently distinguished. . . . To make a comfortable fortune in the public service and to establish those dependent on him in situations of profit was the major and (to contemporaries) the legitimate ambition of the ordinary politician.[37]

Nepotism too was standard practice in eighteenth-century corporations, and an Indian governor inevitably had to cope with what Hastings complained of as "the Curse of Patronage," that is, the "infinitude of claimants for posts of profit" and the pressure exerted by company directors, shareholders, and important politicians for favorable placement of relatives.[38] Indeed, his own survival as governor probably depended on successful negotiation among the various patronage networks and resulting factions within the company.

Notwithstanding these contemporary attitudes and the frequently cynical or resigned acceptance of them, Burke was not sympathetic to such defenses. Far from seeing Hastings as a creature of an established system or the victim of political pressures from without, Burke was convinced he was a principal actor in and initiator of a pattern of corruption that worsened under his governorship. Burke criticized the company directors for permitting the often abused opium monopoly to continue, but he commended their reprimand of Hastings for the Sulivan deal. Noting that these men, as company servants, were bound to promote its interests, Burke wondered "whether a Contract made between Two Servants, contrary to the Orders of their common Master, and to the Prejudice of his known Interest, be a Breach of Trust on both Sides" and thus legally invalid (*Ninth Report*, 285). The Sulivan contract, in Burke's analysis, was just one episode in Hastings's larger scheme of "corrupting the Company's servants in India, and of corrupting the Company itself in England"; his purpose, of course, once he had enriched himself, was to "[secure] a corrupt party to support and bear him out by their evidence, upon the event of any inquiry into his conduct" ("Speech in Reply," 12:297, 299; and "Articles of Charge," 11). Implicitly rejecting the claim that Hastings, like other politicians of the time, needed to cultivate a network of well-placed allies simply to stay in office, Burke argued it was Hastings's accuracy in foreseeing future prosecution for his various offenses that drove him to develop his own patronage system, financed by further offenses such as the contracts in question. Hastings thus built up what at the time was called an "interest" of his own in the company and in British politics, a party or faction united (in this case) by their profitable participation in corrupt dealings and by the determination to protect one another.[39]

Burke's more detailed analysis of Hastings's protective system was threefold. Hastings was, first, able to draw upon the traditional "esprit de corps" of the Indian service, "in which an Informer is the most odious and detestable of all characters . . . as a common enemy of the common profit." Second, there was an element of "terror" associated with the "vast power" Hastings had accumulated. Since all violations were equally illegal,

> the consequence is that he who has taken but one penny of unlawful emolument (and all have taken many pennies of unlawful emolument) . . . dare not complain of the most abandoned extortion and cruel oppression. . . . The great criminal [at least while he was Governor] has the laws in his hand. He is always able to prove the small offence and crush the person entirely who has committed it. ("Speech on Opening," 290–91)

At the same time, he could himself commit great offenses with impunity. But above all, after fourteen years "at the head of the service" in Bengal, Hastings could count on the support and gratitude of numerous men who were beneficiaries of his system.

As a result, Burke admitted, there had been and could be no complaints against Hastings from the only people who were in a position to provide direct testimony against him, whereas he could call on many to give favorable testimony regarding his character ("Speech on Opening," 290–91). It was in the nature of the case, as Burke saw it—and this would seem to be a general problem attending cases of systematic or organized corruption—that the absence of hostile witnesses against the main culprit actually aggravated his guilt, by revealing the extent of his conspiracy, whereas those who testified for the defendant simply demonstrated their own complicity. A charge such as this is not quite nonrefutable, nor is it illogically nonfalsifiable, since the political mechanism alleged to underlie it is quite plausible. To prove such a charge, however, convincing material or documentary evidence was needed, and unfortunately for Burke, the available materials were too complex and ambiguous to be compelling.

The Setting of a Corrupt Regime

The corrupt practices and other abuses of which Burke accused Hastings and many of his colleagues were attributed to men of a distinct class—East India Company servants—operating in a distinctive environment—the British possessions and spheres of influence in India in the early days of the empire. Further consideration of certain aspects of this setting, and of Burke's ideas in relation to it, is appropriate here. The abuses that, according to Burke, occurred during Hastings's governorship (1772–1785) were of the sort that probably flourished on an even greater scale during the preceding period (1757–1772), and the attitudes that underlay them were certainly a continuation of a preexisting outlook. Unsettled conditions in Bengal, combined with the company's sudden accession to political and military power there, provided opportunities for spectacular plunder in the fifteen years after Plassey, a situation that changed only gradually as more orderly procedures of government and revenue collection were developed.[40] Burke's description of the response to sudden power by members of the French National Assembly in 1789 seems to fit company servants in India as well:

> Who could doubt but that, at any expence to the state, of which they understood nothing, they must pursue their private interests, which

they understood but too well . . . [joining in] any project . . . which could lay open to them those innumerable lucrative jobs which follow in the train of all great convulsions and revolutions in the state, and particularly in all great and violent permutations of property[?] (*Reflections*, 131)

One of Burke's worries about revolution or political instability was that they typically provided an opening to adventurers, driven by personal greed and ambition and released from some of the usual restraints.

Furthermore, the Indian empire began as the acquisition of a commercial company, and during its early decades it was ruled by men who regarded themselves as primarily merchants and company servants, whose first duty was to advance the company's (and, within the rules, their own) profit-making ventures. Hastings's era marks the beginning of the transition from this state of affairs to an empire conceived as a public venture, as an adjunct of the British state, ruled by civil servants whose training and ethos clearly differentiated them from merchants. The conduct and attitudes of East India Company personnel in the eighteenth century certainly appeared mercenary and corrupt by the standards of nineteenth-century British imperial officials, just as, for that matter, the eighteenth-century House of Commons was corrupt by later democratic standards, and the patronage-based bureaucracy of Britain at that time fell far short of the standards of a later, professionalized civil service.[41] Even if we make allowances for the times, however, the position the East India Company had attained in Bengal—in Burke's words, "a State in disguise of a Merchant, a great public office in disguise of a Countinghouse" ("Speech on Opening," 283)—seemed dangerously anomalous. By the early 1770s, it is said, nearly everyone outside the company had come to believe it was not an appropriate agency to be governing India; Hastings's period in office, with its objective of internal reform, simply marked the final delay as the company resisted inevitable government control.[42]

Burke, in agreement with this diagnosis, couched the general problem in terms of a theme that is often central in his political thought, namely, the demanding nature of true statesmanship:

We know too that, in the habits of civilized life, in cultivated society, there is imbibed by men a good deal of solid practice of government, of the true maxims of State, and every thing that enables a man to serve his country. But these men are sent over to exercise functions at which a Statesman here would tremble, without any study, without any of that sort of experience which forms men gradually and insensibly in great affairs. These men are sent over to India without maturity, without experience, without knowledge, or habits in cultivated life, to perform such functions as I will venture to say the greatest statesmen are hardly equal to. ("Speech on Opening," 289)

Governing an empire or a major imperial territory such as Bengal called for the highest qualities, moral and intellectual, of statesmanship, always a demanding vocation. The East India Company was evidently not a suitable vehicle for selecting or developing the appropriate qualities.

The lack of maturity to which Burke referred here indicates a theme that was of special concern to him: the youth of the individuals who exercised the power of the British Empire in India. Company servants (both Clive and Hastings, for example) typically began their careers in the East at seventeen or eighteen, rising, if they stayed on and showed ability, to positions of high authority by thirty.[43] Their usual aim, as Burke noted, was to retire early with sufficient wealth to restore the fortune of a decayed family or establish that of a new one. They were ordinary British youth, neither better nor worse than average:

> I think as well of the body of my countrymen as any man can do. I do not think that any man sent out to India is sent with an ill purpose, or goes out with bad dispositions. No: I think the young men who go there are fair and faithful representatives of the people of the same age,—uncorrupted, but corruptible from their age, as we all are. ("Speech in Reply," 12:280)

Given their age, their purpose, and the corrupt surroundings of the company service, however, they were all too likely to fall into the snares that Hastings and other superiors offered, and into the normal temptations of power. Instead of completing the rigorous education appropriate for those who are to act as officials and judges, they

> have been sent there . . . with a perilous independence, with too inordinate expectations, and with boundless power. They are schoolboys without Tutors. They are minors without Guardians. The world is let loose upon them with all its temptations; and they are let loose upon the world, with all the powers that despotism can give. ("Speech on Opening," 288)[44]

Burke's general conception of government as a trust for the benefit of the community presupposed rule by responsible statesmen, persons qualified by education and background to exercise authority in the proper spirit.

Since competent governance involves attention to the experience of the past, it normally depends upon personal experience and hence the maturity that comes with age. At the end of his career, Burke scornfully rejected, in the Duke of Bedford's "few and idle years, the competence to judge of my long and laborious life" (*Noble Lord*, 284). In a similar spirit, surveying the France of 1790, Burke sympathized with a "respectable" older minister trying to comprehend the "fantastick" schemes of "juvenile politicians" suddenly raised to power, men whose youth gave them "a certain inward fanatical assurance and illumination upon all subjects" and who, accordingly, were unwilling to listen to "old men, or to any persons who valued themselves upon their experience" (*Reflections*, 337–38). Likewise in India, "the natives scarcely know what it is to see the grey head of an Englishman. Young men (boys almost) govern there, without society, and without sympathy with the natives." Young men, with no experience to begin with, did not normally remain long enough to acquire it and thus to amend their conduct upon seeing its long-term consequences. In their haste to join the gentry of England, they destroyed the gentry of India, without fully comprehending the import of their actions (*Fox's Bill*, 403).[45] While perspective and responsibility come with age, revolutions, whether in France or in Bengal, were made by the young.

Contributing to the company's corporate goal of returning a profit on its investments was of course the duty of its employees, but everyone had always understood and accepted that these men had come to India in quest of personal fortunes as well. The discomforts of Indian life added to their sense of entitlement in this respect, and the risks created an incentive to move quickly.[46] For this purpose the company, which traditionally paid low salaries, allowed its servants to engage in "private trade": the company maintained a monopoly on trade to Europe, and inland trade within India was supposed to be left to native merchants, but company servants were permitted to engage on their own account in intra-Asian maritime commerce, and many did so to advantage. Thus, in addition to attending to their official duties, Englishmen cultivated a private entrepreneurial spirit, which was subject to abuse in various ways. A long-standing problem, for example, was infringement on the inland trade, which was abetted by a blurring of private and company accounts, as company employees applied to their own dealings the customs exemptions and other privileges that had been granted to the company for its exports.[47]

It is not difficult to see how abuses fostered by this private profit motive and by the customary practice of private trading would have been likely to expand when the company and its personnel became the rulers of Bengal and surrounding areas. Burke analyzed forms of extortion that are all too natural when men with such an outlook suddenly come into positions of power. Commercial abuses also grew as company servants sought to engage in and even monopolize branches of the inland commerce in their local districts.[48] Adam Smith argued that this tendency was inseparable from private trade, and hence from a commercial company's very possession of sovereign powers:

> It is in vain to prohibit them from [trading on their own account]. Nothing can be more completely foolish than to expect that the clerks of a great counting-house at ten thousand miles distance, and consequently almost quite out of sight, should, upon a simple order from their masters . . . abandon for ever all hopes of making a fortune, of which they have the means in their hands, and content themselves with the moderate salaries which those masters allow them.[49]

Even as the government of Bengal was gradually regularized under Hastings, abuses of this kind spread into outlying regions such as Oudh, where company servants and military units were stationed and enjoyed political influence, though they were not formally governing.[50]

Burke's analysis of the Indian problem also took note of Smith's remarks on the relation between corruption and salaries. In India, Burke asserted, at least since the East India Company acquired sovereign responsibilities,

> the emoluments of office do not in any degree correspond with the trust. For under the name of Junior Merchant and Senior Merchant and Writer, and those other little names of a Counting house, you have great Magistrates; you have the administrators of revenues truly royal; you have Judges . . . who pass judgments upon the greatest properties of the Country.

Public service should be adequately compensated and appropriate status maintained: this is a matter of fairness, and moreover, such measures serve to remove illicit temptations. In India salaries were "so inadequate to the dignity of the character that it is impossible . . . to exist in a state of incorruption"; rather, the company's regime resembled the disorderly mercenary armies of the Indian native states—"little pay, but unbounded license to plunder" ("Speech on Opening," 286–87). Arguing elsewhere for "just payment" in a European context, Burke commented that "a Secretary of State, for instance, must not appear sordid in the eyes of the ministers of other nations; neither ought our ministers abroad to appear contemptible in the courts where they reside" ("Economical Reform," 334–35). So also Burke suggested that important but underpaid East India Company servants, such as its "residents" (British ambassadors in effect) in Oudh and Benares, were "[obliged] to have recourse to unfair practices, in order to support their dignity" ("Bill to Amend," 73). Thus Burke acknowledged certain pressures behind these abuses, though, notably, he did not extend such a sympathetic thought to Hastings, whose emoluments he regarded as adequate.[51]

How should public service be compensated? In some countries (including Europe) these labors were sometimes repaid by "glory, family reputation, the love, the tears of joy, the honest applause, of their Country," but these largely aristocratic rewards were not generally available to officials in India, especially those in subordinate positions ("Speech on Opening," 287). Elsewhere, in his lesser-known role as a proponent of rationalized administration, Burke took a different view, founded on the more pessimistic conviction that virtue should not be counted on in systems of public authority. This view seems to fit the Indian case as he saw it:

> Ordinary service must be secured by the motives to ordinary integrity. . . . That state which lays its foundation in rare and heroic virtues will be sure to have its superstructure in the basest profligacy and corruption. An honorable and fair profit is the best security against avarice and rapacity; as in all things else, a lawful and regulated enjoyment is the best security against debauchery and excess. For as wealth is power, so all power will infallibly draw wealth to itself by some means or other. ("Economical Reform," 335)

Once again, the problem in India was that the often irregular arrangements the company had evolved were not appropriate to the power it held in its hands. In his diagnosis of this problem it is apparent that, although Burke vociferously assigned moral blame to individuals (such as Hastings) who he believed were guilty of corruption, he also spoke as a reformer interested in analyzing the structural causes of widespread abuses and devising policies to remedy them. Furthermore, although Burke held that government is a trust and often upheld a large role in it for leisured aristocrats who could be expected to act on the basis of an inbred sense of public duty, he was not above emphasizing the mundane importance of adequate pay for public service. Not all those qualified to hold public positions (including himself) came from backgrounds of independent wealth, or were immune to the temptation of converting offices into riches.

A final feature of the setting for Burke's charges was the sense of solidarity or esprit de corps within the East India Company, which facilitated its resistance to reform and the perpetuation of its own modes of operating. This phenomenon existed at several levels. The civilian or mercantile servants of the company were united by their common careerist interests; by their awareness, according to Burke, that they were a small, alien minority with little real knowledge of or sympathy with the surrounding Indian society; and after their return, by their exotic experiences. Something similar may have been true of the military officers in company employment. Although the army for the most part seems to have performed in a professional manner and did not figure significantly in Burke's charges, there is one suggestive exception. As British influence under Hastings was extended to the neighboring allied state of Oudh, army units stationed there were called upon to suppress disturbances that spread under its ineffectual native government and to supervise revenue collection. There were credible allegations of oppressive practices in outlying districts. Burke, drawing on Hastings's own reports, cited the case of an officer so accused who was unanimously acquitted by fellow officers in a court martial, of what "in times of stricter discipline would have been deemed a crime deserving the severest punishment" ("Articles of Charge," 173). Hastings, the ultimately responsible official, was accused of administrative policies that permitted such indiscipline to persist.

Company solidarity, finally, was apparent in the company's two governing bodies in England. One proposal for internal reform was to concentrate authority in the company directors, who would putatively be more responsive to Parliament and to the larger considerations of public policy, and to remove the checking power held by the much larger court of proprietors (shareholders). The actions of the latter, it was thought, were driven more entirely by the interests in profits, nepotism, and mutual support among returned Indian servants. Arguing instead for direct parliamentary control, Burke saw a decisive objection in the fact that the directors would continue to be elected by the proprietors, who

> will choose undoubtedly, out of themselves, men like themselves; and those who are most forward in resisting your [Parliament's] authority, those who are most engaged in faction or interest with the delinquents abroad, will be the objects of their selection. . . . But if the Directors should slip, and deviate into rectitude . . . it will surely be remembered to them at their next election. (*Fox's Bill*, 441)

This passage indicates Burke's astuteness, as a practicing politician, in analyzing the workings of institutions. The analysis here presupposed that, by the 1780s, the East India Company was pervaded by an ethos that was unified enough to manifest itself through any of the available alternative formal arrangements. Since this ethos was corrupt, Burke concluded that internal reform was impossible and external intervention requisite.

Esprit de corps, then, whether of the Indian servants, army officers, or company leadership, was one of the obstacles to the reform of abuses. Esprit de corps, however, is a social sentiment which, in other contexts, Burke valued highly, accompanying his advocacy of a variety of "corps" or corporate bodies in society. "To be attached to the subdivision, to love the little platoon we belong to in society, is the first principle (the germ as it were) of public affections" (*Reflections*, 135). There is poignancy in the fact that the East India Company, with its customary practices, was the "little platoon" of Hastings and the other prominent "delinquents" whom Burke accused. These were Englishmen who had spent long years working together on the other side of the world, as they saw it, for the good of the body to which they belonged. Once again, Burke was not sympathetic. The French noblemen who deserted their estate and joined the Revolution did so, in Burke's view, out of personal pride and ambition, thereby undermining a useful or at any rate reformable institution. The virtues of loyalty and solidarity, however, ceased to be valuable within a thoroughly corrupt body, however venerable, and were not admissible in mitigation of abuses.[52]

Through their corruption the servants of the East India Company had in Burke's eyes shown themselves to be unfit to rule in the British Empire and had thereby forfeited the position of authority they had acquired for themselves in India. This conclusion leads to a larger theme in Burke's political thought: the qualities he deemed appropriate or necessary in those who rule, and the importance he attached to the characteristics of a ruling group. The privileges held by corporations such as the East India Company were conceived, in eighteenth-century terms, as their "liberties," and any infringement of these liberties by government was jealously resisted. "But liberty, when men act in bodies," said Burke, "is *power*. Considerate people . . . will observe the use which is made of *power*; and particularly of so trying a thing as *new* power in *new* persons, of whose principles, tempers, and dispositions, they have little or no experience" (*Reflections*, 91). In assessing a given regime—and in making a judgment about the value of the liberty or liberties it claims to embody—one must attend closely to the distribution of real power within it and to the people who have power or are likely to acquire it. Accordingly, Burke's forebodings about the French Revolution took shape when he studied the list of persons elected to the Third Estate, subsequently the majority of the National Assembly, men he regarded as unsuited to fill the national political role awaiting them. Political institutions, such as the complex arrangements of constitutional government, were certainly important to Burke. But, he wrote, one must not neglect "the men of whom any system of authority is composed, [as] God, and nature, and education, and their habits of life have made them" (*Reflections*, 128). Again, Burke advised, "Never wholly separate in your mind the merits of any political question, from the men who are concerned in it. . . . Designing men never separate their plans from their interests; and . . . the power of bad men is no indifferent thing" ("Letter to Depont," 13). It is reasonable to suppose that, as Burke wrote these words, he was thinking not only of those ruling in France but also of the men who had been ruling in India, whose leader he was prosecuting at the time.

The simple answer to the question of who should rule is that "there is no qualification for government, but virtue and wisdom, actual or presumptive," wherever these may be found (*Reflections*, 139). Burke thus embraced a version of the classical teaching of Western political philosophy: Special and demanding qualities are needed in the ruling part of the state, qualities that entitle certain individuals to membership in the class of rulers. Among the virtues Burke emphasized was the recognition that power is always, according to the "eternal immutable law," held in trust for the welfare of those over whom it is exercised, and that those who hold it must therefore rule in the spirit of a trustee and "not according to their sordid selfish interest, nor to their wanton caprice, nor to their arbitrary will." They must repudiate "any thing that bears the least resemblance to a proud and lawless domination" (*Reflections*, 192). The appropriate ethical commitment, Burke believed, was most likely to be present if a ruling group was "respectably composed, in point of condition of life, of permanent property, of education, and of such habits as enlarge and liberalize the understanding" (*Reflections*, 129). Hence Burke defended a substantial aristocratic component in government, at least in the context of eighteenth-century society: he called for statesmen of outstanding virtue if they were available, honest gentlemen otherwise.[53] Since prudence derived from experience and respect for the past is another important ruling virtue, Burke expressed particular concern about the danger of abuses when power was suddenly acquired by new men, who were likely to have an attitude of "upstart insolence" toward the restraints and wisdom of tradition (*Reflections*, 121).

By these criteria the East India Company, and especially its personnel in the field, were found wanting. Like the revolutionaries in France, they were "men who are habitually meddling, daring, subtle, active, of litigious dispositions and unquiet minds," men who had not been socialized in the ethos of the traditional ruling class, and who were therefore "intoxicated with their unprepared greatness" (*Reflections*, 130–31).[54] Burke accused Hastings especially of ruling by "arbitrary will," of exercising a "lawless domination," and during the trial he denounced Hastings's sometimes arrogant defense claims as "insolent." Beyond these charges, we may inquire whether Burke believed the company's men were disqualified from political rule simply on the ground that they were in their basic outlook merchants—i.e., that people whose habits and motivations are rooted in the commercial world lack the "actual or presumptive" virtue of statesmen. What were Burke's presumptions on this matter?

There seems little question that Burke accepted with some enthusiasm the modern commercial society of which Great Britain was the leading exemplar in the eighteenth century, admiring the enterprise of successful businessmen and endorsing the character that underlay it. Addressing his (largely commercial) constituents in Bristol, Burke affirmed,

> Our prosperity and dignity arose principally, if not solely, from two
> sources; our Constitution, and commerce. Both these I have spared
> no study to understand, and no endeavour to support.... I have ever
> had my house open, and my poor services ready, for traders and
> manufacturers of every denomination. ("Speech at Arrival," 87)

Some forms of trade were illegitimate, of course. Although he did not dwell on it, Burke condemned the company's contraband opium business—"a smuggling Adventure, of a complicated and expensive Nature, to *China*, where the Importation of Opium is expressly forbidden . . . to the great Disgrace of the *British* Character in *India*" ("Articles of Impeachment," 165).[55] Legitimate international trade, however, was beneficial and respectable, and as we have seen, Burke upheld the imperial system that supported Britain's trading ventures.

It is not surprising, then, that Burke praised the "mercantile constitution" and methods of the East India Company, as these pertained to its strictly commercial operations, and especially its system of exact record keeping (which Hastings occasionally violated in suspect ways). Burke even argued that the company's business methods lent themselves to the development, in its hands, of a relatively efficient system of imperial administration:

> It does so happen that there the Counting-house gave lessons to the
> State.... The regulations made by mercantile men for their mercan-
> tile interest, when they have been able, as in this case, to be applied to
> the discipline and order of the State, have produced a discipline and
> order which no State should be ashamed to copy.... It is perhaps the

best contrivance that ever has been thought of by the wit of men for the government of a remote, large, disjointed empire. ("Speech on Opening," 296)

The state could learn valuable lessons from businessmen about procedural regularity, rational accounting, and the like, but on balance it did not follow that a commercial company should *be* the state, as in India, or even that commercial men should play a large role in government. On the latter question Burke expressed some ambivalence, but his overall view was negative. Speaking for Fox's bill, and alluding to Smith's criticisms of merchant empires, Burke remarked: "My experience in life teaches me nothing clear upon the subject. I have known merchants with the sentiments and the abilities of great statesmen; and I have seen persons in the rank of statesmen, with the conceptions and character of pedlars" (*Fox's Bill*, 387). Nevertheless, his final verdict was in favor of transferring authority from the company to Parliament. Similarly, although he did not condemn them, Burke was disturbed by the number of traders in the French National Assembly; he was afraid that, since they "had never known any thing beyond their counting-house," they would be "overborne and swayed" by the ambitious lawyers and radical theoreticians in that body (*Reflections*, 131).

The more general concern, however, was not the political ineptitude of merchants, but their inappropriate motivation. Burke clearly recognized and praised the "active, awakened and enlightened principle of self-interest" ("Speech on Opening," 296) as the driving force of commercial life, both in individuals and in well-run companies such as the East India Company, insofar as it was concerned merely with commerce. Burke endorsed self-interest, or the private profit motive, in its proper context—the free market—because he believed that markets are self-regulating through the price mechanism when the various agents make decisions based on their own interests. In other words, Burke accepted the familiar "invisible hand" thesis of classical political economy. This is clear in his most extensive work on the subject: "The benign and wise Disposer . . . obliges men, whether they will or not, in pursuing their own selfish interests, to connect the general good with their own individual success" ("Scarcity," 141).

Decidedly, however, Burke did not apply this economic doctrine to all dimensions of human life. In particular, he maintained a clear dichotomy between economic and political life, the market and government, and the kinds of motivation and character appropriate in each sphere.[56] The importance of this distinction rested on Burke's conviction that the true purposes of the state were entirely different from those of the marketplace; therefore, the state was, or ought to be, something entirely different from, say, the East India Company. As he put it in a famous passage: "The state ought not to be considered as nothing better than a partnership agreement in a trade of pepper and coffee, callico or tobacco, or some other such low concern." Rather, it was a collective enterprise aiming at non- or supraeconomic goods or interests (such as art, science, and virtue), goods that transcend a single generation and should be regarded with a spirit of reverence rather than of self-interested calculation (*Reflections*, 194).[57]

Prosperity results when enlightened self-interest guides economic behavior, manifesting itself for example in the methods devised by "mercantile men" for trading in Asia or elsewhere, their proper sphere of expertise. The state is a different kind of association, with respect to its membership, its purposes, and hence its leadership. Burke may have sought to unite a modern, market-based economy with the traditional, largely aristocratic ruling class;[58] certainly it did not follow from the value of modern commerce that government should be in the hands of merchants, in England or in India. As a political philosopher, Burke held that authority was best conferred on a "true natural aristocracy," which he no doubt believed the actual aristocracy of Great Britain approximated to some degree. In a well-known passage, Burke listed some of the experiences conducive to the formation of a true aristocracy: "To be bred in a place of estimation; To see nothing low or sordid from one's infancy; To be taught to respect one's self; To be habituated to the censorial inspection of the public eye," and so forth. Among the many items in this catalogue is: "To be amongst rich traders, who from their success are presumed to have sharp and vigorous understandings, and to possess the virtues of diligence, order, constancy, and regularity, and to have cultivated an habitual regard to commutative justice" ("Appeal," 168). Rulers, that is, should be in touch with these people, learn from them, and acknowledge their legitimate interests, all of which was arguably the case in the politics Burke and his colleagues practiced. But generally speaking, merchants were not themselves the most appropriate candidates for actual political office; and with respect to the empire, where the abuses of outright mercantile rule were apparent, Bacon's advice (we may imagine Burke agreeing) remained sensible: "Let [the governors of colonies] be rather noblemen and gentlemen, than merchants; for they look ever to the present gain."[59] In the end, Hastings was replaced by Lord Cornwallis, who as a general and member of the high aristocracy—and an outsider to the East India Company—was expected to be immune to the temptations and pressures to which Hastings had succumbed.[60] Although Burke was not so sure of Cornwallis personally—a "zealous Courtier . . . no friend of mine" (*Corr.*,

5:297)—one surmises that the appointment of someone of this background was a strategy of which Burke approved.

Political Corruption

We turn now to the political corruption of Great Britain, both actual and potential, a danger that in Burke's analysis was linked to the various kinds of pecuniary corruption already considered. It should be kept in mind that the concept of "corruption" in eighteenth-century British political theory had a number of interrelated meanings, several of which are relevant here. There was, first, the idea that the general moral corruption of a people—corruption of their manners, attitudes, and values—was not only unattractive in itself but could also undermine a healthy political life. This theme was prominent in the rhetoric of republican theory, which viewed political or civic virtue as the most important determinant of liberty; but it was also a concern for thinkers such as Burke who, though not republicans, nevertheless assigned significant weight to public-spiritedness or virtue in public life. Second, the notion of corruption applied to direct but illicit links between money and political power. The most familiar case was when public authority or position was translated into personal enrichment, through bribery or extortion, as Burke alleged of Hastings. Here we are more concerned with the reverse process, in which money purchased political power or office, perhaps for the purpose of making even more money or for protecting corrupt practices, in a vicious cycle. Adjudging this process corrupt presupposes that public office is not properly venal, but rests on some other criterion or procedure. This view, it should be noted, was avialable but was not universal in the eighteenth century. Finally, the term "corruption" was applied to practices (again, usually involving financial interests) that were thought to upset the delicate balance of a mixed constitution such as Britain enjoyed, thereby endangering limited and lawful constitutional government and hence political liberty in this sense.

Regarding both America and India, Burke worried that the possession of empire and the exigencies of imperial government could have a demoralizing and corrupting effect both on British institutions and British political virtues, with dire long-term consequences for the body politic. The principal reason for Burke's advocacy of a conciliatory policy toward the American colonies was his fear that the alternative repressive policy, based on a harsh and authoritarian conception of the imperial relation, would engender increasingly illiberal attitudes at home: "Liberty is in danger of being made unpopular to Englishmen. Contending for an imaginary power we begin to acquire the spirit of domination and to lose the relish of honest equality" (*Sheriffs of Bristol*, 243). America was an especially ominous case because of the means being used, and because what was being suppressed was a genuine expression (in Burke's view) of traditional English conceptions of liberty. The "reduction of a free people to slavery by foreign mercenary armies" was bad enough ("Address to the King," 162), but the willingness of the British government and most of the populace to pursue this policy was especially disturbing, since it marked a deplorable shift not only in political values but also in the underlying national character. Coming as close as he ever came to adopting the outlook of republican theory, Burke wrote in a letter to Lord Rockingham: "We seem no longer that eager, inquisitive, jealous, fiery people, which we have been formerly, and which we have been, a very short time ago" (*Corr.* 3:190). He implied that the loss of these qualities jeopardized free government in Britain. As with Thucydides's Athenians, the privileges of empire were corrupting, and the determination to hold onto an empire by any means bred an attitude toward the use of power that was at variance with the norms of the domestic political system.

The disturbing willingness of Englishmen to see liberty destroyed in America differentiated this case from that of India, where political liberty was not immediately at stake. The organization of a viable empire that allowed for colonial liberty was an intractable problem for Burke, as for other statesmen; with respect to America, Burke admitted to being "deeply sensible of the difficulty of reconciling the strong presiding power, that is so useful towards the conservation of a vast, disconnected, infinitely diversified empire, with that liberty and safety of the provinces" (*Sheriffs of Bristol*, 230). This problem did not arise in full force in India, but in other respects rule over India was also likely to have an adverse effect on British political attitudes. If an erosion of the commitments to law and liberty was a potential consequence of "the unwieldy haughtiness of a great ruling nation, habituated to command, pampered by enormous wealth, and confident from a long course of prosperity and victory," the danger posed by the possession of India was even greater than that involved in rule over America.

A related concern that Burke expressed with respect to America, one that pertains both to the civic virtue of the ruling nation and to equitable standards of rule, also applies equally well to India: "When any community is subordinately connected with another, the great danger of the connection is the extreme pride and self-complacency of the superior, which in all matters of controversy will probably decide in its own favor" (*Sheriffs of Bristol*, 231, 216). Following the general election of 1784, in which the British electorate repudiated Fox's administration and its Indian reforms, Burke complained that—just as in the degenerate period of the Roman Empire—"tyranny, robbery, and destruction" abroad had evidently become "popular and pleasing" in Great Britain (*Corr.* 5:154–55).

Such fears of the morally corrosive effects of imperial rule on the people of the dominant state occasionally appeared in Burke's impeachment speeches. Hence the deeper political importance of Hastings's impeachment: it was "a prosecution not only for the punishing a delinquent, a prosecution not merely for preventing this and that offence, but it is a great censorial prosecution, for the purpose of preserving the manners, characters, and virtues that characterize the people of England." It was not only a matter of bringing Hastings to justice, but of publicly and dramatically airing his and his colleagues' crimes, exorcising their spirit, deterring future occurrences, reaffirming the rule of law, and thus restoring original principles of good government, as republican theory suggested was necessary from time to time. The situation was precarious: "These people pour in upon us every day. They not only bring with them the wealth which they have acquired, but they bring with them into our country the vices by which it was acquired." If the previously "open-hearted, candid, liberal, plain, sincere people" of England should be infected by these vices, or learn from the lords' example to connive at them (assuming the House of Lords were to acquit Hastings), they were in danger of becoming "a nation of concealers, a nation of dissemblers, a nation of liars, a nation of forgers, . . . a people of *banians*, [and] that character of England, that character which, more than our arms, and more than our commerce, has made us a great nation," will be lost ("Sixth Article," 449–50).

The success of the exercise to which Burke devoted so much effort presupposed that the process of corruption had not yet gone too far, and Burke affirmed his belief—or affected to believe, in addressing the lords—that this was the case. Complaining of the subtleties and legalisms of Hastings's defense, Burke asserted:

> The Commons of Great Britain, my Lords, are a rustic people. . . .
> We are not acquainted with the urbanity and politeness of extortion
> and oppression; nor do we know anything of the sentimental delicacy
> of bribery and corruption. We speak the language of truth, and we
> speak it in the plain, simple terms in which truth ought to be spoken.
> ("Speech in Reply," 11:170)

There was a note of challenge here: the Commons had proven their virtue by impeaching; would the House of Lords convict? (Elsewhere, Burke was not so sanguine about the state of the Commons.) In any event, though the welfare of the Indians was the most prominent theme in Burke's Indian speeches, the continuing moral welfare of the British under the impact of imperial rule was certainly among his concerns.

In addition to causing the moral corruption of the people of England, Burke feared that Indian influence would lead to political corruption in the second, more specific sense mentioned above. Reflecting widespread popular suspicions about the returned "Indians," Burke was concerned that Indian wealth could and would be applied to buy political influence in England, both diffusely and directly, through the acquisition of seats in Parliament by members of the "Indian interest." This influence would naturally be used to protect past offenders and perpetuate the profitable system of abuses, while at the same time bringing the unscrupulous methods of Indian politics into the heart of the British government. "Who can estimate the influence of corruption, when supported by all the treasures of India?" Burke asked, alluding to the government's failure to force a recall of Hastings despite mounting criticism ("Almas Ali Khan," 462). Subsequently, during the trial, Burke said, "To-day the Commons of Great Britain prosecute the delinquents of India: to-morrow the delinquents of India may be the Commons of Great Britain." An acquittal, he feared, would accelerate this process, "[letting] loose all the corrupt wealth of India, acquired by the oppression of that country, for the corruption of all the liberties of this, and [filling] the Parliament with men who are now the object of its indignation" ("Sixth Article," 450). The greatness of the House of Commons, he remarked on a different occasion, would continue only "as long as it can keep the breakers of the law in India from becoming the makers of the law for England" (*Reflections*, 133).

Two preliminary comments may be made about this argument. First, it evokes an insightful passage in Hume's political essays that Burke surely knew, to the effect that "free governments" (a category that included Britain) "have been commonly the most happy for those who partake of their freedom; yet are they the most ruinous and oppressive to their provinces." Hume's modern example was Ireland, but his analysis—which harked back to Machiavelli[61]—could apply to India as well. An absolute monarch, he argued, can put newly conquered subjects on the same footing with the old (who are without political rights in any case); but

the conquerors [in a free state] are all legislators, and will be sure to contrive matters, by restrictions on trade, and by taxes, so as to draw some private, as well as public, advantage from their conquests. Provincial governors have also a better chance, in a republic, to escape with their plunder, by means of bribery or intrigue; and their fellow-citizens, who find their own state to be enriched by the spoils of the subject provinces, will be the more inclined to tolerate such abuses.[62]

The liberty of a free state consists in its representative government, which is responsive to the interests of the metropolitan citizens rather than to those of colonial subjects. Sometimes these conflict, and then it acts at the expense of the latter. If influence to this end can be increased by corruption in a free government, as Hume hinted and Burke emphasized, so much the worse. Hume's argument nicely complements Smith's analysis of the defects of merchant empires (with which Burke came to agree), insofar as the merchant companies and their allies enjoyed representation in government. If we assume that Burke, who valued free government as much or more than Hume, was familiar with this argument, we can see his Indian efforts as an attempt to prove that Hume's pessimistic verdict was not universally true. Parliamentary rule need not mean abuse of colonies, and Parliament was not irreparably vulnerable to the power of those with a special interest in this abuse. Sometimes, indeed, Burke turned Hume's argument on its head: the denial of freedom to any "inferior member of the British empire" would tend to destroy freedom at home ("Address to the King," 176). Burke was perfectly cognizant, however, of the dynamics within parliamentary government that made this result possible.

Second, Burke was identifying here an institutionalized vicious cycle, in which ill-gotten wealth was converted into political power, which in turn was used to protect the profiteers, generate more "plunder," and defeat or destroy opponents and would-be reformers of the system. Political power issued from the concerted action of the beneficiaries of the corrupt system and their financial resources, a portion of which was allocated to pay necessary organizational costs and to buy the support of any needed allies. Burke, who as a practicing politician was interested in analyzing the workings of power, discerned the emergence of such a system in the Indian faction in Parliament in the early 1780s; a few years later he saw a similar dynamic at work in the French Revolution:

> The more active and stirring part of the lower orders having got government, and the distribution of plunder, into their hands, they will use its resources in each municipality to form a body of adherents. These rulers, and their adherents, will be strong enough to overpower the discontents of those who have not been able to assert their share of the spoil. The unfortunate adventurers in the cheating

lottery of plunder will probably be the least sagacious, or the most inactive and irresolute of the gang. If, on disappointment, they should dare to stir, they will soon be suppressed as rebels and mutineers. ("National Assembly," 36)

The revolutionary version of this pattern differed from its parliamentary counterpart in that it relied at key points on violence in addition to the political use of money. Furthermore, in the France of 1791, in Burke's view, all remaining actors in politics were similarly motivated competitors for dominance in the system of plunder.

The great danger of such corrupt systems is their capacity for self-perpetuation. If they become entrenched, they can be defeated only by the intervention of an outside force (which Burke advocated in France), by the self-destructive violence of rival factions contending for control of the machine (which Burke suggested was a possibility in France), or by internal decay, as resources available for plunder are exhausted (a possibility he did not consider, either in France or in India). If the system was not entrenched, however, but only incipient, as with the Indian interest in England, it could be thwarted by the efforts of honest statesmen and, in a free state, by public vigilance. Burke's charges of political corruption were designed to elicit such efforts and arouse popular indignation, which he must have believed could still be effective. His support for the provision in Fox's bill transferring control of the empire from the East India Company to Parliament would not have made sense if he believed the company's faction had already achieved a dominant influence in Parliament, though the defeat of this bill and the subsequent fall of the coalition suggested that this remained a serious danger.

Burke explored various aspects of the development of an Indian political machine in England, as a counterpart and extension of Hastings's corrupt conspiracy in Bengal, from the period of his committee investigations in 1781–1783. North's Regulating Act of 1773 had substantially raised the stock value eligibility for voting in the company's court of proprietors in an effort to bring this body in line with the more responsible directors; the underlying assumption was that abuses resulted in part from shareholder pressure. Burke later argued that this policy had failed, and indeed, had merely facilitated dominance of the company by rich returned Indian servants, who could easily meet the new qualification. They then used their voting power in the company as a base from which to defy the "salutary Admonitions" of Parliament and exert political influence: "In Proportion as these Interests prevailed, the Means of Cabal, of Concealment, and of corrupt Confederacy, became far more easy than before" (*Ninth Report*, 202).

Burke was not only worried about the party of returned Indian servants; he also emphasized the personal power of Hastings and the shadow he cast in England. For fourteen years, "he has had himself the means of heaping up immense wealth; and during that whole period, the fortunes of hundreds have depended on his smiles and frowns." At any given time he had "two hundred and fifty young gentlemen, some of them of the best families in England . . . as his hostages for your good behaviour." The result was that, in addition to his despotic power in India, "he domineers with an overbearing sway in the assemblies of his pretended masters; and it is thought in a degree rash to venture to name his offences in this House" (*Fox's Bill*, 434).[63]

Burke's clearest analysis of the problem appeared as a warning in a letter to Henry Dundas, the minister responsible for India in Pitt's government, after Dundas and Pitt had joined the move to impeach Hastings:

> A body of men, united in a close connexion of common guilt and common apprehension of danger in the moment, with a strong and just confidence of future power if they escape it, and possessed of a measure of wealth and influence which perhaps you yourself have not calculated at any thing like its just magnitude, is not forming, but actually formed in this Country. This faction is at present ranged under Hastings as an Indian leader; and it will have very soon, if it has not already, an English [parliamentary] Leader of considerable enterprise and no contemptible influence. If this faction should now obtain a Triumph it will be very quickly too strong for your Ministry.

The only way to forestall this occurrence was to destroy Hastings by a successful impeachment (*Corr.* 5:314). Burke returned to this theme during the trial:

> Great and powerful as the House of Commons is . . . yet we cannot be insensible to the effects produced by the introduction of forty millions of money into this country from India. We know that the private fortunes which have been made there pervade this kingdom so universally that there is not a single parish in it unoccupied by the partisans of the defendant. . . . It is, therefore, to preserve the integrity and honor of the Commons of Great Britain that we have brought this man to your Lordships' bar. ("Speech in Reply," 11:162, 201)

Burke was concerned not only that the Indian faction might prevent reform through its presence in the legislature, but also that it could corrupt the judicial process and obstruct the just punishment of individual offenders.[64] Political corruption of the judiciary, Burke suggested, was even worse than that of the legislature, because of the cynical manipulation of the forms of legal justice involved. "If, from any appearance of chicane in the court, justice should fail, all men will say, better there were no tribunals at all." It would be preferable to follow the example of the dey of Algiers, who admitted he was simply the captain of a robber band, than to wield arbitrary power "under a pretended reverence to punctilious ceremonies and observances of law" ("Speech in Opening," 9:343). The oriental reference in this context, of course, was intended to alert Burke's listeners to the danger that Asian attitudes toward government as well as Asian wealth might be infecting the British polity.

Punishment of the principal offenders such as Hastings required impeachment, however, and for this procedure the legislature sat as the judicial body. The corruption of Parliament and the corruption of justice would coincide in this case. Foreseeing difficulties, Burke privately complained, "We know that we bring before a bribed tribunal a prejudged cause" (*Corr.* 5:241).[65] Somewhat to Burke's surprise, however, the House of Commons impeached Hastings; would the House of Lords (where Indian influence might also be expected) convict him? Burke implored the lords to discount the evidence favorable to Hastings that was offered by many responsible officials who had been his subordinates in India, as the testimony of "persons who derive their fortunes from the ruin of the very people of the country, and who have divided the spoils with the man whom we accuse. Undoubtedly these officers will give him their good word" ("Speech in Reply," 11:358). The more delicate question, however, was whether the lords themselves were sufficiently free of corruption to sit as unbiased judges. Since no higher appeal (other than public opinion) was possible, Burke confronted the issue squarely:

> It is well known that enormous wealth has poured into this country
> from India through a thousand channels, public and concealed; and
> it is no particular derogation from our honor to suppose a possibility
> of being corrupted by that by which other empires have been cor-
> rupted, and assemblies almost as respectable and venerable as your
> Lordships' have been directly or indirectly vitiated. ("Speech in
> Opening," 9:341)

Burke feared that Hastings would be acquitted as a result of an insistence by the lords on strict rules of evidence and other legal technicalities inappropriate in a great political trial.

> I trust that this Cause will put an end to all conjectures . . . which
> have been disseminated with so much industry through this king-
> dom and foreign nations too, that, in order to cover our connivance
> and participation in guilt, and our common share in the plunder of
> the East, we have invented a set of scholastic distinctions abhorrent
> to the general sentiments of mankind, by which we are to deny
> ourselves the knowledge of all that the rest of the world knows.
> ("Speech on Opening," 278)

Given the background corruption that Burke believed to be so widespread, any such legal evasiveness would stand condemned as dishonest.

Burke employed two rhetorical tactics in an attempt to overcome the possible bias of his audience. First, since it was widely expected that Hastings would be acquitted through a corrupt process, Burke urged the lords to secure their reputation by acting "in such a manner as that public opinion may in the end be securely defied, by having been previously respected and dreaded" ("Speech in Opening," 9:341). Punishment of the influential offender would prove the integrity of the court. At first sight, this is a surprising proposal. It is generally improper to suggest that trial judges should allow public opinion to influence their verdict in any manner, and this suggestion seems doubly odd in Burke, who usually defended Parliament's independence from public opinion in all its business. He evidently believed—or hoped the lords might believe—that the general presumption of corruption and the special status of Hastings made this case exceptional. Second, Burke appealed to the lords' sense of honor in the face of the larger opinion of Europe, which he implied would be interested in the quality of British justice in the conduct of her imperial affairs:

> God forbid that, when you try the Cause of Asia in the presence of
> Europe, there should be the least suspicion that the Cause of Asia is
> not as good with you, because the abuse is committed by a British
> subject; . . . that a British subject in power should have rights which
> are denied to our humble allies, to our detached dependents, to those
> who at such a distance depend upon the breath of British justice.
> ("Speech on Opening," 278)

The right verdict would put the process beyond reproach in this larger forum.

These tactics, however, were risky, as Burke surely appreciated. Since they involved a challenge based on a public suggestion that the lords might be either corrupt or lacking in judicial impartiality, they invited defiance, which itself could be construed as a perverse demonstration of independence. Given Burke's suspicions, and his position as a manager of the prosecution, however, it is difficult to see any clearly preferable alternative open to him.

The Arcot Interest

The most important single episode in which corrupt dealings in India were linked to organized political influence in England involved the so-called Arcot interest. The background events took place in the presidency of Madras rather than Bengal, and Hastings was not directly involved in them (though he expressed support for what Burke regarded as the corrupt party); this episode, then, does not figure in the impeachment.[66] It was, however, the subject of another of Burke's most famous Indian speeches, and the danger he believed it posed to the British political system was identical to that represented by the influence of the "Bengal squad" of Hastings's friends in Parliament.

Muhammad Ali Khan, the nawab of the Carnatic,[67] attained his throne against a rival claimant with British assistance in 1749, and he remained their loyal dependent, the nominal ruler of this part of the empire, for many years. His dominions were subject to a pattern of abuses by company servants similar to that detailed by Burke in Bengal, but another insidious scheme developed as well. A group of company servants, acting in a private capacity under the leadership of Paul Benfield, began to lend large sums of money to the irresponsible or inept nawab at exorbitant interest rates, and these debts (running eventually into the millions of pounds) were secured by mortgages on the future public revenues of the Carnatic. As the nawab fell ever more deeply in arrears, his regime fell under the sway of his creditors. At the same time, these individuals acquired a strong interest in the continuing viability and solvency of the nawab's government, from which they were extracting immense fortunes, and they exerted considerable influence to ensure that the company's official policies toward its ally were consistent with their private interest. The nawab was willing to keep on borrowing at high interest, and the creditors were willing to lend, because both were confident that the company, and perhaps ultimately the British government, would bail them out in the end.

In Burke's view, the collusive relations among the nawab, his British creditors, and the East India Company (which permitted or, as Burke saw it, connived at the financial dealings, since the private loans permitted the nawab to repay debts he owed to the company) amounted to a massive

Muhammad Ali Khan, nawab of the Carnatic, by George Willison.
Burke criticized the "Nabob of Arcot" (1749–1795) for his
relations with his British creditors and his annexation of Tanjore.
By permission of the British Library, London.

corrupt scheme for the profit of speculators, a scheme that had detrimental, in fact nearly disastrous, consequences both for the people of the region and for the public interest of the British Empire. In a speech in Parliament, Burke described the complex transactions by which the debt was built up and serviced and the collusion among numerous company officials that allowed the scheme to reach such huge proportions. The outcome, he suggested, was that the nawab had become a mere puppet ruler, kept in place solely as the subject of his financial liabilities:

> The Nabob, without military, without federal capacity, is extinguished as a potentate; but then he is carefully kept alive as an independent and sovereign power, for the purpose of rapine and extortion; for the purpose of perpetuating the old intrigues, animosities, usuries, and corruptions. (*Arcot's Debts*, 536 and passim)

The formerly flourishing Madras region fell into economic decline as vast sums of money were conveyed to England as private fortunes, "the deep silent flow of this steady stream of wealth" mostly passing unnoticed; meanwhile the peasantry were ruined by the rigorous tax-extraction methods of the agents of the "usurious European assignee" who had replaced the nawab's collectors (*Arcot's Debts*, 492, 532–33).

Public debts and the interest on them had to be paid out of public revenues, but when carried too far this policy could become economically ruinous and politically dangerous for any state. Critics of the Whig regime of eighteenth-century Britain worried about the long-term consequences of the fairly novel and increasing British debt: "We have always found, where a government has mortgaged all its revenues, that it necessarily sinks into a state of languor, inactivity, and impotence." This was one of Hume's milder comments.[68] A few years later, Burke was to analyze how "by the vast debt of France a great monied interest had insensibly grown up, and with it a great power," and how the French royal government had been driven into "pledging to creditors the revenue of the state." Fiscal difficulties brought on the French Revolution; the revolutionaries then tried to solve the problem by the even more unconscionable policy of confiscations (especially of Church property). Either course represented a violation of the principle that "it is to the property of the citizen, and not to the demands of the creditor of the state, that the first and original faith of civil society is pledged" (*Reflections*, 209, 207). The irresponsible nawab, and the company that in actuality controlled the public affairs of the Carnatic, were both guilty of sacrificing the real interests and faith of Indian society to an unscrupulous monied interest of British adventurers.

Other deplorable consequences were also related to the nawab's debts. Misgovernment was rampant, to the detriment of the inhabitants; but most ominously, indiscipline and mutiny spread among the nawab's underpaid troops, rendering his state—and ultimately the position of the British at Madras, his protectors—militarily vulnerable. In 1780 Haidar Ali, the ruler of Mysore and one of the most formidable opponents of the company, invaded and devastated the Carnatic, wiped out a small British army, and nearly captured Madras. Burke concluded not only that mismanagement was responsible for the level of destruction but also that the bungling and self-interested influence of the creditors in the nawab's government were among the causes of the war. Haidar Ali, needlessly antagonized, determined "to make the country possessed by these incorrigible and predestinated criminals a memorable example to mankind. . . . Having terminated his disputes with every enemy, and every rival, who buried their mutual animosities in their common detestation against the creditors of the Nabob of Arcot," he gathered his forces into a "black cloud [which] suddenly burst, and poured down the whole of its contents upon the plains of the Carnatic" (*Arcot's Debts*, 519). British forces from Bengal were eventually able to repel the invader and restore the company's position in southeastern India, but the grave public danger and the public costs incurred were attributable to a corrupt scheme for private profits.

Another offshoot of the Arcot debt scandal was the conquest of Tanjore in 1773, a case, in Burke's analysis, of major injustice caused by corrupt pecuniary interests. The nawab of Arcot had claims on the small, neighboring tributary state of Tanjore; his ambition to annex it was encouraged by the British creditors, who advanced funds for the war in exchange for claims on future revenues from the conquered territory. The operation was carried out by British troops placed at the nawab's disposal by the compliant (and financially complicit) company government in Madras.

Although the treaty relations formerly obtaining between Arcot and Tanjore were complex, Burke did not doubt that this was an unjustified act of aggression against an autonomous state. The overthrown raja of Tanjore was friendly toward the British, was the legitimate ruler of Tanjore by hereditary right, and was, moreover, the "natural sovereign" of the country, "a sovereign connected with his subjects in affections, manners, and religion," in contrast to the despotism of the nawab (*Conquests*, 46, 49). Hastings (from afar) and other leading company officials, while disdaining the financial intrigues, regarded the nawab as a loyal ally and favored a policy of supporting his expansionist ambitions on political and strategic grounds. Burke did not entirely dismiss the imperial interest, arguing that the raja too, though weaker than the nawab, could have been cultivated as an ally. For the most part, however, he condemned the conquest and the duplicitous diplomacy that led up to it as unjust and dishonorable:

> The game they play is perfectly new, and well worthy the attention of a reader, who may be inquisitive to know the spirit of British oriental politics. . . . In this scandalous shuffle of prevarication and mutual connivance . . . this extraordinary confederacy has made sport of the faith of the British nation, and of all faith. (*Conquests*, 75)

What was worse, however, was that the real underlying purpose of the plunder of Tanjore was to satisfy the "heroic avarice of the projectors," to help pay off the nawab's obligations to his creditors (*Arcot's Debts*, 518). British public policy in a sensitive area of its foreign relations had been formed and driven to unjust actions, not only by a clear-cut private interest but by a corrupt cabal of speculators and adventurers.

With this background in mind, we may return to the theme of political corruption infiltrating British politics from India. As with the Bengal faction dependent on or loyal to Hastings, the many individuals who had profited from the Arcot debts or who had a continuing interest in them sought to convert some of their wealth into political influence at home, in an effort to use "the junction of the power of office in England, with the abuse of authority in the East," to further the corrupt system (*Arcot's Debts*, 548). Benfield himself entered Parliament in 1780, and Burke alleged that by 1784 he controlled a group of eight MPs. Furthermore, the "Arcot interest" threw its support and its wealth behind Pitt in the general election of 1784—an election which, "managed upon Indian principles, and for an Indian interest," confirmed Pitt in office. In exchange (as Burke and others in the opposition saw it), in 1785 Pitt's government arranged a final settlement of the Arcot debt—without a serious investigation—that was to the advantage of the creditors. The loss of office suffered by Fox, Burke, and the other Whigs was a major blow to their careers, and Burke's anger at the ensuing events is evident: "Do you think that no reckoning was to follow this lewd debauch? that no payment was to be demanded for this riot of public drunkenness and national prostitution?" (*Arcot's Debts*, 543).[69] The government's handling of the Arcot affair, in Burke's view, confirmed widespread suspicions of a corrupt political deal:

> The way to avoid suspicion in the settlement of pecuniary transactions, in which great frauds have been very strongly presumed, is, to attend to these few plain principles:—First, To hear all parties

equally, and not the managers for the suspected claimants only.—
Not to proceed in the dark; but to act with as much publicity as
possible,—Not to precipitate decision. . . . If [these principles] are
violated, a corrupt motive of some kind or other will not only be
suspected, but must be violently presumed. (*Arcot's Debts*, 540)

Pitt's Indian allies, Burke guessed, had also been consulted on the fram-
ing of his India Act, thus assuming the role of "legislator[s] of Indostan."
In these ways, Benfield and his friends had succeeded in taking advantage of "the poor rotten constitution of [their] native country" (*Arcot's
Debts*, 543, 541): the offenders in India had not only concluded their corrupt schemes with success but now actually enjoyed power in the imperial
government.

Let us append several postscripts to this story. Burke was not alone in
believing that a well-organized Indian interest in Parliament was growing
and acquiring a sinister influence in the early 1780s. Although such a group
certainly existed, modern historians doubt that it was ever large or strong
enough to have had a major impact; rather, it has been suggested, many
returned East India Company servants, seeking respectability, preferred not
to call attention to the source of their fortunes by membership in an Indian
group.[70] Hastings's friends in the House of Commons were not strong
enough, after all, to prevent his impeachment. Pitt thwarted the charge that
he was beholden to the East Indian interest when he himself (surprisingly)
voted for the impeachment the year after Burke's speech on the Arcot debt—
unless of course this action was designed to prove his independence in the
wake of Burke's charge.

Meanwhile, Burke and his defenders had to fend off two accusations
impugning Burke's own motives. First, it was charged that he himself had a
special interest in the affairs of the Carnatic, arising from the fact that his
relative William Burke served as an agent in England for the raja of Tanjore;[71] and second, it was suggested that since Burke and his party had been
defeated in their own ambition to serve as "legislators of Indostan" (and
simultaneously acquire patronage for their party) in part through the opposition of the Indian interest, their subsequent prosecution of Hastings was
motivated primarily by partisanship and a desire for revenge.[72] To the second of these charges Burke himself responded: "Why should it ever have
been supposed that we are actuated by revenge? I answer, There are two very
sufficient causes: corruption and ignorance." Through ignorance, some people confounded "the rules of private society with those of public function,"
misinterpreting the harsh language Burke used against Hastings as personal

or partisan animosity rather than the appropriate expression of indignation at great crimes in a court of justice. Through corruption

> an innumerable multitude of people [are disposed] to a fellow-feeling with the prisoner. Under the shadow of his crimes thousands of fortunes have been made; and therefore thousands of tongues are employed to justify the means by which these fortunes were made. When they cannot deny the facts, they attack the accusers. ("Speech in Reply," II:176–77).

In such cases, where issues of justice and injustice were being tried, the evidence and arguments had to stand on their own, regardless of motives; and yet in politics the argument of corrupt or interested motives carries weight, as Burke well knew, responding as he did here to an imputation against himself by returning to the theme of the corruption he thought motivated many of his opponents.

Conclusion: Politics and Interests

Burke's analyses and charges regarding Indian political corruption should finally be placed in the context of certain features of the British political system and of Burke's general view of this system. Relevant topics include: the structure of the eighteenth-century Parliament and the dynamics of parliamentary politics; the idea of the representation of interests; and Burke's particular views on constitutional balance, both between the Crown and Parliament and between the landed and the monied interests, given his conception of an appropriate governing class.

How was it that the East India group in general, and the Arcot group in particular, could so readily obtain political influence in Great Britain and promote their (corrupt) interests? Several responses come immediately to mind. In the British government of the eighteenth century, as in more modern systems of representative government, successful campaigns for election to the House of Commons were often costly, to the advantage of wealthy candidates or candidates who enjoyed the confidence of wealthy donors. Furthermore, seriously contested elections were far fewer than they are today, the electorates much smaller, and the secret ballot not in use. Money could therefore be brought to bear in a concentrated manner on electoral politics. Although overt bribery of voters was officially forbidden, practices suspiciously close to bribery were commonplace in many constituencies. More important, the unreformed (pre-1832) House of Commons was notorious both for its "rotten" or depopulated boroughs, whose franchise-generating property, and hence seats in Parliament, were bought and sold, and for "pocket" or "nomination" boroughs that, through a similar method of controlling the relevant property, were at the disposal of wealthy and powerful patrons.[73] When Burke expressed fears that the "Indian delinquents" were acquiring influence in Parliament, or were appearing there as members, he meant that their money was being applied in the "management" of elections of their allies, that they were finding highly placed borough patrons who shared in the Indian interest, or that they were simply buying parliamentary seats for themselves.

By later standards, of course, the unreformed House of Commons appears not only undemocratic but also thoroughly corrupt, in the ease and openness with which money could purchase influence and even seats in the legislature, and in the degree to which actual politics revolved around the maintenance and management of the various patronage networks or machines, both at election time and during parliamentary sessions. For Burke, however, these practices in and of themselves did not constitute corruption. He himself sat in the House after 1780 as a member for a pocket borough (Malton) in the patronage of the Marquess of Rockingham and Earl Fitzwilliam, as he had done also from 1765 to 1774, and he defended the role of patronage-based parties under the leadership of such notables. Burke also consistently opposed the movement for parliamentary reform that made itself heard from the 1760s onward—a movement that sought to abolish rotten boroughs, expand the electorate, regularize the requirements for the franchise, and shift away from the antiquated system that represented places (counties and boroughs) toward one that represented all the people equally. Burke expressed his conviction that Hastings's system of corruption would be especially abhorrent to a British assembly, since the British nation was distinguished by "less suspicion of pecuniary corruption" in its government than in any other in the world ("Speech on Opening," 376). A note of defensiveness may be detected here, since Burke was well aware of charges of corruption at home but had rejected parliamentary reform.[74] Nonetheless, he regarded Parliament in its existing form as a case of an ancient and evolved institution that, despite its obvious anomalies, was linked in complex ways to all the valuable elements of the English political tradition and was therefore preferable to a more rational but untried scheme.

Burke also defended the existing form of Parliament on functional grounds, as an institution that in fact offered effective governance. Burke appreciated some of the benefits adduced by a modern commentator—that venal and patronage seats permitted the recruitment to Parliament of talented outsiders, of experienced administrators, and of new forms of wealth.[75] Two larger arguments, however, were decisive: the unreformed House of Commons allowed for a satisfactory representation of interests, and it formed an essential component in the system of constitutional balance central to British liberty and stability. In Burke's well-known theory, what was primarily wanted in a legislative assembly was the representation of all the major interests of the country, which legislators, acting in a deliberative capacity as trustees for the national interest, could accommodate in formulating national policy and law.[76] Substantial welfare was more important than formal equality or regularity. If all important interests received their due, the country would flourish; on the whole, this was the case for eighteenth-century Britain. Then, enjoying the confidence of the public and especially of its main propertied groups, Parliament could serve as an effective counterbalance to the Crown or the executive power—could even function as the leading element—in a system of mixed or constitutional government. These desiderata, Burke thought, were largely satisfied in the existing system through irregular but customary practices.

A politics of interest representation seems to be at odds with a politics of public-spirited statesmanship. Burke sometimes upheld the ideal of public-spiritedness, and, like many opposition figures in eighteenth-century Britain, attacked the excessive influence of patronage and special interests as "corruption," which in some cases threatened the constitution itself. As a defender of the independence of Parliament, Burke issued a famous denunciation of the Crown's influence in the House of Commons through royal patronage (*Present Discontents*). Repudiating the claim that venality and self-interest are universal, Burke endorsed the classical opinion "that among a people generally corrupt liberty cannot long exist" (*Sheriffs of Bristol*, 242). In the same spirit, he asserted that "every means, effectual to preserve India from oppression"—that is, the suppression of the independent influence of the East India Company's interest—"is a guard to preserve the British constitution from its worst corruption" (*Fox's Bill*, 383). Special interests such as those pursued by the company were likely to be mercenary and self-serving, and to the extent that they succeeded in infiltrating Parliament, they corrupted the public trust that Parliament was supposed to exercise.

On the other hand, Burke also upheld the more conventionally liberal view that the expression and promotion of a variety of private interests through the political process is a natural and appropriate phenomenon. In the normal course of civil life, he suggested, diversity manifested itself in people's birth, education, professions, and property; accordingly, political arrangements should "furnish to each description such force as might protect it in the conflict caused by the diversity of interests, that must exist, and must contend in all complex society" (*Reflections*, 299–300). As noted above, Burke's normative theory of parliamentary representation—the standard view of the time[77]—focused on the representation of interests (rather than of individuals counted numerically), deeming it appropriate that all the distinct interests of the country have a voice, by some means or other, in legislative deliberations. And among the great interests of eighteenth-century Britain was indisputably the East Indian interest, which had been acknowledged as such and had been closely involved with Parliament and the ministries for a century and more.[78] It would seem unobjectionable, then, that as the Indian empire grew, an organized Indian interest should likewise increase in influence, and that men who had served and prospered in Asia should enter Parliament. Why did Burke condemn these developments as dangerous forms of political corruption?

We may suggest several answers to this question, though none of them is worked out in a completely satisfactory way in Burke's texts. In the first place, we may return to a point made earlier, namely, that while Burke regarded the traditional commerce of the East India Company as perfectly legitimate, as with the other commerce so important to eighteenth-century England, he and others came to believe that a decisive qualitative change had come about when the company acquired effective sovereignty in Bengal and political power in other parts of India. The possession of power led to a transition from bona fide commerce to oppression and extortion, and wealth or profits gained by such means were not permissible. Power had to be exercised according to public norms of justice and be made publicly accountable; a clear distinction had to be made between private (commercial) and public transactions. The East India interest that acquired political force in the 1770s and 1780s sought to blur these distinctions, resist reforms, and so perpetuate an ambiguous situation in which they could continue to make illicit profits. The mere presence of an interested faction in Parliament was not corruption; what made the Indian faction corrupt was that its main purpose was to protect and maintain a corrupt and oppressive operation existing elsewhere, in a vicious cycle. Burke did not systematically develop a distinction between legitimate and illegitimate interests in these terms. Opposition was emerging in this period against the West Indian sugar interest, which was more strongly represented in Parliament than was the East Indian, since it was based on slavery. Such opposition stemmed from the same growing humanitarian sentiment that found reports from India disturbing, but the West Indies sugar trade was not among Burke's major causes.[79] Still,

Burke's views on the responsibilities of power are clear, and his vociferous condemnation of oppression in India (and Ireland) may provide the basis for such a distinction among interests.

Second, Burke's theory of representation had two equally important dimensions. Interests needed to be accommodated in public policy, and it was therefore permissible for interest groups to organize and assert their claims, and even for individual legislators to be drawn from or associated with particular interests, either by personal background or constituency ties. At the stage of parliamentary deliberation and voting, however, members were called upon to transcend any such particularistic ties and act as members of a national (or imperial) legislature, seeking the larger public good. A "spirit of independence" and vigilance against corruption, even when this entailed resistance to immediate popular wishes, were qualities conducive to exercising the trust entailed by a seat in Parliament (*Present Discontents*, 296). To this end it was improper for members to make pledges to constituents or hold themselves bound by their instructions, and parliamentary business was even to be shielded from public scrutiny to a certain extent.[80] In Burke's famous words:

> Parliament is not a *congress* of ambassadors from different and hostile interests; which interests each must maintain, as an agent and advocate, against other agents and advocates; but parliament is a *deliberative* assembly of *one* nation, with *one* interest, that of the whole. . . . You choose a member indeed; but when you have chosen him, he is not a member of Bristol, but he is a member of *Parliament*. ("Electors of Bristol," 96)

In Burke's own case, the special interests of his constituents in Bristol, who benefited from trade restrictions on the Americans and Irish, were at variance with what he saw as the good of the British Empire as a whole, which required conciliation of the disadvantaged parts. Legislators had a particular obligation to consider the welfare of subjects who were not themselves represented in Parliament, including the Indians, the Irish, and the Americans. It is reasonable to suppose that Burke regarded the members of the East Indian interest in the House of Commons as failing to live up to this standard. Not only were they directly and profitably involved in the business of the special interest; they also had no intention of putting this behind them when they entered Parliament. (Benfield, like Clive before him and some others, returned to India after his first stint in Parliament.) They were there precisely and exclusively to act as "agents and advocates" for the interest and to protect their own and their colleagues' stakes in it.

Why were the members of the East Indian interest unable or unwilling to assume the proper outlook of members of Parliament? For Burke, the answer lay in their character and background. We have already noted the emphasis Burke placed on the personal qualities of rulers, and his aversion to power seeking by individuals whose way of life, he believed, was not likely to endow them with the appropriate sense of public responsibility. In addition, Burke shared with many members of the traditional English ruling class a distaste for the "nabobs," as wealthy returned East India Company servants were popularly termed during this period. In part, this antagonism reflected the usual disdain of the older gentry for the nouveaux riches and the conspicuous upstarts of the empire; sinecures, perquisites of office, prize money in warfare, and the purchase of seats in the House of Commons, it has been argued, though acceptable among the traditional elite, were regarded as unseemly in the nabobs.[81]

Although Burke himself was viewed by some members of this elite as an outsider and an upstart, he nevertheless shared or at least encouraged the feeling that the nabobs threatened social order and propriety. He deplored the new "aristocracy" represented by Benfield, "a criminal . . . enfeoffed with an estate, which in the comparison effaces the splendor of all the nobility of Europe" (*Arcot's Debts*, 544–45). He deprecated their influence even while recognizing the vulnerability of old wealth in the face of new:

> Arrived in England, the destroyers of the nobility and gentry of a whole kingdom will find the best company in this nation, at a board of elegance and hospitality. . . . They marry into your families; they enter into your senate; they ease your estates by loans; they raise their value by demand; they cherish and protect your relations which lie heavy on your patronage; and there is scarcely an house in the kingdom that does not feel some concern and interest that makes all reform of our eastern governnment appear officious and disgusting. (*Fox's Bill*, 403)

Hostility toward the nabobs, however, was not entirely a matter of social prejudice.[82] This phenomenon was not apparent in the case of well-to-do East India merchants of an earlier period, but arose in the 1760s as the public began to suspect that great sudden fortunes could have been acquired only through the misuse of the company's new power in the East. Burke labored to provide detailed evidence in support of the assumption of observers such as Horace Walpole, who regarded the nabobs not as merchants but as "banditti" who preyed on the helpless natives of India.[83] So also Burke's disdain for the young man who "goes out an insignificant boy, [and] in a few years returns a great Nabob" (*Fox's Bill*, 443) reflected not mere distaste, but a reasoned conviction that such wealth came at the expense of Indian society.

Finally, the nabobs, who made large fortunes ostensibly through commerce and then settled down to live as investors, were a disreputable element in a larger category that Burke and others termed the monied interest of Great Britain, which by the eighteenth century stood prominently beside the older landed interest. In the eighteenth century, "monied interest" in the narrow sense could refer to financiers or investors in the public debt, a group—which would include the Arcot creditors—to whom Burke, unlike earlier Whigs, was always extremely hostile.[84] In a broader sense the monied interest, comprising manufacturing and financial wealth and the many branches of trade, was for the most part perfectly respectable and included many of the various special interests that were rightly represented in Parliament. The East Indian interest was ostensibly a trading interest; but for Burke, a favorable judgment on the political expression of this interest needed to be qualified, even apart from doubts about the illicit mixture of power and commerce in India. Just as the strength of Parliament within the larger constitutional balance required that all forms of property, and men of independent position, be present in it, so also the maintenance of a reasonable balance between landed and monied property within Parliament was desirable.

Hereditary landed estates were of course the economic foundation of the traditional aristocracy (both peerage and gentry) where Burke located the ethos of public-spiritedness in Great Britain, and from which he expected leading statesmen, to a large degree, to be recruited. Landed property, later under attack by the French Revolution, was "the firm base of every stable government" and had historically been the natural leader of English society (*Regicide Peace 3*, 374). Landed estates were held independent of the state and of politics, and their hereditary holders were not likely to regard politics as a means toward personal enrichment. Monied wealth, on the other hand, which was much more likely to have been acquired through the efforts of the present holder, was associated with other virtues, such as industry and inventiveness; it was also associated with the principle of self-interest and the spirit of private acquisitiveness. The landed interest, being old, was cautious, whereas the "monied interest is in its nature more ready for any adventure [and] . . . falls in more naturally with any novelties" (*Reflections*, 211). Precisely because the monied interest had greater energy, and because its share of the national wealth was steadily increasing, Burke was concerned to bolster the position of the landed interest:

> Nothing is a due and adequate representation of a state, that does not
> represent its ability, as well as its [landed] property. But as ability is a
> vigorous and active principle, and as property is sluggish, inert, and
> timid, it never can be safe from the invasions of ability, unless it be,
> out of all proportion, predominant in the representation. (*Reflections*,
> 140)

Despite the crucial historical contribution of the landed class to parliamentary leadership and to the preservation of free government through resistance to royal encroachment, land was at something of a disadvantage in a
competition with money. Men of the monied or mercantile classes, driven
by envy and aspirations to power, were prominent in the French Revolution.
In Britain, fortunately, commercial wealth enjoyed its "natural weight" in
the House of Commons, where (as we have seen) new money could find the
means to power; but wealth properly shared the political stage with the
Crown and the court, the nobility and the gentry, and with the military and
clerical professions, alongside of which mere money "can never rank first"
("French Affairs," 214–15).

Thus, although Burke frequently praised the contributions of commerce to national life, he looked askance at the growth of the political
monied interest, including the East Indian, lest this growth threaten to
upset the proper distribution of influence. In the end, however, Burke's
conviction that "Indianism" represented such a dangerous form of corruption in British politics went beyond this concern for constitutional and
political balance. As early as 1770, Chatham—despite his role in creating
the empire (and ironically, in view of the Indian origin of the Pitt family
fortune)—had expressed a special concern about East Indian wealth with
which Burke subsequently showed himself in agreement:

> For some years past there has been an influx of wealth into the
> country which has been attended by many fatal consequences, be-
> cause it has not been the regular, natural produce of labour and
> industry. The riches of Asia have been poured in upon us, and have
> brought with them not only Asiatic luxury, but I fear, Asiatic princi-
> ples of government. Without connections, without any natural inter-
> est in the soil, the importers of foreign gold have forced their way
> into Parliament by such a torrent of private corruption as no private
> hereditary fortune could resist.[85]

The size and suddenness (the "torrent") of Asian fortunes, and their lack of
"connections," appeared destabilizing, but the deeper problem, the essence

of their corrupt and corrupting quality, was their illegitimate origin. The East Indian interest was not, in Burke's words, just another "invasion of ability" into the laudably open British political system; it was an invasion of men who had systematically misused their abilities and their power in exploitative rather than productive enterprises, and who sought only to ensure the conditions for continuing to do so.

Chapter Three

The Charges

DESPOTISM

Despotism is the best single rubric for another set of accusations Burke brought against the rulers of British India, exemplified almost entirely in this case by Warren Hastings. *Despotism* as used here covers a variety of offenses against political morality and legitimate rule: unjust or oppressive applications of official power; arbitrary rule unrestrained by law; gross violations of personal and property rights; unnecessary official violence; aggressive war; duplicitous diplomacy and violations of public faith; and in general, the use of government power to the detriment or ruin of subjects rather than for their welfare. These different senses of the term will become clearer as we consider specific episodes and Burke's judgment of them. In sum, he told his fellow members of the House of Commons,

> Every legal regular authority in matters of revenue, of political ad-
> ministration, of criminal law, of civil law, in many of the most essen-
> tial parts of military discipline, is laid level with the ground; and an
> oppressive, irregular, capricious, unsteady, rapacious, and peculating
> despotism, with a direct disavowal of obedience to any authority
> at home, and without any fixed maxim, principle, or rule of proceed-
> ing, to guide them in India, is at present the state of your charter-
> government over great kingdoms. (*Fox's Bill*, 439)

In the eighteenth century, through the writings of Montesquieu, the concept of despotism referred in particular to Asian societies and governments, and in accusing Hastings of despotic rule Burke was associating him with oriental practices (as Europeans perceived them) that clearly violated the moral norms of European political culture. This theme will be pursued more systematically in the following chapter, which considers both Hastings's claim that he was compelled to rule in accordance with local (i.e., despotic) norms and Burke's repudiation of this argument. At the same time, conceptual resources were available to Burke from within the Western political tradition to describe and condemn Hastings's conduct—concepts such as tyranny, illegality, arbitrary power, and Machiavellianism. Burke's attack on what he saw as abuses of power in India provided occasions for enunciating his own normative standards of acceptable and beneficent rule.

Some of the incidents on which Burke based his charges were highly dramatic, or lent themselves to dramatization in his hands. Through his and Sheridan's famous speeches and the writings of Macaulay, some of them became notorious in the annals of British India and prominent in English literature. Although in Burke's larger analysis oppression in India was rarely far removed from mercenary motives in the oppressors, not only were some of the great despotic acts of which he accused Hastings more eye-catching; they also represented more serious types of political crimes than pecuniary corruption, which seems banal by comparison.

At the same time, however, their status as crimes, even if all could agree on the often complex factual circumstances, was more ambiguous and controversial. Burke asserted that "the arguments of tyranny are as contemptible as its force is dreadful"; nevertheless, he recognized the ideological force and persuasiveness of the arguments put forward by the "sophistick tyrants of Paris" (*Reflections*, 207). Hastings's tyranny, or his system of rule, was largely a series of administrative experiments and ad hoc adjustments to a variable political environment, and was comparatively atheoretical; indeed, the lack of ideological fervor or rationalistic schemes for remodeling society was one of the major factors that distinguished the oppressors of India from the revolutionaries of France. Nevertheless, with respect to many of the actions of which he was accused, Hastings defended himself with reasoned arguments, both at the time the actions were committed and later at his trial; and his arguments are not contemptible, but deserve to be taken seriously. Hastings appealed, as we shall see, to state necessity or *raison d'état*, to the exigencies of the despotic traditions of India, and to the need for concentrated authority and local discretion in ruling such an empire. In the end, he rested his case on his success. Burke rejected these arguments, but judgments on such matters can differ, and Hastings has always had his supporters. Burke's thought on such issues is therefore contentious, and must be assessed with a recognition that important and contested principles are at stake.

The charge of despotic rule leveled against Hastings required not only evidence regarding specific actions but also an interpretation of the significance of these actions in their context. Once having formed a suspicion that crimes had been perpetrated, Burke, more than any of his colleagues, labored to acquire an understanding of Indian history and society so that he could take a leading role in discharging Parliament's responsibility for overseeing the authority it had delegated to the East India Company. Seeking to educate his audience on these matters and arouse their sympathy for the Indian victims of oppression, Burke presented his conclusions in lengthy historical discourses and surveys of the Indian scene, which he inserted into his Indian speeches. Before turning to specific episodes, let us follow Burke's efforts, drawing on his background research, to establish two preliminary points.

First, Burke pointed to the generally depressed condition of the areas under British control in order to make a prima facie case for his accusation of misgovernment. How in general does one substantiate the claim that a country has been subjected to oppressive rule? This question, Burke said, must be determined "by a reference to facts," to empirical evidence from which despotism may be inferred as a cause. Citing the cases of "Persia bleeding under the ferocious sword of Taehmas Kouli Khan"[1] and "the barbarous anarchic despotism of Turkey," Burke pointed to situations "where arts are unknown, where manufactures languish, where science is extinguished, where agriculture decays, where the human race itself melts away and perishes under the eye of the observer" (*Reflections*, 231). Burke's point here was that, contrary to the accusations of the revolutionaries, France under the old monarchy, though not free, was decidedly not a despotic regime—or at any rate was "a despotism rather in appearance than in reality"; far from resembling the Hobbesian state of nature evoked in this passage, France had a growing population and economy, and its arts and manufactures were in a flourishing condition, indications of good or adequate government.

The situation in India, however, was different, and not just because of local and ephemeral disorders. Most Europeans in the eighteenth century believed that India had normally been a prosperous country, enjoying sound institutions at the local level, even if there was much political instability at the top.[2] Against this background Burke asserted that Hastings's own description of the district of Farruckabad (in Oudh)—"*almost an entire waste, without cultivation or inhabitants;* . . . [reduced to] *wretched poverty, desolation, and misery*"—was "a true and unexaggerated picture . . . of at least three fourths of the country which we possess, or rather lay waste, in India" (*Fox's*

Bill, 420–21). This was true of Oudh and the Carnatic, but it applied most strikingly to Bengal, traditionally the richest part of India and comparable to Europe:

> Bengal, and the provinces that are united to it, are larger than the kingdom of France; and once contained, as France does contain [in 1783], a great and independent landed interest, composed of princes, of great lords, of a numerous nobility and gentry, of freeholders, of lower tenants, of religious communities, and public foundations. (*Fox's Bill*, 425)

Such social health, however, was a thing of the past. Economic decay in Bengal, Burke noted, had been reported by company servants from the 1760s, and he himself analyzed this phenomenon in his *Ninth Report*. Rather than improving, the situation had only worsened under direct British rule, as a result of the social disruptions caused by Hastings's policies. With respect to the gentry of Bengal, Hastings was the revolutionary; but the French revolutionaries, wrong about France, would have been correct in attributing the calamity in India to despotic government.

Second, Burke strove to place his interpretation of British rule in a historical framework. Despotism, in the sense of an abuse of ruling power, became a possibility for the British only after they became the sovereigns of Bengal, or at least acquired significant political and military power in India. Hastings's despotism was a function of his governorship (1772–1785), which saw the consolidation and expansion of the company's rule. Although the Mogul Empire (or its decadent offshoots) still existed in much of India, it was apparent by the time of Burke's involvement that a new British imperial regime had been firmly established there, and the character of this regime could be evaluated in comparison with previous Indian governments.

Of course, the British could be portrayed as conquerors, but this in itself was not especially noteworthy. The political history of India in general had for centuries been a history of successive invasions and conquest regimes imposed (until the arrival of Europeans) by various groups of Muslim warriors who entered India from the northwest (Persia, Afghanistan, and "Tartary" or Central Asia). Burke surveyed this history from the earliest Arab presence, to the fourteenth-century Tartar invasion of Tamerlane, to the founding of the Mogul Empire, to more recent incursions and dynastic fights, which were a frequent occurrence within the Mogul framework. Although the lengthy period of Muslim conquests was "an era of great misfortune to that Country and to the world in general," and though the events were often violent, Burke concluded that the turmoil and destruction

in India were superficial. The successive Muslim conquerors fought primarily with one another and displaced their predecessors in the ruling elite,
in events Burke compared to the Wars of the Roses in medieval England; for
the most part, they did not interfere with the religion and social institutions
of the ancient Hindu majority. Taxes or tribute were collected, but otherwise Hindu rajas were often retained as subordinate rulers, the gentry held
their lands, and the life of the common people went on according to custom.
Burke exonerated both the notorious Tamerlane and the Mogul founder
Akbar and his successors of the charge of barbarism and despotism and
portrayed them as prudent and lenient rulers ("Speech on Opening," 307–
10). Against this background, Burke sought to demonstrate that Hastings's
oppressive treatment of native rulers was not the standard practice in Indian
politics, and that the disruption of traditional society caused by his policies
reflected an arbitrary use of power that was virtually unprecedented.

It was true, Burke conceded, that the immediate pre-British period of
Indian history, "a troubled and vexatious era indeed," was not so benign as
the larger picture. From the first half of the eighteenth century, the decline
of central Mogul authority led to instability and political violence in the
provinces, which became "a scene of confusion from being the prey and
sport of the infernal ambition of [their] own grandees." Opportunities were
presented for ruthless adventurers to seize power in Indian states either by
invasion or by the assassination of the previous ruler. From 1726 Bengal was
in effect an independent state under a series of strong nawabs who were only
nominally *subahdars* or viceroys of the empire. Of these, Burke agreed that
at least the last two, Alivardi Khan and Siraj al-Daula, were vicious tyrants
and oppressors. This circumstance, and Siraj al-Daula's aggression against
the British, justified his being overthrown by them in 1757, which presented
the British with a memorable opportunity to institute a new pattern of rule,
had their "virtue upon that occasion [been] altogether equal to [their] fortune." Coming from "a learned and enlightened part of Europe, in the most
enlightened period of its time," and indeed being "a Nation the most enlightened of the enlightened part of Europe," the British might have won
glory by bringing to India "all the advantage of the liberty and spirit of a
British constitution." Instead, the company servants on the scene proved to
be primarily interested in extracting plunder by engaging in palace revolutions and other unscrupulous methods characteristic of the political environment in which they found themselves. It was in this tumultuous period, according to Burke, that Hastings as a junior official received his
political apprenticeship, in particular as a participant in the coup of 1760 that
made the murderous Mir Kasim nawab. Subsequently, Hastings brazenly

attempted to justify some of his own oppressive policies by citing precedents from the reigns of Alivardi Khan and Mir Kasim, two of the most notorious offenders ("Speech on Opening," 311, 314–15, 333).

As Burke interpreted this complex historical record, despotism was neither the norm in Indian government nor was it sanctioned by the prevailing moral and religious codes. There were, however, notable instances of Indian despots, and aberrant periods when such rulers and practices were common. Unfortunately, the history of Bengal in the years preceding and during the acquisition of power by the East India Company comprised such a period; even more regrettably, certain local tyrants of this period, who were taken as models, and the methods these tyrants employed, provided company servants with their conception of how India of necessity had to be governed. Thus Hastings's despotism as governor, resting on the more secure foundation provided by British administrative and military efficiency, was in a sense a product of its immediate Indian environment. A deeper understanding of the larger setting of Indian history and society, however, precluded justifying such despotism by appealing to its necessity or inevitability.

We may more easily analyze the issues at stake in Burke's accusation of despotism if we begin with a survey of the most important specific instances that provided him with his evidence. In their speeches, Burke and the other prosecutors cited innumerable specific facts, which they grouped under twenty or so general charges or articles of impeachment. I have organized the most important materials relating to the accusation of despotism (as distinguished from that of corruption) under seven headings. Some of these correspond to charges in Burke's enumeration, including those concerning Chait Singh and the begams of Oudh, which were pursued to the end of the trial in the House of Lords; others synthesize points distributed throughout Burke's presentations. In this chapter, I shall set forth the basic facts (and frequently disputes over the facts) of the cases and briefly indicate both the grounds of Burke's condemnation and the outline of Hastings's defense. In the following chapter we shall turn to a fuller view of Hastings's attempted justifications of his policies in the larger political and cultural context in which he was operating, and to Burke's responses to these efforts.

Treaty Violations

One of Hastings's responsibilities as governor-general was to conduct the company's foreign policy toward the native states or "country powers" of India. Several of these, it must be remembered, were recognized states of

European dimensions which (especially in coalitions) could present formidable threats to the company's regime. In his dealings with Indian rulers, Hastings inherited certain obligations stemming from engagements made by his predecessors, and with the approval of his council he concluded several important treaties on his own initiative. For Burke, the keeping of treaty obligations, and more generally the keeping of faith between sovereigns and nations, was a basic principle of political morality. If there are permissible exceptions to this rule in special cases, Burke did not detail them, in keeping with his well-known attack on Dr. Price's treatment of the right of revolution: statesmen must deal with extraordinary circumstances prudentially, but a practical political theory should not mistake "the deviation from the principle" for the principle itself (*Reflections*, 107). Burke condemned Hastings for violating treaties and refused to accept the excuses he advanced in the name of necessity and statesmanship.

Burke pointed to numerous instances, going so far as to assert that "the Company never has made a treaty which they have not broken" (*Fox's Bill*, 394). I shall discuss two important cases, those of Chait Singh and the begams of Oudh, separately, since in these episodes other factors were more prominent than violations of engagements. Another set of cases arose from the company's complex diplomacy designed to counter the threat posed by the hostile Maratha Confederacy in central India. These included various treaties, before and during Hastings's time, both with the Marathas and with potential allies against them. The very complexity of this situation created moral ambiguity and thence further conflict:

> As to the Marattas, they had so many cross treaties with the States General of that nation, and with each of their chiefs, that it was notorious, that no one of these agreements could be kept without grossly violating the rest. . . . The wars which desolate India, originated from a most atrocious violation of public faith on our part. (*Fox's Bill*, 395)

The most prominent single episode, however, concerned Hastings's dealings with Shah Alam, the Mogul emperor who was the company's nominal superior in this period but who, in reality, was politically and militarily powerless.

In 1764 the company's army defeated the combined forces of Mir Kasim (the nawab of Bengal who had turned violently against his former patrons), Shuja al-Daula (the nawab-wazir of neighboring Oudh, who was worried about the growth of British power), and their common suzerain Shah Alam. In consequence of this victory (at Buxar) Clive concluded the

Shah Alam II, Mogul emperor (1759–1806) and nominal suzerain
of the East India Company's empire.
By permission of the British Library, London.

Treaty of Allahabad with Shuja al-Daula and Shah Alam in 1765, laying the
groundwork for the grand strategy that Hastings was later to pursue. Shuja
al-Daula was converted from an enemy into an ally upon the recognition of
a common interest. The British, viewing Oudh as a buffer state that would
protect Bengal from invasion, acquired the right to station troops there and
undertook to defend their new ally; Shuja al-Daula, while risking increased
company influence in his realm, received in return military support against
his adversaries to the west and south, especially the Marathas. From the
emperor, Clive received the *diwani*—civil and fiscal authority, or quasi-
sovereign status—for the company in Bengal, thus consolidating and for-
malizing its rule there, in exchange for a large annual tribute. In addition,
two significant districts along the Ganges, Kora and Allahabad, were de-
tached from Oudh and transferred to Shah Alam for his support, since the

emperor at that moment was in exile from his capital, which had fallen to
the Marathas.

We shall hear more of the alliance between the company in Bengal and
the nawab of Oudh, which proved to be stable and (from the perspective of
the British Empire in India) advantageous. In contrast, one of Hastings's
first acts when he assumed office in Bengal in 1772 was to cancel both the
tribute payment owed to Shah Alam and the cession of Kora and Allahabad,
which he occupied and restored to Shuja al-Daula, in a clear repudiation of
the treaty. The central factor lying behind this decision, as in British policy
generally in this period, was, in Hastings's words, the "utmost confusion"
that prevailed in the affairs of the Mogul Empire.[3] In the years intervening
since the signing of the treaty, Shah Alam had come to terms with his
Maratha enemies and returned to Delhi; there, in Hastings's view, he was a
captive or puppet of the Marathas, whom the British regarded as their own
most dangerous adversaries. Tribute paid to the emperor would thus have
gone directly into the hands of a hostile power, as would the revenues of
Kora and Allahabad; occupation of these territories by the Marathas, moreover, would have immediately threatened the security of both Oudh and
Bengal, and might have provoked Shuja al-Daula to change sides again and
join the Maratha coalition against the British.[4]

Hastings explained or justified his action in various ways. In one dispatch, he expressed contempt for the weakness of the emperor and the
exigencies of his administration:

> I was surprized and concerned to find on my arrival that the King
> [Shah Alam] still continues to receive the tribute of the provinces. . . .
> I think I may promise that no more payments will be made while he
> is in the hands of the Mahrattas nor, if I can prevent it, ever more.
> Strange! that while the revenue of the provinces is insufficient for its
> expenses and for the claims of the Company and our Mother Coun-
> try, the wealth of the province . . . should be drained to supply the
> pageantry of a mock King, an idol of our own creation![5]

Elsewhere, he argued more legalistically: Kora and Allahabad had been
granted to the emperor in the expectation that he would reside there under
British protection, and he had therefore "forfeited" his claim to them by
handing them over to the Marathas.[6] Hastings seems to have had similar
views about the tribute,[7] though here the argument is implausible, since, as
Burke emphasized, these payments were promised unconditionally in exchange for authority in Bengal ("Articles of Charge," 324). Usually, however,

in this and other cases, Hastings appealed to political or strategic necessity, taking it for granted that the British interest in Bengal had to be secured. In this he has been defended by sympathetic historians.[8] The situation had changed; the beneficiary of the treaty had now aligned himself with the company's enemies; continued adherence to the treaty in the new circumstances would be contrary to company interests and could even jeopardize their basic military security.[9] In this situation, the governor, charged with defending the company's possessions, simply acted according to the dictates of political realism. Hastings justified other treaty violations by similar arguments.

In condemning Hastings's conduct in this area, Burke also rejected these arguments, offering three counterarguments of his own. First, he held that observance of treaties and other solemn engagements was a fundamental element of justice, and hence a strong principle that could be overridden only by the most pressing necessity, if at all. He condemned the French Revolution, for example, for renouncing inherited treaty obligations, and hence the law of nations in which this obligation was expressed (*Regicide Peace 1*, 240). Burke noted that the Bengal Council did not try to justify the cancellation of the tribute "on principles of right and justice, but by arguments of policy and convenience, by which the best founded claims of right and justice may at all times be set aside and defeated" ("Articles of Charge," 324–25). This attitude was clearly unacceptable; part of the point or meaning of a claim of justice, such as that arising from a treaty, was that it had priority over ordinary policy considerations.

Although he was an upholder of moral principles in this sense, however, Burke eschewed dogmatic or doctrinaire adherence to principle, conceding the need to adapt to altered or extraordinary circumstances. With respect to the Indian treaty cases, then, Burke's reading of the situation differed from that of Hastings: he did not see the "necessity" Hastings invoked. In fact, here as elsewhere, Burke believed that Hastings's real motives for breaking the treaty with Shah Alam were mercenary (though not, in this case, corrupt): Kora and Allahabad were transferred to Shuja al-Daula in exchange for a significant consideration (about half a million pounds), and the tribute payments were already in arrears because of shortfalls in the Bengal revenues. Burke thus assumed that the company's financial embarrassment at that time was the real reason for Hastings's handling of the treaty obligations. But a governor's need to raise money, however real and understandable, was not a legitimate ground for abridging a requirement of justice.

Second, with respect both to treaty violations and to other injustices in

India, Burke frequently pointed to the threat such actions posed to British honor. Speaking of the relatively minor episode of the rana of Gohad, an ally whom Hastings allegedly promised to protect in the Maratha War of 1780–1781, and then failed to do so, Burke affirmed that by such conduct Hastings "forfeit[ed] the honor and injur[ed] the credit of the British nation in India" ("Articles of Charge," 74). On the first day of Hastings's trial, Burke told the lords that the case concerned not only the "interest of a great Empire" but "the credit and honour of the British nation"; the issue was "whether the crimes of individuals are to be turned into public guilt and national ignominy" or whether the "honour, justice, and humanity" of the kingdom were to be vindicated ("Speech on Opening," 271). Men—and nations—of honor keep their word: this principle was central to the eighteenth-century code of the gentleman that Burke strongly endorsed, both in private and in public life. This was of course a modern extension of the older aristocratic or chivalric code, reflecting a way of life he admired.

Did Burke's embracing of this concept add anything substantial to his argument for keeping treaties, or did it simply show his facility in deploying the various available political languages for rhetorical effect?[10] Before dismissing Burke's appeals to honor as merely archaic, sentimental, or rhetorical, we should recall that he was not alone in this appeal. Montesquieu, for example, had advanced a very serious argument that the sense of honor among the nobility was the motivational basis for the performance of their function of defending the liberties of European monarchies; and the unsentimental international jurist Vattel held, along with Burke, that nations, like individuals, were or ought to be concerned with maintaining their honor.[11] For theorists such as these, honor supplemented and reinforced morality by providing a useful, perhaps necessary, psychological and cultural basis for what would otherwise be mere abstract duties. Since Hastings had failed to conform to the prevailing social norm of uprightness, Burke appealed to the sense of honor of his countrymen to remove the shame he had brought on them: appropriate punishment would not only be consistent with justice, but would also express and vindicate national self-respect.

As a footnote to the particular episode cited here, we may note that Hastings himself was naturally sensitive to the opinions, or prospective opinions, of his countrymen, but his reading of them did not always agree with Burke's. In one of the anti-Maratha campaigns of 1780 a small British force captured the famous fortress of Gwalior in central India; the British had promised this prize to their ally the rana of Gohad, and their delay in handing it over led to charges of perfidy by him and later by Burke. Conceding the offense, Hastings expressed "regret . . . at the necessity which compelled me to keep the possession of this place against a solemn condition of a public treaty." The political necessity to which Hastings appealed in this instance was partly diplomatic-strategic: in the ever fluid situation, the fortress was needed by the British in their negotiations with the Maratha chief, Mahadaji Sindhia, who was showing signs of coming to terms (as he eventually did). This major political goal simply overrode the promises made to a minor ally. In addition, however, Hastings claimed that the pressure of public opinion at home ("fear of popular reproach") and the actual opposition of his council made it impossible for him to deliver the fortress, seen by many as "the key of Hindostan," even had he wanted to do so. "All the English world was proud of the conquest, and seemed to think it dishonourable to part with it, and imposing terms were used to justify the usurpation."[12] The sense of national honor, or something like it, can be aroused by great victories and imperial conquest, as well as by conceptions of justice and right. Burke appealed to the British sense of honor to uphold the keeping of treaties, but if Hastings was correct here, this sentiment did not necessarily support such an action.

Finally, Burke argued, here as on other occasions, that honesty was the best policy. In contrast to Hastings's understanding of political necessity, the keeping of faith in agreements was conducive to political strength or success in the long run. According to Burke, even Hastings would concede, at least in the abstract, "that British faith is the support of the British empire; that, if the empire is to be maintained, it is to be maintained by good faith; that, if it is to be propagated, it is to be propagated by public faith; and that, if the British empire falls, it will be through perfidy and violence" ("Speech in Reply," 11:388). Speaking here as a proponent of empire, Burke was pointing to a paradox of Machiavellianism: the willingness to violate faith when the prospect of advantage seems so to dictate can be a self-defeating maxim of policy if it eventually prevents one from entering into coalitions and other mutually beneficial agreements.

It was true that Britain's opponents in India were usually disunited, but at this stage of the empire the military power of some Indian states was such that the East India Company needed loyal allies to defend its position. A reputation for unreliability, especially when combined with the growing strength of the British, would drive potential friends away. Burke seems to have believed that keeping faith was the dominant strategy (with respect to long-term success) even in an environment such as India where this was not the prevailing norm. Indeed, given a need for allies, a reputation for "public faith" could be an especially valuable (because scarcer) asset in a frequently "perfidious" political context. As a political realist, Hastings of course would have accepted the logic of this argument. His likely rejoinder, however, would have been that this argument prescribes only relative, not absolute, fidelity; occasions might still arise, especially "in such [an unstable] state of things as exists in India" ("Speech in Reply," II:388), where violations would pay off, and he, as the local expert and skilled tactician, was in the best position to identify them.

Aggressive Wars

Burke regarded Hastings as a bellicose governor whose foreign policy, ostensibly designed to protect the existing British holdings in India, too frequently led to armed conflict with native rulers. He believed that much of this warfare was unnecessary for the proper defensive purpose, that it resulted from inept diplomacy, or, in some cases, that it aimed at the expansion of the company's dominion by outright conquest. Insofar as Hastings's wars involved unprovoked aggression, they violated the traditional European norms of just warfare to which Burke adhered. The use of violence simply to expand one's rule, without an adequate basis in right, was an injustice characteristic of despotism or tyranny.

It is true that Burke, like most jurists and statesmen in the eighteenth century, believed that legitimate sovereignty could arise from the right of conquest in a just war. Military victories had played a decisive role in the East India Company's acquisition of sovereignty in Bengal, and Burke did not object to this original conquest; notwithstanding certain irregularities, he accepted the standard British view that the company had been reacting to unprovoked attacks and massacres perpetrated against it by Siraj al-Daula and Mir Kasim, and that its ensuing political gains were therefore justifiable. Similarly, Burke did not raise questions about the earlier military entanglements with Indian allies and pretenders that led to the company's position of influence in the Carnatic—perhaps because these events did not implicate Hastings or raise other issues with which Burke was directly concerned. National pride in some of these exploits and in the Indian empire, however, could not be taken as an endorsement of any successful conquest; nor could it be allowed to obliterate the morally crucial distinction between just and unjust wars.

In addition to the demands of justice, Burke could also appeal to a prevailing sense among British leaders that further conquests in India were unwise, and to specific policies against them. Pitt's East India Act of 1784 flatly summed up the dominant opinion:

And whereas to pursue schemes of conquest and extension of dominion in India are measures repugnant to the wish, the honour and
policy of this nation . . . it shall not be lawful for the Governor-
General and Council without the express command of the Court of
Directors . . . either to declare war or to commence hostilities, or
enter into any treaty for making war, against any of the country
princes or states in India.[13]

Enacted while Hastings was still in office, this provision amounted to a
public censure of his belligerent policies, as they were widely perceived in
England, and helped precipitate his resignation. It also reflected an ambivalence about the empire as such. Few if any people in eighteenth-century
England imagined, given the size of India and the dangers and costs of
ruling there, that the company could actually govern more than a few en-
claves, much less the entire subcontinent. Offensive wars aiming at expansion of dominion were therefore ruled out, and Hastings's actions to this end
violated policy as well as justice.

Burke believed that Hastings's diplomacy, reflecting his aggressive and
expansionist tendencies, was partly responsible for bringing about the dangerous Maratha War of 1778–1782. Apart from this major crisis (to be examined later), there were two smaller but clear cases of wars of conquest that he
vigorously condemned. The first was the seizure of Tanjore by the nawab of
the Carnatic, with the company's approval and military support, in 1773.
Believing that the raja of Tanjore was a legitimate and independent ruler
by hereditary or prescriptive right, Burke held that his deposition was a
"shocking usurpation." Believing also that the Hindu raja enjoyed the loyalty of his subjects (so far as such matters could be assessed in India), Burke
thought the British-assisted "Mahometan conquest" of the territory was not
only a despotic act in itself but would inevitably be followed by the imposition of a despotic regime in Tanjore. It did not follow that the aggressor
should himself be punished by destruction:

I do not wish that his own principles should be brought home to the
Nabob; I do not wish that any reigning power should be *extirpated*,
though every honest man must wish, that they should all of them be
kept within the bounds of justice; and that we, the English, as an
example of the lesson we teach to others, should keep ourselves
within the same limits. This is what every Englishman has a right to
demand, from those who are entrusted with the management of any
part of the power of this kingdom. (*Conquests*, 110)

Burke argued that Tanjore should be restored to its rightful ruler, and that the British should refrain from such military adventures, however tempting to greed or imperial ambition.

Hastings was not directly involved in the Tanjore business, which was managed from Madras. Later, however, as governor-general, he opposed the restoration of the raja and, in a detailed policy report, called for the permanent annexation of Tanjore to the Carnatic.[14] In Hastings's grand strategy for protecting the British possessions against potential threats, it was imperative that a loyal or dependent ally such as the nawab of the Carnatic be supported and strengthened, as a key element in an elaborate system of alliances that Hastings was trying to construct. From this perspective, the claims of a minor player such as the raja of Tanjore (claims that Hastings regarded as ambiguous in any case, as was common in India) did not count for much.[15] In this instance, Burke, focusing on the rights and wrongs of the particular case, and seeing only the outright conquest of a weaker by a stronger power, did not respond to Hastings's argument of political realism.

The second and most important case of aggression to be considered here was the Rohilla War, notorious at the time and a subject of ongoing controversy. Lending itself to dramatization, the anti-Hastings side of this case was widely publicized in Great Britain by Hastings's enemies and was influential in damaging his reputation. Burke became convinced that a major injustice had been committed, namely, "the extirpation of the Rohillas for a sum of money and giving up the Government of a Country conquered by the Companys arms to the Tyranny of another prince" ("Rohilla Speech," 99). Accordingly, the Rohilla War charge was the first he presented to the House of Commons. Although dismayed when it was defeated as grounds for impeachment, he never changed his view of the events, a view that remained influential in shaping the broader public opinion of the matter for a century.[16]

Soon after taking office, Hastings turned his attention to securing the defense of Bengal, especially with an eye to the Marathas, who were again showing signs of belligerence and growing power. His immediate objective was to reaffirm Clive's strategy of cultivating the ruler of the neighboring state of Oudh as an ally whose country would then serve as a buffer zone between Bengal and the rest of India. To this end, Hastings traveled to Benares in 1773 for a conference with Shuja al-Daula, the nawab of Oudh (and titular wazir or vizier of the Mogul Empire). Among the articles of the resulting Treaty of Benares were the restoration of Kora and Allahabad to

Shuja al-Daula, nawab of Oudh (1754–1775).
By arrangement with Hastings, Shuja al-Daula annexed
Rohilkhand with British troops.
Courtesy of the British Museum, London.

Oudh, the stationing of a British resident at the nawab's court in Faizabad, and the promise of company troops, whose expenses the nawab agreed to pay, to assist in defending his realm against invasion.

In addition, the nawab indicated a desire to conquer and annex Rohilkhand, a sizable country on his northwestern frontier, bounded by the Ganges to the west and the Himalayas to the north. The weakness of the Rohillas, a fierce but not numerous people, was a source of instability in the region. Rohilkhand had been subject to repeated Maratha incursions, and the Rohillas had occasionally shown signs of joining rather than fighting them; either way, there was a danger that the Marathas would acquire a strategically important position in this district from which to stage an attack on Oudh. The nawab had recently assisted the Rohillas in driving back the Marathas; his pretext for now warring against the Rohillas was that they had failed to pay him what they had agreed upon for this service.[17] The real reason for annexation, however, was to give Oudh greater territorial integrity and more defensible borders against the continuing Maratha threat to the west. This objective coincided with Hastings's strategic conceptions, and in a secret clause of the Treaty of Benares he agreed to the nawab's proposal.[18] Accordingly, in the spring of 1774 an army of the nawab's and the company's troops crossed the frontier, defeated the Rohillas in a decisive battle, and annexed the country. As in the case of Tanjore, British military power had been instrumental in assisting an ambitious but valuable Indian ally in enlarging his realm by conquering a smaller neighbor. In the reasoning of officials in India, the policy was dictated in both cases by the fundamental interest in protecting the company's existing holdings in a dangerous environment.

Burke unequivocally condemned Hastings's conduct of the entire Rohilla policy, on a number of grounds. There were, first, the irregular and clandestine circumstances surrounding Hastings's agreement with Shuja al-Daula that led to the war. "[The] whole (both the negotiation and the compact of offensive alliance against the Rohillas) was a mere verbal engagement, the purport and conventions whereof nowhere appeared, except in subsequent correspondence." Although he was committing the company to a risky and controversial military venture, Hastings acted completely alone, initially concealing his undertaking both from the company's court of directors, when he reported the public clauses of the treaty, and then from his own council in Calcutta, until he was sure of majority support for his fait accompli. The vague and undocumented nature of the agreement was an invitation to later "mutual misconstruction, evasion, and ill faith" between the parties, and to a lack of accountability on his part. In exceeding his proper authority and by engaging in procedural irregularities, Hastings showed he was wielding his power in an arbitrary fashion ("Articles of Charge," 311–13).

Second, Burke objected strongly to the mercenary dimension of the arrangement, which he suspected, here as in other cases, supplied Hastings's real motive. In exchange for the company's assistance, Shuja al-Daula agreed to pay about £400,000 and to cover the expenses of the troops during the campaign. To Burke and others it was shocking that British armed forces should be hired out to an unscrupulous Asian ruler, and worse, should take part in an unjust conquest for pay. The Bengal government was chronically short of revenue, and it was certainly convenient to have part of the army profitably employed; even Hastings's defenders concede that his need for funds probably played a role, although a subsidiary one, in his calculations.[19] Subsequently, the hostile majority appointed to the Bengal Council investigated the war and accused Hastings of seeking to "share in the spoils" of an unoffending people, and of "professing to reckon the probable acquisition of wealth among his reasons for taking up arms against his neighbors," words later echoed in Burke's indictment ("Articles of Charge," 312). To this Hastings boldly replied that the "acquisition of wealth" was indeed a good, though admittedly not a sufficient, reason for launching an offensive war; since in this case there was also the strategic reason, and the Rohillas' formal provocation of the wazir, he concluded that the three distinct considerations of justice, policy, and profit coincided.[20] Burke presumably would not have objected to economic gain as a side effect of an otherwise justified war; but he denied that such a convenient state of affairs existed in this case.

Third, Burke was disturbed by evidence that the war had been conducted in "a barbarous and inhuman manner." Unnecessary cruelty and violence had been used, civilians—especially the women and children of the Rohilla warriors—had been mistreated, and the country had been pillaged ("Articles of Charge," 315–16). The Rohilla War violated the canons of just war doctrine with respect to *jus in bello* (the rules of fighting) as well as *jus ad bellum* (the requirement of a rightful cause for going to war), canons Burke sought to uphold.[21] A few years later, for example, Burke was worried that ideological fervor in France would generate a new ferocity in warfare:

> The new school of murder and barbarism, set up in Paris, having destroyed (so far as in it lies) all the other manners and principles which have hitherto civilized Europe, will destroy also the mode of civilized war, which, more than any thing else, has distinguished the Christian world. ("National Assembly," 55–56)

The non-Christian world may not have developed such clearly articulated codes of military conduct as Europe had, but wartime atrocities were barbarism nonetheless. British officials and commanders were bound by the laws of war even when operating in India.

The alleged atrocities, it is true, were committed by the undisciplined troops of the nawab-wazir, not by the company's forces. In fact, the most damning reports on the matter were submitted by the British field commander, who, after his own well-disciplined troops had won the battle, was disgusted by the plundering and cruelty of his Indian allies. The question was whether Hastings had condoned the misconduct or had done all he could to prevent it. It was a "notorious fact" that the kinds of "excesses" alleged in this case, though shocking to Europeans, were commonplace in Indian warfare; and Hastings was certainly aware, from reports on the unsavory reputation of Shuja al-Daula, that his ally in this enterprise was not likely to rise above the prevailing standards.[22] He made at least perfunctory protests, instructing his resident in Oudh "to remonstrate with [the nawab] against every act of cruelty or wanton violence. . . . Tell him that the English manners are abhorrent of every species of inhumanity and oppression, and enjoin the gentlest treatment of a vanquished enemy."[23] Otherwise, however, Hastings argued that he was not in a position to coerce the nawab (an independent sovereign) or control the actions of his army, and so disclaimed responsibility for their offenses. As he wrote in response to the complaints of his commanding officer during the campaign:

> If, in the exercise of his authority, the Vizier is guilty of oppression and other excesses, he only, as the agent, is culpable of it. You have a right, and it is your duty, to remonstrate against any part of his conduct, which may either dishonour the service or prove prejudicial to the common interest; but I protest I do not know what you could do more.[24]

Hastings was no doubt correct in claiming that the events, once in progress, were out of his control. The occurrence of such events, however, surely could have been predicted. In choosing, for greater political reasons, to associate himself in a war with a ruthless and undisciplined Indian ally, Hastings could not so easily disclaim all responsibility for the consequences, even those he deplored ("Rohilla Speech," 110). Other issues aside, the moral problem here was no doubt more ambiguous than Burke suggested, but he was right to raise it.

Another aspect of the cruelty of the war figured as an even more serious accusation against Hastings. Burke frequently asserted, following the phraseology of official testimony on the matter, that what Hastings had agreed to was the "extirpation" or "extermination" of the Rohillas, and that the outcome of the war had in fact been their total destruction or elimination as a nation. The image of ruthless tyranny suggested by these words, which to modern readers suggest genocide, likewise aroused outrage in the England of George III. Two related issues may be discerned here: the status and character of the Rohillas as a nation, and their precise fate. In the light of subsequent historical research, these appear to be matters on which Burke was not fully informed, and yet his protests against Hastings's policy may still carry weight.

Burke certainly considered the Rohillas to be a distinct nation, firmly settled in the country called Rohilkhand. He also portrayed them as an attractive people, "one of the most distinguished of the Tartar nations," hospitable and generous ("Rohilla Speech," 99, 101). Their principal chieftain, Hafiz Rahmat Khan, who was "slain valiantly fighting for his country," was "one of the bravest men of his time, and as famous throughout the East for the elegance of his . . . poetical compositions . . . as for his courage" (*Fox's Bill*, 393). In fact, however, the Rohillas were a small group of warlike tribes of Afghan origin, numbering perhaps about fifty to sixty thousand, who had entered or invaded northern India in the 1720s, alternately offering their services as mercenary soldiers to the weakened Mogul emperor and extorting favors from him. Eventually, they were granted lands in what became known as Rohilkhand and settled there as a ruling elite over the much older and stable population of 1 to 2 million Hindu peasants. They may well have exhibited some of the virtues that eighteenth-century Europeans liked to ascribe to rude peoples, such as fierce courage tempered by a taste for heroic poetry, but they could also be described, as Hastings and some later historians have preferred to describe them, as treacherous marauders and "freebooters" whose only claim to be where they were rested on a fairly recent conquest of their own.[25] Since, like other Muslim ruling groups in India, they had not blended in with the larger population, they might plausibly be characterized as a nation, hence entitled to autonomous existence, as Burke implied. Hastings's main defender, on the other hand, denies them this status, arguing that they were merely a loose assemblage of semi-independent tribal chieftains of common stock.[26] Their very political disunity, which meant that any of their chiefs might defect from a common policy, made them, in Hastings's view, a tempting target for the Marathas and useless as allies for Oudh or the company.

Burke was aware of the circumstances and recent date of the Rohillas' appearance in India, and thus their lack of any ancient prescriptive right to their holdings, though he believed they were there legitimately, with the emperor's consent ("Rohilla Speech," 99–100). He also understood their position as a small ruling class, but this circumstance did not, to his mind, in any way mitigate the injustice of their destruction. Likening the Rohillas to comparable (in number and status) landowning groups in Europe, Burke invited his parliamentary audience to "consider how the people of England would feel . . . were all the principal men of property among their constituents to be driven from the country, to the amount of sixty thousand." It was, after all, "the chief land-holders, the principal manufacturers, the nobles, the superior clergy, and the men of property," and not the peasantry, who were the usual chief victims of conquest and plunder—or of revolution, as Burke would have occasion to observe a few years later ("Rohilla Speech," III). We shall note other cases, too, where Burke sought to understand Indian society and arouse sympathy for persons and groups victimized by Hastings's policies, by assimilating them to European social categories. Doing so was an intellectually and rhetorically reasonable strategy, though it was risky: some of his listeners, like later historians, must have suspected he was idealizing the Rohillas to some extent. Such doubts, however, do not completely undermine his protest against the destruction of an entire social group or nation.

What actually happened to the Rohillas? Here it seems clear that Burke was mistaken in interpreting Hastings's intention, or the outcome, as involving their "extermination." The Persian word used by Hastings in his negotiations with Shuja al-Daula can be translated as "uproot" or "expel" as well as "extirpate," and what seems to have been envisioned was their forcible expulsion from Rohilkhand.[27] As Hastings put it,

> the "extirpation" consisted in nothing more than in removing from their offices the Rohillas who had the official management of the country, and from the country the soldiers who had opposed us in the conquest of it. Nor was the process a sanguinary or hard one, as they had only to pass the Ganges to their countrymen on the other side of it. In a word, we conquered the country from the conquerors of it . . . upon the same principle of right and usage (the right of war being pre-supposed) as a British Commander in Europe would expel the soldiers of a conquered town, and garrison it with his own.[28]

This account no doubt understates the event, which Hastings realized from the start would be controversial in England. After many of their fighting men had been killed in battle, the rest of the Rohillas (except one chieftain, who defected to the nawab's side) were indeed expelled from the country, civilians as well as soldiers. Burke saw in this a "hard process," even for a group of fierce and mobile tribesmen from the Afghan mountains.

Finally, more fundamental for Burke than the harshness with which the war was waged was the justifiability of the war as such; he saw it as a war of outright conquest that reflected a drive for political aggrandizement and economic plunder on the part of both the nawab-wazir and Hastings. A war undertaken exclusively for such reasons had to be condemned under the traditional conceptions of political morality to which Burke adhered. In the relations among independent states, the use of force is sometimes necessary, but, like any application of violence or coercion, a state's recourse to warfare in pursuit of its goals must bear the burden of justification. Traditional morality sought to circumscribe the use of violence between states, appealing to natural law and the consensus of moralists, and promoting the development of rules or conventions to regulate the conduct of sovereigns toward one another. Defining and upholding a distinction between just and unjust wars was one of the principal endeavors in this project. In his impeachment speeches, aimed at securing a legal conviction on specific "crimes and misdemeanors," Burke emphasized that Hastings's Rohilla policy violated explicit and repeated orders from the company's directors forbidding "offensive" wars, including those that sought to enlarge its possessions in India, and in particular (at that time) the use of company troops beyond the borders of Oudh ("Articles of Charge," 307). It is clear, however, that the "uniform, steady, publick anger" to which Burke confessed on this matter did not arise from his view that Hastings had disobeyed his superiors, but from his belief that a great injustice had occurred. In opting to imitate the "mad career of [Indian] conquerors and usurpers," Hastings had violated "the law of nature and nations, the great and fundamental axioms on which every form of society was built," in India as elsewhere {"Rohilla Speech," 104, 108–09).

Unfortunately, however, the criteria for distinguishing just and unjust wars, clear in theory, were (and are) often contestable in practice. Wars fought in self-defense are permissible, but how much latitude do rulers have in pursuing large-scale defensive and preemptive strategies? Although Hastings referred to the Rohilla operation as an "offensive" war, presumably since his and the nawab's army had indisputably initiated it, his principal motive in undertaking it was certainly to enhance the security of Bengal by creating defensible borders for the allied (and British-garrisoned) buffer state of Oudh. Rohilkhand, he argued, stood in relation to Oudh as Scotland had once stood in relation to England, as a grave strategic danger while independent because of its geographic position.[29] As he explained to his military commander,

> We engaged to assist the Vizier in reducing the Rohilla country under his dominion, that the boundary of his possessions might be completed by the Ganges forming a barrier to cover them from the attack and insults to which they were exposed, by his enemies either possessing or having access to the Rohilla country. . . . Security of his possessions from invasions in that quarter is in fact the security of ours.[30]

The orders to which Hastings was bound were also nicely ambiguous, as the following dispatch from the directors suggests: "We also utterly disapprove and condemn offensive wars, distinguishing, however, between offensive measures unnecessarily undertaken with a view to pecuniary advantages and those which the preservation of our honour, or the protection or safety of our possessions, may render absolutely necessary."[31]

The hostile and growing power of the Marathas, and their history of incursions into Rohilkhand, represented a genuine threat to Bengal, and the eighteenth-century law of nations approved of preemptive wars against such potential antagonists as a legitimate mode of defense. The problem was that the Rohilla War was not waged against the dangerous Marathas, but against the relatively innocuous Rohillas, precisely because their weakness rendered them a source of instability in the region. Burke himself approved in general terms of "the true and obvious policy of uniting the power of the Mahometan princes [such as Shuja al-Daula] against the Mahrattas" ("Articles of Charge," 309). This is what Hastings was trying to do. In pursuit of such a policy, however, it was not permissible to destroy a small and "unoffending" nation, even in the name of defense, simply because it would not join, or could not be counted on as a reliable partner, in the common enterprise.

Judicial Murder

Maharaja Nandakumar was a prominent and wealthy Calcutta Brahmin who, over the years, held high administrative and tax-farming positions under both the nawabs of Bengal and successive company governments. Hastings never liked or trusted him but, like his predecessors, found his services useful on occasion, for example, during the sweeping reforms he instituted in the administration of Bengal upon his arrival in 1772.[32] Burke conceded that Nandakumar was not an attractive character: he was "an intriguing man in the time of the last expiring power and the rapid revolutions among the Nabobs of Bengal." In competition with other well-placed Indians, he sought to negotiate among the shifting factions and extract large profits from the prevailing political instability ("Rohilla Speech," 97). As Macaulay remarked, this was a perilous game to play, especially for an Indian whose understanding of British political institutions was imperfect.[33]

In 1775 Hastings's power in Bengal appeared to be seriously weakened through the opposition of a hostile majority of the council. Evidently deciding to cast his lot with the ascendant group, Nandakumar publicly accused the governor-general of having accepted several large bribes in connection with his settlement of the nawab's household several years earlier. While Hastings's British opponents were trying to decide how most effectively to use this information against him, an Indian businessman came forward with a (plausible) charge of forgery against Nandakumar, who in short order was arrested, tried before the Supreme Court of Bengal, convicted, and hanged. The presiding judge of this court was Sir Elijah Impey, an old friend and presumed ally of the governor. Never again was Hastings to be accused of misconduct by an Indian subject.

The circumstances of this case were naturally publicized in England, to great effect, by Hastings's enemies. Burke shared the common assumption that a judicial murder had been arranged by Hastings and his supporters in order to remove an informant who could have been a dangerous tool in the hands of their political opponents. Although no evidence of such a conspiracy has ever been found, the simple facts of the case have seemed to many to warrant the inference. For Macaulay, it was obvious to everyone, "idiots and biographers excepted, that Hastings was the real mover in the business."[34] A modern admirer of Burke has also asserted that Hastings's cool elimination of his enemy was "a major political *coup*, of the type which Machiavelli admired in Borgia . . . decisive, unscrupulous, and ruthless."[35] A prominent modern jurist has endorsed this conclusion; he also questions the Supreme Court's jurisdiction and the propriety of applying English law, in which forgery was a capital crime, to an Indian, in an environment where the offense would normally have been assessed differently. Burke agreed with this point as well (*Ninth Report*, 204).[36]

Some historians, however, pointing to the apparent procedural correctness of Nandakumar's trial and other documentary evidence, have been less sure.[37] Most interesting is a counter-Machiavellian analysis offered on behalf of Hastings by his admirers. If he was guilty as supposed, after all, he certainly miscalculated, since the general belief that he committed judicial murder was surely more damning than the charge of bribery (one of many) that he was supposedly trying to evade; indeed, the charge of murder carries an imputation of guilt in the bribery charge as well. It has therefore been suggested that Hastings's opponents on the Bengal Council, led by Francis, failed to use their influence to have Nandakumar's sentence commuted or his execution delayed precisely because, in their campaign to discredit Hastings, he was worth more to them dead than alive.[38] Whatever the truth of the matter, this episode has always been one of the most damaging to Hastings's reputation.

Burke did not enter into subtle speculations about the details of the incident, which in his view spoke for themselves. In his speech for the India bill of 1783, he not only deplored the hanging as "an insult on every thing which India holds respectable and sacred" but also openly accused Hastings of murder: "The culprit . . . triumphs on the ground of that murder: a murder not of Nundcomar only, but of all living testimony . . . . From that time not a complaint has been heard from the natives against their governors. All the grievances of India have found a complete remedy" (*Fox's Bill*, 435–36).[39] In the impeachment, he returned to the charge and the presumed motive. Nandakumar had been in a position to know the particulars of some of Hastings's dubious financial transactions, and Hastings's reaction to his accusation implied that his evidence was solid. Nandakumar may well have been corrupt himself—in fact, his probable role as an "[accomplice] in guilty actions" is what made him a competent accuser. So it was that, for Hastings, he had to be destroyed: "Nothing less than *stone dead* would do the business." The Supreme Court of Bengal, whose recent establishment Burke had supported, was thus perverted from its proper role in the struggle against corruption through the "close connection" between Hastings and the chief justice ("Speech on Opening," 389–91). The outcome was exactly what Hastings sought:

> [Nandakumar's execution] did not discourage forgeries: they went on at their usual rate, neither more nor less: but it put an end to all accusations against all persons in power for any corrupt practice. Mr. Hastings observes, that no man in India complains of him. It is generally true. The voice of all India is stopped. All complaint was strangled with the same cord that strangled Nundcomar. ("Speech in Opening," 10:30)

Given Burke's conviction and outrage on the matter, however, it is odd that the Nandakumar case did not form one of his impeachment charges against Hastings. Historians have been at a loss to explain this,[40] but it is possible that Burke was sufficiently practical to recognize the legal weakness of the case he would have had to make. Notwithstanding the inferential obviousness of Hastings's guilt in his own mind (and that of many others), witnesses and documentary evidence were simply not available to convince the houses of Parliament sitting as judicial bodies. Burke therefore alluded to the Nandakumar episode only in connection with his charges of bribery against Hastings, making innuendos of murder. This provoked Hastings to declare publicly that he had had "no concern, either directly or indirectly, in the apprehending, prosecuting, or Execution of *Nundcomar*."[41] The absence of a formal charge, however, meant that Hastings never had to defend himself on this issue at any length, and for the most part, he did not deign to mention the matter. Another possible explanation for Burke's omission of this charge is that preparations were under way on the part of some of his colleagues to impeach Sir Elijah Impey on this and other charges; this effort, which would have implicated Hastings as well, failed in the House of Commons in 1788. Subsequently, referring to Nandakumar in arguing his corruption charge before the House of Lords, Burke could not resist asserting that Hastings *"has murdered this man by the hands of Sir Elijah Impey."* Since this was not among the articles on which Hastings had been impeached, and since Impey had been cleared, this statement was inappropriate, and Burke was reprimanded by the House of Commons. His apology was tepid, however, and his embarrassment not very daunting ("Sixth Article," 218, 311–18).

If Burke was correct in his interpretation of the facts, then it is incontrovertible that Hastings was guilty of a heinous crime. Apart from the ruthlessness in the pursuit of power indicated by the events, however, Burke was especially disturbed by the abuse of legal forms for this purpose. Burke's advocacy of the rule of law certainly included the independence of courts from executive pressures, and especially from involvement in partisan political goals. It also included the integrity and impartiality of judicial proceedings, all of which were put in question by the Nandakumar case. Earlier in his career Burke had opposed modifications in English legal procedure aimed at dealing more effectively and harshly with the rebellious American colonists; he was especially opposed to a provision that would have brought Americans accused of treason to England for trial. Governmental convenience or policy, even in circumstances of civil disorder, did not justify a violation of the venerable local jury principle: "All the ancient, honest, juridical principles and institutions of England are so many clogs to check and retard the headlong course of violence and oppression. They were invented for this one good purpose, that what was not just should not be convenient" (*Sheriffs of Bristol*, 193). Even earlier, in 1766, Burke had been upset by the trials and executions of several Irishmen (including a priest) accused of participating in agrarian disturbances, cases he believed reflected the bias of Protestant courts and which he called "judicial murders."[42]

Similarly, with respect to India Burke denounced any encroachments on procedural regularity and legality as tending to destroy the general protection that the rule of law affords. Violence was deplorable, Burke said on another occasion, referring to Hastings and Impey, but violence perpetrated under the guise of law was worse:

> There is no act of violence which, merely as an act of violence, may not in some sort be borne: because an act of violence infers no principle. . . . For at the same time that it pays no regard to law, it does not debauch it, it does not wrest it to its purposes: the law disregarded still exists; and hope still exists in the sufferer, that, when law shall be resorted to, violence will cease, and wrongs will be redressed. But whenever the law itself is debauched, and enters into a corrupt coalition with violence, robbery, and wrong, then all hope is gone. ("Speech in Reply," 12:82)

The view that crimes are aggravated when carried out under cover of law is apparent in Burke's response to another incident as well. Almas Ali Khan was a powerful tax farmer in Oudh whom Hastings regarded as both oppressive and treacherous. Burke produced evidence that Hastings had ordered his resident in Lucknow to explore the possibility of having him covertly killed, playing on local intrigues in the manner of an Asian despot. This plan was not carried out; instead, Hastings came to terms with Almas Ali, dropping his complaints in exchange for an "advance" of funds to the company—"which practice of charging wealthy persons with treason and disloyalty, and afterwards acquitting them on the payment of a sum of money, is highly scandalous to the honor, justice, and government of Great Britain" ("Articles of Charge," 157). Burke appears to have been more disturbed by the pseudolegal extortion than by the prospect of the straightforward assassination of a disreputable figure.[43]

As Burke pointed out, a lasting consequence of the Nandakumar case was to forestall accusations against Hastings by Indians. (It would have had this effect, given native perceptions, regardless of the actual intentions or propriety of the trial.) This in turn partly defeated the purpose for which British-type courts had been established in Bengal, or, as Burke said, "totally vitiated and reversed all the ends for which this country, to its eternal and indelible dishonor, had sent out a pompous embassy of justice to the remotest parts of the globe" ("Speech in Opening," 10:30). It also allowed

Hastings to argue at his trial, to some effect, that the prosecution had failed to produce any victims of his alleged misdeeds to testify against him; on the contrary, he presented a number of testimonials or affidavits from prominent Indians in his favor.[44] This situation presented a problem for Burke similar to that raised by his charge of systematic corruption: just as Hastings's patronage network had put many of his knowledgeable English colleagues in his debt, so the fear of his power deterred complaints from his Indian subjects, thereby making prosecution difficult.

In this case too, Burke (of necessity) took the offensive, ridiculing Hastings's innocent pose. It was not credible that the Indians could be "the only people . . . upon the face of the earth, that have no complaints to make of their government" ("Speech in Reply," 12:367), or that Hastings could have ruled Bengal for fourteen years without provoking any grievances: Burke

> trembled at the enormous degree of power he had to contend with, to which alone could be ascribed the silence in question, since it was not in human nature, situated as Mr. Hastings had been, to preserve so pure, even-handed, and unimpeachable a conduct, as to afford no room for a single accusation to be stated against him. ("Rohilla Speech," 106)

Again running the risk of a circular argument, Burke took the silence to be a further indication of Hastings's despotic conduct, and hence an aggravation of his guilt. The fewer the witnesses against him, the more guilty he must be. The same held true for the Indian testimonials collected on Hastings's behalf—"these flowers of Oriental rhetoric, penned at ease by dirty hireling moonshees [scribes] at Calcutta"—which Burke perfunctorily dismissed either as extorted or as exemplifying the regrettable Asian custom of flattering the powerful ("Speech in Reply," 11:368 and 12:356). Submitted as evidence for the defense at his trial, moreover, these documents were properly viewed not as rhetorical but as fraudulent. Far from being exculpatory, they represented yet another attempt to corrupt the legal process, and thus yet a further offense on the part of the accused. The fairness of Burke's reasoning on these matters, which on the surface appears somewhat perverse, depends upon the other evidence of Hastings's offenses at his disposal and the patterns they revealed.

Abuse of Wardship

Despotism need not involve arbitrary or unjustified physical violence on the part of a ruler, though this may be the case in the most conspicuous instances. Despotic power can also manifest itself in the humiliating treatment of subjects and in contemptuous violations of moral or religious sensibilities and traditions. Burke charged Hastings with what he viewed as serious affronts to Indian society and custom, sometimes but not always accompanied by more violent forms of oppression. For example, Burke regarded Hastings's treatment of two underage Indian notables who fell under his power as both unjust or exploitative in general terms and offensive in relation to local Indian norms.

From 1765 the East India Company exercised its sovereign authority over the fiscal and judicial systems of Bengal indirectly, working through the nawab and his officials in their capital at Murshidabad. By 1772 the company decided that the abuses in this method of government were irremediable and that more direct British rule was required. Immediately upon taking office, Hastings therefore implemented sweeping reforms, transferring the government to Calcutta and establishing direct accountability of the administration (much of it still in native hands) to the central company authority there. The stipend for the nawab, who was retained in a largely ceremonial role, was reduced by half. This coup was made easier by the fact that the office of nawab had recently fallen to Mubarak al-Daula, a minor son of the company's old ally Mir Jafar. In the key position of guardian of the new nawab and director of his remaining household, Hastings installed the notorious (from Burke's speeches) Munni Begam, a widow of Mir Jafar (but not Mubarak's mother). The inappropriateness and putatively corrupt nature of this appointment became one of the most prominent subjects of Burke's rhetoric in his drive to impeach and punish Hastings.

Burke's wrath was aroused in part because he believed the young ruler was being materially despoiled by Hastings's arrangement. He took for granted that Munni Begam received her appointment in exchange for a bribe (this was one of Nandakumar's charges), which she would surely recoup from the nawab's fortune; she was also willing to assist Hastings in carrying out his political program, in return for a free hand in controlling the nawab's household and resources. Hastings should have chosen "a person fit to be a regent to guard the Nabob's minority from all rapacity whatever" ("Sixth Article," 192–93); instead, he favored an ally of his own with an opportunity for plunder.

In this respect the Munni Begam affair resembled another case that caught Burke's attention. In 1780 Hastings settled a succession dispute between the adopted son and the half brother of the deceased raja of Dinajpur in favor of the son, a young child, and there was evidence that his agents in the district had made large profits, both in exchange for the decision and subsequently, by preying on the vulnerability of the minor raja's domain ("Speech in Opening," 10:62ff.).[45] As the ruler of Bengal, within the framework of a quasi-feudal society, Hastings's position was similar to that of feudal monarchs in medieval Europe, who had the right to control—and were frequently tempted to exploit—the estates of vassals who succeeded as minors to major fiefs. Burke claimed that, by manipulating a child-ruler to drain his assets, Hastings had violated both "the laws of that country, [and] the common laws of Nature." In pointing out that Hastings had had, and abused, "the same sacred guardianship of minors that the Chancellor of England has" ("Speech in Opening," 10:125), Burke no doubt hoped to remind his audience that the Magna Carta contained several articles directed at the royal abuse of wardship, and thus that at least some of the offenses of the Indian empire were familiar to European history as well.

Even more than by the material depredations, however, Burke was disturbed by what he understood to be serious violations of custom involved in the appointment of Munni Begam, and the humiliation consequently imposed on the powerless young nawab and his family. In choosing a suitable guardian for him, Burke argued, Hastings ought to have considered the "age, authority, dignity, [and goodness of] manners" of the available "Mahometan and Hindoo princes," selecting a man whose "rank [was] such as at least ought not to wound the Nabob's honor, or lessen his credit in the estimation of the people." Instead, in flagrant disregard of Muslim custom, Hastings appointed a woman, "in a country where no woman can be seen, where no woman can be spoken to by any one without a curtain between them." In addition, he failed to appoint the natural female candidate, the nawab's mother, who also had a rightful claim to superiority in the seraglio—"a large and considerable trust in a country where polygamy is admitted, [for] women of great rank." Instead, he chose Munni Begam, whose lurid story Burke recounted at length. By origin a slave and dancing girl, little better than a prostitute, Munni had caught the attention of the old nawab, Mir Jafar, who had given her a favored place in his harem. When her own son died in infancy, her legitimate claims to precedence were at an end. Her origins and the natural rivalries among the widows of a Muslim ruler and their sons disqualified her both from continuing as head of the women's part of the household and from serving as guardian of her stepson Mubarak, positions in which Hastings nevertheless found it convenient to place her.

> Here is such an arrangement as I believe never was before heard of: a secluded woman in the place of a man of the world; a fantastic dancing-girl in the place of a grave magistrate; a slave in the place of

a woman of quality; a common prostitute made to superintend the education of a young prince; and a step-mother, a name of horror in all countries, made to supersede the natural mother from whose body the Nabob had sprung. ("Sixth Article," 192–97; see also "Speech in Reply," 12:226–27)

The inappropriateness of the appointment convinced Burke that a corrupt deal had been struck. The outrage to the dignity of high-ranking natives whom Hastings had under his authority revealed both his contempt for local custom and his despotic attitude toward the exercise of his power.

Burke's treatment of this episode—indeed, his preoccupation with it—raises questions to which we shall return later. But his attempt to visualize and describe a complex and somewhat startling Indian situation represents the imaginative effort necessary to comprehend a certain type of oppression, that involving an imperial ruler's trampling on the sensibilities of his sub-jects. Once again, if Burke was correct in his interpretation of the facts, including facts about subtle matters on which full and impartial information was impossible to obtain, he made a forceful case.[46] Burke's interpretation, however, should be placed within the perspective offered by the reasons Hastings gave for his action.

Hastings justified his appointment of Munni Begam in two ways, with reference to the welfare of the minor nawab and with reference to the company's interests, for which he was responsible. The most obvious candi-date for the regency was a brother of the late Nawab Mir Jafar, a man "of no dangerous abilities" but with a large family. "If only one of his sons, who are all in the prime of life, should have raised his hopes to the succession, it would have been in his power at any time to remove the single obstacle which the Nabob's life opposed to the advancement of his family." On the other hand, "the Begum, as a woman, is incapable of passing the bounds assigned her; her ambition cannot aspire to higher dignity. She has no children to provide for, or mislead her fidelity; her actual authority rests on the Nabob's life, and therefore cannot endanger it."[47] Such Machiavellian analysis would surely have been distressing to Burke, since it confirmed the view of oriental despotism that he resisted, but Hastings deployed it here on behalf of his ward; and he no doubt understood better than Burke the typical intrigues of an Indian ruler's household. Even if his action was despotic, it might still have been excusable as an adaptation to a despotic environment.

Conveniently for Hastings, moreover, the interests of both the young nawab and Munni Begam coincided perfectly, in his analysis, with that of the company. Munni owed her position entirely to him, and would continue to depend on his support against the likely resentment of her more aristocratic in-laws. "We want the time of [Mubarak's] minority to establish and confirm the Company's authority in the country; and as all her future hopes of protection rest solely in the Company, there is no fear of her opposing our measures or thwarting our views. Indeed, she assents to everything."[48] Thus were empires built: and from Hastings's point of view, building an empire was his job.

Burke protested at the inappropriateness of Munni Begam's appointment, but, practical politician though he was, he failed to recognize that her inappropriateness (by conventional norms) was precisely why Hastings had appointed her. In reference to this case, Burke complained that many of Hastings's "villainies" were perpetrated "through the medium and instrumentality of persons whom they pretended to have rights of their own, and to be acting for themselves; whereas such persons were, in fact, totally dependent upon him, Mr. Hastings, and did no one act that was not prescribed by him" ("Speech in Reply," 12:229–30). Burke condemned as fraud and deceit what for Hastings was a clever and successful political maneuver. An "appropriate" appointee would have been an able adult male member of high standing in the royal family. Under the circumstances, such an individual would have been both a threat to the nawab and a less pliable instrument of the company's policy in its efforts to reorganize the administration of Bengal. These two concerns, and no doubt the latter especially, were foremost in Hastings's calculations. He knew his decision would be resented by "troublesome people" with contrary interests in the nawab's entourage, and he recorded with pride that the installation of Munni Begam was carried out without the use of military force.[49] Given the stakes, he was evidently willing to risk some trouble, and whatever long-term offense his action might cause. In this case, Burke did not challenge the efficacy of Hastings's methods in promoting the interests of the empire, but rather their intrinsic propriety.

Social Oppression

In Burke's opinion, some of Hastings's fiscal and economic policies in Bengal and to some extent in Oudh were severely oppressive of important sectors of the population under his rule. Exorbitant taxes were collected by violent methods, large property holdings were confiscated, and many of the established gentry of the country were ruined. One might say, in modern terminology, that the company government had imposed a social revolution from above on a traditional society, in a futile effort to extract a net profit from its new possessions and sovereign position in India. Indeed, Burke occasionally compared Hastings's actions to socially disruptive anti-Catholic policies in Ireland and to revolutionary policies in France. As in Europe, the result in India was general economic distress, social disintegration, and destruction of the traditional social fabric.

The truth about such a complex situation is difficult to assess. The personnel and information that Hastings had at his disposal for ruling such a huge country as Bengal, whose existing government institutions he believed to be thoroughly corrupt and inefficient, were extremely limited. He regarded his policies as experimental, and he acknowledged that the results were not ideal. Of his revenue program, the "ground-work" of everything else, he remarked, "Who was it that said that he had given such laws to his people as they were capable of receiving, not the best that could be framed?"[50] Whether as classical lawgiver or as modern revolutionary, Hastings set out to rationalize the administration of Bengal with a sweeping set of what he regarded as reforms. His approach, as Burke interpreted it, was indicative of a despotic attitude toward the relationship between government power and society; the inevitable consequence was the destruction of accustomed forms of life without much to show in return.

Money was the central issue. The East India Company had obtained the right to collect and manage the public revenues of Bengal, from which it had to finance the country's police, administration of justice, military defense, and other costs of rule. When early hopes that the riches of India would generate surpluses above these expenses were dashed, and deficits began to mount, Hastings was charged with restructuring the fiscal system. In the event, Hastings's shortage of funds remained chronic, especially as his military undertakings and commitments expanded, and this financial pressure lay behind many of his actions, as Burke sensed.

The existing Mogul system with which Hastings had to work was of a kind familiar in a premodern agricultural society, readily recognizable to eighteenth-century Europeans as a tax-farming system. Assessments based on precedent were levied on local zamindars, large landholders with tax-collecting authority in their districts; their agents then attempted to extract payments from smaller landowners and peasants sufficient to pay the required tax and to yield a comfortable income for their master and his retainers. Dissatisfied with the performance of the system he inherited, Hastings's major policy initiative was to cancel, at one stroke, the revenue-collecting powers of the existing zamindars and to confer these powers over all the lands in Bengal on the highest bidders, in a new system of five-year tax-farming leases. Whether this amounted to a social revolution is not clear. An unknown number of the previous zamindars were successful bidders and stayed on in something like their customary position; others were displaced by new men—including wealthy Indian businessmen and investors, officials carried over from the old regime, and in many cases, the well-placed banians or favored personal agents of East India Company servants.[51] Much controversy ensued over the status and rights of the class of people Hastings had apparently despoiled, and over the justifiability of these proceedings.

Hastings's view was clear. His government was legally the successor to that of the Moguls, and under the Mogul constitution all landed property was ultimately "vested" in the state.[52] As in European feudalism, the local zamindars were originally appointed by their sovereign, and though their position tended to become hereditary, their tenure legally remained conditional on the adequate performance of their duties of collecting revenue and keeping local order. Hastings, their new sovereign, was displeased with their conduct. There was evidence of extortion and embezzlement by their agents; worse, the zamindars were trying to evade his inquiries aimed at compiling a more accurate assessment of the taxable wealth of the country. They "availed themselves of [their long possession] by complex Divisions of the Lands and intricate modes of Collection to perplex the Officers of the Government, and confine the knowledge of the Rents to themselves."[53] Given the zamindars' obstructiveness and the company's necessities, drastic measures were called for, and taken.

Other Englishmen, and later Burke, took a different view. They saw in the zamindars the Indian equivalent of the English gentry, a class of landowners with property rights in their lands and rents, and rights of hereditary succession, as firmly grounded in Indian law and custom as they would have been in Europe. If they also had official responsibilities, these were analogous to English landowners' occasional service as local magistrates or in the county militia; they were not a condition of the tenure of their estates.[54] As soon as the men who were to become Hastings's opponents on the Bengal Council arrived in 1774, they inquired suspiciously into the revenue plan, and their leader, Philip Francis, soon reported to Lord North:

> The Plan of letting the Lands by Auction might seem plausible upon paper. If you would have a true Notion of the Fact, I must intreat you to weigh in your Mind what would be the probable consequence in England, if all the Lands were at once set up to sale by an Act of arbitrary Power, without any Regard to the Rights of Freeholders,

Copyholders and Lords of the Manors: in short, if the Monied Interest . . . were at once to be put in possession of the Lands: and this, not by fair Purchase . . . but by Influence over Individuals in Office."[55]

Thus was initiated a chapter in a larger debate among European observers over the exact status of property rights and tenure in India and in Asia more generally. The scholarly conclusions of the debate were usually preempted in practice, however, by the legal settlements imposed by imperial governments.[56] By the time he returned to England, Hastings realized that British opinion was against him on this matter. From Francis, Burke, and others, the British public had gotten "very high ideas of the rights of the Zemindars in Hindostan," and his land policy, regardless of Mogul precedents, was regarded as oppressive.[57] Pitt's East India Act of 1784, stipulating that "whereas complaints have prevailed that divers rajas, zemindars, and other native landholders have been unjustly deprived of their lands, jurisdictions, and privileges," ordered an investigation and redress of legitimate grievances "consistent with justice and the laws and customs of the country."[58]

Burke's objections to Hastings's land and revenue policy fall into three categories. First, Burke believed that, by the law and custom of Bengal, the land was the "inheritable property" of the zamindars, held solely on condition that they pay a fixed revenue or "quit-rent" to the government, and that under them, as in premodern Europe, the peasants or ryots "held certain subordinate rights of property or occupancy" in exchange for the payment of customary rents. Hastings's policy "destroy[ed] all the rights of private property of the zemindars" and led to extortionate treatment of the peasant cultivators ("Articles of Charge," 79, 82). As he put it more forcefully in opening Hastings's trial:

My Lords, when Mr. Hastings first went into Bengal, the first of his acts was the most bold and extraordinary that I believe ever entered into the head of any man; I will say, of any tyrant. It was no more or less than a general, almost exceptionless, confiscation, in time of profound peace, of all the landed property in Bengal upon strange pretences. . . . He put it up to a pretended public, in reality to a private, corrupt auction; and such favoured landholders as came were obliged to consider themselves as not any longer proprietors of the estates, but to recognize themselves as farmers under Government. And even those few that were permitted to stay had their payments raised at his arbitrary discretion. ("Speech on Opening," 381–82)[59]

Burke could take for granted that his audience agreed with him in holding the rights of private property to be inviolable, and a policy of confiscation to raise revenue, except perhaps in times of dire emergency, to be an impermissible act of tyranny.

Later, Burke was to argue that the confiscation of Church lands and their sale by auction to the highest bidders (to back up the newly issued assignats and to pay off the national debt) was the driving economic dynamic of the French Revolution; it was also the single instance of revolutionary tyranny that was most responsible for arousing his antagonism (*Reflections*, 226). The similarity of the French to the Indian case is striking; and Burke's sensitivity and heated reaction to the French confiscations were probably in part due to his investigation of Hastings and Bengal, which began before his scrutiny of events in France, and continued simultaneously with it. Likewise, when Burke reviewed disapprovingly the seventeenth-century confiscations of the lands of the old Irish gentry, and their sale in a "scandalous auction" to English adventurers ("Richard Burke," 654), Bengal may well have been in the back of his mind.[60]

Second, Burke held that, beyond violating the property rights of individuals, Hastings's policy aimed at destroying the gentry of Bengal as a class and replacing them with an unscrupulous body of ambitious new men whose political loyalty he could count on—a charge reminiscent of his earlier allegation that the Penal Laws were a deliberate plan to destroy the Catholic gentry of Ireland ("Popery Laws," 437). Burke went to some lengths to persuade his listeners in England that the traditional (mostly Muslim) landowning class in Bengal was a genuine aristocracy whose lineage, status, and claims to social position were as legitimate as those of equivalent classes in Europe. Although this class was somewhat decayed, Hastings's victims were "persons of the most ancient and respectable families in the country," members of a social order that antedated even the Mogul regime; they were people who, like European nobles, disdained trade and lived off their rents and the various civil and military employments customarily reserved for them ("Speech in Reply," 12:209). Indeed, some of those whose lands had been confiscated, Burke informed the House of Lords, were "a nobility perhaps as ancient as that of your Lordships" ("Speech on Opening," 382). Burke did not try to make the case that the Indian gentry exhibited the public-spiritedness or performed valuable public functions to the same degree that, in his opinion, the British upper classes did, nor did he respond to Hastings's charge that, in their principal function of tax collection, they were generally corrupt. It was enough that their prescriptive claim to their position (as well as their property) had been infringed upon.

Moreover, Burke did not doubt that the "respectable" established gentry were preferable, as a landholding and socially dominant class, to the new monied men and political favorites who replaced them. In Hastings's auction, the "ancient proprietors [had to] bid against every usurer, every temporary adventurer, every jobber and schemer, every servant of every European" who saw a chance of profit; Hastings's own banian emerged "possessed of territories yielding a rent of one hundred and forty thousand pounds a year" (*Fox's Bill*, 426). When these arrangements were not simply a cover for European profiteering and bribes, they reflected the political objective of replacing an established and thus independent social group with a new class of company dependents and allies, whose loyalty would be cemented not only by their material rewards but also by their collaboration in injustice. Such had been the "despotic" strategy of Henry VIII in transferring the property of the English monasteries and of the "ancient nobility" to his "minions" in the rising middle classes (*Noble Lord*, 303–05). Such also was to be the "grand *arcanum*" of the French Revolution—the arrangement of favorable terms for the purchase of confiscated property by supporters of the Revolution (*Reflections*, 226). Burke was enough of a practical politician to see clearly the political significance of such transactions, but enough of a moralist to condemn them as unscrupulous and tyrannical.[61]

The third objection stemmed directly from the foregoing. Unlike the old gentry, whose position and conduct were largely determined by the customary moral framework, the new owners of the lands or of tax-farming rights would be uninhibited by traditional norms or a sense of social responsibility. Instead, they would be motivated exclusively by their desire for a lucrative return on their investment, and by the need to pay off the purchase price and the bribes or kickbacks that Burke assumed they had to pay to their company patrons. The predictable and actual consequence of their pursuit of maximum profits was the oppression of the peasantry through rack renting and coercive extraction of payments.

Once again, this was to be Burke's expectation in the case of the new class of landed adventurers in France: the "miserable peasantry . . . is to be delivered over to the mercenary and arbitrary discretion of men, who will be stimulated to every species of extortion by the growing demands on the growing profits of an estate held under the precarious settlement of a new political system" (*Reflections*, 226). This prediction could have been based on Burke's prior analysis of the results of the social-revolutionary Bengal land settlement. His most sensational evidence of the hardships suffered by "the poorer sort of people, the yeomen, the husbandmen" as a result of exorbitant rents and extortionate tax collecting pertained to extensive districts that were put in the hands of Devi Singh, a former Calcutta banian and wealthy entrepreneur who was one of the most prominent of the "succession of black tyrants scattered through the country" in Hastings's service: widespread violence, parents reduced to selling their children, tortures applied to force the revelation of caches of grain ("Speech on Opening," 383, 416ff.). The victims of this mistreatment were the people, Burke pointed out, whose labor and produce were ultimately responsible for furnishing his audience with their morning tea ("Speech on Opening," 419).

Among the weapons available to despotic rulers in India—in this case, not to Hastings personally, but to the agents to whom he gave a free hand in raising revenues—were assaults on the religious sensibilities of the populace. For Muslims, the violation of women, or even their exposure to public view, was particularly intolerable, and was accordingly inflicted on women of the zamindar class and on recalcitrant peasants ("Speech on Opening," 415, 420–21). Hindus especially feared loss of caste, which could occur through humiliating treatment at the hands of individuals of low caste, as many of the banians were. Burke was later to compare these Indian religious indignities to certain insulting government proposals for the education of Roman Catholic clergy in Ireland (*Letter to Kenmare*, 572).

Burke's most extensive discussion of the caste system emphasized the vulnerability to which their religious practices exposed Hindus, who could suffer complete loss of dignity and social position not only through "voluntary crimes" but through "certain involuntary sufferings and involuntary disgraces" well known to their tormenters, "so that these miserable castes give one pledge more to fortune than any other nation was ever known to do." He continued,

> Tyranny oppresses upon them. And, accordingly, those who have wished to oppress them, those who have stood imprisonment, those who have stood whips, those who have stood tortures, those who have stood the menaces of death itself . . . have instantly given way when it has been attempted to bring upon them any of those pollutions by which they lose caste. ("Speech on Opening," 303–04)

Such sensibilities and the opening for abuse they provided created a special responsibility for British rulers of India to respect the "laws of religion, the laws of the land and the laws of honour" proper to the country.

And that, my Lords, makes it ten times more necessary for us to keep a strict eye upon all persons who go there . . . and we, if we must govern such a Country, must govern them upon their own principles and maxims and not upon ours, that we must not think to force them to our narrow ideas, but extend ours to take in theirs. ("Speech on Opening," 302–03)

Hastings was accountable for the actions of his agents, who, in using such oppressive methods to carry out an oppressive policy, were doing the opposite of what Burke recommended.[62]

In addition to the revenue policy, one other episode constituted evidence, in Burke's eyes, of Hastings's contemptuous attitude and oppressiveness toward the established aristocracy of the country he ruled. In 1772 Hastings reorganized the household of the minor nawab of Bengal in connection with his larger plan of administrative reform for the provincial government. We have noted how his actions on this occasion led to charges both of corruption (a bribe from Munni Begam) and abuse of wardship. In addition, since the nawab was now demoted to a purely formal role, Hastings reduced his income or household stipend to half the amount Clive had assigned his father in 1765. This meant, in Hastings's words, "retrenching the idle parade of elephants, menageries, etc.," customary at an Indian court. More significantly, it meant sweeping cutbacks in the nawab's traditional pension list, which in recent years had become an even more important source of sinecures for the displaced Bengal aristocracy: "Some hundreds of persons of the ancient nobility of the Country, excluded under our government from almost all employments civil or military, had ever since the revolution depended on the bounty of the Nabob. . . . [This reduction] could not fail to be accompanied with circumstances of real distress."[63] Nevertheless, in the words of a sympathetic historian, Hastings regarded this "[rearrangement of] the Nawab's entourage on a more economical basis" as a necessary step in fulfilling his responsibilities as governor.[64]

Burke, reviewing this incident in connection with Hastings's receipt of illegal presents, took a different view. In dealing this final blow to many of the "decayed nobility and gentry of a great kingdom," Hastings "[is] never corrupt but he is cruel; he never dines without creating a famine; he does not take from the loose superfluity of standing greatness, but falls upon the indigent, the oppressed, and ruined" ("Sixth Article," 236). Nor was the destruction of "ancient Mahometan families" in this manner—part of "a general waste and ravage of the country"—something that Hastings had the legal authority to do.

The Company never had of right despotic power in that country, to overturn any of these establishments. The Mogul, who gave them their charters, could not give them such a power; . . . the government of this country did not by an act of Parliament, and the Company did not and could not by their delegation, give him such a power; the act by which he was appointed Governor did not give him such a power. If he exercised it, he usurped it. ("Speech in Reply," 12:212–13)

Burke's view was that both the arbitrary cancellation of customary rights or expectations, especially on such a large scale and without an adequate showing of necessity, and the deliberate undoing of an entire social group, were not only impermissible but were also further examples of Hastings's despotic mode of imperial governance.

Burke's hostile reaction to Hastings's efforts to economize in the nawab's household raises a series of questions about several larger themes in his political thought. The problem that immediately arises is that Burke himself, throughout much of his career, was known as an economist and took pride in this role. Burke was an *economist* in two common eighteenth-century senses of the word. First, he understood and to a large extent embraced the principles of the emerging science of political economy, as is clear from his "Thoughts and Details on Scarcity"; and second, as a practicing statesman, he was an advocate of frugal and efficient policies in the administration of the public revenue.

Burke studied and presented extensive economic data and arguments both in his American speeches and in his committee reports on India, and a substantial portion of his *Reflections* is devoted to an analysis of the public finances of the French Revolution. Most strikingly, in 1779–1780 Burke led his party's successful program of "economical reform" in Great Britain, including provisions to rationalize the operations of central government offices and eliminate wasteful expenditures.[65] Prominent among the reforms was a reduction in the king's civil list through the abolition of archaic offices and sinecures. Reform, Burke acknowledged, could not be accomplished painlessly:

Very few men of great families and extensive connections but will feel the smart of a cutting reform. . . . Emolument is taken from some; patronage from others; objects of pursuit from all. . . . The cold commendation of a public advantage never was and never will be a match for the quick sensibility of a private loss.

Nevertheless, he went on, the public interest demanded a "system of good management" along the following lines: "of abolishing offices more expensive than useful; of combining duties improperly separated; of changing revenues more vexatious than productive into ready money; of suppressing offices which stand in the way of economy" ("Economical Reform," 269–70, 286, 299). Nor does Burke seem to have had any regrets about his endeavors in this area. At the end of his career, he expressed satisfaction that he had "made political oeconomy an object of my humble studies" from beginning to end, and he defended his "regulation of the civil-list establishment" and other economizing reforms from that period against the charge that he was inconsistent in accepting a royal pension for himself in his retirement (*Noble Lord*, 295, 284–85). How was it that the leader of an assault on the king of Great Britain's civil list in 1780 should have been so disturbed by Hastings's assault on that of the nawab of Bengal a few years earlier?

Burke's speech on "Economical Reform," like his endorsement of political economy, clashes at many points with better-known, more traditionalist or "organic" themes in his thought, as Gertrude Himmelfarb, among others, has emphasized.[66] His proposals for economic reform seem to contradict his arguments elsewhere for prescriptive rights, and they also, along with other "economic" passages, convey a very different spirit from what some students have called the "Gothic" elements in Burke's thought or rhetoric. In a general sense, these were Burke's occasional emotional appeals in favor of old institutions or members of old nobilities through reference to their venerable status and through a nostalgic evocation of medieval or other archaic themes. More specifically, as in the genre of the Gothic novel, the term "Gothic" refers to the aesthetic of terror aroused by violent or criminal disruptions of idyllic traditional settings; this was a device or "paradigm" Burke sometimes used in reference to both France and India.[67] Although Gothic motifs were a familiar feature of the emerging Romantic literary movement, the appearance of a Gothic Burke, most prominently in his *Reflections*, apparently surprised contemporaries, who knew him better as an "oeconomist." There he asserted, in words that have become famous, that Englishmen, "always acting as if in the presence of canonized forefathers," respected their free institutions as an inheritance from the past: "[our liberty, in contrast to that of the French revolutionaries] has a pedigree and illustrating ancestors. It has its bearings and its ensigns armorial. It has its gallery of portraits; its monumental inscriptions; its records, evidences, and titles." He also described, in good Gothic fashion, the horrifying invasion of the queen's apartment, and he deplored the prospect that "the age of chivalry is gone.—That of sophisters, oeconomists, and calculators, has succeeded" (*Reflections*, 121, 170).

Although these passages seize one's attention, they occur in a book that contains many pages of economic analysis. Likewise, his later panegyric on "the British Monarchy . . . like the proud Keep of Windsor, rising in the majesty of proportion" coexists with a defense of his record of economic reform (*Noble Lord*, 310). In his writings and speeches on India, Burke also combined detailed analysis of the economic decline brought about by company misrule with Gothic descriptions—if they may be so termed—of the long-established aristocracies of northern India, whose position and customs, he held, the British were bound to respect. In his impeachment speeches it is the Gothic element, including his accounts of Hastings's assaults on ancient and respectable families, that is more conspicuous.

Various efforts have been made to explain the apparent ambivalence Burke evinces in these two modes of expression. J. G. A. Pocock and others have pointed to the presence in Burke's writings and speeches of several distinct languages, idioms, or "traditions of thought" familiar to eighteenth-century political discourse, for example, those of common law, natural law, Whig political economy, and Gothic sentimentality.[68] It is possible that Burke's use of one or another of these idioms simply reflected his calculated or intuitive sense of what would be rhetorically effective on a given occasion. This view, however, cannot explain why Burke sometimes used conflicting idioms (such as the sentimental and the economic) in such close proximity to each other. Moreover, the "languages" in question reflect conceptual schemes and well-developed arguments about which Burke usually conveys genuine conviction. This is relatively clear with the idioms of natural and common law, but even the Gothic passages, which, in their appeal to feeling, are most clearly rhetorical, rest on claims about the importance of tradition to social and moral stability, which Burke took very seriously and articulated cogently.

Another interpretation, then, is that Burke's rhetorical ambivalence reflected a real psychological conflict within himself. On the one hand, Burke is said to have identified (for the most part subconsciously) with the ambitious or upstart bourgeois spirit, guided by economic rationality and scorn for hereditary privilege. This outlook was sometimes openly expressed, perhaps most vehemently in the "Speech on Economical Reform," where Burke ridiculed the "feudal" vestiges still represented in the royal household—"the cumbrous charge of a Gothic establishment"—which he proposed to abolish. Rejecting the traditional sinecures as "an inheritance of absurdity, derived to them from their ancestors . . . a long and unbroken pedigree of mismanagers that have gone before them," Burke made the radical argument that "when the reason of old establishments is gone, it is absurd to preserve nothing but the burden of them" ("Economical Reform," 303, 305, 279). More often, however, Burke (it is said) repressed this side of his personality and attacked all the more fiercely those who, like Hastings, seemed to exemplify it—in Hastings's case, partly by carrying out in India precisely the kind of rationalizing program that Burke recommended for England in 1780. Burke's more frequently expressed traditionalist and even Gothic sentiments reflected his conservative commitment on behalf of the traditional social order and his strenuous counteridentification with his aristocratic political patrons.[69]

Yet another interpretation attempts to reconcile these apparently conflicting orientations using Marxist categories. C. B. Macpherson argues that Burke defended the interests of capitalism, primarily by embracing the free market and the laws of political economy, and at the same time upheld the traditional hierarchical social order. He could do this consistently—though not without some rhetorical or ideological confusion—because the rising English bourgeoisie was at this stage still willing to accept the political leadership of the older aristocracy, and also because the leading English aristocrats, as improving landlords, had become capitalists themselves. In Burke's thought, natural law was made to coalesce with political economy, and the old idea of social hierarchy disguised the newer subordination of wage labor; in this way, Burke offered a traditionalistic defense of a society in which a "capitalist market economy" was already becoming traditional.[70] This interpretation, however, makes no serious reference to Burke's views on India. In particular, it cannot explain why Burke should have upheld the claims of the established Indian aristocracy, which, unlike the English, was surely neither a class of progressive economic modernizers nor a partner in a procapitalist class coalition. Criticisms of Macpherson's thesis that concentrate exclusively on situating Burke's thought more accurately in relation to the class structure and class ideologies of late eighteenth-century Britain are similarly unhelpful in clarifying his opinions on India.[71]

Finally, Pocock offers a more subtle reconciliation of the two sides of Burke's thought. Like many Englishmen over the preceding century, Burke is said to have abhorred "stockjobbers" or speculators in the national debt while admiring merchants and other productive participants in modern commercial society. As in Macpherson's interpretation, Pocock holds that Burke had no difficulty in defending both commerce and the older landed gentry, since in eighteenth-century England these two classes overlapped and jointly supported the Whig regime. Furthermore, Pocock argues,

Burke's eulogy of the "age of chivalry" (and by extension, similar Gothic passages) is perfectly compatible with this modernist orientation and not at all an indication of Romantic nostalgia. Burke accepted the findings of the Scottish historical school to the effect that "commerce is dependent upon manners" and that "the antient chivalry" had played a crucial role in softening the manners of the feudal nobility, thus initiating a process that led to the "polite" or "refined" commercial society of his own day. The threat to "our civilization" posed by the French Revolution lay in the revolution's contempt for the "spirit of a gentleman, and the spirit of religion," both of which had evolved in a direct line from the European Middle Ages, and which animated modern polite society (*Reflections*, 170, 173).[72]

Plausible and elegant as this interpretation is, however, it too faces a difficulty when we turn to Burke's views on India. The Asian equivalent of chivalry, the manners of the Muslim warriors and their descendants in the Indian upper classes, however cultivated and aristocratic, did not contribute to the development of a commercial society or even to anything resembling the modern European conception of politeness. In fact, Burke argued, it was chivalry and its offshoots that "distinguished [Europe] to its advantage, from the states of Asia" (*Reflections*, 170). Burke admired and defended the "ancient Mahometan families," but it cannot be for the reason Pocock says he admired chivalry. His "Gothic" passages on India cannot reflect the same historical analysis that they may well have reflected regarding Europe.

Let us return briefly to the specific episode that prompted this review of several interpretations of Burke's thought. Burke condemned Hastings's peremptory and drastic reduction of the nawab's household, even though he himself had sponsored a similar reform of the British royal household; he sympathized with the aristocratic Indian victims of Hastings's action and deplored the violation of ancient custom, though in his own "Economical Reform" he dismissed the claims of the officeholders and was scornful of quaintly archaic but wasteful practices. The cases so far seem parallel and Burke's positions thus contradictory. But there is an additional, perhaps distinguishing, element.

Hastings's measure, as Burke perceived it, was purely economizing; he was prepared to ruin a sizable part of the Bengal aristocracy simply because he wanted the funds that supported them. Burke's reform of the civil list and abolition of unnecessary offices in 1780 was likewise presented to the public as an "economical" measure, but in reality it was intended as a political or even constitutional reform of much greater significance. The possibility that the delicate balance of Britain's mixed constitution could be destroyed through excessive royal patronage and hence influence over the House of

Commons was a perennial Whig fear. Burke and his party believed that the independence of Parliament and its proper constitutional position were being undermined by the methods of George III and his advisers. The program to reduce the sinecures available to the Crown for such "corrupt" purposes, and Burke's lack of sympathy for those who were displaced, are thus understandable in terms of his larger political principles. As Burke put it later:

> My oeconomical reforms were not . . . the suppression of a paltry pension or employment, more or less. Oeconomy in my plans was, as it ought to be, secondary, subordinate, instrumental. I acted on state principles. I found a great distemper in the commonwealth: and, according to the nature of the evil and of the object, I treated it. (*Noble Lord*, 289)

By invoking "state principles," Burke claimed to be acting as a statesman, a status he denied to Hastings.[73] Economy for its own sake was not a sufficient ground for overriding prescriptive rights, demolishing tradition, and disrupting the social order. If such things had to be done at all, they required a stronger justification on constitutional principles than Burke thought could be given for Hastings's actions.

We have considered several facets of Hastings's despotism or tyranny, according to Burke's charges, manifested in policies oppressive of Indian society. The oppression was visited on subjects of the empire at different levels, both high and low. Burke registered a strong protest against the exploitation of the peasantry by Hastings's newly appointed and thoroughly mercenary tax farmers, with eloquent descriptions of the hardships and even tortures he believed had been inflicted on them. The bulk of Burke's concern, however, was with Hastings's more well-to-do victims among the gentry and landowners of Bengal who, as the principal property owners and the former social and political elite of the country, naturally had the most to lose from the imposition of the new imperial regime. As Burke asserted toward the end of his career, the principal merit to which he laid claim was in having "[endeavored] to screen every man, in every class, from oppression, and particularly in defending the high and eminent, who in the bad times of confiscating Princes, confiscating chief Governors, or confiscating Demagogues, are the most exposed to jealousy, avarice, and envy" (*Noble Lord*, 303–04).[74]

Burke's solicitude for aristocratic and propertied victims of revolutionary change is especially familiar from his writings on the French Revolution and its "confiscating Demagogues." Many of the things he said in that context seem equally applicable to the Indian case, and indeed, since most of Burke's analysis of Hastings's policies was carried out prior to 1789, it is plausible to suppose that Burke's attentiveness to the consequences of revolution in Europe was motivated by his awareness of the results of what he called the "revolutions" in Bengal. His unequivocal affirmation of the injustice of large-scale confiscations seems to apply to both cases: "I am unalterably persuaded, that the attempt to oppress, degrade, impoverish, confiscate, and extinguish the original gentlemen, and landed property of an whole nation, cannot be justified under any form it may assume" ("National Assembly," 30). This, he believed, was the aim of the French Revolution: "The great object of your tyrants, is to destroy the gentlemen of France" ("National Assembly," 54). And his account of the result—people unjustly deprived of their estates, "reduced from affluence to indigence, . . . driven from indigence to famine, and treated with every possible degree of outrage, insult, and inhumanity" ("Appeal," 84)—is virtually identical to his description of the fate of displaced zamindars and the pensioners of the nawab of Bengal.

Burke's pronounced concern for the "gentlemen" arose not only from the fact that they were most likely to be the primary victims of revolutionary policies, but also from his general approval of the traditional hierarchical social order, whether in Europe or in India. Burke believed that the landed aristocracy in Great Britain, at least, was the class most likely to produce disinterested and competent national leaders. Burke certainly did not have so favorable a view of the traditional Indian political system at the higher levels, but in India as in Europe he believed that the organic solidarity of local society depended on the leadership, in accordance with customary norms, of the traditional gentry. Disruption of the established order invited severe consequences for everyone, in India as in Europe:

> When great multitudes act together, under that discipline of nature, I recognize the PEOPLE. . . . In all things the voice of this grand chorus of national harmony ought to have a mighty and decisive influence. But when you disturb this harmony; when you break up this beautiful order; . . . when you separate the common sort of men from their proper chieftains so as to form them into an adverse army, I no longer know that venerable object called the people in such a disbanded race of deserters and vagabonds. ("Appeal," 169)

In Burke's view, the hardships suffered by the peasantry of Bengal followed from Hastings's violation of the traditional harmony, his replacement of the "proper chieftains" with unscrupulous new men intent only on extracting profits from the countryside.

Finally, Burke was particularly sensitive to attacks on the gentry because of the despotic implications of such policies. Montesquieu had emphasized that the typical moderation and lawfulness of European monarchies depended on the presence of entrenched nobilities, and other intermediate social bodies, that would resist the growth of arbitrary central authority in order to protect their own customary position and privileges. Under despotic regimes, by contrast, nobility was precarious: subjects could hold high rank under despotism only at the pleasure of the ruler, and rulers aiming at despotic power characteristically sought to eliminate intermediate bodies or at least their independence of the central government. As we shall see, Burke was a severe critic of Montesquieu's view of Asian polities, but on the general analysis of despotism and its dangers he agreed. As he summarized the accepted doctrine in an early work: "It is the nature of despotism to abhor power held by any means but its own momentary pleasure; and to annihilate all intermediate situations between boundless strength on its own part, and total debility on the part of the people" (*Present Discontents*, 259–60). Like Montesquieu, Burke thus deplored the violent actions of overpowerful European kings, such as Henry VIII of England, "a *levelling* tyrant, who oppressed all descriptions of his people, but who fell with particular fury on every thing that was *great and noble*" (*Noble Lord*, 303). Later, during the French Revolution, Burke emphasized that despotism or tyranny could take a democratic as well as a monarchical form, but its centralizing and leveling policies were similar. "Who but a tyrant," he asked, in basic violation of "the law of social union," would think of "casting down [men of exalted rank] from the highest situation in the commonwealth, wherein they were maintained by their own landed property, to a state of indigence, depression and contempt?" (*Reflections*, 205). Enjoying the fruits of confiscation while at the same time eliminating political opposition, despotic regimes set "a pernicious example, [teaching] the different descriptions of the community to prey upon one another" ("Letter to Depont," 10).

Comments such as these fit Burke's interpretation of Hastings's social policies as well as of various European episodes; indeed, some of them echo sections of his Indian speeches. This is perhaps most apparent in a passage in which the French revolutionaries were compared to "barbarous" conquerors, a passage that contains an explicit comparison to the Roman Empire and probable allusions both to Ireland and (especially in the "auction" reference) to the British Indian empire: their policy was

> to destroy all vestiges of the antient country, in religion, in polity, in laws, and in manners; . . . to produce a general poverty; to put up their properties to auction; to crush their princes, nobles, and pontiffs; to lay low every thing which had lifted its head above the level, or which could serve to combine or rally, in their distresses, the disbanded people, under the standard of old opinion. (*Reflections*, 298)

The charges listed are too sweeping for India, especially those regarding religion, which even Montesquieu had granted usually restrains despotic rulers. Apart from sporadic outrages, neither Burke nor anyone else ever accused the East India Company of seeking to destroy the religions of India, or for that matter of seeking to remodel the manners of the country. In these respects, the imperial enterprise fell short of the French revolutionary undertaking, in its social ambitions and in its ideological radicalism. Yet in his treatment of Indian property and of the propertied and aristocratic classes— the natural leaders of Indian society—Hastings manifested the classic features of both the despot and the conqueror.

Chait Singh and the Benares Insurrection

In the two famous cases of Chait Singh and the begams of Oudh, Burke accused Hastings of spectacular acts of oppression, not against whole social classes but against specific, high-ranking Indian personages, though widespread civil disorder and violence accompanied both incidents. These cases are noteworthy because they were the two charges of despotic or oppressive rule that Burke and the other managers of the impeachment selected to present in full to the House of Lords; they evidently believed that these episodes contained the most unambiguous and well-documented evidence of criminal conduct on Hastings's part, and that they were suitable for clear and dramatic presentation both in court and in the larger arena of public opinion. The Benares charge, which was the second of Burke's articles to be presented to the House of Commons, is also noteworthy because William Pitt's surprising support of the motion, indicating his decision that the vote on the charges should be nonpartisan, is generally thought to have ensured Hastings's actual impeachment by the House.[75] The more lurid charge regarding the begams of Oudh, on which Sheridan gave the major speeches, most captured the attention of the public and received its share of Burke's attention as well.

The holy city of Benares, "the capital city of the Indian religion" (*Fox's Bill*, 412), situated on the Ganges just beyond the border of Bengal, was the chief city of a district that was both wealthy and strategically important for the British. The East India Company had been on good terms with Balwant Singh, the raja of Benares from 1738 to 1770, who was effectively an independent ruler, though officially a vassal or tributary of the nawab of Oudh, and the company recognized the succession of his son Chait Singh to this position. In 1775 the new nawab Asaf al-Daula (the son of Shuja al-Daula) ceded Oudh's rights over Benares to the company by the Treaty of Faizabad, which reaffirmed the alliance Hastings had forged with his father. Hastings, and even more his council, were interested in securing British control over Benares as another buffer zone for the defense of Bengal. Chait Singh acknowledged his new sovereign, and an agreement was reached in 1776 on his obligations to the company, including both annual tribute or revenue and the maintenance of a military contingent.[76]

Two years later, with a war against the Marathas looming in India, and with news of a new outbreak of war between Great Britain and France received in July 1778, Hastings began putting military and diplomatic arrangements in motion for the defense of the Indian empire. Chait Singh was required to pay special war subsidies beyond his agreed-upon tribute, which he did reluctantly and tardily. In 1780 he procrastinated when called upon to provide the armed forces he was supposed to have in readiness. In the summer of 1781 an angry Hastings went to Benares with a surprisingly small military escort, determined to enforce compliance and impose a large fine on the raja for his recalcitrance. When he found Chait Singh's responses and demeanor to be insufficiently submissive, Hastings had him placed under arrest in his palace. This precipitated an insurrection among the raja's retainers and troops and aroused unrest throughout the city; several units of company soldiers were attacked and killed, Hastings himself was in serious danger, and Chait Singh escaped into exile, which proved to be permanent. British troops gradually suppressed the rebellion, which spread throughout the countryside of Benares and neighboring districts in Bihar and Oudh. A new raja was installed, though the government of Benares was henceforth to be under the close supervision of the company's resident. Another Indian principality that had fallen within the company's sphere of influence, through proximity to its original holdings, had, through a series of apparently unplanned missteps, been effectively added to the British Empire.[77]

Burke adamantly denounced these proceedings on a number of related grounds. The extra demands made upon Chait Singh were at variance with the company's formal agreement with him (another case of a treaty violation). During the confrontation in 1781, Hastings accepted a propitiatory gift from the raja (another case of a corrupt or at least illicit financial transaction), and then violated its spirit by continued harsh treatment. Hastings refused to negotiate or listen to reasonable pleas of hardship on Chait Singh's part, but simply made his demands in a peremptory and arbitary manner. The exorbitant fine that Hastings imposed to punish Chait Singh's delays was out of all proportion to the offense, and represented simply another attempt to supply a shortage of money by arbitrary extortion; in fact, Burke argued, all the various crimes charged against the raja were "pretended for the purpose of exacting money." Hastings's unjust demands, accompanied by publicly humiliating treatment of an Indian prince, provoked the violent response, which was a spontaneous and understandable reaction against intolerable oppression. Indeed, and most damning, Burke maintained that Hastings went to Benares "resolved on the ruin of the Rajah," that he had a premeditated and completely unauthorized design to provoke an incident that would eventuate in Chait Singh's deposition, thus opening the way to the domination and plunder of his dominions ("Articles of Charge," 376, 354–55 and passim). As Burke summarized the episode, it was an unmitigated series of injustices amounting to a conspicuous act of despotic rule that all India could not fail to observe:

> To urge unjust public Demands; to accept private pecuniary Favours in the Course of those Demands; and, on the Pretence of Delay or Refusal, without Mercy to persecute a Benefactor; to refuse to hear his Remonstrances; to arrest him in his Capital, in his Palace, in the Face of all the People;—thus to give Occasion to an Insurrection, and, on Pretext of that Insurrection, to refuse all Treaty or Explanation; to drive him from his Government and his Country; to proscribe him in a general Amnesty; and to send him all over India, a Fugitive to publish the Shame of British Government in all the Nations to whom he successively fled for Refuge;—these are Proceedings to which, for the Honour of human Nature, it is hoped few Parallels are to be found in History. (*Eleventh Report*, 345)

In addition to the main accusation of injustice and oppression, Burke pointed to several circumstances that in his view exacerbated Hastings's offenses. For Burke, it was important to know whether Hastings had violated the letter of the company's earlier agreements with Chait Singh. He believed he had, but there was some confusion on this issue. This was partly because the agreements appeared imprecise on certain key points, but more ominously, because the official records of the transactions in the East India Company files, as transmitted to Great Britain, appeared to be incomplete or altered. The rule of law as a check on despotic government, including the possibility of judicial or parliamentary review of executive actions, depends upon the accuracy and integrity of official records, a sometimes tedious matter to which Burke nevertheless attended. As in financial matters, so in his diplomacy, "it was the particular duty of the said Warren Hastings that all transactions with the country powers should be faithfully entered." Failure on his part to keep clear records was evidence of fraud or, in this case, "strong reason to presume that he did even then meditate to make some evil use of the deeds which he thus withheld from the Company" ("Articles of Charge," 338–39).

Second, Burke condemned the manner as well as the substance of Hastings's dealings with Chait Singh, taking this manner to be a significant indicator of despotism, which characteristically expressed its power through the humiliation of high-ranking subjects and officials. Hastings not only imposed unwarranted requirements on the raja, but "did deliver his demand in proud and insulting language, wholly unfit for a governor of a civilized nation to use towards eminent persons in alliance with and in honorable and free dependence upon its government." Subsequently, Hastings refused to listen to Chait Singh's entreaties, but sent troops "in a manner the most harsh, insulting, and despotic, as if to provoke that prince to some act of resistance" ("Articles of Charge," 342, 345). Burke held that the arrest of the raja was especially ill-judged in light of the sense of honor or loyalty that existed among the raja's subjects and entourage; and "the despotic style, and the extreme insolence of language and demeanour, used to a person of great condition among the politest people in the world, was intolerable. Nothing aggravates tyranny so much as contumely" (*Fox's Bill*, 416). Burke thus portrayed the Benares insurrection as a natural reaction against intolerable abuse.

Third, Hastings's actions throughout this affair were impolitic as well as unjust, which resulted in the failure of his own objectives. Through his bungling, Hastings failed to collect the payments that Chait Singh allegedly owed—a grave sin in the eyes of his employers, "who consider laws, religion, morality, and the principles of state policy of empires as mere questions of profit and loss." Such treasure as was seized in the aftermath of the rebellion was distributed as booty to the company troops who had to be called in, and did not cover all the costs of suppressing the uprising ("Speech in Reply," 11:296–97). Worse, by instigating the revolt, and by exposing his own person to great danger, Hastings had recklessly endangered company interests. Since, by his own admission, his death might have triggered a general insurrection against the British throughout India, he was guilty not only of the "slaughter and devastation which [actually] ensued" but also of "the imminent danger of the total subversion of the British power in India" ("Articles of Charge," 366, 372). In sum, the whole event was disastrous:

> The design on the Rajah proved as unfruitful as it was violent. The unhappy prince was expelled, and his more unhappy country was enslaved and ruined; but not a rupee was acquired. Instead of treasure to recruit the Company's finances . . . they were plunged into a new war, which shook their power in India to its foundation.

As Burke immediately added, of course, "the success is no part of my consideration" (*Fox's Bill*, 416). Success would not have excused an act of oppression. The outcome of the Benares episode, however, well illustrated a point Burke frequently made, that despotic government was often inefficient and counterproductive as well as unjust. Earlier, Burke had argued that in America "tyranny is a poor provider," and that a fair system of contributions would draw more revenue from the colonies than "all the impotent violence of despotism ever could extort from them" (*American Taxation*, 461). Hastings's violence on this occasion also proved impotent, showing once again that "arbitrary power, my Lords, is always a miserable creature" ("Speech in Reply," 11:322).

Finally, Burke protested against the mismanagement and distress of Benares under the British residents and their agents, who replaced the former regime. This was a predictable result of the sudden replacement of traditional authority by usurpers, whose authority was unavoidably arbitrary, yet inefficacious: "By attempting to exercise usurped and arbitrary power, all power and all authority become extinguished, complete anarchy takes place, and nothing of government appears but the means of robbing and ravaging" ("Speech in Reply," 11:354). As with the supplanting of old zamindars by banians as landholders in Bengal, it was also the predictable consequence of the sudden replacement of a traditional ruling elite by new men, whose motives were primarily mercenary. In his final impeachment speech in 1794, Burke reviewed the expulsion of Chait Singh in terms that clearly reflected his concurrent analysis of the French Revolution:

> Those who pull down important ancient establishments, who wantonly destroy modes of administration and public institutions under which a country has prospered, are the most mischievous, and therefore the wickedest of men. . . . The prosperity of a country, that has been distressed by a revolution which has swept off its principal men, cannot be reestablished without extreme difficulty. ("Speech in Reply," 11:308–09)

In Benares as in other instances, Hastings played the role of a revolutionary, albeit without a coherent plan or ideological principles. Some of the consequences were ones that Burke's theory might have predicted.

Hastings did not respond to Burke's charge in all its dimensions, but he did vigorously defend himself on what he took to be the central issue—his authority as governor-general of Bengal to make the demands that he made of Chait Singh and then to punish him for his failure to comply with them. His defense rested on an interpretation of Chait Singh's exact legal position and his obligations toward the East India Company, a matter on which Hastings and his accusers disagreed. Even before his return, Hastings feared that some people in Great Britain might believe that Chait Singh had been an independent prince, "that we had no natural right to his vassalage," and that, accordingly, Hastings had acted toward him on the basis of "the primitive law of nature," that is, sheer force.[78] This was not accurate. The company's authority over the raja of Benares, according to Hastings, had been duly acquired from the nawab-wazir of Oudh and had been lawfully exercised in accordance with the usages of the Mogul Empire. Burke certainly agreed that the company's relations with Indian rulers ought to be constrained by law and by respect for their customary rights. Burke denied, however, that India was a simple despotic empire; it was, he argued, "a Republic of Princes with a great Chief at their head [rather] than a Country in absolute, uniform, systematic subjection" ("Speech on Opening," 309). Thus, whatever rightful power Hastings may have acquired over Benares was subject to lawful limitations. Burke granted that Chait Singh, though a "prince," was a dependent and tributary prince under the sovereignty of the company, but like other such rulers in India, his obligations were specified in charters or treaties and could not be increased by the unilateral will of his superior.

What exactly was Chait Singh's legal position, and what powers did the company legitimately possess over him? On this matter the imperfect information available to Europeans on the complex and historically variable laws and customs of the Mogul Empire led to controversy. Hastings sometimes maintained that in accordance with Mogul practice (pending a parliamentary revision of the legal relationship), he possessed absolute, even arbitrary sovereign authority over the raja,[79] a claim Burke adamantly denied ("Speech in Reply," II:196–98). In other discussions, Hastings maintained that Chait Singh was not properly regarded as a "prince" at all, but was rather a zamindar or subordinate provincial official and landholder (though a notably wealthy and powerful one), and therefore that "every obligation of fidelity and obedience which is due from a Zemeedar to the superior Magistrate by the constitution of Hindostan became as much the right of the Company from Cheit Sing, as it had been due to his former sovereign."[80] As we saw above, however, the exact status of the zamindars of Bengal had to be elucidated by reference to European categories, and disputes could arise when conflicting categories (e.g., landowning gentry or appointed revenue collectors) were applied—though in any event a zamindar was clearly a subject.[81] Similarly, the European feudal category of vassal was occasionally invoked by both sides to explain Chait Singh's relation to the company, but this too was open to ambiguity. For Charles James Fox, speaking for the managers, he was perhaps a "great vassal," implying that though he owed allegiance, he was not subject to arbitrary power on the part of his superior lord.[82] For Hastings, the emphasis in the concept was on subordination and the obligations due from a vassal to his sovereign.[83]

Given Chait Singh's subordinate status and the company's legitimate authority, Hastings justified his conduct on two grounds. First, Great Britain and hence the East India Company were at war with dangerous enemies, and the "political necessity" of this situation dictated that extraordinary subsidies and assistance be required of those who owed "fealty" to them. Whether by the rules of European feudalism or those of the Mogul Empire, a vassal could be called upon to relieve the "pressing exigencies" of his sovereign, especially in wartime.[84] As he asserted at his trial:

> It will not be disputed that the subjects of every empire, generally speaking, are bound to contribute to the support of that empire in a time of war, and that the sovereign power, wherever it be lodged, has an unalienable right to call forth and associate for the public defence the individual strength and power of every member of that state.[85]

This must have sounded familiar to Burke, who had indeed disputed such an unqualified assertion of sovereignty when applied to America two decades before.

Second, when Chait Singh failed or even hesitated to respond appropriately, another, harsher set of considerations came into play. This was the first case of the "open defection" of a subject prince of the British Empire in India, and the whole future of the empire depended on a decisive response. Hastings held that he could not be seen to be negotiating, as if on equal terms, with a vassal in these circumstances, especially one whose behavior seemed to be "aiming at the total subversion of the authority of the Company." Rather, exemplary punishment was necessary—"an example which justice and policy required equally for the reparation of the wrongs which [our state's] dignity had sustained, and for the future preservation of its authority." Always sensitive to the importance of maintaining the appearance of power and firmness in what seemed at the time a precarious regime, Hastings asserted, "I have been the instrument of making known to all the Indian world the constitutional union and resources of our Government, and of proclaiming an example which will deter future attempts to oppose its authority."[86] In these statements we hear the voice, as in the events we see the actions, of a cool political realist obeying what he took to be the necessities of maintaining an empire; and while everything did not turn out quite as he had planned, Hastings was largely satisfied with the result.

Burke claimed that, even if Hastings had reacted in good faith to what he saw as pressing dangers, his doctrine was "subversive of all the principles of just government," since it empowered a governor to act in violation of property, law, and formal agreements merely "on his own private *belief* concerning the necessities of state" ("Articles of Charge," 379). Such uncontrolled authority was unacceptable under British conceptions of government.

In the Benares case as in others, Burke doubted Hastings's good faith, however. He interpreted Hastings's "plain speaking" on the necessities of empire as a mere pretext for the seizure of private wealth to pay the company's bills. Even granted Hastings's questionable claim that Chait Singh was not a prince, "but a mere Zemindar or common subject, holding land by rent," Hastings's view of the terms on which "a land-holder, that is a British subject, holds his life and property under the Company's government" remained extraordinary and disturbing. Hastings seemed to hold that

> at his *discretion* he may demand, of the substance of any Zemindar over and above his rent or tribute, even what he pleases, with a sovereign authority; and if he does not yield an *implicit unreserved* obedience to all his commands, he forfeits his lands, his life, and his property, at Mr. Hastings' *discretion*. (*Fox's Bill*, 413–14)

Not only was Hastings's attitude improper for a British governor exercising authority over British subjects, and contrary to British conceptions of property and legal justice; in addition, by condemning Chait Singh unheard, without due process, Hastings also violated the standards of "substantial and eternal justice" through his "despotic acts" (*Fox's Bill*, 414–15).

The Begams of Oudh

The sensational charges concerning the begams (or, as Burke sometimes said, the "princesses") of Oudh must be considered in the context of developments in that country. Oudh, it will be recalled, was a large Mogul province, in effect an independent kingdom under its nawab-wazir, just to the northwest of Bengal. Clive and Hastings had established a stable alliance with its capable though ruthless ruler, Shuja al-Daula, guaranteeing his defense and helping him to enlarge his dominions (Kora, Allahabad, and Rohilkhand) in exchange for his friendship. Their objective was that Oudh should serve as a frontier buffer zone protecting the company's holdings, especially against the Marathas. Accordingly, British troops were stationed in Oudh, their expenses to be paid out of that country's revenues.[87]

In 1775 Shuja al-Daula died and was succeeded by his son Asaf al-Daula, who was often described by British observers as weak and incompetent.[88] He did, however, resemble his father in proving to be a loyal and pliant ally of the East India Company, the more so since he owed the security of his throne to the company's political and military support. Worried about conditions in Oudh and about the reliability of an important allied state, Hastings began to inquire more closely into Asaf's regime and was disturbed by what he found. Shuja al-Daula had died leaving a large debt to the company, and his successor steadily fell more deeply into arrears, as his government ran an annual deficit. The zamindars and nobles of the realm were uncooperative, the ministers corrupt and inefficient. The "ill-disciplined rabble which [the nawab] euphemistically termed his army" was underpaid and mutinous.[89] Agreements were therefore reached that increased the British military presence in Oudh, first by placing British officers in charge of some units of the nawab's army, and later by stationing armed forces there under direct company control. The need to pay the costs of these troops in turn increased the already indebted Asaf al-Daula's financial obligations to the company. To alleviate this problem, British troops were used to impose order and assist in collecting taxes from recalcitrant landowners in various districts of the country, and the nawab's whole government increasingly came under the supervision of the company's resident stationed in Asaf's capital at Lucknow; this envoy of course received instructions from the governor-general and his council in Calcutta.[90] By a series of incremental steps, each with its own logic, and with the consent of the inept native ruler, an alliance between British Bengal and a major Indian state was transformed into a British sphere of influence and, gradually, into effective imperial dominance.

Burke and other critics of the East India Company believed that the expansion of the company's influence into Oudh was primarily motivated by a desire to plunder the country, and they blamed the continuing disorder and maladministration of Oudh in part on Hastings's policies. Since the readily available wealth of Bengal had been extracted and Bengal was

Asaf al-Daula, nawab of Oudh, by John Zoffany.
The reign of Asaf al-Daula (1775–1797) witnessed increasing
British influence over his government.
By permission of the British Library, London.

gradually being brought under a more regular and effective system of government, company adventurers, it was assumed, turned their attention to this neighboring region, where unstable conditions and indirect company rule created opportunities for quick profits similar to those that had earlier been available in Bengal.[91] Burke offered a striking synopsis of the imperial strategy that served company greed:

> The invariable course of the Company's policy is this: Either they set up some prince too odious to maintain himself without the necessity of their assistance; or they soon render him odious, by making him the instrument of their government. In that case troops are bountifully sent to him to maintain his authority. That he should have no want of assistance, a civil gentleman, called a Resident, is kept at his court, who, under pretence of providing duly for the pay of these troops, gets assignments on the revenue into his hands. Under his provident management, debts soon accumulate . . . until, step by step, the whole revenue, and with it the whole power of the country, is delivered into his hands. The military do not behold without a virtuous emulation the moderate gains of the civil department. . . . Tracts of country are delivered over to their discretion. Then it is found proper to convert their commanding officers into farmers of revenue. Thus, between the well paid civil, and well rewarded military establishment, the situation of the natives may be easily conjectured. (*Fox's Bill*, 407)

As the revenues of Oudh were increasingly anticipated and assigned to pay off the arrears owed the company (Hastings's main policy aim, according to Burke), "the whole civil government, magistracy, and administration of justice gradually declined and at length totally ceased through the whole of vast provinces"; civil disorder and economic decline ensued ("Articles of Charge," 118; "Articles of Impeachment," 202ff.). Nothing in the treaties with Asaf al-Daula authorized British control of his government or the interference in the "interior affairs of his country" that company personnel exercised; rather, Hastings had manipulated his debts and his military dependency to reduce him to "vassalage" ("Speech in Reply," 11:380–81). When, on one occasion, the nawab sought relief through a reduction in the costly military establishment, Hastings at first refused, using the "style of lofty despotism" toward an ostensibly sovereign prince (*Fox's Bill*, 406). The inroads made by the company in Oudh in five or six short years meant that by 1781 Asaf al-Daula was "a monarch deposed, in effect, by persons pretending to be his allies." And, in words that are remarkable for having been delivered in the year following the execution of Louis XVI, Burke asked, "Does the history of tyranny furnish, does the history of popular violence deposing kings furnish, anything like the dreadful deposition of this prince [Asaf al-Daula], and the cruel and abominable tyranny that has been exercised over him?" ("Speech in Reply," 12:24).

The famous begams of Oudh were the widowed mother and grandmother of Asaf al-Daula, imposing royal personages who resided with their large entourages in Faizabad. Although secluded according to custom, the begams, like some other high-ranking Muslim women in India, were not without political awareness and skills. A large income had been settled on these dowager princesses through a number of *jagirs*, or grants of the revenue from specified lands; they were also in possession of a large treasure that had been amassed by Shuja al-Daula and left with them at his death. Asaf al-Daula's chronic financial distress, and the company's demands on him to pay what he owed for the maintenance of the troops, made the begams a tempting target. In 1781, at Hastings's urging, the nawab resumed a large number of *jagirs* throughout his realm, including those of the begams, which he claimed as his sovereign right. Under continuing pressure, and with Hastings's consent and encouragement, he also demanded the transfer of his father's treasure to himself. When the begams refused this demand, military forces under British officers occupied their palace at the nawab's order; the soldiers held the chief eunuchs who administered their households in close confinement, and allegedly tortured them, until they revealed the location of the hidden treasure (or some of it). Of the perhaps 1 million pounds of hoarded wealth thus seized by force, most went to pay obligations owed to the company.

As one can well imagine, Burke raised various objections to these proceedings. In the first place, he held this to be another egregious instance of the forcible extortion or confiscation of wealth, in violation of property rights, to help satisfy the company's apparently unlimited need for revenue. There is no question that Hastings's need for funds motivated his part in the episode. Paying the cost of protecting Oudh with British forces was a continuing problem. Moreover, the incident of the begams followed upon a conference between Hastings and Asaf al-Daula, soon after the suppression of Chait Singh's revolt, and was in a way a continuation of the Benares troubles. Both incidents reflected the financial exigencies arising from the war against the Marathas, aided by the French, in which the company was then engaged. The nawab-wazir of Oudh was ostensibly the principal actor in the affair, though the company resident was on the scene throughout; Burke's charge was that, in his determination to collect undisputed debts,

Hastings condoned unjust and despotic methods, or even urged them upon the weak nawab.

In marked contrast to the emotional speeches of Sheridan and Burke on this topic, Hastings advanced a legalistic argument that the begams had no good title to the treasure. Granted that, in Mogul India, no clear distinction was made between the public treasury and the personal fortune of the ruler, the treasure nonetheless arguably constituted public funds to which Asaf al-Daula, the legitimate ruler, should have had access to pay state debts. If, on the other hand, the treasure were regarded as Shuja al-Daula's personal wealth, there was no clear evidence he had bequeathed it to the begams, and, according to Muslim law, they were entitled to only a fraction of it. In any event, the deceased nawab's creditors (such as the East India Company) had a strong claim on the estate left at his death.[92] Burke scornfully rejected this line of defense as contrived after the fact—"cut with the scissors from a Mahometan law-book" recently translated into English—in order to give legal coloration to the transactions. There was no evidence that Hastings had sought a legal opinion from Chief Justice Impey, or consulted the "muftis and moulavies" available to him for Muslim legal matters at the time. "Mr. Hastings . . . first seizes upon the property, and then produces some Mahometan writers to prove that it did not belong to the persons who were in possession of it" ("Speech in Reply," 12:38, 35). The lack of due process (if this was really a legal matter) and Hastings's transparent attempt to manipulate legal forms aroused Burke's antagonism.

The matter of the *jagirs* necessitated some explanation. "The jaghiredars, the holders of the jaghires," Burke told the House of Lords, "form the body of the principal Mahometan nobility" of India, standing beside the mostly Hindu zamindars, "the ancient proprietors of land." Falling back of necessity on European experience, Burke argued that *jagir* "signifies exactly what the word *fee* does in the English language, or *feodum* in the barbarous Latin of the Feudists." Like medieval fiefs, they "were given in land, as a maintenance: some with the condition of service, some without any condition; some were annexed to an office, some were granted as the support of a dignity, and none were granted for a less term than life." Finally, "by the custom of the [Mogul] empire they are almost all grown, as the feods in Europe are grown, by use, into something which is at least virtually an inheritance" ("Speech in Reply," 12:10–11). It followed that the *jagirdars* of Oudh, including the begams, had strong customary or prescriptive property rights in their holdings, either a life interest in the incomes they had been granted, or perhaps even titles to the lands as hereditary private property, analogous to the landed property in Europe that had developed from once conditional feudal tenures. In addition, the *jagirs* of the begams had been specifically guaranteed by the company in previous formal agreements. Thus the nawab's resumption of these properties was an arbitrary violation of vested rights, and Hastings, at whose behest and for whose benefit he had taken the action, shared in the offense.

Hastings could not deny that specific agreements, at least, had been violated. Rather, he asserted that the begams had forfeited whatever claims they had on the company by the hostility they had demonstrated toward it, in particular by fomenting rebellion against it. The unrest aroused by Chait Singh's uprising the previous year had spread into parts of Oudh, including districts near Faizabad, and Hastings maintained that the begams had deliberately tried to fan the popular disorders into a general insurrection that would drive the British from Oudh.[93] While modern historians' reading of the complex evidence on this issue has tended to uphold Hastings's claims, Burke and his colleagues blamed the disorders themselves on Hastings—on his bungling in Benares and on the widespread resentment against the exploitative conduct of the company's officials and troops in Oudh.[94] If Hastings believed the begams were guilty of rebellion, why had he bothered with complex legal arguments concerning the treasure? "If the fact of the rebellion can be proved, the discussion of the title to the property in question will be totally useless. . . . The law of self-defence is above every other law; and if any persons draw the sword against you, violence on your part is justified" ("Speech in Reply," 12:34). At least one of Hastings's arguments was fraudulent, and probably both were. At best, they were ex post facto attempts to contrive pretexts for oppressive acts: as with his consultation of Muslim law books, it was only after the assault on the begams that Hastings had affidavits collected that tended, primarily through hearsay and conjecture, to support the improbable charge that "the aged women before mentioned had formed or engaged in a plan for the deposition of their son and sovereign, and the *utter extirpation* of the English nation" ("Articles of Charge," 402).

It was far more plausible, Burke held, to view Hastings's policies in Oudh as simple acts of property confiscation, contrary to justice. The resumption of the *jagirs*, which Hastings had recommended to the nawab, was a "violent and unjust measure . . . subversive of property, utterly destructive of several ancient and considerable families" besides the begams, and productive of rack renting and social unrest ("Articles of Charge," 116). This policy fitted the general pattern of British meddling in Oudh, which had ruined the country and left not "one man of property and substance for his rank, in the whole of these provinces . . . which are nearly the extent of

England and Wales taken together" (*Fox's Bill*, 408). As for the begams, they had been summarily deprived of incomes that a peer of England could well comprehend (and envy).

Burke had always upheld property rights, including those of the nobility; but during the course of Hastings's trial the issue of political confiscations took on new importance, and Burke did not hesitate to point out to the lords the general threat implicit in Hastings's mode of ruling:

> If there is anything which will root the present order of things out of Europe, it will begin, as we see it has already begun in a neighboring country, by confiscating, for the purposes of the state, grants made to classes of men. . . . I will venture to say that Jacobinism never can strike a more deadly blow against property, rank, and dignity than your Lordships, if you were to acquit this man, would strike against your own dignity, and the very being of the society in which we live. ("Speech in Reply," 12:10–11)

Once again, the revolutionary acts perpetrated by arbitrary power both in Europe and in Asia bore a certain resemblance to each other.

Apart from the now familiar attack on Hastings's alleged violations of property, Burke's charge regarding the begams contained two other elements, both of which made a greater impression on his audience in Great Britain. First, Burke and his colleagues emphasized in dramatic terms the mistreatment of the begams during the invasion of their palace (though there was no physical harm done to them), and, more luridly, the torture of the obstinate eunuchs.

> To enforce this unjust demand [to give up the treasure], the miserable victims were imprisoned, ironed, scourged, and at last threatened to be sent prisoners to [the British fort at] Chunar. . . . They gave way; and thus were committed acts of oppression and cruelty unknown, I will venture to say, in the history of India. ("Speech in Reply," 12:65)

The violent intrusion into the begams' residence was a humiliating infringement on Muslim norms of propriety, especially for such high-ranking women. Sheridan in particular labored to convey to his English audience the seriousness of the offense in terms of local customs, especially those observed by "these great families, who, inheriting from their Persian ancestors, preserve a purer style of prejudices and a loftier superstition" even than other Muslims.[95] Isaac Kramnick has brought out the degree to which Burke's emotional accounts of the begams contain innuendos of sexual assault.[96] The similar treatment of the event in Sheridan's speeches, however, suggests that this was a rhetorical strategy agreed upon by the managers rather than a reflection of Burke's unconscious obsessions; in fact, Burke's focus on the begams as idealized and exotic female victims of aggression exemplifies his facility at playing to his audience's probable appreciation of Gothic literary conventions.[97] The rhetoric, however, was intended to convey a serious claim about oppression in an unfamiliar cultural context.

Although British soldiers were involved, the dirty work in Oudh was officially carried out on orders from the nawab. In Burke's view, however, Hastings bore full responsibility. He had instigated the episode by his demands for money; he had approved the specific policies; and his resident, whom he had ordered not to allow any "forbearance . . . until the begams are at the entire mercy of the nawab," actually directed the operation.[98] For Burke, the spectacle of "torture or cruelties, [which we] have banished from our courts of justice," being perpetrated in India by British officers and "all that gang of persons that the prisoner used to disgrace the British name," was intolerable ("Speech in Reply," 12:64).

Finally, both Burke and Sheridan dwelt on the shocking violation of filial piety involved in the nawab's attack on his own mother and grandmother, which Hastings had pressured him to carry out.[99] In the outrage committed on the begams, Hastings "did exhibit to all Asia (a country remarkable for the utmost devotion to parental authority) the spectacle of a Christian governor, representing a Christian sovereign, compelling a son to become the instrument of such violence and extortion against his own mother" ("Articles of Charge," 413). Such conduct was to be condemned under religious principles and custom, whether Christian or Indian. It was also unnatural, contrary to normal filial or familial sentiment. The willingness to violate natural relations in this manner was another trait that Hastings shared with other oppressive regimes Burke attacked: the Irish Penal Laws, which deliberately undermined families by decreeing that a Catholic son could automatically acquire his parents' property by converting ("Popery Laws," 437); and the French revolutionaries, who had, among other crimes, endeavored "to subvert those principles of domestic trust and fidelity, which form the discipline of social life" ("National Assembly," 54). In this way, Hastings's oppression of the royal family of Oudh indicated the deeply corrosive implications of the political maxims that guided his actions.

The emphasis Burke gave to the case of the begams of Oudh illustrates the special solicitude for victims of high rank that recurs in his political writings and speeches. Burke sometimes gives the impression that he is condemning certain policies or actions, especially revolutionary ones, primarily because the hardships and suffering were imposed on persons of aristocratic or royal status. Since Thomas Paine, some of his critics have accordingly charged that, "accustomed to kiss the aristocratical hand" of his patrons, he "pities the plumage, but forgets the dying bird."[100] Paine was probably thinking of the famous portrayal of an idealized Marie Antoinette in connection with the insurrectionary events of October 6, 1789 (*Reflections*, 169–70), a passage that invites comparison with Burke's descriptions of the mistreated royal ladies of Oudh.[101] Other examples of this theme can be found in Burke's Indian speeches as well. Burke deplored the pathetic situation and disrespectful treatment accorded Shah Alam, in contrast to the previous status of the Great Mogul. In particular, he accused Hastings of delivering Shah Alam into the hands of his Maratha enemies after the conclusion of the Maratha War ("Articles of Charge," 9:202ff.).[102] Burke offered a clearly idealized picture of the Rohilla chief, Hafiz Rahmat, "slain valiantly fighting for his country," and an affecting glimpse of his widow and children after the war, "begging an handful of rice through the English camp" (*Fox's Bill*, 393). Burke admitted he was especially sorry for the fate of Chait Singh, since "it is wisely provided in the constitution of our heart, that we should interest ourselves in the fate of great personages [who] are therefore made everywhere the objects of tragedy" ("Speech in Reply," 11:308). And, in addition to the begams, Burke sympathized with Asaf al-Daula, an Indian prince of high standing, who suffered the humiliation of being forced into a dishonorable course of action: "I do not know a greater insult that can be offered to a man born to command than to find himself made the tool of a set of obscure men, come from an unknown country, without anything to distinguish them but an usurped power" ("Speech in Reply," 12:23).

There is certainly some truth in this observation about Burke's work, but sycophancy is surely not the only possible explanation. Sometimes, no doubt, it was a matter of a calculated rhetorical strategy, in keeping with the teaching of classical rhetoric that the suffering of noble persons excites special pity.[103] This point has special force given particular circumstances. For example, in his concluding impeachment speech, Burke provided a seemingly interminable description of the indignities and hardships suffered by the begams and by other relatives and dependents of the nawab of Oudh after the expropriation of their wealth ("Speech in Reply," especially June 12, 1794). His decision to emphasize this episode of aristocratic oppression at this time may have owed something to the context, that is, to the preceding year of revolutionary terror in France that had put the fate of nobilities in his listeners' minds.

The rhetorical effect was possible, however, because of the feelings of horror and vicarious distress that Burke believed people naturally experienced when confronted with such events. We "sympathize with all mankind [in conditions of famine, degradation, and oppression] on the ground of the common condition of humanity which belongs to us all," Burke asserted; but "when persons are reduced from ease and affluence to misery and distress, they naturally excite in the mind a greater degree of compassion by comparing the circumstances in which they once stood with those into which they are fallen" ("Speech in Reply," 12:150). This operation of sympathy is a natural psychological fact, but it is the sort of fact that is significant in Burke's moral psychology and hence his political theory. "We are so made as to be affected at such spectacles with melancholy sentiments . . . because in those natural feelings we learn great lessons; because in events like these our passions instruct our reason" (*Reflections*, 175). Shared sentiments not only provide the necessary cement for a stable society; for Burke, natural feelings, at least when nurtured within a tradition, are the most reliable guide to trustworthy moral judgment.

Finally, Burke may have expressed more concern for wealthy or noble victims of oppression simply because such people, having more to lose and being the objects of resentment or fear, were the most likely targets. Wondering how to classify the revolutionary government in France, Burke cited Aristotle to the effect that "a democracy has many striking points of resemblance with a tyranny," including the tendency to "exercise despotism over the better class of citizens" (*Reflections*, 228–29 and n.). Likewise, Montesquieu's theory of Asian despotism held that the standard policy of despots was to suppress any established nobility or wealthy class that might prove independent of the central power and capable of challenging it. In situations of revolutionary upheaval or of emergent despotic government—and Hastings's regime in India counted as both—it was high-ranking individuals and the propertied classes who were most in need of protection. But concern for the aristocracy did not preclude concern for the common people as well. In fact, speaking of Chait Singh, Burke commented that "men of great place, men of great rank, men of great hereditary authority, cannot fall without a horrible crash upon all about them" ("Speech in Reply," 11:308). In a stable society, the prospects of the humble are linked to the welfare of their natural leaders and the propertied, and we have seen that Burke deplored the detrimental consequences suffered by the peasantry when the traditional elites in Bengal, Benares, and Oudh were overthrown. Burke's occasional focus on special cases of suffering among notables should not be allowed to obscure either his underlying political analysis or his more general sympathies.

Chapter Four

Necessity, Despotism,
and Law

The Argument of Political Necessity

In response to Burke's accusations, Hastings sometimes challenged specific allegations, for example, the Rohilla War atrocities. Sometimes he offered a legalistic defense, as when he dismissed the begams' title to the treasure. More often, however, he fell back on two general lines of defense that are of greater interest for political theory, appealing to *raison d'état* and to the prevalent despotic traditions of Asia. In this chapter we consider these two large and mutually reinforcing arguments and their ramifications, together with Burke's repudiation of them.

Hastings asserted that in order to save the British Empire in India and to rule it effectively, he was compelled to employ the power at his disposal in a forceful and discretionary manner, and that in so doing he was warranted not only by political necessity but also by the standard practice of arbitrary government in India and the unstable political environment there. In reply, Burke adamantly denied the thesis of oriental despotism and the permissibility of arbitrary power under any circumstances; he denied in particular that these methods were required for the effective governance of the East India Company's dominions. Rather, Burke insisted here, as elsewhere in his political philosophy, on certain principles of political morality, on the rule of law, and on moderation in the exercise of authority. Although in the Burkean conception of statesmanship there was a recognition of the need for some adaptation of political principles as understood in Europe to the Indian situation, in the final analysis, the prudence and flexibility required in a ruler had to be constrained by the demands of justice and the duty to promote the welfare of the governed. We have here, then, in the special context of empire, a striking confrontation between a capable, successful, and reasonably articulate political realist, and Burke, who, while himself a practicing politician familiar with the workings of power and interest, stands forth as a moralist and legalist. The clash of arguments between these formidable opponents gives Hastings's trial and Burke's speeches their deeper importance.

The concept or doctrine of *raison d'etat* holds that rulers or public officials, by virtue of their role and the circumstances in which they are placed, are sometimes justified in departing from ordinary standards of morality and legality in discharging the responsibilities of their offices. Since rulers pursue public, not private, ends, and since they are charged with responsibility for such all-encompassing and basic values as state security and public welfare, they must be free to act in accordance with their calculations of the most effective means to achieve these ends, even if this entails occasional violations of the standards of conduct that are appropriate in private life or in the routine course of public affairs. State officials are entrusted with the exercise of power, including the instruments of violence and coercion, and their task is to deploy the power at their disposal in a manner that will most effectively advance state or public interests. In doing so, they will encounter opposition, and they must therefore be willing and able to analyze situations and compete in the game of "power politics" in a wholly realistic manner: hence the doctrine in question is sometimes referred to as political realism. Since rulers regard themselves (and are regarded by sympathetic observers) as compelled, by the pressure of circumstances and the limited options available to them, to resort to actions that are unpleasant and morally questionable, they frequently appeal to necessity, that is, to the alleged necessity of such actions as means to the goals prescribed by their official position. Hastings, like other eighteenth-century politicians, usually invoked "political necessity" when defending his policies through an implicit doctrine of *raison d'état* or realism. In this, he and others were more or less consciously echoing Machiavelli, the most famous proponent of the doctrine, who argued that "as all human things are kept in a perpetual movement, and can never remain stable, states naturally either rise or decline, and necessity compels them to many acts to which reason will not influence them."[1]

Several other points from the Machiavellian version of *raison d'état* have a bearing on Hastings's situation.[2] First, this doctrine in its most familiar and influential form referred especially to foreign affairs. Even if the internal administration of the state can be conducted for the most part according to law and under norms of justice, it has often been held, officials responsible for the state's foreign policy cannot be so strictly bound. It is in the international field that the main threats to the state's security or very existence arise, and rulers must do whatever is necessary to defend the state against actual or potential external threats. Furthermore, the anarchic condition of international relations—the absence of enforced law and sometimes even of stable and predictable patterns of behavior—makes for a particularly dangerous environment that requires complex calculations and strategies for ensuring the state's long-term defense and well-being. The absence of effective mechanisms for the peaceful settlement of disputes, and sometimes of any basis for trust or confidence in the motives of rival rulers, renders a state official's position precarious and demanding.

As governor-general, Hastings was responsible for defending the East India Company's possessions in India (especially Bengal, but indirectly Madras and Bombay as well) against external threats, both from the French and from hostile Indian rulers. The environment in which he had to operate was, as he saw it, extremely fluid and dangerous; most native princes were unreliable or untrustworthy. Most of the acrimonious disagreements between Hastings and his council, and most of the charges that Burke later brought against him, involved incidents that occurred beyond the borders of Bengal or actions that were directly or indirectly related to his foreign policy, which was certainly more daring and more complicated than that of his predecessors.[3]

Second, Machiavellianism is sometimes associated with a belligerent and aggressive foreign policy. Machiavelli himself celebrated princes who successfully enlarged their states through conquest, and anyone labeled a "Machiavellian" politician might be suspected of similar ambitions. In its more restrained form *raison d'état* emphasizes the need simply to defend and preserve the state, but an active external policy, the calculated use of violence, and preemptive warfare are among the means that the doctrine endorses if they appear to be instrumentally effective toward this end.[4] Typically, realism differs from more idealistic doctrines in affirming the inescapability of conflict and the need to use force to defend one's vital interests in political life, and especially in international relations.

Hastings was certainly no pacifist. Burke accused him of seeking to extend the empire by force of arms, contrary to both company and British government policy,[5] and Hastings complained that he had been "represented to the public as a man of ambition, and as too apt to be misled by projects of conquest," a charge he firmly denied. On the other hand, he wrote, "I have ever deemed it even more unsafe than dishonourable to sue for peace; and more consistent with the love of peace to be the aggressor, in certain cases, than to see preparations of intended hostility, and wait for their maturity."[6] He admitted he could have adopted more cautious policies toward the Rohillas and the Marathas—"but this is not how the British name got such lustre in India."[7] An effective defense of one's state required an active pursuit of legitimate interests, vindication of all rights, and energetic action against prospective threats. Hastings unabashedly set forth this view of his foreign policy, especially his commitment to the defense of Oudh, in a letter to the prime minister at the close of his career:

> This Government [of Bengal] is now connected with a very extensive, and in some Respect intricate, System of external Policy. It has been wisely interdicted from engaging in new Wars; and it were happy if a Maxim so necessary to the national Repose could be uniformly and at all Times observed. . . . But the pacific, like every other System of Practice, must be received with Exceptions and with Qualifications. It must be armed for Defence, and it ought rather to advance against gathering Dangers on their own Ground than to await their Approach with every Advantage afforded them of Preparation and Maturity. There are also Cases in which Power may be displayed to intimidate without subjecting it to the Necessity of Hazard of actual Employment; and in no Case can this Use of it be so warrantable as in the preservation of a neighboring State from Ruin which stands between our own and an eventual yet distant Enemy.[8]

More details of this policy will follow. Here, Hastings defended his approach in the voice of imperialist realism.

Finally, Machiavelli sometimes suggested that rulers who practiced the methods he recommended actually served the welfare of the majority of their subjects by providing them with the basic desiderata of security and stable government. Machiavelli implied that princes often did this inadvertently, as a by-product of their quest for power and glory. His argument, however, referred especially to princes who were national leaders and founders or builders of nation-states; it seems doubtful that the argument applied to provinces newly conquered and annexed, at least before their thorough unification with the base country.

Burke maintained that the welfare of subjects ought to be not only the objective result but also the conscientiously pursued aim of all rulers, national or imperial, and he argued that such a concern took at best a distant second place to short-term profits for the East India Company. Protesting (in a private letter) against this widespread impression, Hastings affirmed that he had labored "to promote the happiness and prosperity of the people under our jurisdiction."[9] Noting he could have made a great deal more money in India than he did if he had resembled the other "indigent adventurers" who held office there, Hastings also indignantly rejected the suggestion that his own motives were mercenary. On the other hand, he admitted, soon after taking office, that he had "catched the desire of applause in public life," and felt an "honest ambition" to rule in India "for years to come."[10] Burke might have approved of this attitude: he sometimes spoke favorably of the ambition to excel (*Sublime and Beautiful*, 50), and he held that the motives of "fame and glory" were "sublime principles [that] ought to be infused into persons of exalted situations" (*Reflections*, 189). More cautiously, Burke at least granted that "a generous ambition for applause for public services," though not itself a virtue, could "supply its place in some degree" ("Sixth Article," 176). Could Hastings's ambition for fame as an empire builder, if genuine, have had at least beneficial side effects for the people under his power, as Machiavelli had proposed? The larger question of the effects of empire on India cannot be addressed here, but there seems little question that Bengal (and later the rest of British India) enjoyed greater peace under Hastings and his successors than might otherwise have been the case. The problem is that when Hastings did not see himself as a servant of the East India Company, he understood his duty to be the service of the British state, or of "the British nation in India."[11] If his personal ambition and his realpolitik redounded to the advantage of his Indian subjects as well, this was for the most part an even more indirect result than the Machiavellian by-product theory suggests.

It is clear that Hastings understood his role and the growth of the empire under his leadership in Machiavellian terms. What had begun as a commercial enterprise had acquired, primarily during his governorship, a definite "political character"; it had become a formidable system of military and political relations with the surrounding powers. He did not claim to be the sole "author" of this system, nor was it as a whole the outcome of any conscious design. "The seed of this wonderful production was sown by the hand of calamity. It was nourished by fortune, and cultivated, and shaped . . . by necessity."[12] As the responsible official, however, Hastings claimed to have grasped this necessity and responded to its dictates, with successful results. He had

> maintained the splendour of the national character in all its military operations, unalloyed by a single failure of success, or imputed error;

[he had] insured the blessings of peace, security, and abundance to the subjects of [the company's] immediate dominion, while [he] dealt out the terrors of conquest to the remotest enemies of the parent state, and of its own associate members; and while every other member of the British Empire was afflicted with the plagues of war or insurrection.[13]

In his initial reply to Burke's charges before the House of Commons, Hastings conceded that he had used "despotic" methods, arguing they were both appropriate and necessary in the despotic political environment of India. When this line of defense met with an unfavorable response, Hastings and his counsel decided to emphasize "necessity" or *raison d'état* at the trial, though of course necessity as it presented itself in the distinctive Indian context. This was no doubt a sensible strategy, designed to win favor with Hastings's judges, many of whom were themselves practically minded politicians; indeed, he might have done better to rest his case entirely on this foundation, avoiding factual and legalistic disputes altogether.[14] It was not a strategy, however, that was likely to dispel "that fashionable prejudice which ascribes every act of the government of Bengal to improper motives, and brands the authors with criminality."[15] One observer who shared the general antipathy toward the East Indian nabobs remarked to a correspondent that "Mr. Machiavel" was appearing as Hastings's counsel, and that his defense "rested rather on Machiavel's code, than on that of rigid moralists"—not a favorable impression.[16] Burke, although an opponent of overly rigid or doctrinaire principles in politics, nonetheless adopted the position of a moralist in opposition to Hastings's realism, and he might reasonably have expected to strike a favorable chord at least in the court of public opinion.

Raison d'état denotes the skillful adaptation of policy to actual circumstances in the pursuit of power or the defense of the state, and so we must consider briefly both the political situation confronting Hastings and the overall diplomatic and military strategies he framed in response. Hastings took it as a given that he was responsible for defending Bengal—and after 1773, as governor-general, all the East India Company's possessions in India —and providing them with the internal peace and security that would promote their commercial profitability and the welfare of the subjects. From this point of view, the company faced two main threats: imperial competition from France, and intermittent hostility from certain of the major native states of India. Since the enemies of the British could be expected to make common cause, the gravest danger lay in a coalition of these opponents.

In the eighteenth century, the consolidation of the British Empire in

India, as in Canada and the Caribbean, was in large part an offshoot of wars between Great Britain and France, in which India and other areas of imperial competition became theaters in a general armed conflict. During the War of the Austrian Succession and afterwards, in the 1740s, Clive defeated the forces of France and its allies in the Carnatic and reversed Dupleix's ambition to create a French sphere of influence in southern India. During the Seven Years' War of 1756–1763 the company eliminated French influence in northeastern India and acquired effective sovereignty over Bengal.[17] Hastings arrived as governor during a period of European peace, but he was always conscious of the possibility that future hostilities might lead France to try to regain a foothold in India. The outbreak of the American Revolution increased British vulnerability, especially after the defeat at Saratoga in 1777, which coincided with ominous French diplomatic initiatives in western India. The following year Hastings was not surprised to learn that a new Anglo-French war had been declared, once again putting him in jeopardy of attacks by European armed forces. The conclusion of Hastings's impeachment trial, and the rendering of the verdict (1794–1795), occurred when Britain was once again at war with France, a fact that may have enhanced his plea of military necessity in the minds of his judges.[18]

As the Mogul Empire disintegrated, its power devolved onto provincial viceroys who were, in effect, rulers of independent states. Of these, Bengal had been ceded to the company, and the Carnatic was closely tied to the British operating from their base at Madras. An alliance had been concluded, as we have seen, between the company and the rulers of the wealthy and populous state of Oudh. Of major powers, this left the nizam Ali Khan of the Deccan in Hyderabad, and the rulers of Mysore—Haidar Ali, who had been at war with the British in the Carnatic in 1767–1769, and his equally capable son, Tipu Sultan, who succeeded him in 1782. Most important were the Marathas, who controlled large, often rugged territories in central and western India and continually threatened both Delhi and the entire Gangetic plain to their north and east. The Maratha movement, a confederacy of Hindu chieftains based in Poona, in the district of Maharashtra, had originated in the seventeenth century as a Hindu revolt against the intolerant religious policies of Emperor Aurangzeb; historically, their hostility was directed against the Muslim-ruled states of the Mogul Empire, including Bengal, but they had voiced the intention to bring all India under their sway.[19] Hastings perceptively noted a militant (Hindu) national spirit in the Marathas that differentiated them from the mercenary and plunder-seeking armies more common in Indian warfare.[20] The great danger facing the East India Company in the 1770s and 1780s was that these three Indian powers, or even any two of them, might unite in a concerted attack on its possessions, and above all, that they might be urged on and joined in this enterprise by the French, who were still deemed capable of mounting a formidable naval and military offensive on the subcontinent.

These fears were realized during what is commonly called the Maratha War of 1778–1782, which constituted the most dangerous crisis for the British Indian empire since its establishment. The threat first appeared when a French envoy arrived in Poona in May 1777 and succeeded in negotiating an alliance with the Marathas, gaining access to a port on the western coast.[21] When early the following year a succession dispute broke out in the Maratha capital, and an anti-French faction appealed to the British for assistance, the local company authorities at Bombay agreed. Over opposition from some of his council Hastings seconded this decision and dispatched reinforcements, maintaining that the Maratha-French intrigues and the danger that would be posed by a new French military presence in India constituted an emergency that overrode previous treaty agreements between the company and the Marathas.[22] In July 1778, news arrived of war between Britain and France; the nizam invoked grievances against the company government in Madras; and in 1780 Haidar Ali aligned himself with the anti-British coalition and invaded the Carnatic. Initial military reverses both in western India and in the Carnatic, and the combined hostility of most of the powers of India, placed the British position in 1780 in grave jeopardy. By 1782, however, following military and diplomatic successes, the main threat had subsided, and Hastings left India in 1785 with the company's dominions secure and at peace.[23]

Hastings's policies took shape in the threatening environment in which he found himself as follows. First, he had to place the administration of Bengal on a more orderly footing and stabilize its finances. Immediately upon taking office, he was struck by the complexity of the situation, and he appealed to the directors for latitude in implementing changes: "Let me add that it is impossible for this Government not to commit errors. . . . Your affairs will run headlong to ruin if your servants are made responsible for every stumble which in the hurry of your affairs they may make against the forms of law."[24] A year later he reviewed the reforms and achievements of his first year—including some, such as the land settlement, the arrangements of the nawab's household, and the stoppage of payments to the Mogul emperor, of which Burke was to disapprove—and expressed confidence in the solidity of the company's regime in Bengal.[25]

Second, he renewed and strengthened Clive's alliance with the nawab-wazir of Oudh, seeking (successfully) to buttress Oudh as a strong and friendly buffer state between Bengal and the Marathas. This policy led to the seizure of Kora and Allahabad from the emperor, the annexation of Rohilkhand, and indirectly, the company's sovereignty over Benares, with the troubles attending the assertion of its claims there. The alliance with Oudh was concluded with Shuja al-Daula, who earlier had joined Mir Kasim in waging war on the company, and who, in the opinion of a member of Hastings's council, was "a Miscreant [such as] has not existed since the days of Nero."[26] This alliance thus exemplified the realist principle that a beneficial alliance can be formed on the basis of mutual interest regardless of one's partner's moral character or previous record. Later, under the weaker Asaf al-Daula, the alliance led to increasing British involvement in the internal affairs of Oudh, financial pressures, and the incident of the begams. In addition to the Oudh connection and parallel with it, Hastings favored continued support for the company's old ally the nawab of the Carnatic, including his forcible annexation of Tanjore, effective British control over the entire country, and responsibility for its military defense.

Third, Hastings went far beyond his predecessors in formulating a grand strategy to protect the company's interests and in making aggressive diplomatic efforts vis-à-vis the Indian states to realize it. Hastings took pride in this achievement, claiming upon his retirement that he was the first to devise a "system of established policy" for the company's foreign relations.[27] Although he regarded his efforts as defensive, his critics argued that they involved unnecessary and risky entanglements in the complex world of Indian politics, and that they led inexorably to costly wars and to unwanted expansions of the empire.

Hastings's military undertakings on behalf of Oudh constituted an activist foreign policy, as did his acquisition of control over Benares. All these measures were intended to construct a system of buffer zones around Bengal. In addition, Hastings sought new Indian allies on the basis of common interest: for example, he cultivated the nizam of Hyderabad, who had earlier been under French influence, and succeeded in winning his neutrality during the Maratha War through a conciliatory approach on some disputed matters. Rejecting the crude notion that it should be "the fixed policy of our nation in India to enfeeble every power in connection with it," Hastings advocated bolstering the "Sovereign of Hydrabad," who by himself posed little danger to the company but who could be useful as an ally.[28] Finally, he employed diplomatic means to exploit political weaknesses of the Marathas. He did not hesitate to involve himself in internal factional conflict at the Maratha capital,[29] and with more success he capitalized on the Marathas' vulnerability as a confederacy of independent rulers. Most

Warren Hastings, by George Romney, 1795.
This portrait was painted in the year of Hastings's acquittal.
By permission of the British Library, London.

important, his clandestine diplomatic efforts succeeded in winning over Mudhoji Bhonsla, the Maratha raja of Berar, whom he had courted as early as 1773,[30] and whose territory was strategically located in central India. Hastings devoted much effort to analyzing political circumstances and opportunities throughout India, and to strategic calculations of policy. The aim of the "general system" that he developed was, as he put it in 1777,

> to extend the influence of the British nation to every part of India not too remote from their possessions, without enlarging the circle of their defence or involving them in hazardous or indefinite engagements, and to accept of the allegiance of such of our neighbors as shall sue to be enlisted among the friends and allies of the King of Great Britain.[31]

Finally, Hastings, though a civilian, proved himself to be an energetic military commander as well as a diplomatist. He held that "the superiority which the English possess over the other powers of India is derived from two causes, the authority of their government, and their military discipline. . . . Every political measure ought to be carefully avoided that may have a tendency to weaken either."[32] Moreover, Hastings believed that an aggressive use of his military resources was frequently the best means of protecting British interests: "In a Word if you would employ effectual Means for obtaining Peace, you must seek them in the Terrors of a continued War, and in the Incitement of some greater Advantage to be derived from its Conclusion."[33] When the Maratha War broke out, some members of the Calcutta Council urged a cautious policy of retrenchment to defend Bengal. Hastings carefully calculated that Bengal was safe behind its frontiers, so long as the British navy controlled the Indian Ocean. He therefore overruled their objections and went on the offensive, dispatching several armies across India to relieve Bombay, attack the Marathas, and turn back Haidar Ali from the Carnatic. Thanks to capable officers and well-disciplined troops, these efforts proved successful. One of Hastings's initiatives in particular was decisive: a diversionary attack on Gwalior and other possessions of Mahadaji Sindhia was followed by negotiations that induced that important Maratha chieftain to conclude a separate peace with the company. Hastings's dealings with Sindhia and with the raja of Berar, which effectively split the Maratha confederacy, were among his proudest achievements as an imperial statesman, and allowed him to claim credit for bringing the Maratha War to a satisfactory conclusion. Hastings's belligerence can also be seen in his disagreement with Lord Macartney, the governor of Madras,

over the means of ending the Carnatic War. Macartney preferred negotiations with Haidar Ali, while Hastings insisted (successfully) on decisive
military victory.[34] He had stood up to the "necessities" that had presented
themselves; he had served the company and the British state and saved their
empire. This, in the final analysis, was the basis of his efforts to vindicate
himself and his career.

The Counterargument: The Rule of Law

Burke denounced "the odious maxims of a Machiavellian policy,"
which he associated with "tyranny" (*Reflections*, 176), whether they appeared
in a revolutionary upheaval or in imperial policy. Although it was conventional to repudiate "Machiavellian" politics in public utterances, Burke's
sustained attack on Hastings's policies suggests he was serious, and that his
position on this matter marked both a significant difference of opinion with
the imperial practitioner Hastings and an important element of his political
theory.

In the passage from *Reflections* just quoted, Burke argued that Machiavellianism offended people's natural (and generally reliable) moral sentiments, to which he also sometimes appealed in making his case regarding
India. The doctrine of *raison d'état* as the appropriate perspective of statesmen can be formulated in a manner that is more bland and respectable than
the notorious or odious maxims found in *The Prince*, but in any form this
doctrine is bound to clash on occasion not only with moral feelings but also
with general moral and legal principles that might be invoked as guides or
constraints on political action.[35]

Before exploring this conflict between *raison d'état* and moral principles, however, let us note a tension that arises within Burke's thought.
Machiavelli argued that a successful prince must know how to adapt his
conduct to ever-fluctuating circumstances (or "necessities"), always prepared to take advantage of favorable opportunities and to withstand unfavorable turns of fortune. It was the need for such flexibility in the face of
pressures emanating from an unstable environment that led Machiavelli to
insist that a prince could not afford to be bound by strict moral rules.
Although Burke did not teach that an effective ruler must "know how not to
be good" and be willing on occasion to violate justice, he did develop a
conception of statesmanship grounded in political prudence and opposed to
a rigid or doctrinaire adherence to principles, even those that were generally
right.

For example, political systems, according to Burke, grow or evolve incrementally, not according to large-scale conscious designs. Speaking of the American colonies, for instance, Burke pointed out that

> modes of administration were formed in an insensible and very unsystematic manner. But they gradually adapted themselves to the varying condition of things: what was first a single kingdom, stretched into an empire; and an imperial superintendency, of some kind or other, became necessary. Parliament, from a mere representative of the people, and a guardian of popular privileges for its own immediate constituents, grew into a mighty sovereign. (*Sheriffs of Bristol*, 231–32)

In this situation, the proper approach of a practical statesman was to further the process of adjustment to new circumstances, reforming and compromising as might seem desirable. The French Revolution revealed the dangers of attempting to impose entire new schemes derived from general principles, just as the dogmatic insistence of British governments on the abstract right of the sovereign Parliament to tax the Americans had led to failure in the 1770s.

Apparently like Machiavelli, then, Burke endorsed a standard of prudential wisdom for rulers, closely tied to experience; this implied the need for a certain amount of discretion in decision making and for flexibility in policy. In this context, it is suggestive that we sometimes find Burke, like Hastings, using Machiavellian categories in reference to Britain's "great *empire*, extended by our virtue and our fortune to the farthest limits of the East and of the West" ("Electors of Bristol," 97). And strikingly, in light of Hastings's defense, Burke too could appeal to necessity, as practical politicians grasped it, as a legitimate basis for deviations from principle: although hereditary succession of the Crown was a fundamental law of the English constitution, Parliament was driven in 1688 by "*necessity*, in the strictest moral sense," "a grave and overruling necessity," to permissible revolutionary action (*Reflections*, 102, 113). In justifying the violence employed on that occasion, Burke—like Machiavelli—even went so far as to suggest that true necessity provides grounds for just action. Paraphrasing Livy, he wrote: "Justa bella quibus *necessaria*" (*Reflections*, 116).[36]

How, then, does Burkean prudence differ from *raison d'état*, or from the Machiavellianism he condemned in Hastings and others? Sometimes it appears that the distinction is only one of degree. When Burke invoked necessity to justify the departure from legality—and from other principles he usually defended, such as order and continuity in political life—in 1688, he at the same time emphasized that such extraordinary measures were required only on rare occasions, in genuine emergencies, and could not be elevated into a rule of policy. Moreover, their scope should be minimized: in replacing James II, Parliament had striven to retain the principle of hereditary succession and other elements of the established constitution. In Hastings's career, the extraordinary had become standard practice: a whole series of questionable policies and decisions were defended in the name of imperial necessity; and Burke doubted, on his reading of the facts, that the legitimate security interests of the East India Company really necessitated any of the serious violations of moral and legal norms of which he accused Hastings. At this level, the controversy simply turns on differing assessments of the dangers Hastings faced—a matter on which opinions might reasonably differ, and a case where, on a Burkean view, deference should be afforded to the official with the greater local knowledge and experience.

It is possible, however, to distinguish Burke's idea of prudence in a morally qualitative manner from the *raison d'état* outlook he discerned in Hastings. On this interpretation, Burke's position was that, while public officials needed to have a degree of latitude in adjusting policy to circumstances and in dealing with genuine emergencies, and might be excused for occasionally overriding or relaxing lower-order norms, they nevertheless remained subject to higher-order moral norms, including certain fundamental constraints of justice. In deciding to prosecute Hastings (and anticipating his defense), Burke recognized that

> the Commons are too liberal not to allow for the difficulties of a great and arduous public situation. They know too well that domineering necessities will frequently occur in all great affairs. They know that the exigencies of a great occasion, in its precipitate career, do not give time to have recourse to fixed principles, but that they oblige men frequently to decide in a manner that calmer reason would certainly have rejected.

He condemned Hastings not for "errors and mistakes, such as wise and good men might possibly fall into," but for "substantial crimes"—offenses against basic principles of just rule that could not be dismissed as arising from differing policy judgments ("Speech on Opening," 274). Elsewhere, Burke also rejected "petty pedantic scruple[s], in the management of arduous affairs," and argued that "whenever the sacrifice of any subordinate point of morality, or of honour, or even of common liberal sentiment and feeling is called for, one ought to be tolerably sure that the object is worth it" ("Letter to Depont," 13). The sacrifice of higher points of morality would be presumably justified only by a more stringent test, if at all. Finally, in one of his best-known rejections of abstract right in favor of prudence, Burke said he was not guided by "what a lawyer tells me I *may* do, but what humanity, reason, and justice tell me I ought to do" ("Conciliation," 140–41). Burkean prudence was recommended in the spirit of magnanimity, as a reason for sometimes waiving legal claims and relaxing the imposition of duties and rules on others, in accordance with a broad interpretation of the larger values cited; he did not propose it, in the manner of Machiavelli, as a basis for violating one's own duties.

Burke thus opposed Hastings, and rejected his defense, in the name of certain basic principles of political morality. Actual success in building or maintaining an empire was not in itself a sufficient argument, since the exercise of power in any context had properly to be guided and constrained by "humanity, reason, and justice." Humanity in the political sense referred to the ruler's responsibility for promoting the welfare of the governed, which Burke accused Hastings of disregarding. Justice referred to his insistence that the rule of law provided standards for the limited and moderate exercise of governmental power, in contrast to the arbitrariness and despotic methods he accused Hastings of practicing, and that Hastings indeed occasionally claimed were necessary for an imperial official in his position. Reason and justice came together in Burke's invocation of the natural law tradition, which we shall consider in the following chapter.

The general idea of the rule of law—that public power must be exercised through general and publicly announced rules, that disputes both private and public must be resolved by impartial judges according to fair and settled procedures, and that legally determined personal and property rights must be respected—was a central element in eighteenth-century British political culture. Montesquieu had argued that lawful rule and "moderation"—the restrictions on governments imposed by adherence to law—were what distinguished European monarchies from oriental despotisms; the English Whigs with whom Burke associated himself took pride in the claim that they had implemented and reinforced this ideal (against absolutist threats) by means of various constitutional safeguards. The perspective of both Montesquieu and the Whigs suggested that lawful government was an unusual and precarious achievement when viewed in a larger historical or global context. It required vigilant defense against the encroachments of arbitrary centralized power, which often reflected merely the ambition of rulers but which could sometimes acquire plausibility through the apparent benefits it offered. Burke frequently expressed his unsurprising commitment to the ideal of the rule of law and to the institutions through which he

Edmund Burke, by Sir Joshua Reynolds, 1771.
Courtesy of the National Portrait Gallery, London.

believed it was realized in Europe. Among "the *real* rights of men" that he counterposed to those proclaimed by the French Revolution, for example, he listed, first, "a right to live by that rule [of law]," and characterized law as "beneficence acting by a rule" (*Reflections*, 149). The French revolutionaries, in Burke's judgment, were repeating the "vice of the antient democracies" in ruling through "occasional decrees" rather than through consistent law (*Reflections*, 327).

Hastings and his supporters would naturally have had no quarrel with such sentiments in reference to Britain or Europe; rather, their view was that matters were quite different in the context of empire and imperial competition, where arguments from *raison d'état* had force, or in the context of Asia,

203

where despotism had been naturalized. Thus, Burke's position is noteworthy for its insistence on holding the administrators of British India accountable to the standard of lawful rule. Speaking of America, Burke proclaimed that "the spirit of the English Constitution . . . pervades, feeds, unites, invigorates, vivifies every part of the empire, even down to the minutest member" ("Conciliation," 180). As a wish and a prescription rather than a statement of fact this applied to India as well, at least insofar as justice and legality were concerned. Hence, a few years later Burke asserted that "the political maxims of a heathen Prince" were not a fit model for a "christian Governor" such as Hastings:

> The subject of a free state scorned to be directed by the wisdom of a despot. . . . It was a tenet in politics which he ever had, and ever would hold, that all British Governors were obliged to act by law. In India to be sure it could not be expected that they would practise Magna Charta. But there they had the law of nature and nations, the great and fundamental axioms on which every form of society was built. These, in conjunction with the collected experience of ages, the wisdom of antiquity, and the practice of the purest times, formed a system which in every country was venerable and popular. And whoever in high and ostensible situations in India did not conform to a mode of Government thus eligible and indispensable, ought to be found defective in the radical duty of his station. ("Rohilla Speech," 109)

As a British governor forced to defend himself in a British forum, Hastings was clearly on the defensive in the face of such a widely attractive conviction. This was why he occasionally tried to uphold the legality of his acts, but this tactic only made him appear worse to his accusers: Sheridan denounced his plea as "a skulking, quibbling, pilfering, prevaricating state necessity—a state necessity that tries to skulk behind the skirts of justice,"[37] and Burke was as outraged by what he regarded as Hastings's perversions of legal forms (as in the Nandakumar trial, or in affidavits he presented in support of his innocence) as by his substantive acts of injustice. Hastings's real attitude, in Burke's view, had been expressed when he indiscreetly remarked that, in a dispute between the East India Company and an ally, questions about "necessity" would be "decided by the strongest." For Burke this was

> a dangerous and most indecently expressed position, subversive of the rights of allies, and tending to breed war and confusion, instead

of cordiality and cooperation amongst them, and to destroy all confidence of the princes of India in the faith and justice of the English nation. ("Articles of Charge," 100)

Hastings's impeachment and trial were themselves heroic efforts to vindicate the rule of law and justice as understood in Britain, in opposition to the rule of superior force, and to demonstrate to the world that the "laws of England" were not simply for the benefit of "the rich and the powerful" ("Speech on Opening," 278).

Hastings's lawlessness, in Burke's presentation, manifested itself in two ways—in relation to his Indian subjects and in relation to the higher authorities in Great Britain to whom he was supposed to be accountable. Many of the despotic acts that Burke charged against Hastings, including treaty abrogations and property confiscations, could be characterized as violations of legality and of the ideal of government limited by law. Most conspicuous in this respect, perhaps, was the treatment of Chait Singh, whose rebellion, Burke believed, was provoked by arbitrary demands, condemnation, and exorbitant punishment, all imposed without any semblance of a hearing or other judicial due process.

> Now, when any man goes to exact a fine, it presupposes inquiry, charge, defence, and judgment. It does so in the Mahometan law; it does so in the Gentoo [Hindu] law; it does so in the law of England, in the Roman law, and in the law, I believe, of every nation under heaven, except in that law which resides in the arbitrary breast of Mr. Hastings. ("Speech in Reply," 11:252)

In a similar spirit, charged with conniving at the seizure of the treasure in the possession of the begams of Oudh, Hastings asked the House of Lords to believe that these women had no legal title to this wealth. Burke vociferously objected to the propriety of having the lords make an important determination about property rights in such an arbitrary and offhand manner:

> No part of this tribunal is competent to decide upon their title. You have not the parties before you; you have not the cause before you,— but are getting it by oblique, improper, and indecent means. You are not a court of justice to try that question. The parties are at a distance from you; they are neither present themselves, nor represented by any counsel, advocate, or attorney: and I hope no House of Lords will ever judge and decide upon the title of any human being, much less upon the title of the first women of Asia, sequestered, shut up from you, at nine thousand miles' distance. ("Speech in Reply," 12:40)

Burke's point in both of these cases was the same: when the authority of government is applied, whether to punish an offense or to settle a dispute over rights, it must be applied in accordance with norms of procedural justice that are universally recognized; reference must be made to the relevant law, evidence must be heard, affected parties must be allowed to defend themselves, and impartial judgment must be rendered. One of the most disturbing features of the revolutionary capture of the government in France was that arbitrary measures were pursued with official form and force, and even given the perverse appearance of legality: "Government itself, which ought to constrain the more bold and dextrous of these robbers, is their accomplice. Its arms, its treasures, its all, are in their hands. Judicature, which above all things should awe them, is their creature and their instrument" ("National Assembly," 36). Similarly, Hastings used the power available to him through the British government and military machinery in India to attain his policy objectives without regard for the requirements of law and justice.

Finally, Burke accused Hastings of willfully violating the instructions of his legal superiors. As governor-general, Hastings was an employee of the East India Company and answerable to its court of directors in London; he was also subject to legislation enacted by Parliament to regulate the affairs of the company in India. Flagrant disregard for the rules of the larger system of authority in which his office was situated was, for Burke, another instance of Hastings's contempt for the rule of law and his despotic attitude toward the power entrusted to him. Admittedly, there was some ambiguity in Hastings's position, since he and his employers all found it convenient to maintain the legal fiction that the company was exercising powers that had been formally ceded to it by the Mogul authorities, under the continuing nominal suzerainty of the Mogul emperor. Thus Hastings was also in a sense a functionary of the Mogul Empire, and though in a candid moment he could remark to a colleague that official Mogul decrees were no better than "waste paper,"[38] he nonetheless occasionally appealed to the empire's "constitution" and usages—which he argued conferred arbitrary powers on provincial *subahdars* or viceroys like himself—when doing so served to justify his policies. For example, Hastings argued that the company's sovereignty over Benares had been legally ceded to it by the previous ruler, the nawab of Oudh. He naturally acknowledged the paramount authority of the British Parliament to prescribe rules (to him) for the administration of this territory, but since Parliament had not acted on this matter, he asserted that, as governor, he had legally acquired the absolute powers over Benares and over his new

vassal Chait Singh that the Mogul constitution afforded ("Speech in Reply,"
11:197).

Burke agreed that British rulers in India should respect the local laws
and customs: "We claim, that, as our own government and every person
exercising authority in Great Britain is bound by the laws of Great Britain,
so every person exercising authority in another country shall be subject to
the laws of that country; since otherwise they break the very covenant by
which we hold our power there." Burke denied, however, in arguments to be
examined below, that the laws of India conferred arbitrary power on rulers;
and he specifically denied, in the case cited, that the company could have
legitimately acquired "an unlimited power over the life, goods, and property
of Cheyt Sing.... The one [the nawab] had not a right to give, nor the other
to receive such powers" ("Speech in Reply," 11:233, 236). At this point,
however, the question of Hastings's obedience to law became inescapably
blurred, since it merged with the different question of which of several
possibly varying conceptions of law and justice properly applied in the
imperial setting, and with the further complicated question of the actual
content of Indian custom.

There was no question, however, for Burke or for Hastings, that Hastings was accountable for his compliance with orders from the company
directors and with the laws of Great Britain. As we have seen, Burke accused
Hastings of clear violations of rules respecting the taking of presents from
Indians and the awarding of contracts to his colleagues, and he called attention to other disturbing incidents as well. In the mid-1770s Hastings was
confronted by a hostile majority on his council, and he and they frequently
disagreed about both policies and personnel. On one occasion, Hastings
refused to obey an explicit order from the directors to install the council
majority's candidate (a political opponent of his own) in a high office of the
Bengal administration: he "resolved to oppose the lawful Authority of his
Superiors, and to exercise a despotic Power. . . . He directly set up an
independent Right to administer the Government according to his Pleasure." Hastings invoked various pretexts for this disobedience, including a
specious and disruptive claim that the parliamentary Regulating Act gave
him latitude in such a case to overrule the directors. In reality, according to
Burke, he was simply counting on having enough political support in the
long run to get away with it (*Ninth Report*, 322).

Hastings's high-handedness in this and similar cases was symptomatic
of a general attitude of high officials in India, who believed they needed
greater discretion to deal with local situations and who sometimes viewed

orders from London as politically motivated meddling. "Acts of disobedience have not only grown frequent, but systematic; . . . as to amount, in the Company's Servants, to little less than absolute Independence." On this matter, Burke also criticized the negligence of the company directors, who "suffered the most conspicuous, and therefore the most dangerous, Examples of Disobedience and Misconduct in the First Department of their Service, to pass with a feeble and ineffectual Condemnation" (*Ninth Report*, 307, 291). The systemic problem, which the Indian legislation of the 1780s was designed to correct, did not, however, excuse Hastings's illegal conduct.

Finally, though it was not a specific indictment in his impeachment, Hastings faced a general charge that his aggressive diplomatic and military exploits violated repeatedly stated official policy. During this period, it was the general view of both the East India Company directors and of British government ministers that further expansion of the Indian empire was likely to be both costly and dangerous, and throughout his tenure in office Hastings was under orders that prohibited new wars, diplomatic entanglements, and territorial acquisitions.[39] While formally acquiescing in this, Hastings was at the same time responsible for defending the company's existing possessions, and he consistently maintained that a creative diplomatic strategy toward surrounding Indian states, and a readiness to secure the company's claims and deter potential opponents by armed force, were necessary means to this end. A certain logic of empire, historically urged by officials on the scene over resistance in London, seemed to dictate steady expansion of British influence, if only to protect current holdings.[40] And as Macaulay later remarked about this period,

> the situation of India was such that scarcely any aggression could be without a pretext, either in old laws or in recent practice. All rights were in a state of utter uncertainty; and the Europeans who took part in the disputes of the natives confounded the confusion, by applying to Asiatic politics the public law of the West, and analogies drawn from the feudal system.[41]

Hastings regarded his superiors' orders as contradictory, and though he realized he would be open to criticism, he energetically pursued a grand strategy that clearly envisioned new alliances and military commitments.[42] Rohilkhand was conquered, Benares acquired, and control over Oudh consolidated. Although he blamed the initiation of the Maratha War on bungling by the company officials in Bombay, he took credit for prosecuting it aggressively to a satisfactory conclusion.[43] Hastings hoped that what he regarded as the success of his policies would earn him praise, but the appearance of belligerence and expansionism created uneasiness at home. Even before the impeachment, Hastings's political agent informed him that the prime minister was hesitating to recommend a peerage, since Hastings "had attempted to extend the British dominion in India, a system Pitt highly disapproved."[44] For Burke, Hastings's foreign policy as a whole was not only politically unwise; it was another case of his disregard for legal restraints and his lack of the moderation characteristic of lawful government.

Finally, the lawless attitude of an imperial governor such as Hastings posed a potential threat to the rule of law at home, just as the wealth and corrupt practices of the East India Company threatened to corrupt British politics. In India, and to a lesser extent in America, the exigencies of rule over colonies, in the context of international imperial competition, rendered arguments of *raison d'état* plausible and bred habits of rule that could have a detrimental influence on the norms of British public life. The effort to suppress rebellion in America, for example, led to a suspension of habeas corpus, not only for Americans but for any British subjects who had been out of the realm within a specified period. Burke regarded this as an insidious encroachment on the rule of law, worse even than a general suspension of habeas corpus.

> Liberty, if I understand it at all, is a *general* principle, and the clear right of all the subjects within the realm or of none. Partial freedom seems to me a most invidious mode of slavery. But, unfortunately, it is the kind of slavery the most easily admitted in times of civil discord; . . . People without much difficulty admit the entrance of that injustice of which they are not to be the immediate victims. (*Sheriffs of Bristol*, 198)

Policies pursued in India did not have any such direct consequences for the legal rights of Britons, and yet a failure to insist on legal restraints there could have similarly dangerous consequences for British governance. Burke accused Hastings of extensive "obscurity and inaccuracies" in the documentation of his financial transactions, which "constituted a just presumption of fraud"; Burke granted that "a minister in high office may use concealment" from "enemies of his master" and from subordinates, but assuredly not from his employers or legal superiors ("Sixth Article," 396). Likewise, in a more ominous case, Burke reviewed the irregular disposition of official company records pertaining to diplomacy and treaties with the "native powers" of India. In part, this reflected Hastings's desire to conduct his foreign policy independently of the not always amenable Bengal Council, contrary to "the act of Parliament by which he held his office"; it also later obstructed the legal right of Parliament to verify his account of his proceedings and to review his policies ("Speech in Reply," 11:392–93).

Hastings's methods of rule thus indicated a taste for arbitrary executive power in his apparent attempts to evade legal accountability, a fundamental principle of constitutional government in England. Hastings's insubordination was exacerbated by arrogance, which was alarming in an official wielding so much power. When the court of directors reprimanded him in connection with the Chait Singh affair, Hastings responded with a published justification of his actions that, in Burke's view, amounted to a "libel" on the directors ("Articles of Charge," 228ff.). Incidents such as these led Burke to urge the lords "to remember always that you have before you a question and an issue of law; I beseech you to consider what it is that you are disposing of,—that you are not merely disposing of this man and his cause, but that you are disposing of the laws of your country" ("Speech in Reply," 11:305). Hastings's trial was necessary not only to promote better government for India but also to vindicate legal and constitutional government in Great Britain.

Imperial Finance

Financial pressures underlay many of Hastings's questionable policies and, directly or indirectly, most of the charges Burke brought against him. His radical land settlement in Bengal was intended to increase and rationalize the regular revenue available to his government; he canceled Shah Alam's tribute in part to save money; he accepted several large presents from Indian notables and applied the funds (he claimed) to the company treasury in order to relieve financial exigencies; Chait Singh's rebellion was provoked by increased levies on him; and the pressure applied to Oudh during the reign of Asaf al-Daula, including the seizure of the begams' wealth, aimed at recovering debts owed the company. Behind these incidents lay Hastings's active foreign policy, including permanent military commitments in Oudh and elsewhere and the wars he was engaged in, and thus the need for money to raise and pay troops—since British military success depended not only on superior techniques and discipline but also on regular and timely wages, rather than the sporadic plunder expected by most Indian armies.

Upon departing from office, Hastings claimed credit for leaving the Bengal government not only secure but also reasonably solvent, despite having just waged a five-year war against the combined forces of the French, the Marathas, and Haidar Ali.[45] Later, at his trial, Hastings justified his extraordinary steps to raise funds by referring to the necessities of defending the empire, and especially the military emergency facing his regime in 1781: "Every measure of my administration was calculated to relieve the public exigencies."[46]

Government policies must be paid for with funds extracted in one way or another from the productive sectors of society. Burke acknowledged this mundane fact and appreciated its implications for the overall quality of a political regime. The coercive power in the hands of rulers could be used to extract resources from their subject population in violent and arbitrary fashion—one of the hallmarks of despotism. On the other hand, an orderly and fair system of public revenue or taxation, with due respect for property rights, characterized a legal and moderate regime; it was a necessary condition for a prosperous economy, and was likely to meet with voluntary acquiescence on the part of subjects. The additional requirement of more formal consent by taxpayers through a representative assembly, at least to new or extraordinary levies, was a long-standing principle of European government, though not one that Burke or others proposed for India.

The importance of appropriate forms and methods of taxation is therefore one of the themes of Burke's political philosophy. He listed "the collection of an effective and well-distributed revenue" among the "good things"— along with morality, religion, property, peace, and order—with which liberty must be combined if it is to be a lasting benefit (*Reflections*, 91). Returning to this theme in the final pages of *Reflections*, where he attacked the confiscations and other fiscal policies of the French Revolution, Burke went so far as to say, "The revenue of the state is the state. In effect all depends upon it. . . . It is therefore not without reason that the science of speculative and practical finance . . . stands high in the estimation not only of the ordinary sort, but of the wisest and best men" (*Reflections*, 351–52). Hastings, in Burke's judgment, fell well short of this standard. He greedily took bribes and concealed them "like a wild, natural man, void of instruction, discipline, and art," all the while persuading himself, and subsequently trying to persuade his judges, that he was an "eminent financier, a collector of revenue in new and extraordinary ways, and that we should thus at once praise his diligence, industry, and ingenuity" ("Sixth Article," 324). Apart from the private mercenary corruption Burke believed was pervasive in the East India Company, he rejected Hastings's appeal to public financial necessity and condemned his money-raising methods as impermissible.

Imperial finance, and especially the need to pay the costs of the empire's expansion and its defense against France, Britain's major European rival, was an unresolved problem of the eighteenth-century British Empire.[47] Costs incurred in fighting the French and the American Indians in the American theater of the Seven Years' War led the government to impose new taxes on the colonists, who, it was thought, should pay a larger share for their own defense; the consequence was that parliamentary intransigence and American resistance "[shook] the solid structure of this empire to its deepest foundations" (*American Taxation*, 46), provoking rebellion and the loss of much of the western half of the empire. Similarly and simultaneously, the military costs of defending the Indian empire created dilemmas for Hastings and led to extraordinary measures on his part. Like the Americans, the zamindars of Bengal and Chait Singh in Benares were colonial subjects from whom a British government attempted to coerce higher than customary taxes in order to secure these territories against attacks by France and its Indian allies, including dangerous traditional enemies like the Marathas. In contrast to America, resistance to this policy in India, including Chait Singh's armed rebellion, was easily suppressed, albeit with damage to the British claim to offer beneficial rule to its Asian subjects. In the background of both cases was the fact that, to the chagrin of British leaders, the costs of holding these colonies, at least in wartime, greatly exceeded the public revenues they generated, notwithstanding the profits that accrued to private parties; and since an adequate regular system of finance had not been developed, governments were driven to special, ad hoc, and harsh policies that aroused resentment.

Burke had become famous in the 1770s for his opposition to the government's tax policies in America. Deferring to the Americans' insistence on representation, and accepting their argument that the commercial restrictions they were under were equivalent to a significant tax, Burke advocated a system of voluntary contributions by colonial legislatures to imperial defense. By attacking Hastings's irregular methods of raising money, Burke was in effect criticizing the government (and the East India Company) for their similar failure to develop an acceptable fiscal system for India—although it must be said that he did not offer any specific proposals of his own in this regard. Burke denounced Hastings's policies not in the name of a right of representation (an issue that did not arise in the Indian case), but in the name of fairness, customary law and rights, and an ideal of nonarbitrariness in government.

Hastings complained that his supposed love of conquest and certain dramatic incidents of his rule attracted unfavorable attention, while his more solid administrative achievements went unnoticed; these achievements included rationalizing the company's salt monopoly and converting its profits from private to public use.[48] Burke's quarrel was not with such orderly reforms, consistent with traditional Indian law and practices, but rather with Hastings's less routine methods—his arbitrary exactions, his confiscations, his violations of customary property rights. For Hastings as for the French revolutionaries, conspicuous wealth of any kind was an affront to "indigent and rapacious despotism" (*Reflections*, 220), and a temptation to impermissible uses of power to pay public debts and to enrich the members of a politically dominant group at the expense of others. Regarding France, Burke commented:

> The great source of my solicitude is, lest it should ever be considered in England as the policy of a state, to seek a resource in confiscations of any kind; or that any one description of citizens should be brought to regard any of the others, as their proper prey. (*Reflections*, 263)

Hastings's policies in India aroused similar worries.

Burke often supplemented his appeals to principle with the argument that just policies usually turn out to be more effective and successful, whereas unjust ones are frequently self-defeating. If honesty is the best policy, as Burke, along with other optimistic thinkers of the Enlightenment, believed, it is dictated by political prudence as well as by morality. Hence Burke suggested that Hastings's treaty violations tended to destroy British "honor," that is, Britain's perceived trustworthiness as an ally, and thereby undermined the company's long-term diplomatic interests vis-à-vis Indian rulers. Burke maintained that the Maratha War had been caused by duplicitous and aggressive company diplomacy, including Hastings's attempted intervention in the factional intrigues at the Maratha court, in disobedience to orders prohibiting such risky entanglements. Hastings's complex, Machiavellian dealings with various Indian rulers backfired, since in the end they

> did fill the chief of the princes and states of India with a general suspicion and distrust of the ambitious designs and treacherous principles of the British government, and with an universal hatred of the British nation. . . . The said princes and states were thereby so thoroughly convinced of the necessity of uniting amongst themselves to oppose a power which kept no faith with any of them, and equally threatened them all, that, renouncing all former enmities against each other, they united in a common confederacy against the English. ("Articles of Charge," 248–49 and passim)

Burke also accepted Francis's view that Haidar Ali's destructive invasion of the Carnatic had been provoked by Hastings's bellicose policies.[49]

This kind of argument applied to revenue policy as well. Moderate and lawful methods could generally be counted on to produce more revenue, whereas Hastings's arbitrary methods, like those employed in America, were counterproductive as well as unjust. This claim rested on Burke's recognition of reciprocal relations between tax policy and proceeds and the general health of the economy:

> The prosperity and improvement of nations has generally encreased with the encrease of their revenues; and they will both continue to grow and flourish, as long as the balance between what is left to strengthen the efforts of individuals, and what is collected for the common efforts of the state, bear to each other a due reciprocal proportion. (*Reflections*, 352)

Burke's claim also rested on the proposition that the costs of enforcing an extractive policy regarded as illegitimate would tend to cancel out the gains it was designed to achieve. The revenue the British might raise coercively in America, Burke argued, would not even cover the costs of the military force required to suppress the colonists' resistance (*Sheriffs of Bristol*, 237). On the other hand, a lenient policy consistent with the dignity and freedom of the subjects would be more lucrative: "security of property" would "increase the stock" of the community, and "most may be taken where most is accumulated" ("Conciliation," 177).

Burke asserted that "tyranny is a poor provider. It knows neither how to accumulate nor how to extract" (*American Taxation*, 104), and the arguments for this view applied to India as well. Burke pointed out that Hastings failed in the end to collect the payments he demanded from Chait Singh; instead, he incurred the additional costs of quelling the insurrection he had provoked. More generally, Burke held that Hastings's revenue-producing arrangements, such as those he imposed in Benares after regaining control there, were a failure. Violating customary rights and expectations, they were met with passive resistance and noncooperation, which sheer coercive or despotic power was impotent to overcome: "No one dares to tell him a truth, no one dares to give him any information that is disagreeable to him; for all know that their life and fortune depend upon his caprice. Thus the man who lives in the exercise of arbitrary power condemns himself to eternal ignorance" ("Speech in Reply," 11:322). This argument had special force in India, where a small number of Englishmen were attempting to govern a large and complex country of which they had imperfect knowledge.

As a postscript, we may note that insofar as Burke upheld the prudence rather than the moral obligatoriness of a lawful and nonarbitrary policy, he was using an argument of the sort that Hastings as a political realist could appreciate. On occasion, Hastings even expressed agreement with the substance of the Burkean argument regarding financial (and diplomatic) matters. After defending his harsh treatment of Chait Singh as exemplary—necessary to deter future opposition—Hastings informed his agent that he was planning a more lenient strategy to recover the debts that Asaf al-Daula owed the company. He would not "divest him of all his rights, [merely] because I can do it; nor do I think it good policy; for I fear that our encroaching spirit, and the insolence with which it has been exerted, have caused our alliance to be as much dreaded by all the powers of Indostan as our arms."[50] In such a candid (though private) acknowledgement that he may have miscalculated somewhat the pressure he had applied to Oudh, Hastings was simply expressing the sophisticated realist's understanding that moderation in the use of power is sometimes the best route to political success.

Constitutional Government

A central tenet of the classical liberalism prominent in eighteenth-century British political theory was that the rule of law and other important values needed to be safeguarded by constitutional government. A constitution is a fundamental law that carefully prescribes the legitimate powers of government, assigns them to various offices, and specifies the procedures for legislation, for policy and judicial decisions, and for other exercises of public authority. At the same time, a constitution is an elaborate mechanism, characteristically incorporating such devices as a separation of powers among different offices or branches of government, and a system of checks and balances among them, designed to restrain public power and prevent the abuses that would be likely if power were excessively concentrated. A constitutional government is one that is arranged internally so as to be limited to its proper purposes and to appropriate methods. Insofar as constitutional rules have the status of basic law, or of customary practice equivalent to law, they establish the rule of law as a norm for the conduct of government itself, in addition to being a constraint on applications of official power to subjects. Constitutionalism in the eighteenth century was opposed to absolutism, which was in turn historically associated with the doctrine and policy of *raison d'état*. Burke's advocacy of constitutional government is thus consistent with his repudiation of both Hastings's appeal to *raison d'état* and his absolutist approach to rule.

The Revolution of 1688 had vindicated the position of Parliament as an authority independent of the Crown, and Locke had asserted the general desirability of separating a monarchical executive from a legislative assembly; the concept of an independent judiciary soon developed, as it became accepted practice in England that judges, though appointed by the king and speaking in his name, were not removable by him. Montesquieu praised this system of separate powers providing checks on each other as the institutional basis for liberty, the outstanding and distinctive feature of the English constitution, and this verdict was widely accepted by later eighteenth-century Britons. It is thus not surprising that Burke, who in this respect was a disciple of Locke, Montesquieu, and the Hanoverian Whigs, espoused the ideal of constitutional government. His best-known constitutional arguments were directed toward upholding the prerogatives and autonomy of Parliament, as opposed to the Crown, within the overall balance.

"It is not necessary to teach men to thirst after power," Burke said. "But it is very expedient that, by moral instruction, they should be taught, and by their civil constitutions they should be compelled, to put many restrictions upon the immoderate exercise of it." Hence the great difficulty facing a statesman was to consider "the place in which political power is to be lodged, with no other attention, than as it may render the more or the less practicable, its salutary restraint, and its prudent direction" ("Appeal," 158–59). This was not easy: "The machine of a free constitution is no simple thing; but as intricate and delicate as it is valuable. . . . A constitution made up of balanced powers must ever be a critical thing" ("Electors of Bristol," 97–98). Constitutional checks are necessary (negatively) to prevent ambitious men from aggrandizing themselves and abusing their power, and (positively) to assure liberty. In Burke's mind, they were also linked both to the mechanical conception of the control through balance or opposition of physical forces and to the classical conception of a mixed constitution, in which opposed social forces or interests are able to find expression through various channels and thence contribute to moderate policy making. In opposition to the French Revolution's centralization of authority in the name of the nation, Burke defended

> that opposition of interests . . . that action and counteraction which, in the natural and in the political world, from the reciprocal struggle of discordant powers, draws out the harmony of the universe. These opposed and conflicting interests, which you considered as so great a blemish on your old and our present constitution, interpose a salutary check to all precipitate resolutions; . . . they make all change a subject of *compromise*, which naturally begets moderation . . . and render[s] all the headlong exertions of arbitrary power, in the few or in the many, for ever impracticable. (*Reflections*, 122; see also 227)

The absence of checks and balance, or of constitutional rule in this sense, was an invitation to despotism (if, indeed, it was not equivalent to it), in which unlimited and arbitrary authority was vested in a highly centralized and unified sovereign. At the outbreak of the French Revolution, Burke revived the classical idea that despotism could take a democratic or popular form, or at any rate, that it could be exercised by demagogues in the name of the people. In Hastings's case, Burke invoked the more familiar notion of a despotic regime in which a single man, without democratic pretensions or institutional restraints, ruled his subjects by force, fear, and corruption.

Since these ideas were widely accepted among the political class in eighteenth-century Britain, it was natural that the English model of government should have been adapted for use in Britain's overseas dominions. Thus in Lord North's Regulating Act of 1773, the office of governor-general was created, and Hastings (already governor of Bengal) was retained. At the same time, a new Bengal Council was instituted, composed of the governor-general and four other members, which could overrule the governor-general's executive decisions by majority vote. Unlike previous company councils in India, the new councillors were appointed by the British government rather than the East India Company, an arrangement clearly designed to provide a means of oversight of company personnel (including Hastings) and correction of reputed abuses. The council that convened in Calcutta in 1774 included Hastings and another experienced Indian servant who tended to align himself with Hastings; the other three members, however, including Philip Francis, were strangers to India, favored by Lord North and the king. They arrived in Bengal evidently convinced of the corruption and oppressiveness of the existing regime. They immediately reviewed Hastings's prior policies (including the Rohilla War, the nawab's household, and the land settlement) in a highly critical fashion, and for the next two years Hastings was confronted by a hostile majority that frequently defeated his proposals and sent damning reports about the local situation back to London. Hastings recovered and largely retained the initiative in the late 1770s after two of his opponents died, but toward the end of his tenure in office his proposals and policies were again intermittently obstructed by new council majorities.

The Regulating Act also established a Supreme Court for Bengal, with British judges not associated with the company. The court was institutionally separate from both the governor-general and the council—though the first chief justice was a personal acquaintance of Hastings's. Thus, Bengal acquired an elaborate system of government whose threefold structure—governor-council-court—seemed to reflect the familiar separation of powers in Great Britain, with the chief executive's seat on the council paralleling the role of the king in the legislature at home.

In addition, Bengal was one of three geographically separated and largely independent presidencies or governments in British India; its nominal paramountcy over Madras and Bombay was undefined. Furthermore, all three Indian administrations were subordinate to the company's directors in London, and both the Indian governments and the East India Company as a whole were ultimately subject to the supreme authority of king and Parliament. It might thus appear that a multidimensional system of separated powers, and a number of checking mechanisms and opportunities for oversight and control that would satisfy a rigorous constitutionalist, were in place. Burke himself had supported the creation of the Bengal Supreme Court, and he relied on the dissident councillors, especially Francis, for information that could be used to bring Hastings to account. In Burke's view, Hastings nevertheless succeeded in wielding the power of a despot. The court's role in stemming corruption was disappointing; the company failed to impose appropriate controls on its officials in India; and Parliament only really began to investigate Indian affairs in detail in the 1780s. During much of his period in office, Hastings either enjoyed majority support in his council or could use his "casting vote" to break ties. Most of the major offenses charged against him dated from before or after the relatively brief period when he faced effective opposition. From Burke's point of view, then, the checks necessary in any government were not present, or were not working, in India; his eventual conclusion was that much more direct parliamentary supervision of the company's regime was required.

The theory of constitutional checks is generally opposed by the view that, at least in some circumstances, strong and discretionary executive authority is needed to provide effective and stable government. This argument might have special plausibility in relation to India, given the problems of ruling foreign territories in the context of military threats and imperial competition such as those that confronted the British rulers. Both firm governance of colonial subjects (including antitraditional reforms, if desirable), and the consistent direction of a foreign policy in terms of *raison d'état*, might be more successfully carried out by more concentrated, rather than more diffuse or balanced, forms of authority.

Far from agreeing with Burke's assessment of his position, Hastings frequently complained, privately and publicly, about the political obstacles he faced, and called for increases in the powers of the governor-general. The system under which the governor was only as strong as his support in council had been designed for conducting the business of a commercial company; it was a cumbersome method for exercising "the dominion of an extensive kingdom, the collection of a vast revenue, the command of armies, and the direction of a great political system." Emergencies required decisive actions, and therefore the governor should "have the privilege of acting by his own separate authority on such urgent and extraordinary cases as shall in his judgment require it." Consistency of policy, as well as a reduction in the temptation to make a quick private fortune, would be served by a longer guaranteed term of office for the governor.[51] Distance from London precluded detailed supervision of policy from above, while divisions and frequent turnovers of personnel interfered with coherent policy making on the scene:

> I affirm, as a point incontestable, that the administration of the British Government in Bengal, distant as it is from the reach of more then general instructions from the source of its authority, and liable to daily contingencies, which require both instant decision, and a consistency of system, cannot be ruled by a body of men variable in their succession, discordant in opinion, each jealous of his colleagues, and all united in common interest against their ostensible leader.[52]

Furthermore, Hastings complained, his powers as governor were not proportionate to his responsibilities. On one occasion, frustrated by council opposition, he remarked, "We want vigour and unanimity; and I possess but a single voice, though I am charged in all obnoxious measures with the sole responsibility." More ominously, Hastings recognized toward the end of his term in office that "the world"—or public opinion in Britain—"which never waits to listen to long stories, and which wants the understanding to discern the nice points of discrimination between acts done under a collective authority," would hold him alone accountable for any "calamities" or shortcomings of his regime.[53]

Pleas such as these for more concentrated authority in the governorship reflected Hastings's opinion of specific detrimental consequences arising from the divisions of power in the British Indian government. For example, in the late 1770s the Supreme Court came into serious conflict with Hastings and his council when it began to hear and act on complaints from Indian property owners regarding the revenue administration.[54] Hastings, invoking the same psychology of ambition that led some theorists to recommend a separation of powers, attributed this development to the judges' desire to expand their power by taking advantage of conflicts and hence weakness in the political branch of the Bengal government:

> The Love of Power in the Gentlemen of the Law is too notorious to be disputed, and Rome never saw a Pope that contended more vigorously for Supremacy than the Chief Justice hath done at Calcutta. The unhappy division in the Supreme Council gave the Judges an opportunity to extend their power beyond what the Legislature ever intended, and they eagerly seized the occasion.[55]

What a constitutionalist might have interpreted as salutary judicial checks on administrative power in the interest of the rule of law and procedural justice, Hastings viewed only as overall weakness in the imperial regime.

A second problem pertained to the coordination of policy among the three presidencies, separated as they were by great distances and a lack of procedures to give effect to Calcutta's ostensible supremacy. Although he claimed success in the end, Hastings complained that he had not consistently had the unified authority necessary to pursue "so complicated and so vast a plan" as was involved in his large-scale political and military strategy to assure the defense of the company's possessions. Actions taken by Madras had antagonized Haidar Ali and caused diplomatic tension with the nizam of Hyderabad; the major Maratha War had been provoked by diplomatic intrigues followed by military incompetence in Bombay: "I was forced into it. It began with the acts of others unknown to me."[56] Hastings sometimes speculated about what he might have accomplished if he had had more complete power:

> It is too late now to say what would have been the Issue of my plans had I not been counteracted by those whose Duty it was to support them. . . . [I should have raised] the British Empire in India to a Height of more splendid glory, and a Greatness more permanent than any foreign State ever yet acquired over remote Provinces.[57]

It is not clear that such ambitions would have been reassuring to Hastings's superiors in Great Britain, or that greater success along these lines would have contributed to his exoneration in Burke's eyes, given that official policy at this time was opposed to further expansion of the empire, and that many Britons were uncomfortable with notions of imperial glory.

Most often, however, Hastings complained about the weakness of his own position, and thus the weakness of the Bengal government as a whole, as a result of the council system and the factionalism manifested in it. The virtue of a government council or assembly (even if it does not represent the governed), according to classical constitutional theory, lies in its deliberative capacity or collective wisdom, and in its ability to check executive arbitrariness; its characteristic defects are slowness and inconsistency in decision, liability to corruption, and factional or partisan intransigence. On the other hand, a unified executive embodies the "principle of vigour, activity, and decision," in Hastings's words, which is needed somewhere in any effective government.[58] As the chief executive in British India, Hastings naturally upheld the claims of strong individual leadership, especially in a setting such as the Indian empire, and denounced the behavior of many of his councillors as obstructive, self-serving, and dangerous.

In the first place, opposition from the council led to inconsistencies and abrupt reversals in policy, and sometimes to inaction. This was especially troubling when it bore on foreign policy and security, which, Hastings held, should be the province of the governor-general.[59] Treaty obligations with Indian rulers were sometimes renegotiated,[60] and important appointees, such as the British resident in Oudh, were repeatedly replaced by fluctuating council majorities.[61] Even at a moment when a vacancy on the council temporarily gave him the power to carry his measures, Hastings protested to Lord North that he was reluctant to move decisively on pressing business "while I remain uncertain to whose hands the future execution of it may be committed."[62] It is noteworthy that Hastings's main opponent in Bengal, Philip Francis, expressed a similar dictatorial impulse: frustrated by dissensions in council ("not to be equalled by anything but a Polish Diet"), and perhaps imagining himself in the classical role of lawgiver, he too urged the prime minister: "We ought to have a Determination from Home, or one Man ought to be trusted with unlimited Power to give the Country a Constitution."[63] Defending himself in unusually harsh terms at his trial, Hastings placed his authoritarian prescription for the government of India within the clear perspective of imperial realism:

> In a government which is remote from the seat of empire, consisting of a small number of persons who are to govern, and in a country like India where a foreign yoke is to be imposed upon the people, and millions are kept . . . upon the thread of opinion, if it should ever unfortunately happen that there are divisions among those who are to govern, it must have an important effect upon all the operations of government in that country. . . . Those who are disposed to disobey and to avoid the demands of government will be induced to do it, when they can find any body in the Council that will support them in that opposition.[64]

Political opposition in a free or "popular" government such as that of Great Britain is natural and unavoidable, and perhaps even beneficial. Effective rule of an empire must be organized differently.

Second, Hastings believed that much of the opposition he faced represented not bona fide disagreements over policy, but sheer political jealousies and meddling, much of it emanating from home. Like any high-ranking eighteenth-century British politician, Hastings knew he had enemies, and that his position was vulnerable to shifts of parties or factions in London, both in the governing bodies of the East India Company and in Parliament. Hastings was remote from this scene, but his friends tried to keep him apprised of the strength of his own "party" and the intrigues of his opponents.[65] There was no doubt in his mind that the opposition of Francis and others was partisan in nature, designed to discredit and destroy him so that they and their supporters could gain control of the Bengal government and its patronage. Once again, Hastings conceded that partisanship, and the associated "Scramble for Power and Patronage," were normal in British parliamentary government, but he insisted that these practices were dangerous in India, where "the Governor or first executive Member should possess a Power absolute and complete within himself, and independent of actual Control." These were strong terms, as Hastings acknowledged—"an unpopular Doctrine, and repugnant to our domestic Constitution." Nonetheless, imperial necessities required effective and concentrated authority: "A Governor with limited Powers and a Council may subsist under an arbitrary Monarch directing it; but it cannot be too despotic for the Rule of a Province so remote of a free State like that of great Britain."[66] The presence of free and hence partisan government in the imperial metropole especially necessitated authoritarian rule in colonies, lest the disorders of free government pervade and impede the administration of the empire. This in effect was Hastings's response to Hume's argument regarding the governance of provinces by free states. Indeed, it was a vindication of Burke's concerns about the corrosive effects of empire on liberal ideals.

Finally, Hastings argued that divisions and conflicts within the British government in Bengal, especially those associated with the council, could be exploited by Indians, both subjects and enemies, who, though they might not comprehend political liberty in the European sense, were certainly adept at political calculation and maneuver. Hastings remarked that "every [native] state has a vakeel or spy in Calcutta" who was trying to assess weaknesses in the government and establish ties to particular officials.[67] Frequent changes in important administrative or diplomatic personnel invited resistance to company policies by Indians, as did Francis's practice of publicizing directives from England that revealed opposing opinions or breaches in Hastings's support.[68] More specifically, Hastings alleged that Chait Singh's recalcitrance was fostered, and his revolt thus indirectly brought about, by the "unhappy divisions of our government"; the raja's agents were in contact with Hastings's opponents on the council, who may have encouraged him in the hope that the governor-general would soon be recalled.[69] Hastings thus believed he had good reason for advancing one of the more familiar arguments for unified authority and official secrecy: the overt differences of opinion and internal opposition characteristic of a free government may seem to be a source of weakness with respect to the obedience of its subjects and vulnerability with respect to its external opponents.

For all these reasons, then, Hastings consistently maintained that the governor-general (himself and his successors) should have greater—even "absolute"—power, and a greater degree of discretion in formulating policy in response to local exigencies, and that he should be less liable to being checked or overruled either by a council or from England. In 1784 he informed the prime minister: "It has been the fatal Error . . . for many successive Years to degrade the Influence of [this government's] first Member, while its Success always, and its Existence sometimes, has hung by a slender Thread on his Exertions."[70] His resignation shortly afterwards was triggered by the news that his advice had not been heeded and that Pitt's East India Bill retained the council and strengthened government control over the company, an implicit censure of his conduct as governor. Hastings may have felt partially vindicated, however, when his permanent successor, Lord Cornwallis, accepted the office only on the condition that he be granted increased powers along the lines Hastings had advocated.[71]

Burke did not confront Hastings's arguments on these matters directly or in detail, and his general political thought reveals some degree of ambivalence. There are passages, for example, in which Burke acknowledged the need for strong executive authority in some situations, provided that the individuals entrusted with such authority exemplified the personal moderation and sense of responsibility for the public good that Burke looked for in all rulers. Criticizing tendencies to factionalism and anarchy in France, for instance, Burke pointed to the need for leadership in government in terms that Hastings might have appreciated: "The indecision of those who happen to rule at the critical time, their supine neglect, or their precipitate and ill-judged attention, may aggravate the public misfortunes" ("Appeal," 190). The Revolution had retained the king but had unwisely disabled him from performing the function of a chief executive within a balanced constitution: "A political executive magistracy, though merely such, is a great trust. . . . It ought to be environed with dignity, authority, and consideration, and it ought to lead to glory. The office of execution is an office of exertion. It is not from impotence we are to expect the tasks of power" (*Reflections*, 318). Burke astutely analyzed how the Revolution's attempt to divide the power over military appointments (the king's right to appoint was made subject to the assembly's veto) would lead to undesirable factionalism in this domain and the politicization of the officer corps (*Reflections*, 340), a concern reminiscent of Hastings's disputes with his council over appointments in India.

On balance, however, Burke's political theory is thoroughly constitutionalist. Statements in which he advocated strong leadership refer either to special circumstances or (most often) to the relative position of the executive within a constitutional framework. In an early work, Burke rejected the idea that the people should accept "discretionary" power when placed "in hands that they may trust." This was the standard argument "on which every mode of despotism has been defended" (*Present Discontents*, 302), and the argument supported the same tendency when invoked twenty years later by Hastings and his supporters.[72] The alternative to despotism was "a government of reciprocal controul" (*Reflections*, 241), that is, a government embodying internal checks, in which "all its several parts are so constituted, as not alone to answer their own several ends, but also each to limit and control the others"—hence a government, like that of Great Britain, in which "there is a perpetual treaty and compromise going on" ("Appeal," 194–95). Finally, we may note Burke's general view that "every good political institution must have a preventive operation as well as a remedial" (*Present Discontents*, 279). It should be designed so as to "exclude bad men" from office and deter abuses of power, and should contain built-in mechanisms (including impeachment itself) for correcting and punishing offenses after the fact.

Burke did not explicitly apply these general views on government to the imperial regime in Bengal, but there are a few indications that there, as in Europe, he regarded constitutional devices and procedures as a necessary hedge against despotism. Burke adamantly opposed the parliamentary bill of 1786 that increased the powers of the governor-general, since arbitrary power was contrary both to "the privileges of Britons, and the rights of humanity" ("Bill to Amend," 71). He insisted that Hastings could not justify his assumption of dictatorial powers, contrary to Parliament's intentions, by referring to the powers of his successor, since Cornwallis acted under different legal arrangements than had applied to him ("Speech in Reply," 11:273). Burke attributed some of Hastings's irregular financial transactions to his desire to circumvent the opposing majority on his council, thereby undermining the constitutional structure of authority that had been appropriately set up by an act of Parliament.

> The Law had placed the Sense of the Whole in the Majority; and it is not a Thing to be suffered, that any of the members should privately raise Money, for the avowed Purpose of defeating the Sense, or for promoting Designs that are contrary to it: A more alarming Assumption of Power in an individual Member of any deliberative or executive Body, cannot be imagined.

The spirit of constitutional government was also violated by Hastings's usual excuse—his continual effort to "criminate the Majority with Faction" and his insistence on the need for unified government: "No member of any Body, out-voted on a Question, has, or can have a Right to direct any Part of his public Conduct by that Principle" (*Eleventh Report*, 360). Burke further condemned the attempts of Hastings and his allies to interfere with the council's right (analogous to that of Parliament) to conduct investigations of possible wrongdoing in their past actions, on the plea that this should be left to the court. "The Power of Inquisition ought rather to be wholly separated from the judicial, the former being a previous Step to the latter, which requires other Rules and Methods; and ought not (if possible) to be lodged in the same Hands" (*Eleventh Report*, 374).

Even when such niceties of the separation of powers were observed, however, Burke was not satisfied with the results. He deplored the fact that collusion or mutual sympathy between company and judicial personnel, given "the present State of Power and Patronage in India," rendered the Supreme Court ineffectual in prosecuting corrupt practices. A counterbalancing institution had been neutralized by "a Confederacy to defeat the whole Spirit of the Law, and to remove all real Restraints on their Actions . . . between the [company] Servants, Directors, Prosecutors, and Court" (*Ninth Report*, 301–02). As a further check on official misconduct, then, Burke called for maximum publicity in the proceedings of the Indian government. "Every European government is [awed] by an audience formed of the other States of Europe," and restrained to a degree by the awareness that its actions are observed and judged by others. "But if the scene on the other side of the globe, which tempts, invites, almost compels to tyranny and rapine, be not inspected with the eye of a severe and unremitting vigilance, shame and destruction must ensue" (*Arcot's Debts*, 551). Publicity, upheld in liberal political theory as a virtual constitutional principle, would both facilitate parliamentary review of subordinate authorities and permit ultimate judgment by an informed public opinion.

Finally, Burke always looked not only to formal constitutional mechanisms but also to custom as a source of restraints on political power. Under reasonably stable social conditions, at any rate, the surest guarantee of moral inhibitions and just conduct in rulers lay in the traditional moral conceptions and practices handed down by the society around them and embodied in the accepted norms of governance. Even a system of constitutional checks was likely to work well only if it was the product of gradual evolution and was grounded in custom, as was the case in England:

> The parts of our constitution have gradually, and almost insensibly, in a long course of time, accommodated themselves to each other, and to their common, as well as to their separate purposes. But this adaptation of contending parts, as it has not been in our's, so it can never be in your's, or in any country, the effect of a single simultaneous regulation, and no sound heads could ever think of doing it in that manner. ("National Assembly," 68)

This doctrine, however, while generally valid, presented difficulties with respect to India. The social setting of the British regime there was not stable, but in flux, and was characterized by the clash of European and Indian norms and expectations. The East India Company had its own traditional practices, but Burke regarded these as corrupt; while tradition may be a generally reliable source of values, Burke knew that traditional institutions, like any others involving power, could be abused and twisted for private gain if precautions were not taken. In any case, as Burke, Hastings, and many others agreed, the customary administrative methods of a commercial company were no longer appropriate in the radically different situation that obtained once it acquired sovereign power. Therefore, although "sound heads" might worry about the prospects, and vested interests could be expected to resist and undermine reforms, there was no alternative but to impose a newly designed system of government for the new circumstances.

The Regulating Act of 1773 was the "single simultaneous regulation" under which Hastings had to operate. Given Burke's usual doubts about untried new schemes, he should not have been terribly surprised that the governor-council system did not work smoothly—there was no need to impute malice and sabotage to Hastings's opponents or to invoke the sinister possibility that the new arrangements were deliberately designed to fail.[73] When one has no choice but to try a new system, one should do so in an experimental spirit. Hence, when Burke became convinced that neither the company's methods nor the North system were working, he advocated and helped design the equally new and even more radical proposals of Fox's bill. A constitution of checks and balances grounded in tradition (as in England) is the ideal, but when this option is not available (as in India), a nontraditional system of checks and controls imposed to uphold the rule of law from above is the next best choice.

A final dimension of Hastings's impatience with the controls and checks imposed on him concerned the need, as he saw it, for the British to maintain a united front and so make a forceful impression on the Indians. Like Machiavelli, Hastings appreciated the fact that the appearance of strength is a source of actual strength, and that the appearance of weakness in the eyes of one's adversaries can be self-fulfilling, by encouraging resistance. Exercising real power *without* appearing to do so, and being able to disclaim responsibility for one's acts, may be useful Machiavellian techniques for rulers in some settings, for example in constitutional governments,[74] but the opposite strategy seems more appropriate in imperial governments. Indians—whether subjects, enemies, allies, or potential allies—scrutinized the conduct of the British, looking for signs of decisiveness and resolve or of vacillation and disunity. Hastings thus often suggested that the need for rulers to present an appearance of dignity, courage, and mastery was especially great in India (or Asia), the more so since a few Englishmen ruled by force in a country where the prevailing political culture enjoined particular respect for power and its accoutrements. The respect shown by Indian rulers for superior power, moreover, led them to ignore the European principle of trying to maintain a balance of power, and to gravitate to what appeared the stronger or winning side, as Hastings explained in an account of his diplomatic endeavors:

> Arts that proclaim confidence, and a determined spirit in the hour of adversity, are the surest means of retrieving it. Self distrust will never fail to create a distrust in others, and make them become your enemies, for in no part of the world is the principle of supporting a rising interest and depressing a falling one more prevalent than in India.[75]

The maintenance of an empire in India thus required the skillful cultivation and manipulation of the image of a powerful ruler, even if this was at odds with the legal definition of a British governor's office and called for occasional actions that were questionable in light of that office.[76]

Hastings sometimes made this point in connection with the internal divisions of the Bengal government. Besides the actual limitations of his power, he was concerned about the perception of these limitations by Indians, and their likely reaction:

> In a Country the Government of which hath been for ages absolutely
> Monarchical and its Inhabitants have never known nor can ever
> comprehend the Idea of any other form, such a Competition low-
> ers their esteem and Veneration for the Station of the Governor-
> General, and operates powerfully . . . to render it a shadow of an
> office.[77]

Burke charged that Hastings delayed in carrying out orders from London to
make certain unpalatable appointments so that it would not be so obvious to
the Indians that he had been overruled from above ("Speech in Reply,"
11:409–10). Similarly, Hastings complained in 1782 that criticisms of him at
home, including the censures issued by parliamentary committees on which
Burke served, had reached India and were weakening his authority by creating the expectation that he would be recalled.[78]

The role of appearances as a power resource was especially important
for Hastings in his foreign relations. His harsh and disdainful treatment of
Chait Singh was carefully calculated, he later claimed, to be exemplary in
the eyes of other Indian notables, as were the methods he used on that
occasion. Burke criticized Hastings, among other things, for his foolhardi-
ness in going on a punitive mission to Benares with such a small force, a
circumstance that may have helped provoke the revolt. Hastings admitted
later that he could have been killed and the entire empire lost, but he
defended his actions as designed to save face against the resistance of a vassal
and to create an impression of supreme confidence and power in his person,
which in India would have the effect of a "Talisman in the Arabian mythol-
ogy."[79] Subsequently, when the directors reprimanded him over this incident instead of backing him up, he complained that this would encourage
other rebellious subjects and asserted that, had news of the reprimand (and
thus the apparent blow to his authority) arrived in India a little earlier, it
might well have jeopardized his delicate peace negotiations with Mahadaji
Sindhia.[80] Looking back later, Hastings argued that his successful conclusion of the Maratha War, including the peace with Sindhia, was accomplished only as a result of the impressive show of strength by the company's
forces: "The vigorous exertions which we have made for the defence and
security of our possessions, have impressed an idea of our strength and
resources among the powers of India, which will, more than any other
motive, contribute to establish the present peace on a firm foundation."[81] In
the same spirit, Hastings asserted that even if the Maratha War had involved a breach of a treaty on the British side (which he denied), he would
not admit it publicly or make any concessions as a result, since "Confession

in the Language of India is an Acknowledgement of Weakness and an Entreaty for Forgiveness,"[82] and any sign of weakness could imperil the entire imperial enterprise.

In these passages, we glimpse Hastings not only as a determined and calculating practitioner of power politics but also as a Machiavellian politician at a higher level of sophistication, sensitive to the role of images in political contests and concerned to deploy the power at his disposal so as to maximize the appearance of his power in the perception of his adversaries, which in turn would be a means to increasing his actual strength. As we have seen, Burke was a critic both of the *raison d'état* that guided Hastings's policies, and of his efforts to circumvent the legal restraints on his official authority that jeopardized the image of power he sought to project to Indians. Since Hastings pressed the issue of appearances as a justification for some of his actions, we may conclude with a brief consideration of this theme in Burke, who, though he did not respond directly to Hastings's claims, was not oblivious to the role of appearances in political life.

In one passage, indeed, Burke spoke almost as harshly as Hastings of the need for a great state to be respected, and of the danger of humiliation (*Regicide Peace 1*, 193). His best-known comments on appearances in politics, however, have a very different import. Burke defended the "pleasing illusions" of the old regime and the "decent drapery of life," which he accused the French revolutionaries of ruthlessly stripping away in the name of abstract reason. He did so not only on aesthetic grounds, but also because the forms, rituals, and manners he had in mind had political significance. The desirable functions performed by these appearances differed considerably, however, from those Hastings sought. "Decent drapery" was needed, according to Burke, to obscure the usually violent and irregular origins of actual regimes that, having been moderated over time and providing good government, are entitled to obedience in the present. Further, "decent drapery" promoted human dignity by covering "our naked shivering nature." Burke's "pleasing illusions" disguised the actual exercise of political power under customary forms and ceremonies, but this pretense tended to have a self-fulfilling effect, moderating and softening government; the illusions "made power gentle, and obedience liberal . . . [and] incorporated into politics the sentiments which beautify and soften private society." Burke's aim in his appreciative comments on appearances, then, which was to disguise power and thereby help to restrain it, was the opposite of Hastings's, who sought to cultivate the appearance of power so as to augment it in reality. For Burke, the preservation of beautiful and accustomed social and political forms had the cumulative effect of generating legitimacy: "To make us love our country, our country ought to be lovely" (*Reflections*, 171–72). The imperial regime that Hastings built up in India was impressive, but not lovely; it was sublime, possessing the threatening overtones associated with that quality, but not beautiful; and its subjects obeyed not out of love but out of respect.[83]

The Argument of Oriental Despotism

Hastings's other major line of defense, in addition to the political necessities of empire, invoked the prevalent despotic traditions of the Indian environment in which he was situated. The states of India, he said, were and always had been despotisms, and therefore he had little choice himself but to adapt to local conditions and govern despotically, that is, by absolute and arbitrary power, both in appearance and in reality. Since despotic rule was the only type familiar to his Indian subjects, it was the only kind of government they would respect and obey. Since despotic attitudes and practices were standard among the opponents of the East India Company's regime, successful defense of that regime required the use of similar methods against them. Nondespotic—that is, lawful and restrained—government only works (he implied) if it is generally understood and accepted in the surrounding political culture and is practiced by one's rivals on a reciprocal basis. This was not the case in India. Finally, the legitimacy of despotic government in India could be defended in two ways. Formally, the East India Company had received its authority by a grant from the Mogul Empire, which, having a despotic constitution, conferred arbitrary powers on its *subahdars* or provincial viceroys. More generally, insofar as a government's legitimacy is generated by prescription or immemorial custom, a claim Burke himself often endorsed, Hastings could argue that deep-seated Indian traditional practices sanctioned his policies and techniques of rule.[84]

In one of his earlier (1781) speeches on Indian reform, Burke agreed with this general position. Probably influenced by Philip Francis, who accepted the common view that despotism was pervasive in Asia, Burke argued that any system of government had to conform to the opinions and manners of the governed, and he concluded with regret that the British had to govern India on Indian terms:

> It must always be remembered, that the genius of a people is to be consulted in the laws which are imposed upon them. They are to be adapted to the spirit, the temper, the constitution, the habits, and the manners of the people. The free system of Great Britain is consid-

ered by Britons, and justly, as the best and most beautiful fabric of government in Europe; but would the Indians think and speak of it in the same terms? No: Their habits were contrary, their dispositions were inimical to equal freedom. They were familiarized to a system of rule more despotic, and familiarity had rendered it congenial.

An important principle of British freedom was government with the consent of the governed, which in Britain was understood to require the representation of the people in the legislature. In India, paradoxically, the people appeared to consent to their traditional "mental slavery," and nontyrannical government there also had to accede to popular sentiments:

> [If the Indians] love their old constitution, arbitrary and despotic as it is, better than the beautiful and free system of British legislation, what must be done? must we abandon the government of the country rather than agree to rule over them by laws inimical to ourselves? Surely not: men must be governed by those laws which they love. Where thirty millions are to be governed by a few thousand men, the government must be established by consent, and must be congenial to the feelings and to the habits of the people. That which creates tyranny is the imposition of a form of government contrary to the will of the governed. ("Bengal Judicature," 140–41)

Burke continued to adhere to the general principle enunciated here, that countries (including India) should be governed substantially in accordance with the traditions and beliefs of the people; nor did he ever imagine that "freedom" as understood and practiced in Great Britain would be appropriate to India. After more detailed study of Indian affairs, however, he did change his mind on the nature of that country's institutions, arriving ultimately at a decisive and remarkable rejection of the "despotic" thesis. Two years after the speech just quoted, Burke condemned Hastings's plea that his occasional disobedience of orders was necessitated by the need to maintain the appearance of unlimited authority, and rejected his appeal to local custom as cynical and self-serving (*Ninth Report*, 323–25). By the time of the impeachment trial, Burke was denying at length that Hastings's despotic methods of rule were either required or justified by the traditions of India, and he professed to find the governor-general's open defense of "Arbitrary Power" both unprecedented and shocking ("Speech on Opening," 374–75). We will return to Burke's response after further consideration of Hasting's argument.

Hastings could reasonably have expected broad support for his position because of the powerful influence of Montesquieu on the political thinking of the later eighteenth century, among a wide public as well as among philosophers and scholars. Montesquieu made the case, accepted by Burke, Hastings, and most other thoughtful people and statesmen of the period, that laws and political institutions had to be suited to the people to whom they applied, and had to correspond to a variety of prevailing social and cultural circumstances, which he characterized as the "general spirit" of a country. (Only when this assumption was dropped in the nineteenth century was the British imperial mission reconceived as one of transforming and modernizing Indian society.) Furthermore, Montesquieu gave the concept "despotism" unprecedented currency as a central category of his political theory.[85]

Montesquieu was especially concerned to draw a contrast between European monarchies and despotic governments. In the standard European case, kings or central governments were limited in power by the presence of "intermediate bodies," such as nobilities and corporations having well-established legal rights and privileges, and were thereby constrained to rule in a moderate and lawful fashion. In despotic regimes, by contrast, a ruler possessed unchecked and arbitrary power.[86] Although Montesquieu's main purpose was to warn of the danger of despotic tendencies in some European states (such as Spain and even France), he revived and elaborated the ancient Greek idea that despotism was typical of Asia, and supported this thesis with extensive evidence provided by recent European travelers and sojourners in the major Asian countries, from Turkey to India to Japan. Oriental despotism, in Montesquieu's presentation, like European monarchy and ancient republicanism, was not simply a form of government but was a system embracing a distinctive social structure and characteristic manners and attitudes. Although the routine life of the masses proceeded in accordance with custom and religion, which upheld the ruler's absolute authority, the despot's arbitrary will was law, which meant that the regime was unstable and in effect lawless, especially at higher social levels.[87] In contrast to the status of European nobles, the position of the despot's officials, who served at his pleasure, was insecure; laws and legal procedure were simple and subject to the ruler's whim; personal and property rights were precarious or, in extreme cases, nonexistent.[88] Aristotle had asserted that barbarians, being "slavish" by nature, tended to acquiesce in the rule of despotic monarchs, who thus enjoyed legitimacy based on consent as well as custom—a view echoed by Burke in his 1781 speech cited above. In contrast, Montesquieu argued that the sustaining "principle" of despotism, in addition to entrenched custom, was the fear that arose from unchecked and often violent power; such rule was justified, he implied, only in the sense that it was determined and inescapable under certain conditions.

Hastings clearly accepted the thesis that despotism was widespread in the Orient, and that government there, as he more often put it, was both absolute and arbitrary. Although some amelioration of conditions could be expected from British governance, especially an increase in prosperity in consequence of greater security and a more regular administration, the British governors had little choice, particularly at first, but to conform to this tradition. An open defense of arbitrary power was unpalatable in Europe and especially in England, where the existing regime had been founded in a revolutionary repudiation of monarchical absolutism in favor of a "government of laws," and where the attitude of harsh imperialist realism—which had recently backfired in America—was not yet widespread. Hence Hastings was at a certain disadvantage in making this argument, as he did most notably at his appearance before the House of Commons on May 1–2, 1786, notwithstanding the familiarity of Montesquieu's view of Asia; and later the managers of his impeachment quoted some of his stronger statements as shockingly inappropriate for a British official.[89]

Despotism prevailed and was "every where the same, from Cabool to Assam," Hastings asserted. "The whole History of Asia is nothing more than Precedents to prove the invariable Exercise of Arbitrary Power."[90] "Sovereignty in India is a very different thing from European ideas of sovereignty," Hastings explained. "Sovereignty in India means arbitrary power and nothing else." "I know not how we can deny the Existence of many *despotic Principles* in the *Mogul* System of Government, but wherever *those* exist the *Powers* of the Prince will be every Thing, and the *Rights* of the subject nothing."[91] Since he was called upon to govern in this environment, he too was "possessed of an arbitrary and despotic power, restrained by no laws but his own will" (paraphrased by Burke, "Speech in Reply," 11:195).

These opinions were unacceptable to Burke, in reference to India or anywhere else; indeed, they were "repugnant to any principles of government that he had ever heard of" ("Rohilla Speech," 107). Hastings, he said, sought to appear before Parliament "not as a British Governor, answering to a British Tribunal, but as a Soubahdar, as a Bashaw of three tails. He says: I had an arbitrary power to exercise; I exercised it. Slaves I found the people; slaves they are." Unfortunately for him, such a plea grounded in "Oriental principles" was unknown to the laws of England, and the peers of Great Britain, Burke confidently proclaimed, would "sympathize with the Commons in their detestation of such doctrine" ("Speech on Opening," 346–47).

In addition to the general plea, Hastings's arguments invoked or im-

plied several variations on the theme of despotism as constraining his imperial policy. In the modern revival of the Greek concept, some theorists,
notably Hobbes, had defined despotism as a conquest regime, and had
derived its absolutist character from the original submission of the conquered to the conqueror.[92] Montesquieu, more concerned with the social
and systemic qualities of the regime rather than its origin, did not emphasize this point, but he did note that the contemporary despotic regimes of
southern Asia had been established through the highly destructive conquests of the Tartars, who (unlike the Germanic invaders of the Roman
Empire) were themselves subjects of despotic rulers and had acquired further habits of servility from the peoples they subdued.[93] From this origin of
Mogul government several conclusions could be drawn. Ruthless conquerors such as the Tartars and their successors, like despots in general, who
were likely to become enraged at any resistance to their will, were not
restrained by the law of nations in their conduct of warfare or diplomacy.[94] It
followed that those who had dealings with them in the international arena,
or were threatened by them, sometimes had to depart from the norms of
civilized political intercourse, which are obligatory only when they are re-
ciprocated.

Burke challenged both the historical presuppositions and the implications of Montesquieu's sketch of this part of the world. It was true that the
original Arab Muslim conquests, which "extended the influence of that
proud and domineering sect from the banks of the Ganges to the banks of
the Loire," were marked by a combination of enthusiasm and despotism; the
much later Tartar invasion of India under Tamerlane, however, was milder
in its effects and far from lawless in spirit ("Speech in Opening," 9:386–88).
In any case, Burke condemned the spirit of conquest he saw in Hastings, and
denounced the Rohilla War in particular, in which Hastings had joined
forces with an Indian despot in an outright conquest, as unjustifiable both in
its purpose and its conduct under the law of nations, an important element
in the European conception of justice. Hastings, however, though he did
not envisage the British acquisition of the whole of India, anticipated the
justification offered for the nineteenth-century empire by John Stuart Mill:

> The rules of ordinary international morality imply reciprocity. But
> barbarians will not reciprocate. They cannot be depended on for
> observing any rules. . . . A civilized government cannot help having
> barbarous neighbors: when it has, it cannot always content itself with
> a defensive position, one of mere resistance to aggression. After a
> longer or shorter interval of forbearance, it either finds itself obliged

to conquer them, or to assert so much authority over them, and so break their spirit, that they gradually sink into a state of dependence upon itself. . . . This is the history of the relations of the British Government with the native States of India.[95]

Mill's view of Indians as "barbarians," a term that alludes to the classical Greek disdain for peoples whose native political institutions were despotic, was harsher than the views usually expressed by Hastings and his eighteenth-century colleagues; but Hastings agreed that Indian despotism created military dangers that excused and indeed necessitated uses of force on his part that would have been questionable in a different environment.

A second and related feature of the despotic Indian scene was its history of frequent usurpations of political power. This was partly an extension of the original spirit of conquest: political succession, like the founding of new dynasties, was commonly effected by violence. This phenomenon also reflected the high stakes of despotic politics, in which the ruler was everything, and all his subjects equally his slaves; and it was further exacerbated by the failure of despotic regimes, Muslim ones especially, given their lack of fundamental laws, to evolve generally accepted succession rules. Montesquieu related with some relish how new Muslim rulers, including those of India, had to dispose of their brothers to guarantee their claim to the throne, and how the risk of a coup d'état by a servant or relative was endemic in these countries.[96] Burke sometimes implied that in extending British influence Hastings was violating the prescriptive rights of ancient Indian ruling houses. Hastings in reply denied "that we supplanted some old, established, prescriptive form of government in that quarter of the globe. No such thing! Every government with which we were united, or with which we clashed, was itself a crude supersession of some form of government, itself not a very ancient usurpation upon the preceding."[97] Government instability in Indian states was itself a danger (as well as an opportunity) for the East India Company, precluding reliable alliances and creating a continually menacing atmosphere. It also meant that most Indian princes, themselves adventurers or descendants of recent usurpers, were of dubious legitimacy by traditional or prescriptive norms; "modern as our empire is conceived to be," Hastings commented, it was as old as some of the leading "native" regimes it faced.[98] Insofar as it was simply de facto power that justified the authority of rulers in a despotic setting, new dominions acquired by the British through conquest would be as legitimate as the regimes they displaced.

Furthermore, Hastings argued, it was not simply the origins of government in conquest, but the particular nature of historical Indian conquests, that determined the despotic character of rule there. In much of India, including the parts he was directly concerned with, Muslim invaders had established conquest regimes over largely Hindu populations, and the necessity of keeping their numerous and potentially rebellious subjects under control dictated ongoing coercive and arbitrary methods of government on the part of the Muslim elite. India suffered from

> the Informality, Invalidity, and Instability of all Engagements in so divided and unsettled a State of Society; and from the unavoidable Anarchy and Confusion of different Laws, Religions, and Prejudices, moral, civil, and political, all jumbled together in One unnatural and discordant Mass. Every Part of *Hindostan* has been constantly exposed to these and similar Disadvantages ever since the *Mahommedan* Conquests. The *Hindoos*, who never incorporated with their Conquerors, were kept in Order only by the strong Hand of Power. The constant Necessity of similar Exertions would increase at once their Energy and Extent; so that Rebellion itself is the Parent and Promoter of Despotism.[99]

On one occasion, Burke agreed with Hastings's diagnosis of the unfortunate Indian situation, without, however, drawing the same conclusions. As we have noted, Burke condemned the assistance provided by the East India Company in Madras to the nawab of the Carnatic in his conquest and annexation of Hindu Tanjore, which had previously been ruled by a Hindu raja. Burke held this to be an unjustifiable act of aggression, but he also portrayed the nawab as a typically violent and arbitrary Muslim ruler who overthrew the traditional Hindu government of Tanjore and replaced it with his own brand of despotism, to the detriment of the people (*Conquests*, 45–46). Hastings defended the British position in this episode in terms of his larger strategic vision; but neither this, nor the fact that it also may have involved the British in furthering the historic pattern of Muslim political domination, justified it in Burke's eyes. With their own antidespotic traditions, the British should rather have resisted and corrected the abuses of their predecessors.

Hastings disagreed. If the British were to rule in India as a new wave of conquerors over a large and sometimes resistant population, they had to some degree to emulate the methods of the ruling class they were displacing, exercising firm control over Hindus and Muslims alike. Rebelliousness at any sign of weakness in one's superiors, typical of all despotic subjects, was most to be feared from notables such as Chait Singh, who were chafing under the new British regime:

I knew, that from the History of *Asia*, and from the very Nature of Mankind, the Subjects of a despotic Empire are always vigilant for the Moment to rebel, and the Sovereign is ever jealous of rebellious Intentions. A *Zemindar* is an *Indian* Subject, and *as such* exposed to the common Lot of his Fellows. "*The mean and depraved State of a mere Zemindar*" [such as Hastings held Chait Singh to be], is, therefore, this very Dependence above mentioned on a despotic Government—this very Proneness to shake off his Allegiance, and this very Exposure to continual Danger from his Sovereign's Jealousy, which are consequent on the Political State of *Hindostanic* Governments.[100]

Resentment on the part of a despot's subjects was perfectly understandable; their rebelliousness, and the ruler's ongoing use of despotic methods to maintain control, in fact created a self-perpetuating situation.

The British could not, however, abruptly and unilaterally break out of this vicious circle, whatever their judgment of it; Chait Singh's insolence had to be ruthlessly suppressed, as an example to others. The exigencies of imperial rule by a small number of foreigners reinforced this authoritarian conclusion. Hastings's counsel drew the general lesson from the Chait Singh episode:

Obedience in a subject is in all cases necessary: it is most of all necessary in an absolute government. We all know how rapid the progress is from any delay to open resistance. In an absolute government it is bad; in India worse; in the English government in India worst of all; for this reason, because it is an authority maintained by a few foreigners over millions of persons.[101]

Imperial realism, combined with the traditions of the local environment, forced the British to calculate and rule on absolutist principles, however distasteful. In reply Burke urged not only that conquest gave no just title to practice arbitrary government, but that the policy of a prudent conqueror should aim at reversing previous customs of this nature.

Montesquieu suggested that the criminal penalties inflicted by a despotism, consistent with the regime's reliance on fear, were more severe than either European humanitarianism or a rational policy of deterrence could justify. At the same time, the despot's threats, having "more fury than force," tended to be ineffective: irregular application caused them to lose their credibility, the people became inured to cruelty, and the behavior of criminals became more "atrocious," in a perverse reflection of official severity.[102] While not completely embracing this analysis, Hastings found that an unacceptably high level of social disorder and crime was endemic in India, and that previous governments, however absolute, had either tolerated the situation or had been powerless to control it. In particular, Hastings became concerned with dacoity, the phenomenon of large, organized, hereditary gangs of robbers who inflicted depredations on parts of Bengal, extorting payments and creating general insecurity and terror in the countryside. Tackling the problem with the arbitrary power he claimed to have inherited from his Indian predecessors, but with greater efficiency, Hastings deployed his troops, imposed summary procedures of judgment, executed all captured dacoits, and enslaved their families.

Such an approach, he admitted, might seem "severe and unjust," and "repugnant to the equity and tenderness of our own constitution"; nothing less, however, would suffice "to prevail against an evil which has obtained the sanction and force of hereditary practice." Part of the difficulty, contrary to Montesquieu's theory, was that customary Muslim law (which did not impose the death penalty for robbery) failed to deter these crimes because it was too lenient. While "a rigid observance of the letter of the law is a blessing in a well-regulated state," however, "in a Government loose as that of Bengal is, and must be for some years to come, an extraordinary and exemplary coercion must be applied to eradicate those evils which the law cannot reach." This conclusion, Hastings claimed, was not original with him, but in fact reflected standard local practice: it was perfectly "conformable to custom for the Sovereign power [in India] to depart in extraordinary cases from the strict letter of the law." Despotic rulers were, by custom, above the law, and the ineffectualness of the law provoked and justified extralegal exertions of official power whenever the ruler found it necessary. Under traditional regimes, such arbitrary methods of dealing with crime may have been counterproductive, as Montesquieu implied; under Hastings, they may have achieved greater success, though British campaigns to repress organized crime went on into the next century.[103] Hastings was well aware in this case that he was ruling in the manner of an Asian despot, justifying himself by local necessity and tradition. He nevertheless feared censure at home—a fear that proved groundless, at least in the case of Burke, who unfortunately did not comment on this episode.

A final feature that explained the tenacity of despotic practices and attitudes in Asia was the servile spirit of the people. This apparent acquiescence in their own subjection under arbitrary power might in part be understood as a consequence of the coercive force wielded by despots and the fear their rule created. Montesquieu, however, following Aristotle, held that this phenomenon was more deeply rooted, being related to the whole complex (the "general spirit") of customs in a despotic society, and especially to the enervating qualities of the climate; as a natural condition in certain countries, servility could thus be treated as one of the causes of despotic government rather than an effect of it. "The courage of the peoples of cold climates has kept them free," said Montesquieu, whereas "the cowardice of the peoples of hot climates has almost always made them slaves." Indians in particular were "by nature without courage" and timid.[104] Although he did not emphasize the Indian climate, which seems to have bothered him less than it did other Englishmen, Hastings accepted this common view of Asian character and deplored the "spirit of despotism and servitude" among the people of Bengal, which in his opinion invited and facilitated oppression.[105]

Burke denied that despotic government was normal (and therefore justified) in Asia, and in making this case he denied that despotic attitudes were as pervasive there as was commonly believed. He was not prepared to exonerate India completely of this charge, however, or to claim that the despotism of Hastings was a British importation. East India Company personnel had over the years learned techniques of corruption and power and absorbed an arbitrary cast of mind from bad examples offered in Indian society, which they had chosen to imitate. In particular, Burke emphasized the pernicious influence of banians, and of what he sometimes called the whole system of banianism, as a source of corruption of the British in Bengal.

Banians were Indians who served as translators, secretaries, and general agents for East India Company officials, both in their commercial and their administrative affairs. In Burke's interpretation of the situation, they served as conduits for the financial corruption and extortion frequently practiced, and, after the company attained sovereignty, as the direct and sometimes powerful agents of political oppression of the native population. They exemplified the principle that the subordinate officials of a despotism, while servile toward their superiors, transmit the regime's arbitrariness and harshness to those below; and that such figures can sometimes become the real—though precarious—masters of the system through their skills in clandestine maneuvering. Banianism, according to Burke, was the secret but effective reality of the British Empire in India: "Whilst we were proudly calling India a British government, it was in substance a government of the lowest, basest, and most flagitious of the native rabble. . . . [Banians] have ever after obtained the entire dominion over their nominal masters" ("Speech in Opening," 10:73). The servility and deviousness of the banians, and their insolence toward other Indians over whom they acquired power, were related, in Burke's analysis, to the fact that many were of low social origin; however, the prospect of profits was inducing higher-caste individuals to "become menial servants to English men, that they might rise by their degradation." In either case, oppressed themselves and "habituated to misery and subjection," they were "fit to oppress others. They serve an apprenticeship of servitude to qualify them for the trade of tyranny." The banians, however, were often more than simply the agents of their British employers. From their experience of Indian society, they

> know all the ways, all the little frauds, all the defensive armour, all the artifices and contrivances, by which abject slavery secures itself against the violence of power. . . . They know the way they have suffered themselves, and, far from being taught by these sufferings to abstain, they have only learned the way of afflicting others.

Thus, the banians typically became the instructors and corrupters of the innocent young Englishmen who arrived in India with "nothing but simplicity . . . [and] a desire of wealth." Frequently, "it is not the Englishman, but it is the black Banyan that is the Master." Burke suggested some extenuation here for the offenses of lower-ranking and novice East India Company servants, but not for Hastings, who had mastered and developed the whole banian system as the instrument of his policies, placing some of his own personal agents in the highest positions, to domineer over Indian nobility ("Speech on Opening," 292–94). The fact remained, however, that the banians represented a source of corruption and despotism that was native to India, reflecting the traditional social structure and established practices of the country. To this extent, Burke agreed with the view that a strain of deep-seated servility among the people contributed to despotic government there.

Burke's descriptions of the banians and other native instruments of East India Company oppression, more than any other passages in his speeches, put Indian society in an unfavorable light. Nevertheless, in his view, this phenomenon was exceptional, not general; and the claim that despotic government was necessary in India because of the pervasive slavishness of its people was untenable. Burke admitted and deplored the existence of servility, but he denied that this characteristic was distinctively Asian: the miseries of Ireland, he remarked, as well as those of India, were due to "a servile patience under oppression" (*Corr.* 8:147). But no more in India than in Ireland did Burke believe that such a trait was fixed or uniform. To justify his use of arbitrary power, Hastings implied that the people of India had no liberty, no laws, no inheritance, no fixed property, no descendable estate, no subordinations in society, no sense of honor or of shame, and that they are only affected by punishment so far as punishment is a corporal infliction, being totally insensible of any difference between the punishment of man and beast. (Hastings, paraphrased in "Speech in Reply," 11:196)

On the contrary, Burke cited examples from the behavior of Indian women and Hindu soldiers to prove that "the people of India have a keen sense and feeling of disgrace and honor," indications of a spirit of self-respect that is denied in the theory of despotic society. Moreover, as participants in a stable traditional social structure, Indians—and perhaps especially the gentry know well

what is rank, what is law, what is property,—[they are] a people who know how to feel disgrace, who know what equity, what reason, what proportion in punishments, what security of property is, just as well as any of your Lordships; for these are things which are secured to them by laws, by religion, by declarations of all their sovereigns. ("Speech in Reply," 11:220, 224)

Far from inviting despotism, the traditional conceptions of many Indians rendered the arbitrary rule of the British and their banians so much the more oppressive.

Since the conditions of despotism were supposedly determined in Asia both by nature (the climate) and by the customs of the peoples, Montesquieu maintained that rulers in those countries "must" or "ought" to govern in a despotic fashion.[106] Hastings accepted this view that despotism was virtually inevitable under prevailing conditions in India and thus unavoidable by the British rulers for the foreseeable future. At best, the British could aim at a gradual amelioration of conditions, reducing the abuses, severities, and inefficiencies of their predecessors, but even a reforming program would have to be imposed coercively, from above.

Denouncing Hastings's open defense of the arbitrary power he had exercised, Burke expressed further shock that he did not even make the usual excuse of someone in this position, "that by his conduct he had mitigated or purified [the evil system], and that the poison by passing through his constitution had acquired salutary properties" ("Speech on Opening," 375). Responding to this cue, Hastings and his counsel did attempt to make such a case later in the trial. The permanent condition of Indian government prior to the assumption of authority by the British was one in which "the discretion of the sovereign" was everything, and there were "no barriers between the subject and the sovereign for the purpose of defining the rights of the one or limiting the power of the other." The result was "everything that is detestable in the shape of misgovernment and tyranny." By comparison, India was "blessed by the administration of the English," who, despite the need for firmness, introduced some degree of moderation and legality.[107] While asserting the need for arbitrary authority centralized in his own hands, for example, Hastings noted that "it is the invariable consequence of despotism that every inferior agent is equally despotic," and he expressed his determination to correct abuses at the local level by company supervisors and especially their native staffs and banians.[108] Similarly, although despotic methods might continue to be required at the level of high politics, Hastings recognized the existence and legitimacy of customary Muslim and Hindu law for regulating the routine affairs of the population, and he took steps to have these bodies of law compiled and applied in a more orderly fashion.[109]

Reforms indicative of a program designed to negotiate a transition from despotism to a constitutional and legal regime, however, were not prominent in the records of Hastings's government; nevertheless, his counsel argued, it would be preposterous to liken him to the great despots notorious in Asian history, such as Tamerlane, who built pyramids with the heads of his massacred enemies. This was perhaps not a strong argument in Hastings's favor; in any event, Burke doubted its validity. A mercenary and ignoble tyrant "can waste a country more effectually than the proudest and most mighty conquerors" ("Speech in Reply," 11:373), and besides, the suggested comparison implied an inaccurate picture of the normal course of traditional rule in India, as Burke labored to demonstrate. If despotism was in fact neither standard nor inevitable in India, Hastings's claim to have tempered his own despotism with small reforms was not impressive.

Burke's Account of Indian Political Tradition

In order to undercut Hastings's second line of defense, Burke undertook to repudiate the familiar thesis of oriental despotism, especially as it applied to India. This endeavor led him to a deeper study of Indian history and institutions than could be claimed by any of his parliamentary colleagues in Great Britain,[110] and large sections of his speeches were designed to provide them with a more accurate and detailed impression of India than was usually offered. The result of his efforts was a direct and open confrontation with the authority of Montesquieu on this subject, as well as with

Hastings and the many others who accepted Montesquieu's analysis. In denying that arbitrary rule was the standard practice of the subcontinent, Burke was able to vindicate not only Indian tradition but also his own deeply held view that established traditions are usually reliable guides to sound morality and are entitled to respectful treatment by governments. Both his traditionalism and his commitment to lawful and moderate government are important features of Burke's political philosophy, familiar from his writings on European affairs; both themes were also asserted in his Indian speeches and received reinforcement from his favorable findings about the practices of Asia.

In repudiating despotic government for India, Burke evidently meant to advocate its contrary, of which there were various formulations. Despotism could be contrasted to liberty, held by many to be distinctive of European political tradition and especially of England. In one well-known passage, Montesquieu defined liberty as the legal security of the subject, guaranteed by institutional arrangements that prevented official arbitrariness.[111] In this sense, liberty is related conceptually to the rule of law; Burke agreed on the value of liberty so understood and insisted it be implemented in British India. In its more familiar political sense, however, liberty connoted a form of government arranged so as to reflect the active consent of the governed, and in particular, to be responsive to their wishes through a system of representation. Burke did not defend this conception either as part of Indian tradition or as a requirement of the British Indian regime; although he was a strong defender of an appropriately qualified or "regulated" liberty at home (*Reflections*, 89), Burke did not often speak of "liberty" in connection with India.

Second, despotism implies a system of rule that gratifies the desires or whims of the ruler, standing therefore in contrast to government that promotes the welfare of the society as a whole. Burke frequently maintained that "power has no other rational end than that of the general advantage" (*Reflections*, 115), and he often rebuked the East India Company on this account. Hastings also claimed (cynically, Burke believed) that he had the welfare of his Indian subjects at heart, and that his government had brought unprecedented peace to Bengal. Apart from the question of Hastings's sincerity, the difference between them was Hastings's conviction that arbitrary methods were a necessary means toward substantive benefits. A later utilitarian conception of the imperialist mission was expressed by John Stuart Mill in his dictum that "despotism is a legitimate mode of government in dealing with barbarians, provided the end be their improvement."[112] Neither Hastings nor Burke shared the nineteenth-century conviction of European superiority that could classify Indians (as Mill did) as "barbarians," but Hastings agreed with Mill on the instrumental necessity of despotism in the interest of welfare. Burke not only disagreed with this analysis; he took the opposite position: despotic rule, which produced an atmosphere of personal insecurity and hence economic stagnation, was inconsistent with the general welfare.

Finally and most important, despotism could be contrasted to what Montesquieu termed "moderate" government, which is restrained procedurally by the rule of law and substantively by higher norms of justice, including due respect for persons and property. Burke's rejection of oriental despotism and his condemnation of Hastings's claim to "arbitrary power" relied principally on this last sense of the concept.

Burke's concern with despotism was twofold. On the one hand, he criticized the theory that such regimes were commonplace in Asia; on the other, he accused the East India Company, and Hastings personally, of establishing a despotic regime and practicing forms of oppression characteristic of it. Montesquieu was wrong about Asian custom and necessity, but his theory of oriental despotism illuminated—and may indirectly have helped inspire—certain features of Hastings's mode of arbitrary rule.

As Montesquieu's *The Spirit of the Laws* suggests, despotic states are lawless, or alternatively, the law is simply "the momentary will of the prince," which is equivalent to lawlessness, since the constant presence of arbitrary power renders all legal rights precarious.[113] Property is insecure. Confiscations of private wealth, often itself ill gotten, are commonplace, and excessive taxes are arbitrarily imposed.[114] Burke accused Hastings of destructive taxation and confiscations—but of legitimate property holdings—both in Bengal and in Oudh. The most oppressive kind of despotism, according to Montesquieu, occurs when the prince claims to own all the land, which erodes the incentive to labor and causes neglect of both agriculture and industry; this, he asserted, was the case in the Indies, as indeed Hastings was later to claim in justification of his land policies.[115] Since an established nobility would threaten or constrain the despot's power, despotic policy promotes instability of rank and seeks to keep important people in a state of fear.[116] In a similar spirit, Hastings undermined the old gentry of Bengal. Official positions in a despotism are held entirely at the ruler's whim, and individuals of low origin are often raised to high rank,[117] just as Hastings elevated Munni Begam and numerous parvenus to administer Bengal. Since familial loyalty and honor (especially among the prominent) can generate resistance, despots do not hesitate to violate filial piety,[118] as Hastings did with respect to Asaf al-Daula and the begams of Oudh. Since power is concentrated around the person of the prince, a fearful tranquillity prevails in the country; court politics and palace revolutions, and in Muslim states, the intrigues of the seraglio, predominate.[119] With his appointment of Munni Begam, his indirect control over the court of Oudh and its weak ruler, and his diplomatic maneuvers at other Indian courts, Hastings showed himself an adept player in this style of politics. His whole approach to the governance of British India, and his open proclamation of his arbitrary power, demonstrated his assimilation of the theory of despotism.

Montesquieu's model of despotism is useful in clarifying certain aspects of Hastings's policies. One of the most striking features of Burke's Indian speeches, however, was his opposition to the theory that despotism was prevalent and customary in Asia, a view that might have justified those policies. Like most British political thinkers of the late eighteenth century, Burke had previously admired Montesquieu on many grounds and no doubt felt his influence, for instance, in his appreciation of the complexity of societies and traditions.[120] In rejecting this central organizing thesis of Montesquieu's work, however, Burke was explicit and harsh.

The politics of the Ottoman Empire, and the absolutism of the sultan or *grand seigneur*—Bodin had earlier translated the Greek word "despotism" as "seigneurial monarchy"[121]—had become familiar to Europeans through long diplomatic contact. To document his extension of the concept, Montesquieu relied on accounts provided by European travelers in books that were themselves well known among the educated public. The leading authority on Persia, for example, Sir John Chardin, admired Persian art and literature but confirmed that the shah's government was a despotic monarchy; François Bernier, who had resided at the court of the last great Mogul emperor, Aurangzeb, in the late seventeenth century, argued that Turkey, Persia, and India were similarly despotic, and emphasized that the resulting insecurity of property obstructed the prosperity of these fertile countries.[122] Burke, however, denounced "these wild, loose, casual, and silly observations of travellers and theorists," as well as "the wild systems which ingenious men have thought proper to build on their authority." Hastings and his supporters cited this "rabble of travellers" and Montesquieu himself, in order to make the point that the people "have no laws, no rights, no property movable or immovable, no distinctions of ranks, nor any sense of disgrace," and thus that "despotism is the only principle of government acknowledged in India." Views such as these had an insidious, self-fulfilling effect when inculcated into young Englishmen going out to India: "We shall not treat persons well whom we have learnt to despise. . . . People whom we suppose to have neither laws nor rights will not be treated by us as a people who have laws and rights." Such an attitude was inexcusable, however, in an experienced Indian official such as Hastings, who had access to more accurate and detailed knowledge about the country and people; in his case, invocation of the old despotic stereotype was merely a cynical pretext for oppression. Drawing upon what he believed was more recent and more reliable information, Burke set out "to prove that every word which Montesquieu has taken from idle and inconsiderate travellers is absolutely false" ("Speech in Reply," 11:202–07).

As a distinguished opponent of the theory of oriental despotism, Burke was not alone, though his contribution has been overlooked in surveys of the subject.[123] Montesquieu's interest in comparative political science was genuine, but some readers suspected that his model of oriental despotism was constructed as an ideological weapon against European absolutism and in defense of the French nobility and *parlements*. Voltaire, who nourished hopes for the reforming potentiality of enlightened central governments, was the "international patron" of those who questioned the reality of despotism as standard practice in major Asian nations.[124] Voltaire was a particular admirer of the sound morality and tolerance of the Chinese government—which he in his turn offered as a worthy model for Europe. He also argued that European monarchs were sometimes as arbitrary as those of Persia or India, and he rejected the thesis that there was no stable property in the Mogul Empire, since such a thesis was incompatible with the wealth of India.[125] Like Burke later on, Voltaire drew antidespotic inferences from such bits of empirical and legal evidence as he could assemble, and he argued that the image of pure arbitrariness conjured up in Montesquieu's account was incoherent or inconsistent with large-scale social life over time.

There is irony in this affinity. "We are not the disciples of Voltaire," Burke proclaimed in a famous passage (*Reflections*, 181), disturbed by Voltaire's irreligion, and indeed, he did not enlist the *philosophe*'s authority in his arguments against Hastings. Nor does Burke give evidence of familiarity with the work of Anquetil-Duperron, another traveler-scholar, whose *Législation orientale* (1778) provided the best-grounded arguments against oriental despotism, and indeed, against exploitative Western imperialism that used despotism as a pretext. (Anquetil-Duperron, however, remained far less influential than Montesquieu.)[126] Burke did refer to a number of firsthand accounts, some of them by former East India Company employees, to support his view of the normal—or previous—prosperity and stability of Indian society. Prominent among the works he cited was Nathaniel Halhed's *Code of Gentoo Laws* (1776), a "good authority" on "probably the most ancient laws in the world, if we except the Mosaic," "a work which I have read with all the care that such an extraordinary view of human affairs and human constitutions deserves." In another irony of the debate, this particular work, the first compilation and translation into English of customary Hindu law, had been commissioned by Hastings to serve as a guide for judges presiding over native cases in Bengal. Subsequently, Halhed was a supporter of Hastings and assisted in the preparation of his impeachment defense. The spectacle of the leading English scholar of Indian law lending his weight to Hastings's claim that India was traditionally lawless and despotic was "alarming" in Burke's view, another example of the corrupt collusion among old company colleagues ("Speech in Reply," II:223, 207, 202).[127]

Some curious twists in the eighteenth-century debate over despotism appear in European views of the Tartars, as the peoples of central Asia were generally called. The Mogul rulers of India claimed to be the successors of Tamerlane (or Timur), the notorious Tartar chieftain who invaded northern India in 1398, and Europeans regarded the Muslim elites of India as in large part descendants of the Tartars, combined with other invaders of Afghan and Persian stock. The popular image of Tamerlane, like that of his reputed ancestor Genghis Khan, was of a ferocious and destructive conqueror who wreaked havoc from Turkey and Baghdad to Delhi. As noted above, Hastings's counsel invoked the murderous Tartar as an exemplar of true oriental despotism, to underscore Hastings's comparative mildness; Burke in reply slipped into the same stereotype, calling Hastings "this successor of Tamerlane, this emulator of Genghis Khan" in connection with his annexation of Benares ("Speech in Reply," II:304).

Sophisticated opinion, however, including Burke's own, was more ambivalent. Montesquieu regarded the Tartars (in contrast to the ancient Germans) as living under despotic rule, but unlike most despotic nations they were warlike and courageous; he therefore suggested that their servile manners, and perhaps their political institutions, had been acquired from the warmer countries (such as China and India) that they overran.[128] Voltaire offered a mixed picture of Tamerlane and refrained from calling him a despot: a fierce barbarian, he was inferior to Alexander, since he was a destroyer rather than a founder of cities; still, most of the disparaging stories about him derived from the chronicles of his enemies, and in his wars he seemed to have observed some principles of the law of nations.[129] Similarly, Gibbon balanced accounts of atrocities and pillage against a rather chivalrous portrait of the man; in contrast to his view of the Turks, for example, Gibbon did not label Tamerlane despotic.[130] Europeans were clearly impressed by the scope of Tartar conquests, and some were inclined to admire their energy, cruel and barbarous though it was; since the similarly barbarous "Goths" originally came from the central Asian steppes, some suspected there might be a connection between the two peoples, and thus that some vestiges of Gothic liberty might even be glimpsed among the Tartars.[131]

As if to bear out this more positive image, a work entitled *Institutes Political and Military . . . by the Great Timour* was published in England in 1783; it indicated that the Tartars of Tamerlane's period had had conceptions of law and government that bore comparison to medieval conceptions in Europe. Hastings had said that it would be a happy (though distant) day for India "when the despotic Institutes of Genghiz Khan, or Tamerlane, shall give place to the liberal spirit of a British Legislature." In response, Burke not only cited a more favorable view of the infamous Genghis but also quoted at length from the Tartar document, asserting,

> There is no book in the world, I believe, which contains nobler, more just, more manly, more pious, principles of Government than this book called the Institutions of Tamerlane. Nor is there one word of arbitrary power in it, much less of that arbitrary power which Mr. Hastings supposed himself justified by. ("Speech on Opening," 355–61)

Hastings's trial counsel tried to dismiss Burke's view of Tamerlane as a fantasy that reflected the European fashion of portraying noble barbarians on stage.[132] Undaunted, Burke returned to this theme in his summation of the prosecution's case. The best available evidence showed that Tamerlane, far from being a despot, was an elective monarch, indeed "duly elected by the princes lawfully assembled in general diet," and that

> a Tartarian sovereign could not obtain the recognition of ancient laws, or establish new ones, without the consent of his parliament; that he could not ascend the throne without being duly elected; and that, when so elected, he was bound to preserve the great in all their immunities, and the people in all their rights, liberties, privileges, and properties. ("Speech in Reply," II:212–13)

The Mogul Empire, to be sure, had been founded through violent invasion and conquest, but if it in any way preserved the political conceptions of its founders—which were recognizable to anyone familiar with the medieval political development of Europe—Hastings's argument that arbitrary power was sanctioned by immemorial Asian tradition would collapse.

Burke's rejection of the oriental despotism thesis in his impeachment speeches must be qualified in three ways. First, Burke did occasionally express the more common opposite view, sometimes in passing, and usually with reference to the most familiar case of Turkey ("Conciliation," 126; *Reflections*, 231, 236).[133] In the well-known passage in which he deplored the passing of the "age of chivalry," Burke appeared to endorse Montesquieu's analysis of comparative world institutions by saying that European chivalry had given a special character to European government, in contrast to "the states of Asia" (*Reflections*, 170). Although "chivalry" probably refers here to the late medieval softening of aristocratic manners, the implied characterization of Asian government conflicts with the favorable picture of Mongol-Mogul institutions that Burke offered against Hastings. There is of course a double tactical explanation for the references to despotism in Burke's *Reflections*. In opposition to the revolutionaries, Burke did not recognize "the despotism of Turkey" amid the achievements and culture of France under the old regime; on the other hand, Burke accused the revolution of creating a despotic or arbitrary government in France—a "despotism of the multitude" rather than of the monarch, but a despotism on which the standard Asian model offered some insight (*Reflections*, 236, 227, 142). Montesquieu's contrast between oriental despotism and European freedom constituted one of the well-known languages or discourses that Burke deployed for rhetorical purposes in reference to European or American affairs; but in doing so, he contradicted the more considered views he expressed when addressing the affairs of Asia. In opening Hastings's trial (in 1788), Burke asserted that even the "grand seigneur" or emperor of Turkey did not exercise arbitrary power and was in fact bound by Muslim religious law ("Speech on Opening," 353–54).

Second, in one of his earlier approaches to Indian affairs, Burke adopted the view held by many Englishmen that despotic regimes on the subcontinent had been imposed by successive waves of Muslim conquerors on a largely Hindu population that continued to live according to an extremely conservative and custom-bound way of life. Muslim regimes figured prominently among the examples of despotism provided by Montesquieu, who neglected Hinduism and Hindu polities. The long-standing image of Islam as a violent and conquering religion, and the proximity of the Ottoman sultan, further reinforced the particular connection between Islam and despotism in the popular European view. The British in India, on the other hand, were impressed by the complex and apparently stable body of customary rules that defined the Hindu way of life, and they realized that this was the more venerable tradition in most of India, whereas Muslim rule had been imposed by force in relatively modern times. In both these respects,

Hindu institutions in India seemed more legitimate, and less despotic, than Muslim ones. In establishing their rule in India, the British had to deal primarily with existing Muslim rulers and elites, and Hastings's argument that the despotic environment of India compelled him to use despotic methods referred almost entirely to the pressures and dangers he faced in this sphere. At the same time, this distinction between the two political cultures of India permitted the British to see themselves as simply displacing a previous set of invaders, despotic ones at that, and thereby bringing better conditions for the Hindu majority.[134]

Burke adopted this interpretation in his analysis of the affairs of Tanjore, but he applied it not to justify British imperial policies but to further criticize the actions of the East India Company. The company had assisted the nawab Muhammad Ali in securing the throne of the Carnatic in the 1740s at the expense of another Muslim contender, and he remained their close ally thereafter. In 1773, moreover, the company provided the military means for the nawab to conquer and annex the neighboring Hindu state of Tanjore, and Hastings later upheld this policy on the grounds that strengthening the dependent nawab's state served the company's larger strategic interests. Burke condemned the policy both as an unjust act of aggression and as a move motivated by the corrupt interests of the nawab's English creditors. He also denounced it as a violent and illegitimate imposition of Muslim despotism on a Hindu state that had hitherto been governed by its Hindu rajas according to its lawful traditions. Burke embraced a widespread opinion of the virtues of the peaceable and hard-working Hindus:

> The native Indians, under their own native government, are, to speak without prejudice, a far better people than the Mahometans; or than those who by living under Mahometans, become the depressed subjects, or the corrupted instruments of their tyranny; they are of far milder manners, more industrious, more tractable, and less enterprising. (*Conquests*, 113)

These people had been exposed repeatedly to the "ferocious rapacity of Mahometan despotism," whether Arab, Tartar, or Persian, which they detested as alien and exploitative. It was the duty of the English to try to mitigate "the horrors of the Mahometan government in India," and to its credit the East India Company had checked some of the "excesses" in areas under its influence, such as the Carnatic. In Tanjore, however (as later in Rohilkhand), the company had allowed "English arms [to be] employed by a ferocious and insatiable Mahometan, to exterminate near twenty native hereditary princes, of very ancient, and in that part of the world, illustrious families," and to extend his corrupt and destructive regime (*Conquests*, 110, 114–15). On this occasion, the English aligned themselves with the historical pattern through which despotism had been imposed by foreign conquerors on traditional Indian society, and at the expense of mild and lawful native rulers. By defending the annexation, Hastings demonstrated his willingness to side with the unjust party in an Indian conflict when *raison d'état* seemed to dictate it. The entire episode illustrated the process by which the British were acquiring despotic attitudes, in emulation of their Muslim predecessors or collaborators, through their own policy of Indian conquest.

The speech just quoted, in which Burke ascribed despotism to the Muslim conquerors of India but not to the native Hindus, was delivered in 1779, just before he embarked on his intensive investigations of the situation in Bengal. By the time he initiated the impeachment of Hastings a few years later, he had evidently changed his mind: the Muslim-Hindu distinction was replaced by a general denial of the thesis of oriental despotism on which Hastings's defense relied. Muslim political ideals included the principle of lawful rule, and Muslim regimes on the whole observed this requirement. As a third qualification of his main argument, however, Burke did concede that there were conspicuous exceptions in practice. Some Indian rulers with whom the British had close relations—all Muslim, as it happened—were in fact despots or tyrants, but as such they acted in violation of the tenets of their own religion and national traditions (just as European and Christian tyrants sometimes did).

Burke agreed in particular that the nawabs of Bengal just before the British acquisition of sovereignty (Siraj al-Daula and Mir Kasim) were vicious tyrants whose actions justified their overthrow by the East India Company. He did not retract his condemnation of the conquest of Tanjore by the nawab of the Carnatic or his view of its despotic character, and he later portrayed Shuja al-Daula of Oudh, and his conquest of the Rohillas, in the same manner. Hastings argued that Bengal lacked a regular constitution or orderly system of government prior to the British takeover, that it was ruled instead by the "exertions of individuals in power."[135] Burke held that, in a larger view, Indian states did possess constitutional norms, and his charge against Hastings and other high company officials was that they chose to imitate the worst, and in fact aberrant, examples of Indian politics, rather than trying to restore and uphold the respectable laws and traditions of the country:

> The practice of Asia, as the Gentleman at your Bar has thought fit to say, is what he holds to; the constitution he flies away from. Un-

doubtedly much blood, murder, false imprisonment, much peculation, cruelty and robbery are to be found in Asia; and if, instead of
going to the sacred laws of the Country, Mr. Hastings chooses to go
to the iniquitous practices of it, and practices authorized only by
public tumult, contention, war and riot, he will find as clear an
acquittal in the practices, as he would find condemnation in the
institutions. ("Speech on Opening," 354)

When Hastings decided to punish Chait Singh, he did not consult the laws
or "approved authorities in this country," or even the *Institutes of Timour;*
rather, as if perversely following Longinus's advice to imitate the greatest
models, he emulated the oppressive practices of Shuja al-Daula, Mir Kasim,
and other great tyrants in his experience ("Speech in Reply," 11:250).[136]
Hastings attributed the problems of Oudh to the "faulty system of government" that he found in place there; but Burke, who held that the company
was taking advantage of Oudh's weakness to despoil it, replied that "systems
never make mankind happy or unhappy, any further than as they give occasions for wicked men to exercise their own abominable talents" ("Speech in
Reply," 11:377–78). Where others would have set out to reform abuses, Hastings's plea was that he was compelled to copy and perpetuate them.

Burke's considered judgment, then, was that both normatively and
traditionally Indian government was lawful rather than despotic, and therefore that Hastings's despotism could be justified neither by prescription nor
by necessity. Burke arrived at this view through his work on a parliamentary
investigative committee in the early 1780s, and he explained it in his official
report, trying to render the exotic comprehensible:

> Your Committee conceive, that it is a great Error to imagine, that the
> People of those Countries lived without any fixed Law before the
> British Establishment. The Mahomedans were subject to the Ma-
> homedan Law, as it is found in the Book called the Alcoran, and its
> authorized Interpreters; and all Persons, from the lowest Slave to the
> most powerful Prince, was [*sic*] bound by it. Their Judges and Mag-
> istrates were also bound to observe, and to judge by, the Reaje ul
> Mulk, or ancient Custom and Usages, or Common Law of the
> Country.

The Hindu population likewise acknowledged a normative conception of
legality and were bound by a parallel and well-developed legal system:

> That a body of Law existed for the Gentu Inhabitants, is certain; and
> Mr. Hastings [through his patronage of Halhed] has the Merit of

bringing that to the View of the Public. . . . The Gentus have also their Professors in that Science, who, as it appears in Evidence to Your Committee, are Persons highly revered by the Natives, on Account of their Learning and Integrity of Life.

If the prescribed rule of law was sometimes violated in practice, this was because the rulers of Bengal had acquired an "Exorbitance of Power" in making good their de facto independence from Delhi, and because there were no other effective checks on them. But "Acts of Abuse can never be made the Standard of Legality" (*First Report*, 171).

Burke elaborated these points in greater detail in his striking survey of Indian society in the speech opening the impeachment trial. He had undertaken, he affirmed, a "minute inspection" of the constitutions of Asia, and he found no case of "Oriental Governors claiming to themselves a right to act by arbitrary will." Most of Asia was under Muslim rule, and "to name a Mahometan Government is to name a Government of law"—indeed, a God-given law having "the double sanction of law and of religion." Not one text of the Koran, which Burke asserted he had read, "authorizes in any degree an arbitrary power in the Government" ("Speech on Opening," 353). Religious principles served as the foundation for a highly developed legal tradition and legal profession in Muslim nations; Burke outlined the unfamiliar categories of this tradition in terms that would be understandable to the peers, bishops, and judges of the House of Lords:

> The first foundation of their law is the Koran. The next part is the Fetfa, or adjudged cases by proper authority, well known there. The next is the written interpretation of the principles of jurisprudence; and their books are as numerous upon the principles of jurisprudence as in any country in Europe. The next part of their law is what they call the Kanon, which is equivalent to Acts of Parliament. . . . The next is the Rage ul Mulk, the Common Law or Custom of the Kingdom, equivalent to our Common Law. Therefore they have laws from more sources than we have, exactly in the same order.

Burke then surveyed the judicial system of the Mogul Empire: government authority in the provinces was divided between a "Soubahdar or Viceroy," whose duties included the administration of criminal justice, and a "Dewan or High Steward," in charge of "Revenue and all Exchequeur Causes." The law of inheritance was entrusted to local judges called Kadis, whose verdicts had to be approved by Muftis or legal scholars. The point was that "these powers of magistracy, revenue, and law are all different and consequently are not delegated in the whole to any one," contrary to Hastings's picture of unified despotic power and to actual concentration of power in the British regime in Bengal ("Speech on Opening," 364–65; also "Speech in Reply," 11:216–17).

Hindu society was similarly regulated by a conception of law administered by learned practitioners, as Halhed's compilation showed.

> The Gentoos have a law which positively proscribes in magistrates any idea of will. . . . These people in many points are governed by their own ancient written law, called the *Shaster*. Its interpreters and judges are the *Pundits*. This law is comprehensive, extending to all the concerns of life, affording principles and maxims and legal theories applicable to all cases, drawn from the sources of natural equity, modified by their institutions, full of refinement and subtilty of distinction equal to that of any other law. ("Speech in Opening," 9:482)

Hindu law prescribed a complex social system, dividing the people into "classes and ranks, with more accuracy of distinction" than in other countries. Burke thus noticed the caste system but did not dwell on it or note its centrality in Indian life; his knowledge of this phenomenon was apparently sketchy.[137] Certain other features of Hindu law did catch his attention. He observed that property rights and inheritance rules were defined in detail: for example, "a Brahmin's estate comes by descent to him; it is forever descendible to his heirs, if he has heirs; and if he has none, it belongs to his disciples, and those connected with him in the Brahminical caste." Criminal punishments were limited, Brahmins in particular enjoying immunity from the death sentence and from confiscation of property. "Rules of evidence and of pleading" were spelled out—"in short, all the rules which have been formed in other countries to prevent this very arbitrary power [in the magistrate]." This was, in sum, an "enlightened jurisprudence" that assuredly did not sanction the powers of arbitrary punishment or seizure of property claimed and exercised by Hastings ("Speech in Reply," 11:208–211). Insofar as there was a legitimate element of discretion in the governor-general's authority, he was bound to use it in accordance with "political morality, humanity, and equity." This meant that, if there were any ambiguity in the laws of his Indian subjects, he was "bound to act according to the largest and most liberal construction of their laws, rights, usages, institutions, and good customs" ("Speech in Reply," 11:194–95).

The expected consequence of a developed and equitable system of law, and indeed the "grand test of all law," was that "wherever it has prevailed, the country has been populous, flourishing, and happy" ("Speech in Opening," 9:482). The rule of law was not only required by justice but could also be defended in terms of the general welfare it promoted. Burke believed that this test had been met for the most part in India prior to the disruptions caused by the British conquest and the plundering of Indian wealth by unscrupulous East India Company personnel. Burke's *Ninth Report* attempted to document the economic decline of Bengal under British administration; and the same pattern, he believed, manifested itself in other districts that came under British control—in Oudh, for example, "a country which, before our acquaintance with it, was in the same happy and flourishing condition with Benares, and which dates its period of decline and misery from the time of our intermeddling with it" (Speech in Reply," 11:370). Since lawful governance was a necessary condition of economic prosperity, the previously flourishing condition of India served to refute Hastings's claim that Indian rulers were generally harsh and despotic.

To these arguments Hastings might have responded that conceptions of law and the observance of customary law among the Indian masses did not in themselves disprove the simultaneous existence of a despotic tradition there. The prevailing theory held that oriental governments were lawless in the sense that the despot's arbitrary will, backed up by the coercive force at his disposal, could at any time be imposed on any of his subjects, but one would expect to observe instances of arbitrariness primarily at the level of high politics. As Voltaire suggested against Montesquieu, totally arbitrary rule is virtually inconceivable, since any stable society requires a degree of order, which presupposes some regularity of law or custom; and Asian societies appeared to be relatively stable and unchanging. A sensible despot, moreover, would desire such order and would therefore impose rules or, more likely, confirm and enforce the rules prescribed by custom and religion, especially for the routine affairs of the population at lower social levels. Although a despot could overrule law at any time, most of his exertions of arbitrary power would probably be aimed at either notable subjects or other princes who could threaten his position. The policy Montesquieu emphasized of maintaining a climate of fear or insecurity would also have been directed at potential rivals for the most part.

Hastings was aware of Muslim and Hindu customary law and did indeed, as Burke pointed out, seek to have it administered for the ordinary business of life in Bengal. The arbitrary or discretionary power for which he claimed a sanction from Indian political tradition was expressed almost entirely at a higher level of policy, in the name of either imperial necessity or reform—in military and diplomatic affairs, toward Indian rulers who threatened or obstructed British authority, and against established aristocracies.

Burke implicitly though briefly replied to this argument by pointing to the dignity and customary rights of the various local rulers within the Mogul Empire from the time of Tamerlane, which "resembled more a Republic of Princes" than the centralized despotism imagined in Europe. Thus the exorbitant fine levied upon Chait Singh was inappropriate, and his rebellion was understandable in terms of traditional norms:

> These principal Rajahs, instead of being called wretches and treated as such, were, even when they were at arms against their Sovereign, admitted to easy reconciliations; because in reality they were not rebellious subjects, but Princes, often asserting their natural liberty and the just constitution of the country. ("Speech on Opening," 309–10)

In the political tradition of India, a strong sense of constitutional rules and rights was preserved at the upper levels, among rulers and notables, while customary law prevailed at the lower.

Hastings also argued that despotic government was associated with and was partly determined by the history of conquests in that country, of which the British regime was simply the last in a long series. The rights of conquest (he held) overrode preexisting law, just as conquest regimes depended on the continuing use of force. While conceding that Muslim rule in India originated in invasion and conquest, Burke denied Hastings's conclusion. Tamerlane's violence had been directed at the previous Muslim rulers in India; he had been "just, prudent and politic" toward the Hindu rajas and inhabitants, and his successors had by and large perpetuated a "constitution" that was mild and orderly, apart from occasional insubordination within the ruling class, which resembled that of great vassals in feudal Europe ("Speech on Opening," 308–10). More important, though Burke was willing to concede that the East India Company had acquired a legitimate title to rule Bengal by right of conquest, given the circumstances there, he denied that a justifiable conquest generated specific (i.e., absolute or unlimited) rights of rule or abrogated existing law and the rights of subjects.

> Your Committee [of the House of Commons] find the Question of the Rights derived from Conquest in the Abstract, dark and arduous. But they are unwilling to believe, that Parliament ever intended [when it restructured the company's Indian government in 1773] to act upon a Supposition of the utter Extinction of all the original Laws and Rights of the Natives. (*First Report*, 172)

Arguing that all ruling power is ultimately "of God" and is therefore constrained by justice and concern for the welfare of the ruled, Burke asserted that "the title of conquest makes no difference at all. No conquest can give such a right [to rule by arbitrary will]." Conquest, like any other procedure through which authority is acquired, is accompanied by moral obligation: "By conquest, which is a more immediate designation of the hand of God, the conqueror succeeds to all the painful duties and subordination to the power of God which belonged to the sovereign whom he has displaced." Furthermore, a prudent conqueror realizes that, in this case, his long-term interests coincide with his duty:

> Every wise conqueror has gone much further than he was bound to go. It has been his ambition and his policy to reconcile the vanquished to his fortune, to show that they had gained by the change, to convert their momentary suffering into a long benefit, and to draw from the humiliation of his enemies an accession to his own glory.

All these objectives were best attained by implementing a regime of "law and liberty" in the newly acquired country. This was well understood not only by Parliament, but by the company's court of directors, whose instructions to their servants in India reflected these ideals ("Speech in Opening," 9:456–57).

The reference to conquest, finally, raised the question of the source of whatever authority Hastings possessed in India and the implications for the extent of his powers. Burke did not dispute the fact that conquest played a role in the acquisition of the empire, but he was reluctant to insist on this as the exclusive foundation of the British government in India or to specify the rights it conferred on the victors. Like other beneficial revolutions considered by Burke, the recent political upheaval in Bengal was neither self-justifying nor justified in the abstract by its formal qualities, but needed to consolidate its legitimacy through the beneficial results it brought over time. Fortunately, like the Revolution of 1688 in England, the revolution of 1757–1765 in Bengal soon acquired a form that was as legal and regular as was possible under the circumstances, since it was both confirmed by a formal grant from the Mogul emperor and then ratified by an act of Parliament. These constitutional measures defined the structure of authority in British India and the powers exercised by East India Company officials.

> Formally and in Style, the Company do not act as a Sovereign deriving a Title from absolute and unconditional Conquest, whatever Right such a Title may be supposed to confer. They have accepted by [the] Treaty [of Allahabad, in 1765], from the ancient sovereign Power of that Country, a Patent, under which they act as Duan, or

Administrator of Civil Justice and of the Revenues. By accepting that Office, they accepted the Duties inseparable from it; which were undoubtedly to protect the People committed to their Charge, in all their Possessions, moveable and immoveable, and in all their Rights, religious and civil. The Acceptance of this Instrument was virtually a Convention entered into in Favour of the Natives, then delivered over to the Government of British Subjects.

As British subjects, the company's employees also had to obey Parliament, which had taken upon itself the obligation of seeing that the spirit of this agreement was complied with. Parliament could not be supposed to have conferred arbitrary powers, or powers repugnant to the agreement, on the responsible officials. Even if it were true that the company's immediate predecessors in Bengal were lawless usurpers who ruled arbitrarily, this was neither the norm of the Mogul Empire nor the standard that Parliament had endorsed for British governors there (*First Report*, 172, 170).

It followed that there was no formal basis for Hastings's claim to despotic power, and that his actual exercise of such power was itself a usurpation. The East India Company derived its corporate existence and prerogatives from Parliament, to which it remained responsible ("Speech on Opening," 280–81). Hastings's office as governor-general was likewise created by an act of Parliament, and its delegated sovereign powers, shared with a council, were far from personal despotism (*Fox's Bill*, 415). In addition, and with parliamentary approval, the company had acquired powers by a charter from the Mogul Empire, by which it bound itself and its servants "to observe the laws, rights, usages and customs of the Natives, and to pursue their benefit in all things" ("Speech on Opening," 281). Hastings's claim that he exercised a kind of constitutional despotism over Benares, since this is what the company had received from its previous sovereign, the nawab of Oudh, was fallacious; Asaf al-Daula, like his father, may have been an arbitrary ruler in practice, but as a vizier or minister of the Mogul Empire, and subject to its law and to Muslim law more generally, he could not transfer powers that he did not legitimately possess ("Speech in Reply," 11:236). The central Mogul authority, it was true, was too feeble to be in a position to enforce the terms of its grant to the company, but the company's "duty to the people below" was certainly not suspended or annihilated by this fact. In this situation, indeed, Parliament undertook to ensure that the company discharged its responsibility. By agreeing that "an English Corporation [become] an integral part of the Mogul Empire," Great Britain itself "made a virtual act of union" with India and its people, and was obliged to respect (at least) the "rights, laws and liberties" that were traditional there ("Speech on Opening," 281–82).

How, then, could Hastings have had arbitrary power, as he insisted? As Burke declaimed at the opening of the trial, and repeated toward its conclusion: "My Lords, the East India Company have not arbitrary power to give him; the King has no arbitrary power to give him; your Lordships have not, nor the Commons, nor the whole Legislature." Arbitrary power was not inherent in the government of Great Britain, and therefore could not be transmitted to its representatives. Moreover, arbitrary power was illegitimate per se: "We have no arbitrary power to give, because Arbitrary power is a thing which neither any man can hold nor any man can give away" ("Speech on Opening," 350; also "Speech in Reply," 11:200). For Burke, it followed, and the evidence confirmed, that arbitrary power was not sanctioned by the traditional conceptions and laws of Asia. Hastings called for concentrated central authority in British India and defended his own occasional use of power that was arbitrary by European standards on two grounds: they were required by "necessity" to maintain the empire, especially in the emergency conditions he sometimes faced, and were thus justifiable according to the doctrine of *raison d'état*; and they were legitimized prescriptively by the prevailing despotic customs of India. These two arguments coincided and reinforced each other. If India really presented a despotic environment, in which the company's enemies, rivals, and subjects all took despotic methods for granted and could not be trusted to behave lawfully, then the argument of political necessity had all the more force. Hastings's answer to Burke's rhetorical question, then, was that Indian custom was the source of his maxims of rule, and a combination of necessity and local custom was their justification.

The widely accepted theory of oriental despotism was thus crucial to Hastings's position, and Burke's refutation of its validity in India was a major element in his attack on Hastings and on the attitude Hastings shared with many of his East India Company colleagues. The theory served several ideological purposes. Generally disparaging to Asia, it provided a justification for European imperialism, since European rulers of Asian societies could claim to bring with them the previously unknown benefits of lawful government, personal liberty, and stable property rights. The planting of these institutions in an unreceptive cultural setting, however, was likely to be a long and gradual process. In the short term, the theory of despotism could have the opposite import, justifying the use of arbitrary or coercive methods by imperial rulers as temporarily necessary and validated by local custom. Hastings no doubt valued British political institutions and believed that his regime was laying the foundation for eventual qualitative improvements in Indian government, but his attention was almost entirely focused on the immediate tasks of securing the empire, which required measures that would have been both impermissible and unnecessary in Europe.

Burke agreed that British rule could and should be beneficial to Indians: the responsibility of persons in positions of authority for the welfare of their subjects was a constant theme of his political philosophy. Furthermore, he held that the potential benefits could be realized only if British rulers in India adhered to norms of lawfulness and justice, consistently and from the start. Finally, Burke repudiated the argument that arbitrary rule was a necessary means to future improvements, by rejecting the idea that despotism was pervasive in India and was therefore the only workable system of rule there. Rather, India had its own admirable moral and legal traditions, which, on careful scrutiny, embodied basic values similar to those acknowledged in Europe. The required commitment to lawfulness and justice on the part of the British rulers, therefore, should be expressed in respect for local law and custom. The missing component of this argument was why, if Indian society already reflected adequate conceptions of justice, was British rule needed at all.

Chapter Five

Political Philosophy

Burke's Traditionalism

A number of philosophical themes in Burke's political thought can be assessed in relation to his views on the Indian empire. An adequate general interpretation of Burke as a political theorist must accommodate his statements on India and Hastings—the most neglected major part of his corpus—and consider the extent to which his positions on these matters constitute important evidence in debates about his leading ideas.

Interpreters who view Burke as an important political theorist have argued for the centrality of a number of themes that figure in his speeches and writings. These include: his conservatism, manifested especially in opposition to parliamentary reform and the French Revolution; his hostility toward abstract theory and theory-oriented intellectuals in politics; his trusteeship conceptions of representation and of government in general; his commitment to such classical liberal or Whig values as property, the rule of law, and constitutionalism; and his conception of statesmanship, informed by notions of prudence, expediency, and practical wisdom. Some of these themes have been discussed already. In this chapter, however, we concentrate on two other themes in Burke's philosophy: first, his traditionalism, or his usual attribution of value and normative force to social customs, prejudice, and time-sanctioned institutions and usages; and second, his embrace of a "higher law" tradition, or a theory of natural right that posits universal moral norms as standards for government and positive law. The rich diversity of Burke's ideas, and of the practical issues to which he applied them, has led to continuing questions about his consistency; certainly, there appears to be some tension, most fundamentally between his traditionalism and his invocations of natural law, as well as between these two concepts and other ideas that he expressed. The problem of reconciling the various guiding threads in Burke's theory will therefore be addressed in relation to their application to India.

We may begin with Burke's theory of traditionalism, a term that is often linked to the "conservative" label most frequently applied to him. References to Burke as a traditionalist conservative may initially stumble on Michael Freeman's claim that Burke does not actually use the word "tradition," and that tradition should therefore not be taken to be a category of his thought.[1] If correct, this omission is odd, since the literal meaning of the word—a "handing down" from past to present—connotes a social process that Burke often invokes approvingly. Burke's works do contain a rich panoply of words and concepts that may reasonably be associated with the idea of traditionalism: *custom, prescription, inheritance, the ancestral,* "the spirit of our old manners and opinions" (*Reflections,* 173), and the like; thus, we may follow Pocock and the common view that a "doctrine of traditionalism" is indeed central to Burke's thought.[2] In what follows I shall analyze Burke's traditionalism in three stages: as a sociological theory, as an account of the practical basis of morality, and as a normative doctrine. Although Burke is best known for his defenses of traditional institutions against revolutionary threats in Europe, the objective here is to consider this orientation in relation to his views on British imperial policy in India. It will lead us to substantial agreement with the thesis that Burke's appreciation of Indian traditions made him one of the first to develop a "conservative theory of Indian society, culture, and government."[3]

At the level of sociological analysis, Burke recognized that, in any reasonably stable society, many or most of the rules and practices that order people's interactions and provide social cohesion are traditional or customary in nature—handed down from the past—rather than, for example, imposed by fiat and enforced by political authority, or produced by the rational calculation of individuals. Old institutions and laws become venerable and are strengthened through habitual compliance, in addition to whatever other kinds of legitimacy or sanctions they may have. People normally derive great benefits—moral as well as material—and significant elements of their identity from membership in a community with a historical existence, a community that looks back to ancestors and forward to future generations. Such views were readily applicable to India. The integration of individuals into a profoundly, even rigidly, customary community seemed especially obvious in Hindu India, where, as Burke explained, the laws of the land, of religion, and of honor coincided in the ancient rules of the caste system ("Speech on Opening," 303). But the general point has universal validity.

In developing this theme, Burke adopted a historical approach to politics and society in which tradition, as the residue of historical experience, constitutes a key element in any analysis. In doing so, he opposed the abstract, ahistorical, and universalist approach to moral and political theory sometimes ascribed to eighteenth-century thinkers, although this view of the Enlightenment is, in fact, one-sided. In a famous argument, for example, Montesquieu claimed that an adequate interpretation of laws and governments had to take into account numerous underlying social and cultural factors, which themselves were grounded in custom and history. We have seen that Burke accepted Montesquieu's contention that laws had to be adapted to the particular conditions of a given country.[4] Burke was also acquainted with the work of Scottish theorists such as Hume, Ferguson, and Smith, who were deeply interested in historical perspectives on contemporary society, and whose theories of sympathy and mental association offered a psychological explanation for the importance of habits and custom.

Second, Burke held that well-established traditions were likely to contain valuable elements or to serve to promote important social values; he thus often expressed a favorable, even affectionate, attitude toward traditions and recommended they be conserved as much as possible, and not lightly altered or violated. Burke's endorsement of gradual reform, in contrast to revolutionary or radical change, rested in part on his belief that traditional rules and institutions usually embodied beneficial adaptations to social needs—ones that, on the whole, were more advantageous than alternative schemes that people might try to design in the abstract, at a distance from the complexity of actual experience. In prosperous societies, at any rate, Burke ascribed a strong (though rebuttable) presumption of utility to traditional institutions, and he warned against the tendency of would-be reformers to overlook the valuable ingredients in such institutions that were usually intermixed with their defects, and thus to underestimate the losses that would attend reform (*Reflections*, 173, 285).

This perspective was applicable to India, whose native laws and institutions, far more ancient than those of Europe, had two features "which entitle them to respect: first, great force and stability; and next, excellent moral and civil effects." Their stability, "with all the reverence of antiquity," and with "roots deep in their native soil," had enabled them to withstand foreign conquests; their beneficial effects could be glimpsed in the normally flourishing condition of Hindu polities, unless disturbed by "the rapacity of a foreign hand" ("Speech in Opening," 9:382–84). With such an opinion of the value of tradition in India and elsewhere, Burke was all the more "stupefied," upon studying the history of the East India Company,

> by the desperate boldness of a few obscure young men, who having obtained, by ways which they could not comprehend, a power of which they saw neither the purposes nor the limits, tossed about, subverted, and tore to pieces, . . . the most established rights, and the most ancient and most revered institutions, of ages and nations. (*Fox's Bill*, 427)

Equally if not more important, Burke held that morality is in practice necessarily associated with stable traditions. People ordinarily do not and cannot engage in deliberate ethical reasoning on most occasions of action, and indeed the results would be unreliable if they tried. Rather, people absorb the moral principles that are prescribed by the traditions of their communities—"the moral, civil, and social habitudes of the people" ("Speech on Representation," 95)—in the form of "prejudices," which in turn serve as a trustworthy guide to moral practice. Prejudices, in this sense, according to Burke's doctrine, perform both a cognitive or learning function in moral life, transforming the "latent wisdom" of social and historical experience into a practical guide for individual action, and a motivational function, "render-[ing] a man's virtue his habit" (*Reflections*, 183). The "empire of [traditional] opinion," moreover, strong everywhere and the foundation of human happiness, possessed "a pure, unrestrained, complete, and despotic power" among the people of India ("Speech in Opening," 9:379).[5]

Burke thus stands in a venerable tradition of moral theory that includes Aristotle's emphasis on the practical need for habituation in virtue, the Scottish Enlightenment's account of a socialized moral sense, and contemporary assessments of the role of internalized social norms in explaining social order.[6] Burke's admonitions against revolution rested in part on his fear that any large-scale disruption of tradition would undermine everyday morality, which could not be easily reconstituted. This is the principal reason why it is unwise for governments to "set at defiance the general feelings of great communities" ("Address to the King," 165), and why "when antient opinions and rules of life are taken away, the loss cannot possibly be estimated" (*Reflections*, 172).

Finally, Burke's traditionalism is a normative doctrine insofar as he maintains that traditional status confers legitimacy on institutions and creates valid claims of right or obligation. He held, for example, that we ought to venerate our ancestors, a sentiment he believed was linked psychologically to our acceptance of duties to posterity through an appropriate sense of ourselves as members of an ongoing community (*Reflections*, 119), one having "continuity . . . in time as well as in numbers and in space" ("Speech on Representation," 95). This idea is related in turn to the Burkean ethic of regarding our social institutions and cultural heritage, including our laws and liberties, as an inheritance comparable to an entailed estate passed down to us from our predecessors. We should therefore consider ourselves "temporary possessors and life-renters," or trustees, bound to pass it on intact to our descendants (*Reflections*, 192). Accordingly, Burke claimed to make "what the ancients call *mos majorum*, not indeed his sole, but certainly his principal rule of policy, to guide his judgment in whatever regards our laws" ("Appeal," 134).

More formally, Burke enunciated a conception of prescriptive right, which some readers have taken to be central to his normative philosophy. Prescription was the familiar legal doctrine—found in different versions in natural and civil law, and in English common law—that custom or usage generates right, and especially, that long possession creates a valid title to property.[7] Pocock has argued that this idea is the key to Burke's traditionalism and that its prominence shows his indebtedness to the common law, which he once studied.[8] Burke not only recognized the importance of prescriptive property rights but also applied the concept to the legitimacy of governments, to the rights of certain individuals or groups to occupy positions of authority, and to the liberties or rights that subjects might claim against their rulers. Political rights were assimilated to property rights—not remarkable in an age when ownership of property did in fact often carry political rights with it—and a legal principle expressing the normative force of the past (tradition) was incorporated into Burke's political theory.

Burke's use of prescriptive right in his political theory blurs several legal distinctions. Common law differentiated between rights or titles by local custom, which were possessed by everyone or by members of certain groups in a given locality, from prescriptive rights, which were strictly personal, claimable by a particular individual by virtue of the practice of his ancestors or legal predecessors.[9] By these criteria, the liberties of Englishmen, which Burke treats as prescriptive, were properly speaking customary—as were analogous rights belonging to the various castes and regional or religious groups in India. For purposes of Burke's political arguments, custom and prescription in their technical senses merged in the contention that genuine rights were the product of tradition or past usage.

Another distinction holds that customary rights arise from "immemorial" usage—uncontested practice for which no beginning can be shown, or running as far back as the records indicate. Prescription, by contrast, like the modern legal principle of adverse possession, refers to rights derived from usage or possession extending back only a limited period of time, which is stipulated by law. Custom and prescription in these senses are similar in that they both acknowledge the legal force of "long possession," and derive valid right from past practice. They differ significantly, however, in that prescription can confer right on a present practice or possession that demonstrably deviates from earlier practice and that may even have originated in a usurpation, so long as a certain period of time has elapsed. The point of such a rule is to stabilize present titles and reduce disputes and litigation based on the revival of old (and thus often uncertain) claims, as well as to uphold expectations that are reasonably grounded in a long-established state of affairs.[10]

The doctrine of prescription in this sense differs in an important way from the argument of custom, especially when it is taken from the law of property and applied to politics. The doctrine of prescription can legitimize present systems of authority or government that stem from irregular transfers or usurpations of power, or even from revolutions, in the past, if they have been stable and effective over a sufficient period of time. In the case of political authority, the condition that possession be uncontested must normally be dropped, and other criteria may be combined with pure prescriptive right. Hume, for example, withheld judgment on the rightfulness of the Revolution of 1688, but argued in precisely this fashion for the legitimacy of the Hanoverian successor regime half a century later, pointing both to long possession and to the beneficial quality of the governance actually provided.[11] Burke, as we have noted, justified the Revolution directly by referring to its "necessity," but in other cases, including that of Great Britain's possession of its empire in India, Burke was prepared to grant that merely long—not ancient—possession of ruling authority constitutes a sufficient title, or at least contributes to the case for one. "Decent drapery" must be drawn over the exact origins of most governments, which do not bear close scrutiny. The political version of prescription in the sense of "adverse possession," then, is less conservative than appeals to custom; it is also less purely a traditionalist position, since, in Burke as in Hume, it looks to the past but combines the claim that past usage as such generates right with utilitarian arguments regarding the undesirability of reopening old controversies and the advantages of maintaining a stable de facto government, at least if its rule is reasonably effective and just.[12]

Burke invoked the idea of prescriptive right, both to property and to political authority, in both the senses just discussed. In his best-known declaration, he used "prescription" in the sense of immemorial custom. Denying that individuals had a natural right to be directly represented in government, and pointing to the hereditary rights of Crown and peerage, Burke said: "Our Constitution is a prescriptive constitution; it is a constitution whose sole authority is, that it has existed time out of mind. . . . Prescription is the most solid of all titles, not only to property, but, which is to secure that property, to government" ("Speech on Representation," 94). The striking claim here that prescription is the sole basis of legitimate authority is surely overstated, since Burke clearly used other normative criteria for assessing governments. Even the lesser claim that it constitutes the "most solid" title is surprising, since prescriptive claims were considered relatively weak in law, used only when title to property could not be established on any other basis. Clearly, Burke was giving prescriptive right greater weight than was usual and was granting it a novel importance in controversies over political authority.[13] Here, however, prescription seems to be equivalent to custom, which would have been the more correct term. Burke was expressing the standard common lawyers' view that the common law itself, and the rights of the various agencies of English government enshrined in that law, were institutions so ancient that their origins could not be documented, and that their authority rested on this fact.

On other occasions, however, Burke used the idea of prescriptive right to justify existing titles of questionable origin. The French revolutionaries claimed that the lands they confiscated had originally been wrested unjustly from the nation; rather than disputing the factual basis of this allegation, Burke condemned them for violating rights founded on "law, usage, the decisions of courts, and the accumulated prescription of a thousand years" (*Reflections*, 206). The "insolent men calling themselves the French nation" could themselves assert a right to "the territory called France" only by virtue of "prescription and descent from certain gangs of banditti called Franks" who had anciently seized the country ("Appeal," 166). The French nobility may have originally seized their lands by violence, but then again, so had the entire French nation; both sets of rights could be made legitimate only through the passage of time. More proximately, titles to land, peerages, and franchises in Britain and Ireland ultimately rested on prescription in this sense. In his bitter rejoinder to the duke of Bedford, who had criticized Burke's acceptance of a pension from the Crown, Burke pointed out that the duke's estates originated in Henry VIII's tyrannical confiscation of English monastic property, and could be defended now only by the length of time that had elapsed since the original injustice: "The Duke of Bedford will stand as long as prescriptive law endures; as long as the great stable laws of property, common to us with all civilized nations, are kept in their integrity" (*Noble Lord*, 516). And although Burke frequently criticized the oppressive rule of the Protestant Ascendancy in Ireland, he maintained that Protestant estates there, many of which had originated in confiscations in the previous century, were now solid by prescription: "It is *old violence*; and that which might be wrong in the beginning, is consecrated by time, and becomes lawful" (*Corr.* 6:95). In all these cases, prescription upheld titles based on long, but not immemorial, possession, in the interest of present peace and the stability of property and government. "Sacred veils" had to be drawn over origins, in these cases as in Bengal, where prescription (even after only a few decades) appears to have supplemented the rather weak argument that the British had received a formal grant of authority from the Mogul emperor as a basis for Burke's willingness to accept the legitimacy of the empire.

Burke's traditionalism, then, led him to embrace prescription as a principle of law and of stable political institutions—but in two different senses that were not always compatible with each other. Prescription as adverse possession is a paradoxical doctrine, since it upholds existing rights against disruptive change or revolution in the present, while simultaneously dictating acceptance of revolutions in the past. Prescriptive rights in this sense can also be opposed to prescription based on ancient or immemorial custom; the prescriptive rights of rulers derived from stabilized conquests (like those of the East India Company) can conflict with the customary rights of subjects to their property and established local practices. If Burke accepted the right of the company or the British to rule in India at least partly on the basis of prescription, he also asserted that they were bound to rule in accordance with the customary rights of their Indian subjects, and he condemned Hastings for violating this duty.

According to Burke, the formal charters which the East India Company had obtained from the Mogul Empire obligated it to "observe the laws, rights, usages and customs of the Natives," and, by accepting a position of authority in India, Great Britain "made a virtual act of union with that country, by which they bound themselves as securities for their subjects, to preserve the people in all rights, laws and liberties, which their natural original Sovereign was bound to enforce, if he had been in a condition to enforce it" ("Speech on Opening," 281–82). Both formally and implicitly, Britain had correctly acknowledged a duty to observe preexisting customary rights; indeed, the greater "versatility" of European manners, compared to the restrictiveness of Hindu custom, imposed a special duty to "govern them upon their own principles and maxims and not upon ours . . . [and not] to force them to our narrow ideas, but extend ours to take in theirs; because to say that people shall change their maxims, lives and opinions, is what cannot be" ("Speech on Opening," 302). Referring to the caste system, Burke asserted that it was not appropriate for Englishmen "to commend or blame the institutions and prejudices of a whole race of people, radicated in them by a long succession of ages." Deliberate violations of caste—used, Burke charged, as a form of torture to extract taxes—were impermissible offenses against valid customary norms or, in the case of high-caste victims, customary privileges ("Speech in Opening," 10:89). Early in the Indian phase of his career, Burke helped draft legislation to ensure that British courts in Bengal would administer native law on Indian subjects ("Bengal Judicature," 140). Toward the end he reaffirmed that Hastings had been "bound to proceed according to the laws, rights, laudable customs, privileges, and franchises of the country that he governed . . . to which the people of the country had a clear and just claim" ("Speech in Reply," 11:230).

Burke's charge that, in their quest for power and profits, the officials of the East India Company wantonly and ruthlessly trampled on the traditional culture and society of India, has often been seen as misguided or exaggerated, even by those who sympathize with other aspects of his indictment. In part, this assessment looks backward from the nineteenth century, when British officials, influenced by reforming utilitarianism and by evangelical humanitarianism, consciously attempted to transform and modernize India. No one concerned with the Indian empire in Hastings's period advocated or even imagined such a project; thus, by later standards, Burke and his adversaries ironically appear to agree that India had to be governed on its own terms. Fearing disorder, for example, the East India Company prohibited Christian missionaries in the parts of India under its control, until it was overruled by Parliament in 1813, under pressure from evangelicals;[14] accordingly, although Burke accused Hastings's agents of occasional violations of religious sensibilities, he did not accuse the company of any general attempt to destroy Indian religions, or of religious persecution and harassment comparable to that which he accused the English and Anglo-Irish authorities of perpetrating in Ireland, causing "intollerable hardship" for the Roman Catholic population (*Letter to Kenmare*, 576). On this score, at least, the East India Company of the period appeared as a protector of tradition.

More particularly, Hastings himself has frequently been defended on this matter. A weak version of this position holds that he, along with the other "adventurers" and "gentlemen warriors" who created the empire, was aiming at commercial and national advantage but was, in keeping with his eighteenth-century background, "unexcited by questions of morality." Lacking both the high-mindedness and the sense of racial superiority of their successors, Hastings and other adventurers "conquered India but did not despise it."[15] More strongly, Hastings has been defended as someone who, more than most of his colleagues, admired Indian culture and sought to promote knowledge of it.[16] For the most part, he agreed with Burke that Indians should be ruled in accordance with their own customary law. Although it was sometimes grounded in "superstitious" religion, he reported to the company directors, since local law was

> consonant to the ideas, manners, and inclinations of the people for whose use it is intended, I presume that on these grounds it will be preferable to any which ever a superior wisdom could substitute in its room. . . . The people of this country do not require our aid to furnish them with a rule for their conduct, or a standard for their property.[17]

Most strikingly, Hastings patronized the study of Hinduism, an enterprise that produced not only Halhed's edition of Hindu laws (which Burke later cited against him) but the first translation of a classical Sanskrit work into a European language.[18] Hastings sometimes justified these efforts in political terms, as facilitating imperial rule: "Every accumulation of knowledge . . . of people over whom we exercise a dominion founded on the right of conquest, is useful to the state." He also, however, expressed genuine appreciation for the "sublimity" of Hindu works and argued that their publication would be "the gain of humanity" and would lead to greater respect and "benevolence" toward Indians on the part of the English.[19] To Samuel Johnson he wrote, "It has been one of my first wishes to be able to free the inhabitants of this country from the reproach of ignorance and barbarism which has been undeservedly cast upon them by the too precipitate information of those who have wanted opportunities of knowing their real state."[20]

Burke may have been uninformed about some of these efforts and hence unfair to the governor-general on this issue. On balance, however, it seems likely that Burke would not have been impressed by any attempt to portray Hastings as genuinely sympathetic to Indian tradition, given the numerous violations of local customs and sensibilities of which he accused him.[21] When Hastings aligned himself with local tradition, in Burke's view, it was usually in a cynical or self-serving spirit. He defended the oppressive conditions maintained among the workers in the company's salt monopoly, for example, as being "customary from Time immemorial" (*Ninth Report*, 288); and a "Mahometan college" that Hastings established in Calcutta quickly became a "scene of peculation," in keeping with the general corruption of his regime ("Speech in Reply," 12:354). Moreover, it was generally the worst customs of the country, rather than the more respectable ones, that Hastings found it convenient to follow for his own purposes. The Indian practice of accepting large entertainment allowances from subordinate officials, for example, as Hastings had done when he visited Munni Begam in Murshidabad, was a "lewd custom" that a British governor ought to have repudiated ("Sixth Article," 268). The prevalence of giving and receiving presents or bribes may in fact have been a traditional practice, but Burke judged it to be bad in itself, as well as forbidden to British officials by their own laws. The fact that Hastings's predecessors had long enjoyed such perquisites did not confer on him a prescriptive right to do the same; or at least, this was not a right that a new company or parliamentary regulation could not summarily cancel. In Burke's view, Hastings was wrong to claim that his embrace of a despotic mode of governance was in line with the general practice of Asia; but Burke conceded that there were many instances of local despotic rulers whom the English could imitate if they chose. His accusation in this respect was that Hastings was culpable for following an aberrant custom he should have rejected.

These considerations make it clear that tradition was not always authoritative for Burke; it was not invariably the case—even if it was usually true—that "latent wisdom" and sound morality were embodied in venerable customs and prejudices. Some traditions might incorporate injustice; contrary to Burke's view of the usually benign effects of evolutionary adaptation, practices that had once been sound might become corrupt or dysfunctional in changing circumstances, as Burke believed was the case with the East India Company's system of rule in India. Thus, the British were bound to uphold not tradition as such in India, but only the "laudable customs" of the country ("Speech in Reply," 11:230), or at any rate, those that were not clearly bad. The duty of Burkean rulers to rule well conflicts with the duty to respect and conform to custom, unless one is convinced, as Burke evidently was not, that customs are invariably good. If Burke was prepared to distinguish between good and bad traditions, however, he must have recognized standards above tradition from which such distinctions could be derived. Tradition, however important and usually valuable an element in social life, was not always a decisive consideration.

Finally, we may consider the possibility that Burke's appreciation of tradition and his acknowledgment of its normative force—in some if not all cases—led him to a position of relativism or historicism. To recognize the moral and political authority of tradition is to recognize the authority of norms and practices that exist, on a more or less solid historical foundation, in a particular place, culture, or society. Since moral beliefs and practices apparently differ considerably from one society to another, this amounts to acknowledging the rightfulness of a variety of different, and no doubt sometimes conflicting, norms. Relativism in the sense that might apply to Burke is the doctrine that different norms are equally valid in the social or cultural settings in which they are traditional. Since norms also vary over time, and since traditional norms are the product of history, relativism is closely related to historicism, the doctrine either that history and historical practices are self-justifying, or that it is pointless or inappropriate to evaluate or condemn a given historical culture or a historical process by moral standards external to it. The doctrine of prescriptive right, in the sense of adverse possession, implies that successful possession over time can convert an injustice into a rightful title; prescription in the looser sense of immemorial custom implies the existence of diverse cultures, defined by their deeply rooted customs, whose validity and claim to respect rest on their antiquity and their coherence over time. Both these versions of traditionalism, referring as they do to the temporal character of practices and institutions, involve a relativistic denial of general and unchanging standards.

To accept tradition as absolutely authoritative—that is, to hold that tradition is the only source of value and right—implies complete relativism (except insofar as some norms happened to be universal). As we have just seen, Burke was almost certainly not absolutist in his traditionalism, which, after all, would have meant taking a rigidly doctrinaire and simplistic position on complex moral matters, a stance he often condemned. At the same time, Burke clearly upheld prescriptive or customary right in some form and to some degree, and this implies that he was convinced of the validity of historically variable practices and institutions, and hence of at least partial relativism. For this he has been both praised and blamed. Ernest Barker took Burkean "prescription" to be "the historic process behind any system of institutions, which forms their connecting cement," or a process of "objective mind" that both explains and legitimizes social reality; he accordingly commented admiringly that Burke had "an Hegel within him."[22] Leo Strauss also asserted that Burke's use of prescription formed a "preparation for Hegel" and thus for modern historicism, though he appraised this tendency very differently and found other, more valuable elements in Burke's theory.[23] More recent scholars have noted the problem of historicism in Burke while downplaying its significance or pointing to ambivalence in Burke's theory.[24]

To make the case that Burke was a historical relativist, one would first have to show that he recognized the existence of significant and deep-seated cultural or moral differences among societies, and that these differences legitimized or prescribed different institutions and different standards for government organization and policies. We may find support for this in Burke's defense of the appropriateness of somewhat different political and religious institutions in England, Ireland, America, and France—for example, in his claim that he was not "a friend or an enemy to republics or to monarchies in the abstract. He thought that the circumstances and habits of every country, which it is always perilous and productive of the greatest calamities to force, are to decide upon the form of its government" ("Appeal," 114). This evidence is weak in that, in Burke's own view, the various European institutions shared a family resemblance; the case of India, however, provides much more dramatic evidence that Burke could confront a society that was fundamentally different from Europe in some respects, could urge understanding of and sympathy with it on its own terms, and could argue that it should be governed in conformity with its traditions.[25] To complete the case for relativism, however, one would also have to argue that Burke believed that the only norms pertinent to ruling India were local ones, and that he was unwilling to invoke extraneous (i.e., European) moral values, or universal norms, to supplement, restrict, or interpret the claims of Indian tradition. In the following section it will become clear that this case for a strong version of relativism or historicism cannot be sustained.

Nonetheless, Burke immersed himself in Indian history as much as possible and made imaginative efforts to comprehend Indian culture and the meaning of imperial events through Indian eyes. In his descriptions of India, Burke did his part to roll back "the Great Map of Mankind," thus encouraging appreciation of foreign societies among Europeans.[26] In the process, he occasionally gave vivid expression to the different and alien quality of the people and society with which he was concerned, as the rhetorical strategies of his trial speeches dictated. To secure the condemnation of Hastings from an assembly of British politicians (or by British public opinion), Burke had to urge that justice be done in a context that was extremely obscure and exotic for nearly all in his audience, yet vast in scale and importance:

> It is not from this district or from that parish, not from this city or the other province, that relief is now applied for: exiled and undone princes, extensive tribes, suffering nations, infinite descriptions of men, different in language, in manners, and in rites, men separated

by every barrier of Nature from you, by the Providence of God are blended in one common cause, and are now become suppliants at your bar. ("Speech in Opening," 9:340)[27]

The strangeness of India was most strikingly evident in the Hindus, "who extend their good-will to the whole animal creation," but whose caste restrictions made them, "of all nations, the most unalliable" to outsiders. Caste Hindus could not share meals with others, which "renders it difficult for us to enter with due sympathy into their concerns, or for them to enter into ours, even when we meet on the same ground." Nor were they allowed to cross the ocean, the element that otherwise "unites mankind." This prevented them from pleading their cause in person: "It is a great gulf fixed between you and them,—not so much that elementary gulf, but that gulf which manners, opinions, and laws have radicated in the very nature of the people." Burke urged that this circumstance "imposes upon us a stricter duty to guard with firm and powerful vigilance those whose principles of conscience weaken their principles of self-defence" ("Speech in Opening," 9: 378). That duty, however, entailed an arduous effort to understand and respect the Indians' peculiar sensibilities and all the principles of their laws and customs.[28]

Similar obstacles to sympathy arose in the case of Muslim India, especially in connection with the position of women. A correct assessment of Hastings's mistreatment of the begams of Oudh depended on grasping "the general Sanctity of women in that Country, the general homage paid to maternal authority wherever the Mahometan Religion prevails," though this was something that might instead arouse ridicule in England:

It is our nature and we cannot help it; it is the most difficult thing in the world to bring ourselves to a proper degree of sympathy when we are describing those circumstances which are not ingrafted in our nature by custom. I believe that the first thing that creates laughter throughout mankind by general sympathy is distress which arises not from our nature but from local institution. ("Evidence," 478)

Physical pain is readily understandable anywhere, but "the sufferings which touch our moral nature have a wider range, and are infinitely more acute." They arise from the fact that

man, in his moral nature, becomes, in his progress through life, a creature of prejudice, a creature of opinions, a creature of habits, and of sentiments growing out of them. These form our second nature, as inhabitants of the country and members of the society in which Providence has placed us. ("Speech in Reply," 12:164)

In Burke's view, it was Providence—the "Sovereign Disposer"—who placed the British in Bengal as the rulers of Indians. With this authority came the obligation not to inflict the moral suffering caused by wanton violations of local tradition and the "second nature" it defined.

Burke frequently and in various contexts expressed the idea that "government . . . ought to conform to the exigencies of the time and the temper and character of the people with whom it is concerned" (*Sheriffs of Bristol*, 230; also "Conciliation," 141). This could be taken as a maxim of practical statecraft, and may sometimes have been intended as one: any other course might provoke resistance and lead to failure. Or it could be taken as a prudent recognition of circumstantial constraints on ideal policy: sometimes one must settle for compromises or approximations of justice. Or it could indicate the (at least partial) role of popular desires and consent in legitimizing government policies. On the traditionalist interpretation of Burke's theory, however, it is an acknowledgment of the reality of prescriptive and customary rights as understood within a particular historical society, and thus of the genuine moral claims of tradition on the holders of power.

The Moral Law

Others have held that the ethical foundation of Burke's political theory is his adherence to a higher moral law prescribing rules or principles whose validity is independent of human choice or social convention, and whose applicability is universal. Objective and fixed standards of justice would constitute a source of normative constraints on political conduct and a basis for evaluating both the performance of governments and the content of existing practices and institutions, whether new or old; commitment to such a higher law would therefore provide a clear alternative both to *raison d'état* and to traditionalism as a fundamental moral orientation in politics. Burke's writings and speeches on Indian affairs bear out the view that he held such a position; indeed, they offer the strongest textual evidence for this view.

According to the best-known interpretation of Burke along these lines, he adhered to the venerable natural law tradition of Western moral philosophy. Strauss, who drew a clear distinction between classical and modern doctrines of natural right, argued that Burke attempted to revive, "at the last minute, as it were," the "premodern," "classical or Thomistic" version of natural right, with special emphasis on the classical virtue of prudence. This interpretation accords well with the common view of Burke as a venerator of the received moral and political heritage of Europe. Strauss, however, detected ambivalence on two counts: Burke, he thought, also helped pave the

way for modern historicism, which eventually displaced natural right altogether; and Burke occasionally employed the "language of modern natural
right whenever that could assist him in persuading his modern audience of
the soundness of a policy." This practice has led some to suspect that all
of Burke's references to natural law were merely rhetorical, a conclusion
Strauss rejected.[29]

Subsequently, Peter J. Stanlis and Francis P. Canavan portrayed Burke
in more detail as both a sincere and an unambivalent adherent of traditional
or Thomist natural law. Stanlis admits, however, that Burke's references to
this philosophy are most explicit in the early, unpublished "Tract on the
Popery Laws," and especially in the Indian speeches; they are absent, brief,
or only "implicit" in most of his other works.[30] It would seem, then, that
study of Burke's ideas on India and the cogency of his statements on a higher
law in that context would be crucial to the interpretation of his political
theory in general. In a different reading, Frederick A. Dreyer, taking Burke
at his word, characterizes him as a Whig of the Glorious Revolution and
hence an adherent of the most important Lockeian political principles,
including Locke's theory that the state is limited by the "dictates of natural
justice." Despite Burke's respect for custom in general, bad customs can be
identified and repudiated in light of this moral principle.[31] Wilkins offers
a synthetic interpretation, questioning the Straussian distinction between
classic and modern natural right, and arguing that Burke and Locke are both
essentially within the tradition of Thomist or Christian natural law, with its
classical roots.[32] All these commentators agree that Burke's thought constitutes a substantial normative political theory grounded in his acceptance
of moral principles that can for the most part be identified with natural law,
as this doctrine had been variously expounded by earlier philosophers.

We need to make two qualifications to this thesis. First, Burke should
not himself be regarded as a natural law philosopher, in the sense of having
systematically theorized about it; apart from his treatise on aesthetics, Burke
wrote political, not philosophical, works. Rather, the claim is that Burke
was familiar with natural law philosophy, accepted it, and often invoked or
alluded to it in his political arguments, presupposing familiarity with it on
the part of his classically educated and Christian audiences. Oddly, given
the Thomist interpretation, Burke never refers to Thomas Aquinas; but he
does frequently and approvingly cite Richard Hooker, a major expounder of
Christian natural law, as well as ancient figures in the tradition such as
Aristotle and Cicero.[33] Second, Burke rarely speaks of "natural law" directly,
but he often appeals to concepts equivalent or linked to the idea of natural
law: "moral law," "eternal law," "natural justice," or "justice," "equity," and

"humanity" in the abstract. These terms and phrases seem to imply a higher moral law or set of moral principles—higher in that their validity transcends the beliefs and conventions of any historical society—from which Burke drew his ethical commitments and judgments in political affairs.

A moral philosophy such as that expressed by Burke's higher law provides standards by which to evaluate positive laws and customs, political institutions, and political action and programs. Natural law can be invoked to justify existing institutions that are held to correspond to its dictates, and Burke sometimes employed the notion in such a conservative fashion: the "latent wisdom" he thought could usually be discovered in the moral prejudices of a well-ordered society expressed the truths of the moral law; and he defended the political system of Great Britain as a reasonable approximation of its requirements. Equally, however, natural law can provide a critical standard for challenging or condemning laws and practices that violate its provisions, and even for identifying moral "crimes" against justice. Insofar as Burke invoked natural law with reference to Ireland and India, the two cases where he was most consistently and severely critical of existing policies, his use of the theory exemplifies the latter function, which is historically most familiar.

For some portions of his case against Hastings, Burke argued like a lawyer, from within the positive structure of British law and government, maintaining that Hastings had violated specific company rules or parliamentary statutes, or that he had transgressed conventions of behavior or honor accepted in British public life at that time. In his long speech on the "sixth article" of impeachment, for example, which dealt with allegations of bribery and illegal contracts, Burke did not refer to natural law, since he believed Hastings's guilt could be clearly established in relation to positive laws and regulations.[34] For his more important and dramatic charges, however—that the East India Company's rule was generally oppressive to its Indian subjects, and that Hastings had personally ruled in a despotic manner—he needed a higher standard of justice or political morality. In particular, he needed a standard sufficiently fundamental to defeat both Hastings's relativistic appeals to local practice and above all the defense of his actions in the name of "state necessity" or *raison d'état*. The need for extraordinary and forceful measures to "save the empire" or simply to deal with military and financial threats to its security constituted a strong argument for the practical men who were to judge the case; state necessity plausibly overrides mere customs, regulations, and even laws, at least occasionally. Most of Burke's audience shared his belief in natural law or justice in some form; only by appealing to these ideals could Burke defeat Hastings's various appeals to the constraints of imperial reality.[35] Thus we find Burke announcing to the House of Lords, at the beginning of the trial, that Hastings was charged with "crimes, not against forms, but against those eternal laws of justice which you are assembled here to assert . . . not in formal and technical language, but in real and absolute effect, High Crimes and Misdemeanours" ("Speech on Opening, 275). Most of the charges against Hastings discussed in chapter 3, including treaty breaking, aggressive war, property confiscations, denial of due process to Chait Singh, abuse of wardship, and violations of filial duty (in the case of the begams of Oudh), were presented as crimes against natural law or justice.

Drawing on what indeed appears to be traditional natural law doctrine, Burke had no difficulty in developing moral principles that served his practical purposes in his criticism of the East India Company and the prosecution of Hastings. The moral framework he evokes in his Indian speeches, however, is frequently echoed throughout his works. Moral law prescribes duties to people, who are understood to be naturally sociable beings. These duties are therefore not created or chosen by human will but are rationally connected to our status as members of civil society. Without such duties, social relations would be determined simply by "the will of the prevalent power" ("Appeal," 160). Civil society requires authority or government, which natural law accordingly endorses. Citing a passage from Cicero with which Christian natural lawyers could readily concur, Burke asserted that God was the ultimate "institutor, and author and protector of civil society," without which man could not "arrive at the perfection of which his nature is capable." As a further means to that end, God also "willed therefore the State" (*Reflections*, 196). The general duties of rulers, which Burke sometimes conceived in terms of the legal category of a trust, were similarly prescribed by natural law, and their legitimate powers limited by it. Government, though not necessarily directly accountable to its subjects, was for their benefit, and was thus bound both to promote material prosperity and social order and to uphold justice and rights. "Equity and utility," as Burke put it in an early declaration, were the two foundations of all valid law ("Popery Laws," 456). As principles drawn from a general moral law, these strictures applied to government in India as well as to government in Ireland or England.[36]

Above all, and especially important in the context of imperial rule, government power could not simply express the arbitrary will of the rulers. In his writings on France, especially, Burke emphasized that will could not be the sole basis of legitimate power. The revolutionaries, he held, had not only concentrated power in the National Assembly but had also renounced the most important restraints on arbitrary rule, such as religion, custom, prescriptive right, "fundamental law," and natural law in its traditional form as a source of limits on power (*Reflections*, 133). All government, whether in the hands of select individuals or in the hands of the people more broadly, "to be legitimate must be according to that eternal immutable law, in which will and reason are the same." No one was ever entitled "to use any arbitrary power whatsoever" (*Reflections*, 191–92). Government in accordance with the moral law would be lawful rule in one sense; Burke's additional insistence that government be constitutional, structured so as to ensure the rule of law in its positive enactments, represents a complementary commitment to limits on power and to procedural justice.

While Burke was denouncing willful or arbitrary government in his *Reflections* on events in France, he was simultaneously carrying to its culmination, in the impeachment trial, his decade-long campaign against Hastings and misrule in India. In this case too, a central theme was the repudiation of arbitrary or despotic rule in the name of a higher standard of morality and justice.[37] Burke's application of higher law norms to the Indian empire, however, had begun earlier. Apart from numerous scattered phrases, there are three main passages that express this aspect of his thought: in his speech supporting Fox's East India Bill, and then in the opening and closing speeches of the impeachment trial.[38]

Burke opened his famous 1783 speech by declaring that "a substantial reform in our Eastern administration" was demanded "by humanity, by justice, and by every principle of true policy," implying, as he often did, that the requirements of morality were likely to coincide with an enlightened view of interest—in this case, Britain's interests in sustaining a flourishing commercial empire and in preserving its own constitution from corruption. The moral emphasis quickly became paramount: if Great Britain was to govern India, it had a duty "of governing India *well*," and "preserv[ing] India from oppression." A failure in that respect would require a "separation" of the two nations. This claim led directly to a clear statement of Burke's conception of government as trusteeship:

> All political power which is set over men . . . being wholly artificial, and for so much, a derogation from the natural equality of mankind at large, ought to be some way or other exercised ultimately for their benefit. . . . Every species of political dominion, and every description of commercial privilege . . . are all in the strictest sense a *trust*.

This argument was made in the context of a contrast between the East India Company's artificial, chartered right to its dominion and privileges, and a set of more fundamental rights—"the rights of *men*, that is to say, the natural rights of mankind, [which] are indeed sacred things." The natural rights Burke cites here are rights "against [arbitrary] power," against oppressive rule. Rights imply duties; the rights of subjects therefore correspond to the duties of rulers and officials. The general duty implicit in the idea of government as a trust, the duty of rulers to promote the well-being of those under their authority, is thus evidently derived from natural law, since its correlate is a natural right of subjects to expect or demand government that meets this standard.

In a later passage, it becomes clear that Burke was appealing to such a higher law: he asserted that for him, as a member of Parliament, to support the continuance of the legal arrangement by which the East India Company exercised—and abused—its authority in India would be to "break the faith, the covenant, the solemn, original, indispensable oath, in which I am bound, by the eternal frame and constitution of things, to the whole human race." It is true that Burke also said in this speech that "the situation of man is the preceptor of his duty": the fact that the members of the Parliament of Great Britain found themselves in a position to exercise power over Indians, and hence with a responsibility to ensure that this power was used correctly, was the result of an improbable and unplanned sequence of events that ultimately had to be accepted as providential. Moral duties are specific and local, as well as general and eternal. If we combine these two statements, we find the outline of a doctrine to the effect that, while natural law prescribes duties that can be stated abstractly and universally and that potentially apply to "the whole human race," one's actual duties arise from the application of the general principles to particular persons and cases, and depend on circumstances, engagements, and particular histories. Practical wisdom or judgment must be called upon to work out how a general adherence to higher morality binds one in a given situation (*Fox's Bill*, 381, 383, 385, 425, 404).

Burke's most extensive and unequivocal invocation of natural law occurred on the second day of his long speech opening Hastings's impeachment trial (February 16, 1788). Indeed, this passage—intertwined with a condemnation of Hastings's argument that the despotic traditions and environment of India authorized him to exercise arbitrary power—is the most extensive presentation of the moral basis of Burke's political theory.

Laying out the background of the prosecution's case, Burke completed a lengthy survey of the history of the East India Company with an examination of some of the more unsavory events of the 1757–1765 period, in which company officials enriched themselves by sponsoring a series of coups in the native government of Bengal and by accepting large presents from rival Indian office seekers. Englishmen, holding effective power, had taken advantage of the prevalent political instability for personal advantage, and had done so by adapting to what Burke regarded as the worst aspects of the local political scene, imitating the despotic practices that admittedly were all too frequent in India during this period. This was inadmissible: "We call for that spirit of equity, that spirit of justice, that spirit of safety, that spirit of protection, that spirit of lenity, which ought to characterise every British subject in power; and upon these and these principles only, [Hastings] will be tried."

Against this position, Hastings had articulated a view that was probably shared by many of the men who had actually served in India—the view, in Burke's summary, "that actions in Asia do not bear the same moral qualities as the same actions would bear in Europe." Hastings and his supporters had

> formed a plan of Geographical morality, by which the duties of men in public and private situations are not to be governed by their relations to the Great Governor of the Universe, or by their relations to men, but by climates, degrees of longitude and latitude, parallels not of life but of latitudes.

The theory of "geographical morality," a version of what today would be called moral relativism, holds that standard practices, institutions, and conduct vary in the different societies around the world, and that moral judgments about them can be made only with reference to the varying cultural norms acknowledged in those societies. It is therefore inappropriate to judge the political practices of India, with its deep-seated despotic customs, by the values of an alien (British) political culture, or by abstract ethical principles that are unknown or unobserved there. Furthermore, Hastings assumed that foreign rulers should—or at any rate may—conform to local traditions, either because people are entitled to preserve their own laws and customs and be governed by them (*this* principle has general validity), or more likely because in practice any other course would prove futile. "This Geographical morality," responded Burke, "we do protest against." As we have seen, Burke disputed Hastings's opinion of the actual content and moral quality of Asian traditions; but now he adopted the antirelativist argument that

> the laws of morality are the same every where, and . . . there is no action which would pass for an action of extortion, of peculation, of

bribery and of oppression in England, that is not an act of extortion, of peculation, of bribery and of oppression in Europe, Asia, Africa, and all the world over. ("Speech on Opening," 345–46)[39]

The principal issue at stake in the ethical controversy was the permissibility of arbitrary methods of rule in the Indian empire. At this point in his speech, Burke reviewed Hastings's arguments to the effect that despotism was universal in Asia and was therefore not only acceptable but was the sole feasible mode of governance there. In reply, Burke denied that despotism was actually normal or sanctioned by the laws and religions of India. Furthermore, he suggested that, to the extent that despotic practices were in fact present, it was the duty of a British governor to reverse the pattern rather than conforming to bad customs. Most important, however, and as the moral basis for this claim, Burke unequivocally denied the permissibility of arbitrary rule under any circumstances, by referring to a higher law. Hastings could not rightfully have ruled arbitrarily because there was no legitimate source or procedure by which such power could have been conferred upon him:

> We have no arbitrary power to give, because Arbitrary power is a thing which neither any man can hold nor any man can give away. No man can govern himself by his own will, much less can he be governed by the will of others. We are all born in subjection, all born equally, high and low, governors and governed, in subjection to one great immutable, pre-existent law, prior to all our devices and prior to all our contrivances . . . by which we are knit and connected in the eternal frame of the universe.

Although Burke's focus on the prohibition of arbitrariness was somewhat distinctive, his allusions to the philosophy of theistic natural law were traditional:[40]

> This great law does not arise from our conventions or compacts. On the contrary, it gives to our conventions and compacts all the force and sanction they can have. . . . All dominion of man over man is the Effect of the divine disposition. All power is of God: and if it be, it is bound by the eternal laws of him that gave it which no human authority can dispense neither he that exercises it nor even those who are subject to it.

Conquest makes no difference: whatever it may have contributed to British authority, the legitimate rights of a conqueror, like any ruler, are circumscribed by the moral law. Nor could the East India Company have acquired arbitrary power by succession or grant from a despotic Mogul emperor, since (whatever his practice) he could not have rightfully possessed or conveyed such power. Nor can arbitrary power rest on "compact, covenant, or submission." And although Burke did not specifically mention prescription in these passages, a natural law requirement of lawful rule in states and empires evidently overrides all contrary positive or customary institutions: "Law and arbitrary power are at eternal enmity" ("Speech on Opening," 350–51, 470).

Apart from the pretext offered by the theory of oriental despotism, Burke suggested that the "idea of arbitrary power" had arisen from a "gross confusion" that the lords of England would have no difficulty escaping. "It does so happen by the necessity of the case that the Supreme power in every Country is not legally and in any ordinary way subject to a penal prosecution for any of its actions."[41] The king and the houses of Parliament in Great Britain were thus not accountable by any legal procedure, and so it was "in the Eastern governments, and the Western, and in all governments." Hastings, however, was not a sovereign in this sense, but exercised an authority delegated by law, for which he was criminally answerable. More important, while "the supreme power in every constitution of government must be absolute" in the sense of legally sovereign, it does not follow that it may be arbitrary, though there is always a danger that it may be "corrupted into the arbitrary." Sovereign powers must be exercised in conformity with the higher law, and "all good constitutions have established certain fixed rules for the exercise of their functions . . . [as] security against that worst of evils, the government of will and force instead of wisdom and justice." Along the same lines, Burke argued that if there were any favorable or defensible sense of the concept "despotism," it was "a mode of Government bound by no written rules; and coerced by no controlling Magistracies." But even without these checks, it was not morally permissible for a "despot" to rule arbitrarily, or to "cancel the primaeval, indefeasible, inalterable Law of Nature and of nations" ("Speech on Opening," 351, 470; cf. variants in "Speech in Opening," 9:459–61). Natural law thus indicates the necessity of the rule of law in states and the desirability of constitutional government to ensure this. Burke could thus invoke natural law to reinforce his central case against arbitrary and oppressive rule in India.

Burke returned to these themes six years later on the first day of his speech closing the trial (May 28, 1794). Granting that Hastings had been vested with a certain amount of "discretionary power," he nevertheless declared that "he was bound to use that power according to the established rules of political morality, humanity, and equity." More precisely, Hastings had been obligated to rule in a lawful manner, under several different bodies of norms:

> In all questions relating to foreign powers he was bound to act under the Law of Nature and under the Law of Nations, as it is recognized by the wisest authorities in public jurisprudence; in his relation to this country he was bound to act according to the laws and statutes of Great Britain . . . ; and we affirm, that in his relation to the people of India he was bound to act according to the largest and most liberal construction of their laws, rights, usages, institutions, and good customs.

As noted above, Burke needed a higher standard of justice to distinguish good from bad customs, and he closed this day's speech by reaffirming that such a standard was available in the form of a moral law whose validity was universal, and whose force was not abrogated by any contrary precedents to which Hastings might appeal:

> The law is the security of the people of England; it is the security of the people of India; it is the security of every person that is governed, and of every person that governs. There is but one law for all, namely, that law which governs all law, the law of our Creator, the law of humanity, justice, equity,—the Law of Nature and of Nations. ("Speech in Reply," II:194–95, 225)

These passages make clear Burke's convictions regarding the reality of a moral law and its applicability to political affairs. Let us conclude the present discussion with a few comments on Burke's view of the status and sources of natural law, bearing in mind that he did not himself attempt to develop a philosophical doctrine on these matters, and that his offerings were therefore fragmentary and allusive.

First, theories of natural law or natural justice have frequently, though not invariably, been presented within a theistic framework by Western philosophers, who have incorporated the philosophical theology of the ancient Stoics or combined it with Christian doctrine in the Middle Ages and later. God is identified as the legislator of natural law or the creator of nature, including human nature, to which the rules and principles of natural law apply. It appears that Burke absorbed the traditional Christian version of natural law associated with Aquinas and Hooker, and it is apparent from several of the passages cited above that he believed God to be the source or guarantor of the validity of the natural law or of the standards of "justice"

and "equity" that he invoked. That is, Burke's personal religious faith reinforced the political morality on which he insisted in accusing Hastings.[42]
The difficulty is that, if natural law is too closely linked to Christianity, its
application to non-Christian societies is problematic; its application to Indian affairs might seem to contain an implicit critique of Indian religions
insofar as they did not acknowledge a similar ethical doctrine. Burke was not
seeking to make such a point. He did not address the question, soon to be
raised in British politics, of whether Christians ought to be allowed to
proselytize in India, but he spoke respectfully of Indian religions. However,
while he believed that Indian laws and traditions generally conformed to
basic principles of justice, Burke did not attempt to argue that Islam or
Hinduism as such contained a theology that supported natural law morality
in the way Christianity did. All we can say is that Burke sometimes referred
to God, in relation to the moral law, in the abstract manner of eighteenth-
century deism, as the "Creator" or "Author" of the world, a conception he
may have believed was acknowledged in all the major world religions.

Second, natural law prescriptions can be derived from a conception of
human nature and basic human needs in the context of social life. In the
traditional doctrine, people are regarded as sociable, hence capable of sharing in the benefits of a well-ordered society, and possessed of higher faculties
or potentialities such as reason, conscience, and a variety of virtues whose
realization is considered to constitute an objective human good; all these
ideas are generally consonant with Burke's outlook. Perhaps the most noteworthy tenet of natural law philosophy for present purposes is its assertion
of a common or universal human nature as the foundation of its universalist
ethics. Just as moral duties are essentially the same in all times and places, so
human nature and human goods are essentially similar—in India as in England—notwithstanding relatively superficial cultural differences.

Did Burke embrace such a position? Burke's traditionalism and his
appreciation of communities displaying both moral coherence and historical
continuity have led some commentators to regard his work as contributing
to the historicism and awareness of cultural diversity that became more
pronounced in nineteenth- century thought; at the same time, he adamantly
rejected "geographical morality" of the sort that might accompany histor-
icist doctrine, and his writings correspondingly contain many references to a
common human nature or humanity.[43] Burke certainly took this position in
his only (early) philosophical treatise, arguing that "it is probable that the
standard both of reason and Taste is the same in all human creatures"
(*Sublime and Beautiful*, ii).[44] In pre-Indian political writings Burke sometimes appealed to a general consensus about justice that reflected a common

humanity: practices that "differ from the general informed sense of mankind" are at least suspicious ("Popery Laws," 453), and legislators ought to be bound by "the great principles of reason and equity, and the general sense of mankind" (*Sheriffs of Bristol*, 196–97). Thus, in ending the dramatic speech that opened Hastings's trial in the House of Lords, Burke accused Hastings "in the name of the Commons of Great Britain . . . in the name of the people of India, whose laws, rights and liberties he has subverted . . . [and] by virtue of those eternal laws of justice which he has violated." And he concluded, "I impeach him in the name of human nature itself, which he has cruelly outraged, injured and oppressed, in both sexes, in every age, rank, situation and condition of life" ("Speech on Opening," 459). Later, toward the end of the process, Burke reflected to an Irish correspondent on the arduous, twelve-year campaign he had waged on behalf of "a very remote people . . . with whom I have no tie, but the common bond of mankind." Burke's conviction of the moral solidarity of mankind regardless of religious differences underlay his concern for just treatment of the "Pagans" and "Mussulmen" of India, and of the "Papists" of Ireland (*Letter to Langrishe*, 637).

In attempting to vindicate the cause of India before Parliament, Burke faced the difficulty of arousing the concern of a largely parochial British audience for a distant and unknown people. His difficulty was increased not only by the obscurity of many of the facts he alleged but also by the abstract quality of the standards, such as "natural law" or "eternal justice," that he sought to apply—despite the widespread formal assent such phrases commanded. According to the moral psychology that Burke shared with some other thinkers of the period, appropriate application of general moral rules was likely to be furthered if emotions such as indignation could be aroused, and if a lively sympathy for victims of oppression came into play. Burke's detailed descriptions of particular events were designed to assist his listeners in making the necessary imaginative effort to grasp and sympathize with the situation of their Indian subjects.

Burke proclaimed this intention and attempted to further it in what O'Brien calls the "extraordinary panegyric on 'sympathetic revenge'" on the first day of his "Speech in Reply"—a good illustration of Burke's "Great Melody" against oppression.[45] Responding to accusations that the prosecution of Hastings was motivated by personal or partisan revenge, Burke defended the propriety of a "becoming indignation" in the face of crimes. Citing Bacon's famous dictum, he argued that the natural feeling of revenge underlies justice, so long as the instinct "passes from the private to the public hand," or is "transferred from the suffering party to the communion and sympathy of mankind" ("Speech in Reply," II:178–79). Sympathy was most likely, and the charge that natural law had been violated was most plausible, when the suffering was readily comprehensible. This was no doubt why Burke returned so often to the breach of the natural human feeling of filial piety in the case of the begams of Oudh: "Forcing a son to violate the property of his mother must everywhere be considered a crime most portentous and enormous" ("Speech in Reply," 12:75). Burke also returned to charges that Bengali peasants had been forced to sell their children, or flee their country, under pressure from Hastings's tax collectors. This could not have been a "common practice" in India, as some had said. "No man ever sold his children, but under the pressure of some cruel exaction," since the love of children is "stronger than all laws; for it is the Law of Nature, which is the law of God."

> Next to the love of parents for their children, the strongest instinct, both natural and moral, that exists in man, is the love of his country. . . . All creatures love their offspring; next to that they love their homes; they have a fondness for the place where they have been bred, for the habitations they have dwelt in. . . . We have seen, therefore, Nature violated in its strongest principles. ("Speech in Reply," 11: 422–23)

In the previous section we saw that Burke sometimes had to try to arouse sympathy for Indian customs (such as the position of Muslim women) that were clearly exotic, alien to the cultural norms of Europe. When he appealed to natural law, however, he had to make the opposite case, that Englishmen and Indians shared a common humanity that supported certain universal moral principles, notwithstanding legitimate cultural differences. Getting his countrymen to see things this way was not likely to be easy, but it was a "glorious sight," he told the lords, that the Commons of England, separated "from a remote people," but nevertheless "united by the bond of a social and moral community" ("Speech on Opening," 457–58), had responded to the dictates of justice.

Finally, Burke held that natural law could in part be equated with principles embodied in the law of nations, to which he also held Hastings accountable. Philosophers and jurists in the eighteenth century, as in the preceding two centuries, sought to derive the basic rules of international law, or the law of nations, from natural law, or conversely, to show that rules and practices of international intercourse that were widely acknowledged and observed by diverse nations accorded with dictates of reason for peaceable and just relations among different peoples.[46] Following this program, European jurists had articulated a well-developed body of legal doctrine paralleling and supporting the emergence of the European system of sovereign states.

During this same period, however, European explorers and merchants were encountering most of the non-European states and societies of the world for the first time, conquering and settling some areas, and developing diplomatic and commercial ties with others. The emerging law of nations addressed the problems raised by this experience, specifying normative rules to order the relations of European and non-European, Christian and non-Christian peoples. Most important for our purposes, as Europeans made contact with southern Asia or the "East Indies"—from Persia to India and the Indonesian archipelago—they discovered highly civilized societies, well-established Muslim and Hindu states, and a preexisting system of diplomacy and trade throughout the region. European jurists did not hesitate to recognize the legitimacy of the states and sovereigns of Asia, including the Mogul Empire, which, like China, was clearly an impressive and powerful state at the time of its first direct contact with Europeans. Moreover, the East Indian states had their own well-developed version of a law of nations, which on many basic issues (such as diplomatic relations and etiquette, the inviolability of ambassadors, formalized treaties, and commerce) resembled the European version. Discovery of such common ground furthered the conviction of European thinkers that a truly global law of nations, reflecting natural law, was possible. Equivalencies were worked out, not always without ambiguity, between European and Asian legal terms;[47] and the European powers and trading companies gradually entered into a large number of commercial treaties, and occasionally formal diplomatic relations, with Asian sovereigns.[48]

Thus the world in which the English East India Company operated had always been a legal world, and the company's ties to the Mogul Empire and the various other "country powers" of India were formally set forth in numerous legal instruments. The law of nations was supposed to be regulative, even after European military power began to play a significant role on the subcontinent in the eighteenth century. It was therefore reasonable for Burke to invoke the law of nations against Hastings, and it was in keeping with prevailing doctrine to identify certain basic rules of this law with moral principles contained in natural law.

Simultaneously with the trial, Burke was continuing his militant opposition to the French Revolution, partly on the ground that, both in its domestic and its international policies, it had repudiated the traditional law of nations as well as lawful rule in general:

France, since her Revolution, is under the sway of a sect, whose
leaders have deliberately, at one stroke, demolished the whole body
of that jurisprudence which France had pretty nearly in common
with other civilized countries. In that jurisprudence were contained
the elements and principles of the law of nations, the great ligament
of mankind. (*Regicide Peace 1*, 239–40)

France had shared such institutions as Church, nobility, and prescriptive
property rights with the rest of Europe, "in a great politick communion with
the Christian world." The Revolution thus threatened the common heritage
and the common law of Europe. Even in this passage, however, Burke,
while emphasizing European unity, added that the French were destroying
institutions common to civilized countries not only in Europe but also in
"Asia, or even in Africa on this side of Mount Atlas" (*Regicide Peace 1*, 240).

Earlier, in his first major effort to convey a sense of India to a parliamentary audience, Burke had presented an extended comparison of the
Indian empire to the German empire, similar in its extent, diversity, population, nobility, priesthoods, cities, commerce, manufactures, and other at-
tributes of civilization—"a people for ages civilized and cultivated; cultivated
by all the arts of polished life, whilst we were yet in the woods" (*Fox's Bill*,
389–90). His stated purpose here was to "awaken something of sympathy"
for the people of India, but the effect of this account was also to demonstrate
India's clear eligibility for inclusion in the society of civilized nations, hence
its rightful claim to lawful governance. Against the Jacobins, Burke conceived of Europe as a single great community with common traditions, a
community under the law of nations. By an even greater effort of the moral
imagination, Burke sought to conceive of India as a participant in the same
law of nations, bound in the same "ligament of mankind."

Burke believed, and asserted against Hastings, that

the Law of Nations is the law of India as well as of Europe, because it
is the law of reason and the law of Nature, drawn from the pure
sources of morality, of public good, and of natural equity, and recognized and digested into order by the labors of learned men. ("Speech
in Reply," 11:240)

The law of nations, incorporating natural justice, provided standards and
constraints on government action that applied in several of the important
categories of charges that Burke brought, including treaty violations and
arbitrary confiscation of property. Agreements and property rights, for example, were both swept aside when Hastings, "contrary to justice and equity

and the security of property, as well as to public faith and the sanction of the Company's guaranty," authorized the nawab of Oudh to seize the begams' wealth ("Articles of Charge," 400). The best examples appear in the Benares charge. Chait Singh was subjected to arbitrary demands, and then summarily condemned, in Burke's view, without anything resembling due process and in disregard of the rights of his position, whether as a subordinate ruler or as a major vassal of the Mogul Empire.[49] Burke cited Emer de Vattel, the leading European authority on the law of nations, to establish that Chait Singh, as "a subordinate sovereign dependent upon a superior, according to the tenor of his compact," was entitled to protection, retained rights against his superior, and was fully justified in protesting against despotic treatment ("Speech in Reply," 11:240).[50] The vagueness of Hastings's accusations against the raja, the lack of proof, the denial of "a fair and impartial trial and inquiry" or of an opportunity to present a defense, and the exorbitant punishment all infringed upon the "essential principles of natural justice," and on legal principles recognized in English and Indian law alike ("Articles of Charge," 359; "Speech in Reply," 11:242). Chait Singh's actual arrest was executed by Hastings's resident or ambassador in Benares— who, "being a public minister representing the British government at the court of the said Rajah, [was] bound by the law of nations to respect the prince at whose court he was Resident, and not to attempt anything against his person or state" ("Articles of Charge," 361). Finally, after deposing Chait Singh, "without any form of trial, inquisition, or other legal process, for forfeiture of the privileges of the people to be governed by magistrates of their own, and according to their natural laws, customs, and usages," and in disregard of the former treaty, Hastings arbitrarily rearranged the government of Benares under his own appointees ("Articles of Charge," 381).

Burke's agreement with leading jurists that a recognizable version of the law of nations was understood in India, and was thus applicable to rulers there, served several purposes, in addition to providing him with a standard for condemning Hastings. The fact that Indian political culture embraced the law of nations was further evidence that Indian tradition was fundamentally lawful, contrary to Montesquieu's and Hastings's assertions that Asian politics were uniformly despotic. Insofar as the law of nations coincided with or included principles of natural law, the existence of an Indian law of nations suggested that Indians grasped the essentials of natural law, even though the concept of "natural law" as such might not exist in Indian thought. Finally, evidence that Asians acknowledged basic principles of the natural law or law of nations provided heartening evidence of the supposed consensus of mankind on the truth of the higher moral law, a supposition that formed one of the traditional arguments of natural lawyers and was implied by the claim that the law of nature was simply the law of reason.

Although Burke's arguments suggested these ideas, it must be admitted that he did not develop them as explicitly as he might have. Despite his laborious study of Indian affairs, in the end it may be that Burke remained uncertain about the extent of the moral similarity between Europe and Asia, though he surely believed there was significant common ground. The doctrine of natural law as such was undoubtedly a European and Christian achievement, part of Western, not Eastern, philosophy. Burke could readily assume that his British audience accepted natural law, that they believed its principles were embodied in British law, and that they were prepared to judge Hastings by its standards. This causes a certain ambiguity, in that Burke's major statement regarding the reality of a universal moral law, in opposition to "geographical morality," was immediately preceded by the assertion that Hastings ought to have governed according to "British [not despotic] principles . . . that spirit of equity, that spirit of justice . . . which ought to characterise every British subject in power; and upon these and these principles only, he will be tried" ("Speech on Opening," 344–45). Similarly, Burke occasionally suggested to the lords that the trial was taking place on a European stage as a way of upholding British honor and British justice before European peers: "We have raised and exhibited a theatre of justice which has excited the admiration of all Europe" ("Sixth Article," 308). British principles or universal principles? There was no conflict here, since natural law was both a British (or European) principle and one that purported to have universal validity. Burke hoped and asserted that it was not an alien standard being imposed upon the world of Indian politics, but he lacked sufficient materials to prove it conclusively, as Hastings was to argue in his own defense.

Rights and Rebellion

In this section we consider two related issues in Burke's political theory: did his acceptance of natural law lead him to endorse some version of a doctrine of natural rights? And was a right of popular resistance, even armed rebellion, against oppressive government, among these rights? Although one does not usually think of Burke in such terms, his positions on India confirm scattered passages elsewhere in his writings that suggest an affirmative answer to these questions.

Historically, Burke has been best known for his uncompromising attack on the French Revolution, based on his analysis of its probable self-defeating and destructive course, and on the misguided ideology of the "rights of man" that motivated it. Burke accordingly (and correctly, on the whole) has been read as a theorist of conservatism, expressing the values of social tradition and continuity and hence of stable authority; and he has correspondingly been interpreted as reaffirming an old-fashioned doctrine of natural law that supported individual duty, social hierarchy, and the authority of rulers, against the modern tendency to convert natural law into an assertion of individual rights.

Against this view, however, it is striking to recall that of the four major revolutions on which he commented—the English Revolution of 1688, the American Revolution, the "revolutions in Bengal" of 1757–1765, which created the British Indian empire, and the French Revolution—Burke openly justified or accepted three.[51] Looking more closely at India, we may note that the Benares charge concerned an armed uprising by Chait Singh and his followers against what they and Burke regarded as unjust exactions, and in condemning Hastings's policy here Burke explicitly defended the revolt. In addition, Burke described sympathetically a number of cases of more diffuse popular opposition and resistance against forcible attempts to extract tax payments in various districts of Bengal and Oudh. Burke consistently upheld what he took to be the interests of Britain's Indian subjects and sought redress for the victims of the East India Company's misrule.[52] This reminds us that Burke frequently spoke on behalf of the Catholic majority of Ireland against what he openly denounced as oppressive rule by England and the Irish Protestant Ascendancy.[53] Burke not only pleaded eloquently for the oppressed and invoked the higher law of justice on their behalf; he also occasionally affirmed a right to act against oppressive acts perpetrated by those in power.[54]

The interpretive difficulty raised here clearly stems not only from the prominence of the *Reflections* in Burke's corpus but also from the special character of the French Revolution as he saw it. The French Revolution was a more profound upheaval than any of the other events mentioned—a social revolution, radically forward-looking and hostile to traditional institutions, and guided by abstract doctrine; it also occasioned what Burke regarded as a perversion of the idea of natural law and rights. Early in his career, Burke embraced the standard Lockeian or Whig principle that the "secure enjoyment of natural rights" is the fundamental purpose of civil society ("Popery Laws," 463). In his speech on Fox's East India Bill of 1783 Burke declared that the "natural rights of mankind" (as opposed to mere chartered rights) "are indeed sacred things," and in his early impeachment speeches (1786–1788) he often asserted that the basic rights and liberties, as well as the

customs and usages, of Indians were entitled to protection. Burke was therefore confronted with a theoretical difficulty when the French revolutionaries, from 1789 onward, justified their actions in the name of natural rights,
or the "droits de l'homme et du citoyen."

The revolutionary doctrine of rights was mistaken, in Burke's analysis,
on two counts. First, the revolutionaries were asserting individual rights
without a corresponding emphasis on the individual's duty toward others or
responsibility for the manner in which the rights were exercised, and without a balancing concern for the larger good of the social whole to which the
individual belonged. For Burke, natural rights were properly understood as
one element in a larger conception of the human good, and of a good society,
as expressed in traditional natural law doctrine; rights, like liberty, could not
simply be counted a benefit in the abstract, without being combined with a
variety of other desirable practices and institutions (*Reflections*, 90–91). Proclaimed without reference to the appropriate context, rights were simply
a vehicle for egoistic self-assertion, willfulness, and power struggles; and
without the restraints and guidance provided by other norms, both moral
and legal, a system of rights was likely to be unstable.[55]

Second, the revolutionaries prominently asserted a right whose validity, at least as a natural right, Burke denied: the right of all people to
participate, directly or through elected representatives, in the government of
which they were subjects, or (alternatively stated) the right to a system of
political authority based on popular sovereignty, in which the general will
of the people or nation determined laws and policies. Burke endorsed the
traditional English form of government, in which representation of the
more capable and property-owning segment of the population formed an
important element within the larger, balanced constitution, and in which
representatives were supposed to act as trustees of the public good rather
than as agents of their constituents. He denied, however, that a democratic
form of representation was either a basic right or a desirable institution, and
he held that political rights in any form were artificial creations of the law of
particular countries rather than natural rights of human beings as such
("Speech on Representation," 93; *Reflections*, 150). The desirability of political institutions was properly determined through a prudent assessment of
their likely effects and their conformity to the traditions and other circumstances of a given country. On these grounds, Burke supported both the
American colonists' demand for representative government and a Roman
Catholic franchise in Ireland, while opposing British parliamentary reform
and the removal of civil disabilities for English Dissenters.[56] He also found
it ominous that the National Assembly's claim to sovereignty destroyed any

real constitutional balance in France. And, although Burke sometimes upheld the "liberties" of Indians in the sense of their legal or customary rights, he never suggested that the subjects of the British Empire in India were entitled to political liberty in the sense of a representative form of government, much less one that embodied so foreign a concept as popular sovereignty, as a matter of natural right. For Burke, such questions regarding the organization of political authority were to be worked out through practical wisdom, exercised with reference to context and within the constraints of historical circumstances, rather than through appeal to abstract right.

Faced with what he regarded as a dangerous distortion of natural law theory, Burke attempted, even in his *Reflections*, to distinguish and defend the "*real* rights of men" from the "metaphysic rights" and "pretended rights" of the revolutionary theorists (*Reflections*, 149–53). Later too, even while attacking the Revolution, Burke could invoke "the fundamental sacred rights of man" (*Regicide 1*, 212); and in the same late period of his life, toward the close of the trial, Burke once again denounced Hastings's argument that Indians had never been anything but rightless slaves of despotism, asserting that in India as elsewhere "the rights of the people are every thing, as they ought to be, in the true and natural order of things" ("Speech in Reply," 11:232). Thus, throughout his career, Burke was not averse to defending individual rights—fundamental or natural as well as legal rights—as part of a higher political morality, even though he did not make this theme so central as other political theorists have done.[57] This should not be surprising in view of the logical correlation of rights and duties: all rights can be restated as correlative duties of other parties, and many duties can be restated as corresponding rights. Hence the duties of natural law imply the existence of natural rights in some cases; whether the doctrine is phrased in terms of duties or rights may have important procedural implications, but is often a matter of emphasis.[58]

What natural rights, then, did Burke accept? His most explicit statement is as follows:

> If civil society be made for the advantage of man, all the advantages for which it is made become his right. It is an institution of beneficence; and law itself is only beneficence acting by a rule. Men have a right to live by that rule; they have a right to justice; as between their fellows, whether their fellows are in politic function or in ordinary occupation. They have a right to the fruits of their industry; and to the means of making their industry fruitful. They have a right to the acquisitions of their parents; to the nourishment and improvement

of their offspring; to instruction in life, and to consolation in death. (*Reflections*, 149)

In this passage, Burke applies the concept of right to values associated with his conception of society as a partnership in the attainment of higher goods than mere security and material welfare—a conception he believed was realized in traditional Indian society as well as in Europe. More concretely, however, he affirms natural rights to lawful rule, justice under law, and property, institutions on which he insisted for British India and which he prominently accused Hastings (as well as the French revolutionaries) of violating. In general, Burke's mature understanding of "real" natural rights derived from his normative view of society and government. The purpose of civil society was not to secure a preexisting set of individual rights; rather, natural law in the first instance acknowledged the necessity of social life, indicated the benefits available to people only from membership in a well-ordered society, and authorized government to supply these goods. While not insisting on any particular form of government, natural law also endorsed the trusteeship conception of authority, imposing on all rulers an obligation to rule justly and to promote the welfare of the governed, on whose behalf they held their trust. From this there followed a general right of subjects to expect or demand good government; and although particular claims under this general right might vary in different societies, Burke held that certain fundamental rights of subjects—to the rule of law, procedural justice or due process, liberty in the sense of personal and familial security, equitable sharing of burdens such as taxation, and property as defined by law or custom—obtained everywhere.[59] Burke unequivocally maintained that the East India Company, like any ruler, had a duty to provide beneficial government for its subjects; from scattered passages it appears he also thought that its failure to carry out this duty amounted to a violation of the rights of Indians.

Among the fundamental rights frequently asserted in modern political theory is the right of people to resist oppressive rule, or more specifically, a right of revolution by armed force against abusive governments. Burke's idea of government as a "trust" is reminiscent of Locke's use of the same term, which in legal usage implies accountability of the trustees to the principals, the magistrates to the people from whom they have received their authority on well-defined and limited terms. For Locke, clear violations of the trust, or even simply a dispute about its terms, justified a revocation of the government's authority by the people and, if necessary, recourse to arms—an "appeal to heaven"—as the means of exercising their right to protect themselves from tyranny. In chapter 1 we considered Burke's well-known general arguments against revolution, with the violent disruptions of social order and tradition they bring; but both there and in references to 1688 we have also noted that he was prepared to make occasional exceptions in cases of grave abuse or "necessity." Burke criticized Dr. Price for giving undue centrality to the people's right to "cashier [their governors] for misconduct" (*Reflections*, 99), and he did not think it wise to try to spell out the conditions under which such a right might exist. Nevertheless, Burke's unambiguous conviction that rulers have duties led him to view resistance by subjects to misrule, even violent resistance, as sometimes justifiable, and as a natural course of action that could be expressed as a right. "None of us who would not risk his life rather than fall under a government purely arbitrary," he remarked of the Americans in 1775, granting their claim that arbitrary rule canceled the benefits that empire might otherwise have offered ("Conciliation," 169); and two years later, with armed rebellion under way, he openly asserted that "the hostile mind of the rulers to their people did fully justify a change of government" (*Sheriffs of Bristol*, 211).

These ideas are applicable to the Indian empire as well, given Burke's opinion of the arbitrariness of Hastings's rule, and his "hostile mind" vis-à-vis Indians who stood in the way of his plans. And accordingly, we find Burke opening the impeachment trial by declaring that "nothing but absolute impotence can justify men in not resisting [arbitrary rule] to the best of their power." If a government were not constrained to obey the law of nature and nations by constitutional checks, or by the ruler's moderation, it could be resisted or coerced by "downright revolt on the part of the subject by a rebellion divested of all its criminal qualities" ("Speech on Opening," 351, 470).

These general statements pertained to specific episodes in India, notably Chait Singh's rebellion and several instances of popular resistance to tax collection. In considering these cases, we may advance three refinements of Burke's theory regarding the permissibility of resistance. First, Burke held that "the speculative line of demarcation, where obedience ought to end, and resistance must begin, is faint, obscure, and not easily definable." However, in a faint echo of Locke, he suggested that "it is not a single act, or a single event, which determines it. Governments must be abused and deranged indeed, before it can be thought of; and the prospect of the future must be as bad as the experience of the past." In such circumstances, revolution may be undertaken as the "last recourse" of upright people (*Reflections*, 116–17). These qualifications were presumably met in the case of the Benares insurrection, as Burke understood the record: Hastings's actions were abusive if not deranged; the original demands, the refusal of a hearing, the exorbitant fine, the humiliating treatment, and finally, the arrest of the raja constituted a long series of abuses adding up to what Burke (or Locke, or the Americans) would have recognized as a settled "design" of tyranny; and Chait Singh might reasonably have regarded his future prospects as bleak in light of this pattern and of the growing British power in Bengal. Burke thus regarded Chait Singh's resistance as justifiable, and believed the violent revolt that broke out among his subjects to have been provoked by Hastings. "It was Warren Hastings's rebellion.—a rebellion which arose from his own dreadful exaction . . . from his abominable tyranny, from his lust of arbitrary power" ("Speech in Reply," 11:249). "The subjects of this unfortunate prince did what we should have done" in such a situation; "the whole country rose up in rebellion, and surely in justifiable rebellion. . . . Surely, if ever there was an occasion on which people, from love to their sovereign and regard to their country, might take up arms, it was this" ("Speech in Reply," 11:281–84). Similarly, an armed peasant insurrection in Rangpur, Bengal, broke out in 1783 as a "last recourse" against the tortures imposed by tax collectors to extract hidden wealth, and only after the people's usual recourse of flight had been prevented by soldiers ("Speech in Opening," 10:91).[60]

Second, Burke distinguished between revolutions organized and led by dissident elites and more spontaneous popular uprisings against oppressive rule. It is true that the English Revolution of 1688 was carried out by Whig notables whom Burke viewed as the natural leaders of society in a necessary cause. The French Revolution, however, he attributed not so much to genuine popular discontent as to a "cabal" of doctrinaire intellectuals and other social and professional groups whose references to the "people" masked their own ambitions for power. Unorganized disturbances or rebellion on a wide scale, by contrast, were more plausible indicators of genuine grievances and suffering. Burke saw the American revolt, following upon decentralized disorders throughout the colonies, in this light: "*General* rebellions and revolts of a whole people never were *encouraged*, now or at any time. They are always *provoked*" (*Sheriffs of Bristol*, 217).

In order to increase his revenues and create a clientele directly dependent on himself, Hastings removed tax-farming authority from the established zamindars in many cases and assigned it to new men, to banians such as Devi Singh and Ganga Govind Singh. Unrestrained by customary norms and seeking a profitable return on their investment, these agents employed harsh measures that resulted in widespread disorders and sometimes open rebellion among the peasants in certain districts of Bengal: "My Lords, the people of India are patience itself. . . . But here they burst at once into a wild universal uproar and unarmed rebellion. The whole Province of Rungpore and a great part of Dinagepore broke out into one general rebellion and revolt" ("Speech on Opening," 422). The unorganized nature of these uprisings led to their quick suppression by regular troops, but for Burke it also confirmed the legitimacy of the grievances and the truth of eyewitness accounts of the torments that provoked them. Similar disorders, including a "general Insurrection" of local landowners, were reported in the district of Gorakhpur in Oudh, where British troops were directly employed in tax collecting; Burke inferred that unjust methods had similarly been to blame for that revolt—"rapacious and oppressive Revenue Exaction, and a violent, disorderly, and licentious Military Tyranny"—and condemned the brutality of its suppression ("Articles of Impeachment," 219–22).

One further episode is of interest. Chait Singh's rebellion in Benares quickly spread and engulfed large areas of eastern Oudh, including the region of Faizabad where the begams resided. Hastings claimed this revolt was not spontaneous, but had been fomented and coordinated by the begams and other dissident aristocrats who were being displaced from positions of power as British control of Oudh intensified—that the entire disturbance resulted from a deliberate conspiracy to expel the British from the country.[61] This provided one of his main justifications for later encouraging Asaf al-Daula to seize the begams' wealth. Burke is sometimes said to have been attracted to conspiratorial explanations of disturbing political events, such as the king's double cabinet system of his *Present Discontents*, or the French Revolution. In this instance, however, Burke went to great lengths to refute Hastings's allegation, analyzing detailed but murky evidence ("Speech in Reply," 12:111–12 and passim). The genuinely popular quality of the uprising both undermined Hastings's pretext for attacking the begams and implied that the grievances were more legitimate than if they had merely reflected the discontents of a displaced clique.

Finally, Burke sometimes came close to arguing that resistance and rebellion, when broadly based, are self-justifying, since they strongly imply the reality of oppression and injustice as causes. Burke may have had second thoughts about this view in the case of France—or perhaps this was why he was so concerned to emphasize the role of self-serving elites in that revolution. In any event, in his early work on Ireland Burke argued that the "genuine voice" of Irish history (as opposed to the official English histories) revealed that the rebellions in that country had been responses to government "persecution" and "the most unparalleled oppression," and he warned that "the real danger to every State is to render its subjects justly discontented" ("Popery Laws," 479).[62] Similarly, with respect to America, Burke bluntly asserted that the revolt there was "owing to the usual and natural cause of such disorders at all times, and in all places, where such have prevailed;—the misconduct of government;—that they are owing to plans laid in error, pursued with obstinacy, and conducted without wisdom." Overly harsh repressive policies, like excessive or inequitable revenue demands, are likely to backfire by provoking resistance, "inflaming discontent into disobedience, and resistance into revolt." And it is "the duty of those who claim to rule over others"—and an elementary maxim of statecraft— "not to provoke them beyond the necessity of the case" ("Address to the King," 163, 167, 170). If Burke really meant this thesis to apply to "all places," India provided him with new confirming evidence a few years later. Hastings's misgovernment and the obstinacy of his repressive responses to resistance, in Burke's view, inflamed both Chait Singh and rural taxpayers and provoked their revolts. Predictably, justifiable insurrection "rent in pieces that veil of fraud and mystery that covers all the miseries of all the provinces" subject to oppressive rule ("Speech in Opening," 10:92).

Principles Embodied: A Magna Charta for Hindustan

Burke's traditionalism, a doctrine that ascribes legitimacy to customary or evolved practices and moral beliefs, and that derives right and obligation from particular histories, is potentially in conflict with his expressions of support for a higher moral law containing principles of general validity, even though these two normative orientations may converge in certain cases. Burke's arguments for both justice and respect for local tradition in Ireland and India may obscure this conflict in his thought, but the universalist prescriptions of a doctrine such as that of natural law or natural rights clearly may be at variance with the actual practices of a given time or place, and indeed, the practical point of higher law philosophies has often been to identify and criticize "bad customs." Let us finally consider how these two sets of standards can be reconciled in Burke's thought, and then briefly consider how the proposed solution might apply to the British Empire in India. We shall be wrestling here, as Burke was (no doubt inconclusively), with the age-old question of Western political philosophy—whether justice or a pattern for a good regime exists by nature, or whether these matters are settled inescapably by custom and convention.

The problem posed here bears on the larger and much-discussed question of Burke's consistency as a political philosopher. Commentators have disagreed on this matter (or on the depth of Burke's inconsistency), while arguing for the centrality in his theory of a variety of different standards.

Some have focused on prescriptive right, an idea that is present in some of his writings but surely not pervasive or fundamental. Others have pointed to natural law in a traditional (perhaps Christian) form, still others to a more modern conception of natural rights, often in conjunction with other eighteenth-century Whig principles such as property and constitutional government. Some have attributed to him, as a central value, a corporate or organic conception of a society arranged hierarchically, an idea that was both old-fashioned and in some respects forward-looking, anticipating later theories of society. Others have held that Burke's ultimate standard was utility, or the general welfare, interpreting his occasional calls for expediency in statecraft as a commitment to a utilitarian calculation of beneficial consequences of policies.[63] Burke's famous conservatism is held to incorporate some of the foregoing elements, combined with a diagnosis of the dangers of revolutionary interventions in society and a systematic critique of overly rationalistic or doctrinaire politics. Finally, Burke's ideal of statesmanship is sometimes linked to the classical conception of prudence or practical wisdom (which in turn suggests an interpretation of his antirationalism and his favorable references to expediency) and to his aristocratic sympathies and trusteeship conception of government.

Working out all the relations among these ideas would be a lengthy task. In general, there need not be major contradictions among them, at least if they are interpreted with a view to a synthesis. The forward-looking criterion of utility might seem at odds with a backward-looking defense of custom or with a strong or rigid principle of prescription; and yet a utilitarian might think there are good reasons for ascribing a presumption of utility to evolved and established institutions, for placing a high value on continuity and on stable property rights, and for protecting expectations based on long possession. Burke explicitly sought to distinguish the reforms undertaken by a sensible and experienced statesman, concerned to promote the welfare of society, from impermissible revolution. When Burke said that "in all political questions the consequences of any assumed rights are of great moment in deciding upon their validity" ("Appeal," 175), he might be interpreted as establishing a priority rule to govern conflicting standards (utility overrides rights); less contentiously, he may simply have been trying to balance the two, with appeals to consequences settling disputes arising from different interpretations of rights. The classical doctrine of natural right, above all, is broad enough to subsume many of the prominent elements of Burkean theory. The dominant Aristotelian version of the doctrine was closely linked to an endorsement of statesmanship and the need for prudence in applying principles of justice in particular circumstances. Aristotle, followed by Aquinas, recommended a conservative approach to legal reform on the "Burkean" ground that legal continuity facilitates the cultivation of the virtue of law-abidingness, and perhaps the habituation of other virtues as well. Burke himself emphasized that prescriptive property rights formed part of the law of nature (*Reflections*, 260), having been drawn from that source into the law of "all civilized nations" (*Noble Lord*, 309). More generally, he believed that the legal force of ancient custom was a fundamental maxim of traditional jurisprudence and equity, also presumably reflecting (via Roman law) the law of nature and nations (*Regicide Peace 1*, 251).[64] Finally, natural law imposed upon rulers a duty or responsibility to govern lawfully, respecting the legal or customary rights of their subjects and promoting their welfare.[65] Hence it is understandable that Burke, an eclectic and admittedly unsystematic thinker, who explicitly acknowledged the complexity of moral life and the danger of simplistic doctrines, should have assumed the ultimate compatibility of these various strands.[66]

A tension remains, however. Natural law may recognize the value of custom and continuity as aspects of its doctrine of human sociability, but if "respect custom and prescriptive rights" is its dominant principle, then natural law would collapse into traditionalism (and perhaps relativism). If, on the other hand, natural law contains any substantive principles other than respect for tradition, it is possible that they might conflict with particular customs. Natural law would then have to determine its priorities; and the distinctiveness and practical aim of the doctrine have historically lain in its formulation of general criteria such as justice, rights, or nonoppression, with reference to which existing and customary practices may be assessed and revised if necessary. In the Indian portion of his political theory, as elsewhere, it is clear that Burke was predisposed to admire deeply rooted traditions and to presume their latent wisdom; but his denunciation of geographical morality, his rejection of bad customs (both in India and in the East India Company), and his repeated insistence on general standards such as justice and the rule of law lead to the conclusion that he accepted this logic of a higher law tradition.

Perhaps the most promising approach to Burke is indicated in some remarks of an admiring nineteenth-century commentator, to the effect that Burke's "theorising is always checked and verified by the test of specific instances, and yet in every special case he always sees a general principle," and that it was "his habit to regard principles as embodied in concrete facts."[67] In his famous attacks on "metaphysical" reasoning in politics, Burke did not mean to reject general moral principles, but only to insist that abstract principles must be applied or embodied in concrete cases and institutions. The real problem of political life is doing this appropriately and successfully. In his own words, principles

> must be embodied in circumstances; for, since things are right or wrong, morally speaking, only by their relation and connection with other things, this very question of what it is politically right to grant depends upon this relation to its effects. ("Unitarian Petition," 55)

Burke no doubt sought the valuable principles (the "latent wisdom") that were frequently to be discovered in customs, "prejudices," and evolved institutions. His conception of statesmanship—combining leadership with political judgment—pointed to the importance of specifying and adjusting general principles in applying them to particular situations ("Unitarian Petition," 41). He held that assertions of principles could be dangerous if made in disregard of actual—usually complex—circumstances; and political values were secure only if institutionalized, or better, firmly rooted in tradition.

Stephen's remark about embodied principles recalls another promising approach—Strauss's comment that, of the classic theorists of natural right, Burke most resembles Cicero.[68] Like Burke, Cicero was a politician as well as an (unsystematic) philosopher, and his theorizing was similarly informed by the politician's respect for practical experience, complexity, and the constraints of circumstance. Although Cicero accepted the Greek idea of natural justice, he was comparatively uninterested in its metaphysical basis, and in its ideal realization in an imagined state. Rather, he sought to exhibit its approximate or adequate realization in Rome, with its historically developed constitution, laws, and customs. For Cicero as for Burke, a central concern was to see how the higher law could be or could come to be embodied in concrete actuality, and how, through the actions over time of many leading statesmen, this result had been satisfactorily achieved in their respective countries.

Burke greatly admired Cicero, which was of course not unusual in the eighteenth century; beyond the matter of literary taste, however, Burke's political thought is akin to Cicero's, and as a practicing politician and orator he seems to have identified with his ancient predecessor as a *novus homo* on the political stage.[69] Furthermore, of all Burke's various causes, the lessons to be drawn from Roman experience were perhaps clearest in India. England's vigor as a free state (in reality a republic in the guise of a monarchy, as Montesquieu said) manifested itself, as had the Roman republic's, in the acquisition of an empire; now, ill-gotten wealth, corruption, and arbitrary habits of rule on the part of its imperial officials were returning, as they had done in Rome, to undermine England's political virtue and balanced constitution.

This parallel and the dangers it signaled were familiar to Burke's audiences, as he frequently reminded them.[70] The profits of the Arcot creditors surpassed the "exemplary plunder of Roman iniquity," and their corrupt political machine resembled Nero's largesse to his praetorian guards (*Arcot's Debts*, 510). Wars caused by British intrigues left the Carnatic in the condition of Carthage as described by Sallust (*Fox's Bill*, 422). Mrs. Hastings's receipt of presents from Indians, in evasion of restrictions, served as a reminder that Roman provincial governors were not allowed to take their wives with them during the best period of the commonwealth ("Sixth Article," 438). Hastings's arrogance before his judges contrasted with the decorum that would have characterized a similarly placed Roman defendant ("Speech in Reply," 11:166), just as the maxims of his rule clashed with the normally mild and equitable government of the Roman Empire ("Speech in Reply," 11:234). It was more difficult to prosecute a British than a Roman governor charged with crimes in office ("Rohilla Speech," 106); nevertheless, the passion shown by members of the House of Commons to avenge the wrongs done in India burned "like the Vestal fire" ("Speech in Reply," 11:180), reflecting not only their sense of justice but also their knowledge that "Rome never felt within herself the seeds of decline, till corruption from foreign misconduct impaired her vitals" ("Motion for Papers," 63). Most directly, Burke openly compared his prosecution of Hastings to Cicero's prosecution of Gaius Verres, the corrupt governor of Sicily, and drew inspiration from the Verrine orations for his own attacks on Hastings's conduct (*Fox's Bill*, 416). In composing his impeachment speeches Burke turned to Cicero, who showed "what course a great public accuser in a great public cause ought to pursue, and, as connected with it, what course judges ought to pursue in deciding upon such a cause" ("Speech in Reply," 12:350).[71]

The deeper affinity suggested by Strauss between Burke and Cicero, however, lies in their common approach to the problem of reconciling the moral law and particular traditions, natural right and history. Burke, like Cicero, sought to characterize and justify the institutions of his own country as embodying justice and the other values of natural law, and thus as satisfactorily realizing the proper ends of social life. This was Burke's conviction about British institutions, and to the extent that he could vindicate this belief, the problem of a plurality of normative standards in his political theory was solved, in this case, by congruence: a set of institutions, consistent with natural law, was at the same time grounded in custom or prescription and conducive to the welfare and flourishing of society.

Burke's theory not only deems a society fortunate when such congruence occurs; it also offers a number of reasons for expecting an approximation to this state of affairs as normal in any stably functioning society, and for regarding it as the only way in which social values can be reliably attained. The principles of the moral law can be stated as abstractions, but their purpose is to be embodied in concrete practices and institutions, and their implementation can legitimately vary to a considerable extent in accordance with the circumstances and cultures of different societies. Furthermore, custom, in addition to making virtue habitual and to satisfying the natural desire for continuity in experience, may be expected frequently, though not invariably, to incorporate morality. When it fails to do so, cautious reform is called for on the part of statesmen working within the framework of an existing system of laws and customs; indeed, repeated applications of practical wisdom in the past, along with the operation of a general moral sense and an undirected process of adaptation, are responsible for such convergence of tradition and morality as does exist. Finally, moral values and principles are secure only to the degree that they are firmly embedded within a network of customs and established institutions.

Burke was confident that a reasonable congruence of natural justice and tradition had been achieved in England, which is why, with relatively minor exceptions, he was a conservative in that context. With respect to British imperial arrangements, however, matters had not evolved so smoothly or equitably, and therefore Burke frequently assumed the role of a prudential reformer: Irish laws were distorted by a particular political history of oppression; American governance had failed to adapt to the rapid growth and self-assurance of the colonists; and even more rapidly changing conditions in India had placed immense power in the hands of men who were inappropriately motivated and who lay beyond the control of effective law. There were no doubt defects in France's traditional constitution as well—for example, an excessively privileged and exclusive nobility—but moderate reform could have addressed them. England, however, remained the model for Burke's theorizing, just as reflections on Rome's success and Roman law provided the guiding themes of Cicero's political thought. English common law evidently provided Burke with his conception of how latent wisdom comes to be embodied in custom or prejudice through a gradual process of adjustment, and Burke followed famous English jurists in holding that traditional common law principles were congruent with the dictates of natural law.[72] "The science of jurisprudence, the pride of the human intellect . . . is the collected reason of ages, combining the principles of original justice with the infinite variety of human concerns" (*Reflections*, 193). English liberties, Burke argued in a famous passage, were an "*entailed inheritance* derived to us from our forefathers," stabilized and secure both because they were embodied in a system of positive law extending back for centuries, and because they therefore enjoyed the veneration that normally attaches to tradition. In all these respects, the people of Great Britain had achieved a "conformity to nature in our artificial institutions" (*Reflections*, 119–21). Nature supplied the basic principles, the pattern of inheritance, and the sentiment of respect for the ancestral, all of which were incorporated into the traditional constitution. Nature and convention were reconciled.

Burke was averse to theorizing an ideal in the abstract, apart from actual circumstances. Rather, he found his ideal, or an approximation of it, in the English pattern. To what extent did he believe a similar pattern existed elsewhere? In particular, did he see in Indian tradition a similarly satisfactory embodiment of natural moral principles? To the extent that Burke espoused a uniquely English common law traditionalism, or praised the British constitution and its distinctive historical pedigree, his theory seems parochial.[73] The same holds true of the interpretation of Burke as fundamentally an "Anglican" theorist, upholding in the manner of Hooker the religious basis of civil society, as expressed in the close relation between the English Church and the state.[74] It is apparent, however, that Burke understood British institutions—religious, political, and legal—as local variants of a general pattern found throughout Western Europe and reflecting a common set of historical influences. From the start, Burke maintained that the French revolutionaries were repudiating "the old common law of Europe," which England and France shared (*Reflections*, 123), and his later militancy against the Revolution in its international phase was likewise grounded in a vivid sense of Europe as a single "commonwealth," with similar institutions and values (*Regicide Peace 1*, 248).[75] If natural justice and sound morality were embodied in traditional English institutions, then the same held true, to varying degrees and with superficial variations, for Europe as a whole. The question is whether the same could be said for non-European societies or, if we read Burke as a Christian natural law theorist, beyond the Christian world.

Burke never directly addressed this question, but there is reason to suggest a qualified affirmative answer on the basis of his Indian writings and speeches taken as a whole. In keeping with the direct and personal epistolary style of his *Reflections*, Burke said that "we" value "our" prejudices, venerate "our" ancestors, and appreciate the historical background of "our" constitution. He also said that the French would have been wise to do the same, and it is certainly tempting to read these statements (and many others throughout his works) as adding up to a general theory of traditionalism. All venerable and well-established traditions, especially those of large and flourishing societies possessing admirable civilizations, should be presumed to contain latent wisdom; all the major religions and bodies of moral doctrine, and not only Christianity, should be presumed to express some version of the moral law which, in its most fundamental principles, is the same everywhere. Burke's portrayal of India, and especially his concern to deny the oriental despotism thesis, bear out this interpretation. Basic conceptions of legal rule and justice, dignity and honor, personal and property rights, and familial duty were as well known in India as anywhere; and the religions of India, both Hinduism and Islam, inculcated these and other norms through their respected priesthoods and ancient bodies of doctrine.

> I must do justice to the East. I assert that their morality is equal to ours as regards the morality of Governors, fathers, superiors; and I challenge the world to shew, in any modern European book, more true morality and wisdom than is to be found in the writings of Asiatic men in high trusts, and who have been Counsellors to Princes. This is to be set against that geographical morality to which I have referred. ("Speech on Opening," 361)

Indians were traditionally governed

> not by the arbitrary power of any one, but by laws and institutions in which there is the substance of a whole body of equity, diversified by the manners and customs of the people, but having in it that which makes law good for anything, a substantial body of equity and great principles of jurisprudence. ("Speech on Opening," 365)

India no doubt possessed its share of malefactors and tyrants, but in the overall picture morality and tradition were brought together in ways that were recognizable to anyone who took the trouble, as Burke did, to become acquainted with the history and customs of the country. Hastings and the other officials of the East India Company, having in their "British principles" a sound guide, should have endeavored to bring just rule to India in any case; that their unjust rule frequently violated these principles as they were embodied in the customary life of India simply worsened their offense.

This favorable view of Indian tradition should be qualified in one important respect. A stable pattern of customary social life, and of sound morality grounded in religion, were among the key elements of a good society for Burke; but at the level of government Burke may have shared the view—which was steadily to gain ground among the proponents of European empires—that India, like other non-European countries, was deficient.

In Great Britain, in the European world generally, and in the East India Company's Indian regime, Burke strongly endorsed constitutional government. Although natural law does not specify a form of government, it does, according to Burke, prohibit arbitrary power, require the rule of law and the observance of basic rights, and insist that all authority is held in trust, to be exercised for the well-being of those subject to it. These conditions and ends are likely to be realized with consistency only in a balanced government with institutional limitations or checks on the power of officials, in addition to the guidance and inhibitions provided by customary norms and religion. India, however, lacked a tradition of constitutional government, not to mention a tradition of political liberty in the sense of representative institutions; and without constitutional government the other political values that were acknowledged there—law, justice, rights, property—were in continual jeopardy.

It is true that Burke occasionally suggested that the Mogul Empire had an elaborate constitutional structure, with an orderly subordination of local rulers and well-defined partitions of authority under the emperor; but he admitted that this system was in a state of disintegration when the British acquired their empire. He even briefly conjectured that the Tartar predecessors of the Moguls had had the rudiments of something like the estates of medieval Europe; but his evidence was not very convincing, and such constitutional ingredients as may have existed had in any case failed to develop as they had in England. As Burke conceded, instances of arbitrary and tyrannical rulers were all too common in Indian history, especially among eighteenth-century usurpers, notwithstanding the normative tradition of lawfulness. Burke placed great weight on refuting Hastings's allegation that the entire history of Asia revealed nothing but despotic rule. Despotism was not sanctioned by Asian philosophy and custom, nor was it, in a large perspective, the norm in practice. In making this point, Burke undercut one of Hastings's main defenses, vindicated his own traditionalism, and reinforced his conviction that basic moral values enjoyed universal assent. Nevertheless, deviations from the norm of lawful rule, especially at the level of high politics, were conspicuous enough to imply a defect in Indian government, and to indicate one important respect in which England might claim superiority.

We return, then, to a subject touched on in chapter 1. In supporting radical reform of the East India Company's government, Burke and others in his party had to overcome their initial objection to overriding the company's "chartered rights," and the vested interests and expectations that were bound up with them. Taking such an action was indeed regrettable, but the company had abused the responsibilities that accompanied its rights, and moreover, the rights in question were not natural or fundamental, but merely privileges granted by law. Burke's willingness to abrogate a charter in this case, however, should be viewed in the context of the great importance he generally attached to charters and to the idea of chartered rights. To "charter" a right was to embody it in a document of positive law, to give it clear content and operational force, and to initiate a process by which it might over time acquire the additional sanction of custom (especially in a political culture in which the idea of such charters was familiar). Chartered rights, as embodied principles, therefore had the "pedigree," the solidity, and the reliability that the abstract "rights of man" of the French Revolution lacked. Hence Burke, in defending the true natural rights of mankind, said that "if these natural rights are further affirmed and declared by express covenants, if they are clearly defined and secured against chicane, against power, and authority, by written instruments and positive engagements, they are in a still better condition." This is what the *great* charters of English history, in contrast to the East India Company's charter of commercial privileges, accomplished (*Fox's Bill*, 383–84). Similarly, Burke traced English laws and liberties, and the basic elements of England's constitutional government, back to the Magna Carta, itself probably a reaffirmation of still more ancient laws: "From Magna Charta to the Declaration of Right, it has been the uniform policy of our constitution to claim and assert our liberties, as an *entailed inheritance*" (*Reflections*, 118–19).

Great charters, then, charters of rights and charters of limited government, were a hallmark of English, and to some extent European, political history. They were the basis of constitutional government, and hence the guarantor of other valued practices. And while the Mogul Empire sometimes conferred privileges or issued grants of authority, as it did to the East India Company, by means of legal documents called charters, there were no "great charters" in India, no charters providing for constitutional government or legal protection of rights on a constitutional level. It was this defect that led Burke to hope that his and Fox's East India Bill might prove to be "the *Magna Charta* of Hindustan. . . . Whatever the great charter, the statute of tallage, the petition of right, and the declaration of right, are to Great Britain, these bills are to the people of India." Traditional in Europe, such enactments could be transplanted in some form to India, where they could initiate a tradition of constitutional rule and a process by which Indians could learn to complement their "laudable customs" with political liberty.

Of this benefit, I am certain, their condition is capable; and when I know that they are capable of more, my vote shall most assuredly be for our giving to the full extent of their capacity of receiving; and no charter of dominion shall stand as a bar in my way to their charter of safety and protection. (*Fox's Bill*, 386)

Burke's denial of Asian despotism, and his praise of Indian culture and society, might raise doubts about the very purpose or legitimacy of British rule there, apart from the fact that the British were simply and fortuitously placed there by the Sovereign Disposer. This passage, which suggests the superiority in one respect of European political conceptions, merely hints at the kind of liberal justification for imperialism that was to be greatly elaborated in the following century.

NOTES

Introduction

1. References to Burke's works will be incorporated into the text, using abbreviated titles. See bibliography.

2. Kant's call for "moral politicians" and his denunciation of Machiavellian maxims are found in his *Perpetual Peace*, appendix 1 (in *Kant's Political Writings*, ed. Hans Reiss [Cambridge: Cambridge University Press, 1970], 116–25). *Perpetual Peace* appeared in 1795, the year of Hastings's acquittal. Kant is primarily criticizing the politics of the European states system, but he also notes disapprovingly the conduct of Europeans overseas, including in India (106). Without pressing the comparison any further, we may observe that Kant's definition of a moral politician—"someone who conceives of the principles of political expediency in such a way that they can co-exist with morality" (118)—matches Burke's ideal.

3. According to Carl B. Cone, *Burke and the Nature of Politics*, 2 vols. (University of Kentucky Press, 1957), 2:95.

4. The nineteenth-century idea of a British imperial mission was driven by the otherwise antipathetic forces of utilitarianism and Evangelicalism. Paradoxically, these movements—moralistic, high-minded, and ostensibly benevolent—sometimes led to harsh rule grounded in contempt for cultures deemed backward or superstitious. See Eric Stokes, *The English Utilitarians and India* (Oxford: Clarendon Press, 1959); Ainslie Thomas Embree, *Charles Grant and British Rule in India* (New York: Columbia University Press, 1962); and Francis G. Hutchins, *The Illusion of Permanence: British Imperialism in India* (Princeton: Princeton University Press, 1967), 4 and passim.

5. Burke's plan for gradually abolishing slavery included efforts to "civilize" the freed slaves and the societies on the coast of Africa ("Negro Code," 259–60), but he never imagined that such a program was necessary for India.

6. Gerald W. Chapman, *Edmund Burke; The Practical Imagination* (Cambridge: Harvard University Press, 1967), 244.

7. Isaac Kramnick asserts that Victorian liberals such as Morley "captured" Burke for the cause of progress by emphasizing his American and constitutional writings while downplaying the aristocratic sympathies expressed not only in the *Reflections* but also in

the Indian speeches. Isaac Kramnick, "The Left and Edmund Burke," *Political Theory* 11:2 (1983): 196. There is, of course, much more than this in the Indian material.

8. Conor Cruise O'Brien, *The Great Melody: A Thematic Biography and Commented Anthology of Edmund Burke* (Chicago: University of Chicago Press, 1992). Unfortunately, this book is unreliable on India; it fails to cite recent historical scholarship on the events there, and is overly partisan in favor of Burke at the expense of Hastings. It nonetheless presents a powerful interpretation of Burke that provides a useful corrective to the view just summarized.

9. Ibid., 309.

10. Regina Janes, "Edmund Burke's Flying Leap from India to France," *History of European Ideas* 7 (1986): 509–27.

11. Thomas H. D. Mahoney, *Edmund Burke and Ireland* (Cambridge: Harvard University Press, 1960), 323.

12. Michael Freeman, *Edmund Burke and the Critique of Political Radicalism* (Chicago: University of Chicago Press, 1980), 198; and F. P. Lock, *Burke's Reflections on the Revolution in France* (London: George Allen and Unwin, 1985), 27, 150–51. In *The Problem of Burke's Political Philosophy* (Oxford: Clarendon Press, 1967), Burleigh Taylor Wilkins argues that the logic of Burke's theory, in which traditional institutions are normally expected to be sound, drove him to attribute problems to blameworthy human agents and conspiracies (167). France, India, and the schemes of the "King's friends" are plausible cases. No such tendency is apparent in Burke's analysis of America, however, where the troubles were due to gradually changing circumstances combined with simple stubbornness on the part of British governments. In Ireland and India too, Burke analyzed long-term historical conditions as the setting of particular injustices.

13. In his introduction to Burke's *Reflections*, J. G. A. Pocock writes that Burke feared not the "bourgeoisie" so much as "the power of the human intelligence when divorced from all social restraints" (xxxix). This formulation could apply to people such as Hastings, since it omits any reference to political "metaphysicians"—carriers of revolutionary theory—who are prominent in *Reflections*.

14. John Morley, *Edmund Burke, a Historical Study* (New York: Knopf, 1924; first published 1866), 170; and idem, *Burke* (London: Macmillan, 1913; first published 1888), 191.

15. Stephen regarded Hastings as the creator of the British administration in India, who was "called upon" to surmount his legal authority and "act the part of an absolute sovereign." Sir James Fitzjames Stephen, *The Story of Nuncomar and the Impeachment of Sir Elijah Impey*, 2 vols. (London: Macmillan, 1885), 1:25–26. The tough-minded Stephen praises what Burke condemned.

16. In addition to his books on India and the impeachment, Marshall has provided an invaluable service in editing volumes 5 and 6 of the new Oxford edition of Burke's *Writings and Speeches*, which contain the Indian works.

17. For example, John Strachey, *Hastings and the Rohilla War* (Oxford: Clarendon Press, 1892), xii. While exonerating Burke, Strachey accused James Mill, who had access to fuller information, of "criminal" dishonesty in distorting the record against Hastings

(vi). Some contemporary writers in the pro-Hastings tradition express a more unequivocally hostile opinion of his prosecutors. See, for example, David Musselwhite, "The Trial of Warren Hastings," in Francis Barker et al., eds., *Literature, Politics, and Theory* (London and New York: Methuen, 1986), 94.

18. A defect of O'Brien's *Great Melody* is that, by accepting Burke's version of events at face value, he makes Hastings into a caricature villain, and thus inadvertently also diminishes Burke's stature.

19. Warren Hastings, "Minutes of What Was Offered by Warren Hastings, Esquire, late Governor General of Bengal at the Bar of the House of Commons . . ." May 1–2, 1786, *Journals of the House of Commons* 41:670.

20. See Lock, *Burke's Reflections*, 90. According to Lock, Burke's *Reflections* "expresses its author's social and political values but not in the ordered and systematic manner of a work of philosophy."

21. As Francis P. Canavan remarks in *The Political Reason of Edmund Burke* (Durham: Duke University Press, 1960), 46. The one exception is Burke's early treatise on aesthetics, *Sublime and Beautiful*.

22. Frank O'Gorman, *Edmund Burke: His Political Philosophy* (Bloomington: Indiana University Press, 1973), 13–14.

23. Frederick A. Dreyer, *Burke's Politics: A Study in Whig Orthodoxy* (Waterloo: Wilfrid Laurier University Press, 1979), 4.

24. Sir Leslie Stephen, *History of English Thought in the Eighteenth Century* (New York: Harcourt, Brace, and World, 1962; first published 1876), 2:186.

25. Ronald Paulson, *Representations of Revolution (1789–1820)* (New Haven: Yale University Press, 1983), 71, 65. A good corrective to such nonsense is J. G. A. Pocock's "The Political Economy of Burke's Analysis of the French Revolution," in *Virtue, Commerce, and History* (Cambridge: Cambridge University Press, 1985). In this essay, a serious student of Burke's thought argues that the decisive theme of the *Reflections* is Burke's hardheaded analysis of revolutionary finances.

26. Regina Janes, "Edmund Burke's Indian Idyll," in *Studies in Eighteenth-Century Culture*, ed. Roseann Ruate, vol. 9 (Madison: University of Wisconsin Press, 1979).

27. Neal Wood, "The Aesthetic Dimension of Burke's Political Thought," *Journal of British Studies* 4 (1964): 41–64; Stephen K. White, "Burke on Politics, Aesthetics, and the Dangers of Modernity," *Political Theory* 21 (1993): 507–27.

28. Wilkins, *Problem*, 129. Lock, however, who emphasizes Burke's rhetoric, admits that his oratory was less emotional than that of his colleague Fox. See *Burke's Reflections*, 8. Emotionalism can be calculated, and one must allow for the oratorical conventions of the period.

29. Sara Suleri, *The Rhetoric of English India* (Chicago: University of Chicago Press, 1992), 26 and passim.

30. Leo Strauss, *Natural Right and History* (Chicago: University of Chicago Press, 1953).

31. Richard Speer, "The Rhetoric of Burke's Select Committee Reports," *Quarterly Journal of Speech* 57 (1971): 315. Speer does not consider the possibility that arguments of

national interest, addressed to members of Parliament, may have been designed to accomplish a humanitarian purpose.

32. J. G. A. Pocock, "Burke and the Ancient Constitution: A Problem in the History of Ideas," in *Politics, Language, and Time* (New York: Atheneum, 1973); and idem, "Political Economy."

33. J. C. D. Clark, *English Society 1688–1832* (Cambridge: Cambridge University Press, 1985).

34. Christopher Reid, *Edmund Burke and the Practice of Political Writing* (Dublin: Gill and Macmillan, 1985), 24. This point is exemplified by Burke's "Appeal from the New to the Old Whigs" and his "Articles of Charge" and "Articles of Impeachment" against Hastings.

35. Frans de Bruyn, "Edmund Burke's Gothic Romance: The Portrayal of Warren Hastings in Burke's Writings and Speeches on India," *Criticism* 29 (1987): 415–38.

36. Ernest Barker, "Burke and his Bristol Constituency, 1774–1780," in *Essays on Government*, 2d ed. (Oxford: Clarendon Press, 1951), 201.

37. Those who believe history has been unfair to Hastings point out that he had the bad luck to become the target of three of the most famous orators of the eighteenth century (Burke, Fox, and Sheridan) and of one of the best-known essayists of the nineteenth (Macaulay). Curiously, as we learn from G. R. Gleig, in 1803 Hastings was reading Burke's *Sublime and Beautiful* for insights into eloquence. Was he trying to grasp the rhetorical power of which he had been a victim? See G. R. Gleig, *Memoirs of the Life of the Right Hon. Warren Hastings, First Governor-General of Bengal*, 3 vols. (London: Richard Bentley, 1841), 3:387.

38. Iain Hampsher-Monk, "Rhetoric and Opinion in the Politics of Edmund Burke," *History of Political Thought* 9 (1988): 455–84; and Lock, *Burke's Reflections*, chap. 4.

39. For a reasonable approach, see Harvey C. Mansfield Jr., *Statesmanship and Party Government: A Study of Burke and Bolingbroke* (Chicago: University of Chicago Press, 1965). Granting that Burke was a rhetorician (21), Mansfield provides a careful study of the argument of *Present Discontents* and its place in Burke's political philosophy, taking account of its manner of presentation. Stephen H. Browne plausibly analyzes Burke's rhetoric as a vehicle for presenting a doctrine of virtue, which "is made meaningful in and through the public vocabulary" that Burke developed to suit various occasions. Stephen H. Browne, *Edmund Burke and the Discourse of Virtue* (Tuscaloosa: University of Alabama Press, 1993), 5.

40. Gertrude Himmelfarb, *Victorian Minds* (New York: Knopf, 1968), 6, 20.

Chapter 1. "Opulent Oppression"

1. Donald Winch, *Classical Political Economy and Colonies* (Cambridge: Harvard University Press, 1965), 1–2.

2. Paul Langford, *A Polite and Commercial People: England 1727–1783* (Oxford: Clarendon Press, 1989), 619. Linda Colley agrees that Britons liked to contrast their beneficent trading empire with the conquest empires of the Romans or Spaniards, but notes

that this contrast was more difficult to maintain after the Seven Years' War issued in British rule over numerous non-Protestant and nonwhite subjects. See Linda Colley, *Britons: Forging the Nation 1707–1837* (New Haven: Yale University Press, 1992), 102.

3. Burke's imperialism—combined with pleas for just rule—with respect to Ireland is emphasized by Mahoney, *Burke and Ireland*, 51, 119–35, 312–13. Burke privately opposed the Rockingham government's grant of legislative independence to Ireland in 1782, partly for fear it would lead to a complete break. He even opposed a tax on absentee Irish landlords as contrary to common imperial citizenship ("Letter to Bingham").

4. J. R. Seeley's famous remark that the British Empire had been acquired "in a fit of absence of mind" expressed, in its self-deprecating manner, the confidence of Victorian imperialism; see Hutchins, *Illusion of Permanence*, 84. This was not Burke's meaning, but the problem he and his colleagues faced arose from the enterprising activities of English merchants and adventurers in the absence of any prior plan or deliberation by responsible public officials.

5. Cf. Morley's rather tepid defense of the empire, given his pessimism about England's ability to carry out the "noble task" of improving India. The best that could be said was that the British takeover was probably less damaging than the alternatives to the declining Mogul power, and that, once Great Britain had acquired power, to abandon it would bring "disaster and confusion" to the inhabitants. Morley, *Edmund Burke*, 161–63.

6. Peter J. Stanlis, *Edmund Burke and the Natural Law* (Ann Arbor: University of Michigan Press, 1958), 93. Quebec and parts of the West Indies, as well as Bengal, fell into this category.

7. See Dreyer, *Burke's Politics*, 39–44. Burke's version is said to correspond to trusteeship in the English law of equity, in which the trustee is given discretion to act on behalf of the beneficiaries and is not immediately accountable to them (72).

8. James Conniff suggests that, for Burke, "a bond of interest or affection" between trustee and beneficiary could substitute for formal accountability, but that such a bond—insufficient in the case of America—was surely lacking in India. See James Conniff, "Burke and India: The Failure of the Theory of Trusteeship," *Political Research Quarterly* 46 (1993):298. Some passages in Burke's Indian speeches may be seen as attempts to arouse sympathy—not an easy task, given the great gulf of distance and unfamiliarity.

9. As Dreyer notes, in several important cases Burke opposed the actions of a governing authority possessing formal rights—the right of the king to choose his ministers, of Parliament to govern the Americans, of the East India Company to rule Bengal. Rather than challenge the legality of the power, Burke invoked "trust" as a constraint on the manner in which all power must be exercised. Dreyer, *Burke's Politics*, 45.

10. As testimony to the commonplace nature of the term, we might note that Hastings acknowledged that he exercised a trust—though on behalf of his employers, not his subjects. Hastings, "Minutes," 669.

11. In "Idyll" (10), Janes explores Burke's usually contrasting pictures: America as energetic and progressive, India as stable and traditional.

12. See M. E. Monckton Jones, *Warren Hastings in Bengal 1772–1774* (Oxford: Clarendon Press, 1918), 4.

13. Gleig, *Memoirs*, 2:149.

14. Ibid., 139, 203; see also 111.

15. A leading modern historian of the empire agrees with Hastings's view. See P. J. Marshall, *Problems of Empire: Britain and India 1757–1813* (London: George Allen and Unwin, 1968), 52.

16. In Ireland, however, the failure of the English conquerors to blend in with the native Catholic population led to oppression, even though they settled there as a ruling class. Burke, *Letter to Langrishe*, 614.

17. Well, hardly anyone. Langford cites the case of the English radical Granville Sharp, who in 1780 called for representative government in India. This appeal illustrates the difficulty that many Englishmen of that period had in conceiving of India except in English terms. See Langford, *Polite and Commercial People*, 619–20.

18. Burke gave as his opinion "that publick contributions ought only to be raised by the publick will," but he based this on "the judicious form of our constitution" rather than natural rights. Burke, *Regicide Peace 3*, 351. Even with respect to America, Burke did not endorse the Lockeian claim, since he and his party were committed to the Declaratory Act, which declared that Parliament had the authority to tax the colonies; he simply questioned the prudence of doing so, given the American situation. This is an admitted exception to Dreyer's Lockeian interpretation of Burke. See Dreyer, *Burke's Politics*, 19, 70.

19. Since Russia was an ally at the time, Burke prudently refrained from mentioning that Catherine became empress by having her Russian husband murdered, and did not indicate whether this was in accordance with local custom.

20. The claims of the "nation," both democratic and antidynastic, were central to Jacobinism, the only phenomenon that Burke, toward the end of his career, regarded as worse than "Indianism." The intense popular hostility to Queen Marie Antoinette as a foreign princess and its role in the Revolution is pointed out in Simon Schama, *Citizens: A Chronicle of the French Revolution* (New York: Knopf, 1989). Burke's sympathy for her will be noted below.

21. Cone, *Nature of Politics*, 2:79.

22. Janice E. Thomson, *Mercenaries, Pirates, and Sovereigns: State-Building and Extraterritorial Violence in Early Modern Europe* (Princeton: Princeton University Press, 1994), 32–42. Thomson suggests (43) that eighteenth-century European rulers invented the convenient stance of "plausible deniability" vis-à-vis company exploits overseas, a stance Burke rejected.

23. In *North India Between Empires: Awadh, the Mughals, and the British 1720–1801* (Berkeley: University of California Press, 1980), Richard B. Barnett analyzes this process and provides an account of the independent state that briefly took shape in Oudh.

24. Jones, *Hastings in Bengal*, 24.

25. The adjacent province of Bihar was united with Bengal proper under its Mogul government. The name "Bengal" is used throughout this book to refer to this entire unified territory over which the British acquired control.

26. A hundred or so English, most of them civilians, were also killed by suffocation while confined in the "Black Hole" of Calcutta, a military prison cell. Although this was a notorious atrocity, Burke mentioned but did not emphasize it in his condemnation of Siraj al-Daula. "Speech on Opening," 316.

27. Hastings's counsel, in E. A. Bond, ed., *Speeches of the Managers and Counsel in the Trial of Warren Hastings*, 4 vols. (London: Longman, Brown, Green, Longmans, and Roberts, 1859), 2:548.

28. The *Boston* edition (9:401) gives "sacred veil" in this passage.

29. P. J. Marshall, *East Indian Fortunes: The British in Bengal in the Eighteenth Century* (Oxford: Clarendon Press, 1976), 15. In 1756, the total number of Europeans in Bengal is estimated to have been about fifteen hundred, approximately half of them company soldiers. See Jones, *Hastings in Bengal*, 34.

30. Montesquieu, *The Spirit of the Laws*, ed. and trans. Anne M. Cohler et al. (Cambridge: Cambridge University Press, 1989), 21.21. I have modified the translation slightly. Montesquieu was especially worried that the Habsburg or Bourbon ambition for territorial empire in Europe might lead to "universal monarchy" there. Britain's maritime empire was more appropriate for a free state and did not threaten the liberties of Europe. See John Robertson, "Universal Monarchy and the Liberties of Europe: David Hume's Critique of an English Whig Doctrine," in *Political Discourse in Early Modern Britain*, ed. Nicholas Phillipson and Quentin Skinner (Cambridge: Cambridge University Press, 1993) 360, 364, 367.

31. Adam Smith, *An Inquiry into the Nature and Causes of the Wealth of Nations*, ed. Edwin Cannan (New York: Modern Library, 1937), 600–03. An admirer of Hastings has claimed he tried to put an end to abuses by autocratic army officers stationed in the countryside; it was difficult, however, for a "company of merchants" to exert their control over professional military men, given the ethos of the military. Jones, *Hastings in Bengal*, 176.

32. Burke's clear allusion to Smith in *Fox's Bill* demonstrates that Kirk Willis is incorrect in stating that Burke, unlike some of his famous contemporaries, "never invoked Smith as an authority in a parliamentary debate." Kirk Willis, "The Role in Parliament of the Economic Ideas of Adam Smith, 1776–1800," *History of Political Economy* 11 (1979): 523.

33. Hastings shared the view that the participation of the "magistrate" in the trade of Bengal was ruinous to it, at least in the abstract. See Gleig, *Memoirs*, 1:228. Changing the system was another matter.

34. This comment anticipates Burke's later defense of the free market in "Scarcity," namely, that it was ordained by the laws of nature. The free trade called for was local, however, not international. Burke upheld a mercantilist empire and did not challenge the East India Company's monopoly on maritime trade. Mansfield gives undue weight to this phrase and to this issue, at least in the impeachment, as distinguished from the *Ninth Report*. See Mansfield, *Statesmanship and Party Government*, 148, 150, 160.

35. Marshall, *East Indian Fortunes*, 31–32, 261–62.

36. Ibid., 144. Hastings blamed the economic problems of Bengal, including specula-tion in rice during the famine, on the former regime, and especially on the highest-ranking native official, whom he removed from office. Gleig, *Memoirs*, 1:283.

37. Quoted in David Kopf, *British Orientalism and the Bengal Renaissance* (Berkeley: University of California Press, 1969), 13–14.

38. Smith, *Wealth of Nations*, 73.

39. Marshall, *Problems*, 32; and Jones, *Hastings in Bengal*, 112. Burke cited the dis-appointment of hopes of a net revenue from Bengal a few years later in arguing against overly exacting taxation of America ("Conciliation," 178). The benefits to be expected from empire lay in trade.

40. Lucy S. Sutherland, *The East India Company in Eighteenth-Century Politics* (Ox-ford: Clarendon Press, 1952), 138. For a review of Burke's scattered and brief antireform speeches during this period, see O'Brien, *Great Melody*, 257, 260–72; and Holden Furber, "Edmund Burke and India," *Bengal Past and Present* 76 (1957): 11–21. In Burke, see especially "East India Settlement," "East India Select Committee," and "North's Reso-lutions." As a newcomer, Burke naturally followed his party and feared North's potential control of Indian affairs. It is also true that he had not yet studied the Indian situation closely.

41. Cone, *Nature of Politics*, 1:237. O'Brien concludes that a whitewash was intended. O'Brien, *Great Melody*, 263–64.

42. Cone, *Nature of Politics*, 2:121.

43. Marshall, *Problems*, 43–44.

44. The brief history of the Fox-North ministry as a whole amounted to a "constitu-tional crisis," in that this was the first time a British monarch had been forced to appoint a government to which he was openly hostile on the basis of its support in Parliament. The king's public expression of displeasure with Fox's East India Bill, which precipitated its defeat in the House of Lords, was also unprecedented in this period and was consid-ered illegitimate by the Whigs. See John Cannon, *The Fox-North Coalition* (Cambridge: Cambridge University Press, 1969).

45. The impossibility of politically neutral reform can be illustrated by the case of Hastings's principal antagonist in India, Philip Francis: his proposal that sovereignty over Bengal be vested directly in the Crown was accompanied by the hope that, having won favor with the king, he would replace Hastings as governor under the proposed system. See Sophia Weitzman, *Warren Hastings and Philip Francis* (Manchester: Man-chester University Press, 1929), 31. Motives are difficult to discern; since even bona fide reform efforts could be portrayed as self-serving or partisan, they were usually conten-tious.

46. These events were presented as a "reform movement" by Burke and other political leaders, and have been viewed as such by later historians. The opposing view was that, as the East India Company became richer and more powerful, politicians were seeking to control it and capture its patronage.

47. Marshall, *Problems*, 23.

48. Cone, *Nature of Politics*, 2:129; and Cannon, *Fox-North Coalition*, 111. Cannon

points out that there was a shortage of patronage available to the government as a result of Burke's own recent "economical reform." The fact that there was some confusion about whether Indian patronage would strengthen the king or the Fox-North government reflected the constitutional ambiguity of the period, when it was still a controverted issue whether ministers were responsible to the king or to Parliament (116).

49. Cone, *Nature of Politics*, 1:241–44, 2:130; Marshall, *Problems*, 22. Pitt warned that Fox was trying "to secure to the Gentoos their natural rights, but let him take care that he did not destroy the liberties of Englishmen." Cannon, *Fox-North Coalition*, 115.

50. Edward Gibbon, *The Letters of Edward Gibbon*, ed. J. E. Norton (New York: Macmillan, 1956), 2:384. Not surprisingly, the Court of Proprietors of the East India Company was worried and resolved that Fox's bill authorized a "total confiscation" of their property. Cannon, *Fox-North Coalition*, 117.

51. The only permissible changes in the law would be Pareto-efficient ones, under which some are made better off, and no one is made worse off; such measures are few and far between.

52. In *East India Company* (397–400), Sutherland confirms Burke's authorship of Fox's bill and calls it the "most radical" Indian measure of the century.

53. A few minor comments on Indian appointments are found in *Corr.* 7:233, 246ff., 252, 266. Burke's silence on postindependence events in America, after his deep involvement in them in the 1770s, is similarly striking.

54. In *Burke and the Natural Law* (118), Stanlis writes that Burke's persistence shows his principled commitment to a just cause. Elsewhere, however, Stanlis emphasizes the high place Burke accorded to prudence, a virtue that calls for making the best of circumstances with a view to future benefits. Could the impeachment have embodied a combination of justice and prudence?

55. By voting in favor of impeachment, Pitt undercut this maneuver and left the opposition with a time-consuming matter on their hands. Burke insisted on carrying it through to the end; some of his colleagues wanted to drop it when it no longer promised partisan advantage. See L. G. Mitchell, *Charles James Fox and the Disintegration of the Whig Party 1782–1794* (Oxford: Oxford University Press, 1971), 105–15.

56. Burke proclaimed that Hastings's impeachment was the first for "abuse of authority and misdemeanour in office" in sixty-three years, since 1725 (a Jacobite lord had been impeached after the rebellion of 1745, however). He commented that the revival of impeachment after long disuse gave it "some appearance of novelty." The same could be said for the simultaneous resuscitation of the Estates-General in France; a Burkean might well be wary of the consequences of such revivals ("Speech on Opening," 272).

57. Hastings was already out of office. In England, unlike the United States, removal from office was not the only possible consequence of impeachment; (undefined) criminal penalties could have been imposed had Hastings been convicted.

58. Cf. Mansfield, *Statesmanship and Party Government*, 146.

59. And by political observers in Europe with an interest in the development of constitutional government. When Kant referred disapprovingly to the English in India who abused the right of hospitality by conquering countries with which they traded

(*Political Writings*, 106), he may have been alluding to Hastings. Benjamin Constant, wrestling with the problem of ministerial accountability, argued that legal punishment of offending officials in a representative government was difficult to achieve but largely unnecessary. The case of "the oppressor of India appear[ing] on his knees in front of the House of Lords" showed that public investigation of official conduct and the termination of careers could suffice. Benjamin Constant, *Principles of Politics Applicable to All Representative Governments*, in *Political Writings*, ed. and trans. Biancamaria Fontana (Cambridge: Cambridge University Press, 1988), 240.

60. This is the judgment of P. J. Marshall, *The Impeachment of Warren Hastings* (Oxford: Oxford University Press, 1965), 40, 70.

61. Burke's eloquence constitutes an exception to Hume's argument that modern legal systems, with their strict rules of procedure and evidence, had "banish[ed] oratory from Westminster-Hall." David Hume, "Of Eloquence," in *Essays Moral, Political, and Literary*, ed. Eugene F. Miller., rev. ed. (Indianapolis: Liberty Classics, 1987), 103. Of course, the nature of impeachment dictated a political, not a narrowly forensic, quality to the speeches. Some have questioned the effectiveness of Burke's rhetoric at the trial: most strikingly, in *Rhetoric of English India*, Suleri argues that the vastness and "unspeakability" of the crimes alleged were "self-disempowering," since they precluded a focus on specific legal charges (63). In "The Trial of Warren Hastings," Musselwhite adjudges Burke's "invective" excessive and "inept" (90), but then says that in the end Burke won in the "tribunal" of "public opinion" to which he and Hastings both played (92). In *Impeachment* (189), Marshall suggests more cautiously that the length of the trial led to a decline in public attention. Surely the interposition of the French Revolution and renewed war with France influenced public perceptions. In any case, these are all impressionistic judgments that would be difficult to verify.

62. This interpretation concurs with Cone, *Nature of Politics*, 2:185; and O'Brien, *Great Melody*, 382.

63. Sheridan, though not Burke, candidly said of the prosecution that "some example is necessary to retrieve the character of the British nation in India." Bond, *Speeches*, 1:482.

64. See Mansfield, *Statesmanship and Party Government*, 36.

65. Conor Cruise O'Brien, "Warren Hastings in Burke's Great Melody," in *The Impeachment of Warren Hastings*, ed. Geoffrey Carnall and Colin Nicholson (Edinburgh: Edinburgh University Press, 1989), 72.

66. David Hume, "Of Commerce," in *Essays,* 255.

67. Isaac Kramnick, *The Rage of Edmund Burke* (New York: Basic Books, 1977), chap. 7. In a sense, Burke could have *been* Hastings, since he was offered a supervisory position in India in 1772.

68. O'Brien, *Great Melody*, 271.

69. Suleri, *Rhetoric of English India*, 25–26, 45, 55. This charge, however, is anachronistic. Since Burke openly supported a justly governed empire, it is not clear why we should suppose he felt unconscious guilt about imperialism, which he then had to project onto Hastings. Besides, far from evading it, Burke attempted a systemic analysis in his *Reports* and *Fox's Bill*.

70. Could Burke have sensed a parallel between the prosecution of Hastings and the egregiously political trial of Louis XVI early in 1793? He would have had to dismiss any such thought quickly.

71. The forms were not all completely clear, however. Procedural controversies that affected prosecutorial strategy arose and were duly settled by the lords, generally to the disadvantage of the prosecution, in the course of the trial.

72. Gleig, *Memoirs*, 3:296.

73. Bond, *Speeches*, 2:486.

74. See Bernard Schwartz, "Edmund Burke and the Law," *Law Quarterly Review* 95 (1979): 370.

75. Weitzman, *Hastings and Francis*, 256; Gleig, *Memoirs*, 2:350.

76. Hastings, "Memoirs Relative to the State of India," in G. W. Forrest, ed., *Selections from the State Papers of the Governors-General of India*, vol. 2, *Warren Hastings: Documents* (Oxford: Blackwell, 1910), 68.

77. Bond, *Speeches*, 2:519.

Chapter 2. The Charges: Corruption

1. This was the Rohilla War charge (see chapter 3).

2. For an outline of all the charges, see Marshall, *Impeachment*, introduction, and his notes to the Oxford edition of Burke's *Writings and Speeches*, 6:127.

3. Montesquieu, *Spirit of the Laws* 5.15: Embezzlement is common among officials of a despotic government; (8.10): While other governments may be corrupted and destroyed by "particular accidents," despotism is permanently corrupt "by its nature."

4. For the directors' mandate, see Gleig, *Memoirs*, 1:219–20.

5. Macaulay regarded Hastings as an unscrupulous statesman, "but still he was a statesman, and not a freebooter." His monetary transactions were "indelicate and irregular" by later standards, but not corrupt; otherwise "he would infallibly have returned to his country the richest subject in Europe." Thomas Babington Macaulay, "Warren Hastings," in *Critical and Historical Essays* (London: Dent, 1966), 1:557, 618. In *Bribes* (New York: Macmillan, 1984), John T. Noonan Jr. voices a view different from the common one, concluding that Hastings's fortune was suspiciously large, given his salary (396). Noonan generally endorses Burke's case against Hastings (chap. 14).

6. Weitzman, *Hastings and Francis*, 52–53.

7. Ibid., 21.

8. David Hume, "Independency of Parliament," in *Essays*, 42. Hastings too shared the assumptions of this political culture. Complaining of misconduct by officers stationed at a remote post (but not blaming them harshly), he remarked, "It is not possible that a body of men should refrain from illicit advantages, when the means are easy, not expressly forbidden, no penalty or disgrace annexed to them, and, falling within the reach of all, receive the sanction of general practice." Gleig, *Memoirs*, 2:178. Hastings sought to impose checks on power at lower levels; from Burke's point of view, however, his statement could have applied just as well to himself.

9. Virtue for Burke had to be "given structure" or expressed within a "proper order," according to Browne, *Burke and the Discourse of Virtue*, 86. The moral chaos embodied in Hastings arose from his position outside the legal community.

10. See Marshall, *East Indian Fortunes*, 163. Marshall estimates that £2 million in presents were received by company servants from Indians in the period 1757–1765 alone.

11. Marshall, *East Indian Fortunes*, 166; Marshall, *Impeachment*, 131.

12. Noonan, *Bribes*, xi.

13. Marshall, *East Indian Fortunes*, 176.

14. Ibid., 175; Marshall, *Impeachment*, 131.

15. Warren Hastings, letter to Willam Pitt, Dec. 11, 1784, in C. Collin Davies, "Warren Hastings and the Younger Pitt," *English Historical Review* 60 (1955): 618.

16. In a private letter to his supporter, Lord Thurlow, just before his impeachment, Hastings conceded that questionable private enrichment in India was inevitable, if regrettable: "That the government of a great kingdom, equal in extent and population, and with natural resources superior to Great Britain itself, exercised by a power held at the distance of half the globe by foreign agents, who are precluded by the difference of complexion, manners, religious and political habits, and language, from assimilating with the native inhabitants of it, should be productive of the evil of which your Lordship complains, is a consequence so necessary, that all the powers of legislation, control, and executive, however complete in each, never will, nor is it possible that they should remove it." Gleig, *Memoirs*, 3:260–61. This is a strikingly pessimistic retrospective view of the empire he had in large part created.

17. After reviewing the evidence, Noonan writes that "it is a reasonable conclusion that [Hastings] received the money for a corrupt purpose"; discrepancies in testimony and poor records tend to discredit Hastings. Noonan, *Bribes*, 408.

18. William Blackstone, *Commentaries on the Laws of England*, facsimile of the first edition of 1765–1769 (Chicago: University of Chicago Press, 1979), 4:139.

19. Marshall, *Impeachment*, 145.

20. Such perquisites of office were common for the well placed in England too, and were paralleled by irregular payments in kind to supplement the wages of laborers. Standards were being tightened in the latter part of the century, however. Calls for a more honest or more rational administration were paralleled by a clamp-down on "pilfering" from the work site. Hastings's trial on corruption charges may therefore be viewed as analogous to an exemplary Tyburn hanging of a lower-class thief in support of the new standards. See Keith Thomas, "How Britain Made It," *New York Review of Books*, Nov. 19, 1992, 37.

21. Marshall, *East Indian Fortunes*, 178–79.

22. This phrase probably alludes to Francis Bacon's plea in connection with his impeachment trial for bribery, a reference Burke may have expected his audience to recognize. See Francis Bacon, "The Humble Submission and Supplication of the Lord Chancellor," in *The Works of Francis Bacon*, ed. James Spedding et al. (1874; reprint, New York: Garrett, 1968), 14:244.

23. Montesquieu, *Spirit of the Laws* 5.17.

24. Hutchins, *Illusion of Permanence*, 58.

25. Jones, *Hastings in Bengal*, 57. In *Warren Hastings and Oudh* (London: Oxford University Press, 1939), C. Collin Davies writes that venality remained standard in the East India Company until "the reforming zeal of the incorruptible Cornwallis," Hastings's successor, ended it (xiii).

26. Marshall, *Impeachment*, 140.

27. The language of the 1773 Regulating Act, quoted in Noonan, *Bribes*, 399. Munni Begam's gift actually preceded this law, but was arguably contrary to similar company regulations.

28. Marshall, *Impeachment*, 159.

29. Noonan's analysis supports Burke's accusations in this case too. Noonan, *Bribes*, 409–11.

30. Marshall, *Impeachment*, 167.

31. See Wood, "Aesthetic Dimension," 44.

32. Hastings, "Minutes," 703.

33. Hastings, "State of India," 78; See also "Minutes," 705, where Hastings argues that the company was better off than under previous arrangements.

34. Warren Hastings, *Warren Hastings' Letters to Sir John MacPherson*, ed. Henry Dodwell (London: Faber and Gwyer, 1927), 108.

35. Marshall, *Impeachment*, 168; idem, *East Indian Fortunes*, 202; Cone, *Nature of Politics*, 2:135.

36. John Brewer, *The Sinews of Power: War, Money and the English State, 1688–1783* (London: Unwin Hyman, 1989), 209.

37. Sutherland, *East India Company*, 51. Cf. 298 on Hastings's distribution of "jobs" and contracts to allies.

38. Hastings's letter to Pitt, in Davies, "Hastings and the Younger Pitt," 618; Gleig, *Memoirs*, 2:374 and 1:268–69; and Marshall, *East Indian Fortunes*, 11, 183.

39. One of Hastings's protégés in India was William Markham, whose father, the archbishop of York, strongly supported Hastings in the House of Lords. Noting this family's fortune was built on the spoils of Chait Singh, Burke deplored the corruption of even high religious figures (*Corr.* 8:438).

40. Marshall, *East Indian Fortunes*, 181.

41. Ibid., 3, 205, and passim. Marshall suggests that Hastings was both a scapegoat for the sins of his predecessors and a victim of changing standards of public service in Great Britain.

42. Weitzman, *Hastings and Francis*, 54.

43. In "Minutes" (670), Hastings pleaded in extenuation of his errors that he had left England "while yet but a School Boy" to fill a responsible position.

44. The "schoolboy" reference here echoes an epithet sometimes used by opponents of Pitt, who at the age of twenty-four had displaced Burke's party from office. The still youthful Pitt voted for Hastings's impeachment, however.

45. Burke often refers to the company's servants in India as "English"; actually, during Hastings's time there, about half of them were Scots—partial outsiders, like Burke

himself—responding to imperial opportunities. Michael Fry, *The Dundas Despotism* (Edinburgh: Edinburgh University Press, 1992), 112. In this period of anti-Scottish sentiment, many English tended to regard enterprising Scots as unscrupulous profiteers, and as tainted with absolutist political attitudes, especially if they were from Jacobite families. Colley writes that Hastings may have drawn opprobrium because of his Scottish associates, but she offers no evidence for her suggestion that Burke shared this prejudice. Colley, *Britons*, 128–30.

46. The mortality rate for company servants in India exceeded 50 percent in the eighteenth century. Marshall, *East Indian Fortunes*, 218.

47. Jones, *Hastings in Bengal*, 40.

48. At one point, Hastings complained of the virtual enslavement of native weavers under company contract. Gleig, *Memoirs*, 1:305.

49. Smith, *Wealth of Nations*, 603.

50. Marshall, *East Indian Fortunes*, 148–49, 155. In *Rulers, Townsmen and Bazaars: North Indian Society in the Age of British Expansion 1770–1870* (Cambridge: Cambridge University Press, 1983), C. A. Bayly describes the well-developed domestic Indian commercial system, which company personnel infringed upon.

51. Hastings agreed with this analysis and on the need for higher salaries. Gleig, *Memoirs*, 1:388.

52. Two of the three references to Burke in Judith N. Shklar's *Ordinary Vices* (Cambridge: Harvard University Press, 1984), raise doubts about the "little platoon" (160 and 185): local loyalties can conflict with larger responsibilities rather than provide training for them.

53. According to Mansfield's *Statesmanship and Party Government*, Burke expressed the hope (in *Present Discontents*) that constitutional and party government under men of principle would replace reliance on extraordinary virtue, just as a regularized opposition would replace the occasional need for conspiracies to resist tyranny (as in 1688). But Burke did not repudiate statesmanship if it was available.

54. Burke's language here evokes the Greek concept of *polypragmosyne* (meddlesomeness) and related notions, qualities that were held by critics to constitute the disposition behind Athenian imperialism. See Frederick G. Whelan, "Socrates and the Meddlesomeness of the Athenians," *History of Political Thought* 4 (1983): 1–29.

55. Various "criminal" abuses relating to the opium business formed part of Burke's original impeachment charges, but do not seem to have attracted much attention at the time ("Articles of Charge," 63–70). The production of opium for sale in China, where it financed the purchase of tea, was an important element of the East India Company's overall economy. The actual marketing (and smuggling) of opium in China and elsewhere in Southeast Asia was done by independent merchants—an important part of the "private trade" in which company employees could engage. P. J. Marshall, *The New Cambridge History of India*, vol. 2, *Bengal: The British Bridgehead. Eastern India 1740–1828* (Cambridge: Cambridge University Press, 1987), 110–11. Hastings's defense assumed that the prevailing view was that smugglers took their chances, and that their activities were not a matter for grievance between states: "I do not know that it ever was

matter of much complaint between France and us, that they run their brandy into this country, or we our woollen cloths into that. Each is subject to the penalty of confiscation if caught, and, further than enforcing the general laws of the country, I believe no state interferes in that matter." Bond, *Speeches*, 2:675.

56. In *Political Radicalism* (41), Freeman holds that market behavior was the major exception for Burke to the traditional moral view that self-denying duty is virtuous and self-seeking behavior a vice.

57. Since pepper and calico were East Indian commodities, India was evidently in Burke's mind when he wrote this famous passage.

58. This is the thesis of C. B. Macpherson, *Burke* (New York: Hill and Wang, 1980).

59. Bacon, "Of Plantations," in *Francis Bacon's Essays* (London: Dent, 1968), 106.

60. Jones, *Hastings in Bengal*, 321. Burke viewed governing well a matter of experience, condemning the members of the Third Estate as men of theory who lacked "practical experience in the state" (*Reflections*, 128). Cornwallis was an experienced public figure, but he had no experience in India; in this case, his outsider status was a virtue. Hastings had plenty of experience, but the wrong kind. His case showed that one should never "employ a man who has been bred in base and corrupt practices, from any hope that his local knowledge may make him the fittest person to correct such practices" ("Speech in Reply," 12:284).

61. "The hardest of all servitudes is to be subject to a republic." Niccolò Machiavelli, *Discourses* 2.2 (p. 287), in *The Prince and the Discourses*, trans. Luigi Ricci and Christian E. Detmold (New York: Modern Library, 1950).

62. David Hume, "That Politics May Be Reduced to a Science," in *Essays*, 18–19.

63. Burke's warning is partly borne out by the profile of the network of protégés and supporters Hastings organized on his return to England, as described by Rosane Rocher, *Orientalism, Poetry, and the Millennium: The Checkered Life of Nathaniel Brassey Halhed 1751–1830* (Columbia, Mo.: South Asia Books, 1983), 122–27, 131–47. This "Bengal squad" was more a group of publicists and pamphleteers than a political party.

64. Ironically, Hastings agreed, though (naturally) not in his own case. Referring to his colleague the governor of Madras, whom he regarded as especially corrupt, Hastings wrote, "The Evidence against Rumbold is strong enough to convict twelve Felons . . . but he will surmount it all. There is not Virtue in England for the punishment of wealthy Villainy." *Letters to MacPherson*, 154. For a pro-Hastings account of Hastings's conflict with Rumbold, see A. P. Dasgupta, *The Central Authority in British India 1774–1784* (Calcutta: Calcutta University Press, 1931) chap. 2.

65. Burke's party was a minority or opposition group in Parliament at the time of the impeachment. Thus, aside from corrupt motives, a more realistic fear of failure arose from the possibility that the impeachment would be treated as a party issue.

66. Hastings was stationed at Madras just before assuming the governorship of Bengal. According to Keith Feiling, he was one of the few there not involved in the scheme. Keith Feiling, *Warren Hastings* (London: Macmillan, 1954), 71.

67. He was more commonly known at the time as the nabob of Arcot, after his capital.

68. David Hume, "Of Public Credit," in *Essays*, 360.

69. See Cone, *Nature of Politics*, 2:165. Dundas, in charge of India in Pitt's government, acknowledged that this was a "rotten deal," in the words of his biographer. Fry, *Dundas Despotism*, 120.

70. Marshall, *Problems*, 29; *Impeachment*, 24–25.

71. Cone, *Nature of Politics*, 1:308. Furber argues that Burke's shift to the position of antagonist of Hastings and the company occurred during a period encompassing the years when William Burke served as the agent of the raja (1777–1778). Furber, "Burke and India," 13–14. See also Noonan, *Bribes*, 418–20. While upholding the corruption charges against Hastings, Noonan also details Burke's participation in practices (patronage, nepotism, partisan sinecures, etc.) that might appear corrupt by later standards. Cf. J. Riddy, "Warren Hastings: Scotland's Benefactor?" in Carnall and Nicholson, eds., *Impeachment*, 32.

72. According to Mitchell, the prosecution was a partisan issue and an attempt at self-vindication for Fox, but not for Burke, whose attacks on Hastings in the name of political morality had begun before the fall of the coalition. Mitchell, *Charles James Fox*, 105–07.

73. See Frank O'Gorman, *Voters, Patrons, and Parties: The Unreformed Electoral System of Hanoverian England 1734–1832* (Oxford: Clarendon Press, 1989), especially 18–21 (on nomination boroughs, which generated perhaps a third of late eighteenth-century MPs), 27–67 (on "proprietary" boroughs and other forms of electoral influence), and 158ff. (on the problem of bribery of voters).

74. Morley chides Burke for failing to embrace the conception of democratic government that was beginning to make itself felt. As if in compensation, he suggests, Burke was "indefatigable in his enmity to everything that savoured of abuse and maladministration," and attacked the corruption of those who failed to behave as true statesmen within the old constitution. Morley, *Edmund Burke*, 11, 135.

75. Sir Lewis Namier, *England in the Age of the American Revolution*, 2d ed. (London: Macmillan, 1961), 3–6.

76. See Hanna Fenichel Pitkin, *The Concept of Representation* (Berkeley: University of California Press, 1972), chap. 8.

77. J. R. Pole, *Political Representation in England and the Origins of the American Republic* (Berkeley: University of California Press, 1966), 441.

78. Sutherland, *East India Company*, 19 and passim.

79. Ibid., 19, 58; Cone, *Nature of Politics*, 2:385–88. Burke condemned the African slave trade as an "incurable evil"; in accordance with his usual approach as a practical politician and a cautious reformer, he proposed a scheme for its gradual abolition and the manumission of the slaves. "Negro Code," 258 and passim. Opposition to the slave trade elicited a moral fervor in politics similar to that which Burke evinced against Hastings. Leaders of that opposition, such as William Wilberforce, were supporters of Pitt, however. See P. J. Marshall, introduction to volume 6 of the Oxford edition of Burke's *Writings and Speeches*, 5.

80. Barker discusses the degree to which Burke shared the usual expectation that a member of Parliament would exert himself on behalf of constituency interests. Barker, "Bristol Constituency," in *Essays on Government*, 194.

81. James N. Holzman, *The Nabobs in England: A Study of the Returned Anglo-Indian, 1760–1785* (New York, 1926), 15, 21, 45, 49–50.

82. Macaulay's account of the unpopularity of the nabobs is irresistible: "That they had sprung from obscurity, that they had acquired great wealth, that they exhibited it insolently, that they spent it extravagantly, that they raised the price of everything in their neighborhood, from fresh eggs to rotten boroughs, that their liveries outshone those of dukes" etc. Thomas Babington Macaulay, "Lord Clive," in *Critical and Historical Essays*, 537–38.

83. Holzman, *Nabobs*, 20.

84. J. G. A. Pocock, "Edmund Burke and the Redefinition of Enthusiasm: The Context as Counter-Revolution," in *The French Revolution and the Creation of Modern Political Culture*, ed. François Furet and Mona Ozouf (Oxford: Pergamon Press, 1989), 3:28.

85. Quoted in Michael Edwardes, *Warren Hastings: King of the Nabobs* (London: Hart-Davis, MacGibbon, 1976), 37. For the context, see Stanley Ayling, *The Elder Pitt* (New York: David McKay, 1976), 387.

Chapter 3. The Charges: Despotism

1. Also known as Nadir Shah, he invaded India from Persia and sacked Delhi in 1738–1739, dealing a near fatal blow to the Mogul Empire. Burke does not mention the fact that India also bled, perhaps to avoid the impression that India suffered from despotism and disorder prior to British rule there. Janes, "Flying Leap," 510.

2. Marshall, *Problems*, 60.

3. Gleig, *Memoirs*, 1:294.

4. Jones, *Hastings in Bengal*, 170.

5. Quoted ibid., 147.

6. Gleig, *Memoirs*, 1:352, 358.

7. Strachey, *Rohilla War*, 97.

8. See, for example, Strachey, *Rohilla War*; Weitzman, *Hastings and Francis*; Jones, *Hastings in Bengal*; Davies, *Hastings and Oudh*; Penderel Moon, *Warren Hastings and British India* (New York: Collier, 1962).

9. See especially Strachey, *Rohilla War*, 102–05.

10. In his *Rhetoric*, Aristotle recommends appeals to the "noble" (or honorable) as well as to the just and the advantageous. Note, however, that such appeals would not have worked if the noble (*to kalon*) had not been a genuine standard of value for the Greeks.

11. Frederick G. Whelan, "Vattel's Doctrine of the State," *History of Political Thought* 9 (1988): 79.

12. Gleig, *Memoirs*, 2:379.

13. Weitzman, *Hastings and Francis*, 161.

14. Gleig, *Memoirs*, 2:145.

15. Dasgupta, *Central Authority*, 34–35. Hastings held that imperial security require-

ments as he saw them overrode explicit orders from the company directors to restore the raja.

16. James Mill, Macaulay, and Morley, for example, all echo Burke's interpretation and condemn Hastings on this incident. Strachey's *Rohilla War* reversed the received view.

17. Strachey, *Rohilla War*, 69–74 and passim.

18. Davies, *Hastings and Oudh*, 31, 36.

19. Strachey, *Rohilla War*, 118, 256. Hastings argued that he was under orders from the directors to increase remittances and reduce military expenses. Hastings "Minutes," 683.

20. Hastings, in Strachey, *Rohilla War*, 256–57; and "Minutes," 672.

21. See Jennifer M. Welsh, *Edmund Burke and International Relations: The Commonwealth of Europe and the Crusade against the French Revolution* (New York: St. Martin's, 1995), 32–33, 157ff. Burke's advocacy of a "holy war" against the French Revolution contrasts with his usual embrace of just war doctrine.

22. Strachey, *Rohilla War*, 208, 231–33.

23. Gleig, *Memoirs*, 1:438.

24. Ibid., 425–26.

25. Strachey, *Rohilla War*, 10, 22–26.

26. Ibid., 25.

27. Ibid., 187; Davies, *Hastings and Oudh*, 59–60. As an example of contemporaneous linguistic usage in a similar situation, compare Hume's statement that the policy of William the Conqueror was to "entirely extirpate" the English gentry in favor of the Normans. David Hume, *The History of England* (Boston: Phillips, Sampson, 1849), 1:194.

28. Hastings, in Strachey, *Rohilla War*, 180; and "Minutes," 673.

29. Gleig, *Memoirs*, 1:358.

30. Hastings, in Strachey, *Rohilla War*, 148.

31. Weitzman, *Hastings and Francis*, 255.

32. Gleig, *Memoirs*, 1:262.

33. Macaulay, "Hastings," 579.

34. Ibid., 580. The biographer was G. R. Gleig. The commentary in his edition of Hastings's papers is highly adulatory.

35. O'Brien, "Hastings in Burke's Great Melody," 70.

36. Noonan, *Bribes*, 402–03. The status of the crime of forgery has been a secondary issue of the case. Forgery had been made a capital crime in England in 1729, where the seriousness of the offense was related to the emergence of a commercial society. In 1773 Parliament investigated the events of 1757, and Clive admitted he had deceived an important Indian official by forgery in the conspiracy preceding the battle of Plassey. The disparity in the treatment of Clive and Nandakumar for the same offense was shocking to Macaulay and other nineteenth-century moralists, as was the fact that an Englishman had descended to what were regarded as Indian standards of dishonesty. The judgment that Nandakumar's punishment was overly severe and culturally inappropriate was thus combined with a disparaging opinion of Asian moral standards. As Morley commented, praising Burke, "Nobody now believes that Clive was justified in

tricking Omichund by forging another man's name; that Impey was justified in hanging Nuncomar for committing the very offence for which Clive was excused or applauded, although forgery is no grave crime according to Hindoo usage, and it is the gravest according to English usage." Morley, *Burke*, 196.

37. The pathbreaking revisionist work is Stephen, *Story of Nuncomar;* see 1:139 and 186 and 2:37, for the conclusion that the conduct of the trial, including Impey's summation, was fair. Cf. Marshall, *Impeachment*, 142.

38. Weitzman, *Hastings and Francis*, 36. Stephen also argued that murdering Nandakumar made little sense from Hastings's point of view, and questioned the council majority's refusal to seek a reprieve. Stephen, *Story of Nuncomar*, 1:74–75 and 233; 2:110–111.

39. The insult to the sacred probably refers to the hanging of a Brahmin and to the fact that the circumstances of Nandakumar's imprisonment obstructed the performance of the ritual obligations of his caste, both of which were major issues in Calcutta at the time.

40. Marshall, *Impeachment*, 141.

41. Hastings, "Minutes," 708.

42. On the "Munster disturbances," see introduction to part 2 of the Oxford edition of Burke's *Writings and Speeches*, 9:414–15; and *Letter to Kenmare*, 570.

43. See also *Corr.* 5:253, where the text of Hastings's order is given.

44. Bond, *Speeches*, 2:488.

45. See Marshall, *Impeachment*, 153–54.

46. For example, it is apparent that Burke's sense of propriety in relation to social rank was offended by Munni Begam's origin as a slave. Montesquieu, however, had said that marriages between princes and slaves, and the sudden elevation of slaves, were unexceptionable in Asia, since the distinction of ranks was generally unstable under despots, and all subjects little better than slaves. Montesquieu, *Spirit of the Laws* 6.1.

47. Gleig, *Memoirs*, 1:253–54.

48. Ibid., 269–70.

49. Ibid., 270.

50. Ibid., 268. Hastings compares himself to Solon.

51. Jones, *Hastings in Bengal*, 255–56 and passim.

52. Gleig, *Memoirs*, 1:388.

53. Hastings in Forrest, *Selections*, 267.

54. Weitzman, *Hastings and Francis*, 82–83; Jones, *Hastings in Bengal*, 11–14. The zamindars were not be easily understood in terms of European categories. Were they government officials, tax farmers, local magistrates, feudal-type lords, gentry, or rent-collecting landowners? The difficulty was heightened by regional variations and by the distinction between their original or formal position and the customary position they had acquired by the late eighteenth century.

55. Quoted in Weitzman, *Hastings and Francis*, 235–36.

56. In its land settlement of 1793, the British administration attempted to create an English-type gentry in India, based on firm landed property rights; this policy reflected the victory of Francis's (and Burke's) view over that of Hastings, according to Ranajit

Guha, *A Rule of Property for Bengal* (Paris: Mouton, 1963). See also Marshall, *Problems,* 63–64.

57. Hastings, "State of India," 72.

58. Weitzman, *Hastings and Francis,* 161.

59. Burke asserted that the revenue charge—auctioning off the landed interest of Bengal—was the most atrocious, with the exception of the Rohilla War (*Corr.* 5:328).

60. O'Brien has argued both that Burke's repressed hatred of the Protestant Ascendancy surfaced in his attack on the French Revolution (introduction to Burke's *Reflections*) and that the causes of Ireland and India came to be fused in his mind (*Great Melody*). The idea of large-scale revolutionary "confiscations" followed by "auctions" may have triggered an association of all three cases. To this catalog we should add Burke's attack on Henry VIII in *Noble Lord,* and perhaps also his rejection of property confiscation as contrary to the law of nations in connection with the Saint Eustatius incident. Stanlis, *Burke and the Natural Law,* 91. In "Burke's Flying Leap" (512), Janes points to the Bengal-France link. It should be noted that in *Reflections* (270), Burke does not absolutely rule out "violent revolutions in property through extensive confiscation," but says they must meet a very rigorous test of public utility.

61. In elevating new men and depressing the old aristocracy, Hastings was following Machiavelli's advice on how a prince should administer a newly acquired province. Machiavelli, *Discourses* 1.26.

62. On the second day of his opening speech, Burke's descriptions of tortures created a sensation, and Hastings's supporters vigorously denied Hastings was responsible for the actions of Devi Singh's agents. Burke replied that he blamed the "Collusion" of Englishmen who "ought to have been a check" on their underlings (*Corr.,* 5:381).

63. Hastings, quoted in Jones, *Hastings in Bengal,* 191.

64. Jones, *Hastings in Bengal,* 171.

65. Cone, *Nature of Politics,* 1:363–73.

66. In *The Idea of Poverty: England in the Early Industrial Age* (New York: Knopf, 1984), Gertrude Himmelfarb focuses on Burke's opposition to the Poor Laws in the 1790s in the name of the laws of political economy. She concludes only that this tension in Burke foreshadows the ambivalence of later conservatives between paternalism and the attractions of the free market (66–73).

67. For a discussion of "Gothic" in this second sense, see Bruyn, "Gothic Romance."

68. Pocock, "Ancient Constitution"; idem, "Political Economy," 193–94; Reid, *Political Writing,* 58, 68; and Bruyn, "Gothic Romance," 419.

69. Kramnick, *Rage of Edmund Burke,* 130, 161, and passim.

70. Macpherson, *Burke,* 62–63.

71. Kramnick, "The Left and Burke," 206–10.

72. Pocock, "Political Economy," 195–200.

73. Burke failed to acknowledge that Hastings's reforms of the household were indeed linked to a larger government reorganization of Bengal as a whole.

74. The confiscating princes, governors, and demagogues were, respectively, Henry VIII vis-à-vis the monasteries, Hastings, and the French revolutionaries.

75. Marshall, *Impeachment,* 46–48.

76. For these and the following facts, see Marshall, *Impeachment,* chap. 5; Davies, *Hastings and Oudh,* 82–84 and chap. 5.

77. Suprakash Sanyal argues that Hastings was encouraged (perhaps misled) by local opponents of Chait Singh, especially the local Brahmins; he therefore concludes the raja was the victim not only of Hastings's "high-handedness" but also of "caste-ridden India" and the endemic "divisions and conspiracies" there. Suprakash Sanyal, *Benares and the English East India Company, 1764–1795* (Calcutta: World Press, 1979), 102, 113. Such complications escaped Burke's notice.

78. Hastings, "A Narrative of the Insurrection Which Happened in the Zemeedary of Banaris in the Month of August, 1781, and of the Transactions of the Governor-General in that District," in Forrest, *Selections,* 134.

79. Hastings, "Minutes," 696.

80. Hastings, "Insurrection," 135. In "Minutes" (690–92), Hastings argued in detail that Chait Singh and his father were originally appointed tax farmers, with fewer rights than a hereditary zamindar.

81. Davies calls Chait Singh a "tributary landholder." Davies, *Hastings and Oudh,* 113. On the ambiguities of zamindar, see ibid., 118–20. Marshall calls him "a chieftain very similar to the major *zamindars* in neighbouring Bihar" and interprets the regional uprisings as "the last bid by the Bihar *zamindars* to reassert what they saw as their traditional right to limit the claims which any ruler of Bengal could make upon them." Marshall, *Cambridge History,* 95. The suppression of the insurrection, in other words, was an integral part of the gradual imposition of British authority in eastern India. See, however, C. H. Alexandrowicz, *An Introduction to the History of the Law of Nations in the East Indies* (Oxford: Clarendon Press, 1967), 20–23. Alexandrowicz supports Burke, holding that Chait Singh was comparable to a high-level feudal vassal, or at least closer to such a vassal than to a zamindar.

82. Bond, *Speeches,* 1:205.

83. Hastings's counsel, in Bond, *Speeches,* 2:651. Hastings's counsel calls Chait Singh a "haughty vassal" who refused reasonable requests.

84. Hastings, "Insurrection," 139; cf. Marshall, *Impeachment,* 92.

85. Hastings's counsel, in Bond, *Speeches,* 2:717.

86. Hastings, "Insurrection," 133–35; Gleig, *Memoirs,* 2:420–21.

87. This policy toward Oudh, called a system of subsidiary alliances, was continued by Hastings's successors as well.

88. Hastings cited one such writer, Alexander Dow, who had called Asaf al-Daula the "infamous son of an infamous Persian peddler," as if to justify his contemptuous treatment of him. Burke indignantly defended Asaf's ancestry as being among the highest Persian nobility. "Speech in Reply," 11:375–76.

89. Davies, *Hastings and Oudh,* 89. In *North India,* Barnett provides a more detailed and sympathetic view of Asaf's regime and the pressures it was under in the transitional period between Mogul and British dominance.

90. The British alliance was effective in that Oudh was never again invaded after

British troops were placed there; however, Barnett confirms Burke's analysis of the "vicious circle" produced: increased revenues were needed, primarily to pay for the troops, and the main function of the troops was often collecting the taxes. Barnett, *North India*, 92, 154. Other costs of the British presence led to an "open season" on the nawab's treasury. Ibid., 145.

91. This was the opinion of Francis, who rejected Hastings's view of the strategic importance of the British presence in Oudh. Weitzman, *Hastings and Francis*, 84. The trade routes along the Ganges and Jumna Rivers created natural economic ties between Oudh and Bengal. The rulers of Oudh sought unsuccessfully to resist British economic penetration, which was detrimental to local mercantile interests, and which they correctly realized would endanger their sovereignty. Jones, *Hastings in Bengal*, 227; Barnett, *North India*, 84–88.

92. Hastings, in Bond, *Speeches*, 2:496; Davies, *Hastings and Oudh*, 168; Marshall, *Impeachment*, 112–16.

93. Hastings, in Bond, *Speeches*, 2:495; and "Minutes," 699–700.

94. Davies, *Hastings and Oudh*, 138, 169–70; Marshall, *Impeachment*, 119. Barnett (*North India*, 192–205) confirms both that the larger rebellion was organized and led, and that the begams were the central figures in an extensive "power network" of opponents of Asaf al-Daula and his British alliance.

95. Bond, *Speeches*, 1:492–93.

96. Kramnick, *Rage of Edmund Burke*, 137–38.

97. Bruyn, "Gothic Romance," 420, 430–31.

98. Quoted in Davies, *Hastings and Oudh*, 164. Hastings actually censured his resident for not having used greater force. Barnett, *North India*, 214.

99. Sheridan especially dwelt on the "monstrous quality" of this crime, giving more emphasis than Burke to the personal effects of tyranny rather than the public issues. Bond, *Speeches*, 1:689ff.

100. Thomas Paine, *Rights of Man* (Harmondsworth: Penguin, 1969), 73.

101. Janes suggests forcefully that Burke's prior preoccupation with the begams inspired the famous passage in *Reflections*: "Marie Antoinette emerges from the zenana." Janes, "Flying Leap," 524. More precisely, it may have been the effect made by Sheridan's speeches that inspired him. Burke's own lengthy descriptions of the begams came after the *Reflections*, in his closing speech.

102. Janes suggests that Burke's image of Shah Alam, a humiliated king in the hands of his enemies, contributed to his reaction to the treatment of Louis XVI in 1789. Janes, "Flying Leap," 513.

103. Aristotle, *Rhetoric*, trans. W. Rhys Roberts (New York: Modern Library, 1954), 2.8 (p. 115).

Chapter 4. Necessity, Despotism, and Law

1. Machiavelli, *Discourses* 1.6 (p. 129).

2. Recent scholars have sought to emphasize Machiavelli's adherence to the civic

humanist tradition and have dated the prominence of *raison d'état* doctrine to the later sixteenth century, in conjunction with the spread of absolutism and a more pessimistic view of human nature. See Richard Tuck, *Philosophy and Government 1572−1651* (Cambridge: Cambridge University Press, 1993), esp. chap. 2. While agreeing with this larger picture, Maurizio Viroli correctly points out that Machiavelli's writings belong to both traditions (*From Politics to Reason of State* [Cambridge: Cambridge University Press, 1992], 6, 8). *The Prince* is surely a textbook of the "art of state" (in Viroli's terms), even though Machiavelli did not use the phrase *ragione di stato*. It is therefore not difficult to see how *raison d'état* and "Machiavellianism" later came to be more or less synonymous in popular usage.

3. Weitzman, *Hastings and Francis*, 83.

4. Viroli emphasizes the domestic application of *raison d'état* in its early (seventeenth-century) form—keeping internal order rather than enlarging the state (*From Politics to Reason of State*, chap. 1). On the other hand, Meinecke emphasizes growth or expansion as an "organic necessity" of the state. Friedrich Meinecke, *Machiavellism: The Doctrine of Raison d'Etat and its Place in Modern History*, trans. Douglas Scott (London: Routledge and Kegan Paul, 1957), 1. It seems to me that the doctrine posits state security as its fundamental end; it endorses expansion when and if this is a necessary means to that end, and stresses the likelihood of international conflict and external threats to the state.

5. Janes ("Flying Leap," 517−20) suggests that the progressive militarization of the Indian empire contributed to Burke's prediction that a military dictator would eventually step into the vacuum created by the destruction of traditional institutions in France. Burke, however, had no quarrel with Hastings's predecessor or successor—Clive and Cornwallis—who as military men might have provided somewhat better models for this scenario.

6. Hastings, "State of India," 61, 67.

7. Hastings, "Minutes," 685.

8. Hastings, "Letter to Pitt," 619.

9. Gleig, *Memoirs*, 3:338.

10. Ibid., 1:377, 375.

11. Hastings, "State of India," 60.

12. Ibid.

13. Ibid., 22. Cf. *The Prince*, chap. 6, where Machiavelli discusses fortune, ability, opportunities provided by calamity, and the necessity of being armed as factors in the acquisition of new dominions.

14. "The argument of state necessity" was persuasive to "politicians who customarily found the justification of a policy in its success, utility, advantage, or mere convenience. Specifically, Hastings had saved the British Empire in India, and of what effect was a lofty moral argument against that indisputable fact?" Cone, *Nature of Politics*, 2:205−06. See also Marshall, *Impeachment*, 42.

15. Hastings, "State of India," 47.

16. Horace Walpole, *Selected Letters of Horace Walpole*, ed. W. S. Lewis (New Haven: Yale University Press, 1973), 270.

17. The very extent of British territorial gains in the Seven Years' War made British governments nervous about defending them, according to Colley (*Britons*, 101). This helps explain why official policy prohibited further expansion of the Indian possessions.

18. The effect of these wars and the transition from a commercial to a military empire is apparent in the numbers: in 1740 there were 2,000 British troops in India; in 1782 (at the end of the Maratha War), 115,000. Geoffrey Parker, "Europe and the Wider World, 1500–1750: The Military Balance," in *The Political Economy of Merchant Empires*, ed. James D. Tracy (Cambridge: Cambridge University Press, 1991), 181–84.

19. Davies, *Hastings and Oudh*, 2. The Marathas had raided Bengal on a number of occasions in the 1740s and established control over parts of Orissa. Marshall, *Cambridge History*, 70–71.

20. Hastings, "State of India," 52.

21. For Hastings's detailed assessment of the danger, see Gleig, *Memoirs*, 2:194–207.

22. Weitzman, *Hastings and Francis*, 114.

23. Since the war in India coincided with the American Revolution, a sense of imperial crisis set the stage for the Indian reform movement of the early 1780s. The parliamentary select committee on which Burke served was established to investigate abuses in the government of Bengal; shortly afterwards, in April 1781, a secret committee was formed under Henry Dundas to investigate the causes of the Carnatic War; news of Yorktown followed in the autumn.

24. Hastings, quoted in Jones, *Hastings in Bengal*, 207.

25. Gleig, *Memoirs*, 1:284–85.

26. Weitzman, *Hastings and Francis*, 228.

27. Hastings, "State of India," 60.

28. Ibid., 58.

29. For Hastings's analysis of the situation, see "State of India," 52–53.

30. Gleig, *Memoirs*, 2:198.

31. Ibid., 136–37.

32. Ibid., 143.

33. Hastings, *Letters to MacPherson*, 100.

34. Dasgupta, *Central Authority*, 288.

35. Burke cites "reason of state" approvingly in *Regicide Peace 1* (261), but only in support of a mild conclusion (the occasional need for secrecy).

36. Burke is paraphrasing Livy 9.1. Machiavelli quotes the same passage at greater length, both in *The Prince* 26 (p. 96), and *Discourses* 3.12 (p. 453).

37. Quoted in Bond, *Speeches*, 1:533.

38. Gleig, *Memoirs*, 3:192.

39. Jones, *Hastings in Bengal*, 116–22.

40. Davies, *Hastings and Oudh*, 50.

41. Macaulay, "Clive," 489–90.

42. Gleig, *Memoirs*, 2:140ff.

43. Ibid., 3:25.

44. Ibid., 178.

45. Hastings, "State of India," 12.

46. Bond, *Speeches*, 2:498, 514–16.

47. See Colley, *Britons*, 102.

48. Hastings, "State of India," 77; Gleig, *Memoirs*, 3:301.

49. Marshall, *Impeachment*, 12.

50. Gleig, *Memoirs*, 2:424.

51. Ibid., 1:290, 292, 373–74.

52. Hastings, "State of India." 93.

53. Gleig, *Memoirs*, 3:45–46.

54. Weitzman, *Hastings and Francis*, 128–29.

55. Hastings, *Letters to MacPherson*, 72.

56. Gleig, *Memoirs*, 3:310, 25; 2:325. The Regulating Act subordinated the other presidencies to Bengal with respect to hostilities and treaties, except in cases of "imminent necessity." The most detailed study of this system concludes it was unworkable, supporting Hastings's view that it forced the governor-general to prosecute wars that others began. Dasgupta, *Central Authority*, 6–8 and passim.

57. Hastings, *Letters to MacPherson*, 150–51.

58. Gleig, *Memoirs*, 1:371.

59. Ibid., 3:81.

60. Weitzman, *Hastings and Francis*, 30.

61. Davies, *Hastings and Oudh*, 65, 94.

62. Gleig, *Memoirs*, 2:110.

63. Quoted in Weitzman, *Hastings and Francis*, 231, 244, 224.

64. Hastings's counsel, in Bond, *Speeches*, 2:778.

65. Gleig, *Memoirs*, 2:342; Weitzman, *Hastings and Francis*, 212.

66. Hastings, "Letter to Pitt," 616; cf. "State of India," 94.

67. Gleig, *Memoirs*, 2:388.

68. Ibid., 191–92, 329–30.

69. Hastings, "Insurrection," 130–34; idem, "Minutes," 693; and Davies, *Hastings and Oudh*, 140. For confirmation and discussion, see Sanyal, *Benares and the English Company*, 85, 90, 111.

70. Hastings, "Letter to Pitt," 615.

71. Weitzman, *Hastings and Francis*, 199. Burke observed that Lord Macartney, the able governor of Madras who was offered the governor-generalship, also wanted greater power (*Corr.* 5:207).

72. Mansfield emphasizes the antimonarchical thrust of Burke's defense of constitutional and party government in *Present Discontents*. This would apply to Hastings insofar as he was claiming the position of absolute monarch in British India. Mansfield, *Statesmanship and Party Government*, chap. 6, esp. 130.

73. This is suggested by Hastings's admiring biographer, Gleig, *Memoirs*, 1:446.

74. Harvey C. Mansfield Jr., *Taming the Prince: The Ambivalence of Modern Executive Power* (Baltimore: Johns Hopkins University Press, 1993), 13 and passim.

75. Gleig, *Memoirs*, 2:358.

76. In a very early, pro-East India Company speech of 1772, Burke defended Clive's use of "arbitrary" power as necessary to keep the Indians in awe in a lawless environment ("East India Select Committee," 373–74). This is exactly the position he rejected ten—and again twenty—years later, after studying Indian affairs more closely.

77. Hastings, *Letters to MacPherson*, 72.

78. Gleig, *Memoirs*, 3:23.

79. Hastings, "Insurrection," 160.

80. Gleig, *Memoirs*, 3:57, 73–74, 82.

81. Hastings, "State of India," 70.

82. Hastings, *Letters to MacPherson*, 101.

83. Like Machiavelli's prince, Hastings hoped his policies would win the love as well as the fear of Indians, but in the final analysis it was fear he counted on. See Wood, "Aesthetic Dimension," 58. Wood argues that, for Burke, some degree of sublimity or fearsomeness had to attend any effective government—though not, of course, the pervasive reliance on fear characteristic of despotism. See also Wilkins, *Problem*, 151: Sublimity makes for better art than politics, and the sublimity of power is one reason constitutional restraints are needed.

84. In 1792 Burke worried that the theme of "the supposed oriental despotism" might arouse more support for Hastings in the House of Lords than in the Commons, particularly among "those Lords who may be lovers of power, especially when . . . Indian power may possibly be exercised [as a future governor] by one of their own body." *Corr.* 7:113.

85. For the background of the term, see R. Koebner, "Despot and Despotism: Vicissitudes of a Political Term," *Journal of the Warburg and Courtauld Institutes* 14 (1951): 275–302; and Melvin Richter, "Despotism," in *Dictionary of the History of Ideas*, vol. 2 (New York: Scribner's, 1973).

86. See especially Montesquieu, *Spirit of the Laws* 5.14–19.

87. Ibid., 5.16, 19.13.

88. Ibid., 6.1.

89. One oddity of Hastings's trial in the House of Lords is that some of the strongest evidence against him was drawn by the managers from his own previous defense statement to the Commons. Stephen regards this as unfair, but it is not clear why, since the self-incriminating material was freely offered. Stephen, *Story of Nuncomar*, 1:72. Most of Hastings's "Minutes" actually consists of detailed defenses of the legal propriety of his actions.

90. Hastings, "Minutes," 696. Burke quotes this passage in "Speech on Opening," 348–49, and "Speech in Reply," 11:198.

91. Hastings, "Minutes," 692; and Fox, in Bond, *Speeches*, 1:202; cf. "Speech in Reply," 11:196. Hastings was referring in particular to the powers over Chait Singh that he had received from the nawab of Oudh.

92. Koebner, "Despot," 289.

93. Montesquieu, *Spirit of the Laws* 17.5, 18.20.

94. Ibid., 5.14.

95. John Stuart Mill, "A Few Words on Non-Intervention," in *Essays on Politics and Culture*, ed. Gertrude Himmelfarb (Garden City: Anchor, 1963), 377−78.

96. Montesquieu, *Spirit of the Laws* 5.14. The point is confirmed for India by Davies, *Hastings and Oudh*, 70. Asaf al-Daula had no sooner succeeded as nawab of Oudh in 1775 than he faced a "mutiny" or rebellion in favor of his half brother Saadat Ali, which, though quelled with British help, weakened his regime from the outset. See Barnett, *North India*, 113−20.

97. Hastings's counsel, in Bond, *Speeches*, 2:545.

98. Bond, *Speeches*, 2:546.

99. Hastings, "Minutes," 696, quoted by Burke, "Speech on Opening," 348.

100. Hastings, "Minutes," 696, quoted by Burke, "Speech on Opening," 349.

101. Hastings's counsel, in Bond, *Speeches*, 2:812.

102. Montesquieu, *Spirit of the Laws*, 6.9 and 13.

103. Hastings's reports, quoted in Jones, *Hastings in Bengal*, 210−11, 330. Marshall questions Hastings's success in dealing with dacoity, which was sometimes hard to distinguish from frontier rebelliousness. Marshall, *Cambridge History*, 97−98.

104. Montesquieu, *Spirit of the Laws*, 17.2, 14.3.

105. Gleig, *Memoirs*, 1:394.

106. See Judith N. Shklar, *Montesquieu* (Oxford: Oxford University Press, 1987), 69, on the meanings of *doivent*.

107. Hastings's counsel, in Bond, *Speeches*, 2:533−37.

108. Hastings, quoted in Jones, *Hastings in Bengal*, 148−49.

109. Gleig, *Memoirs*, 1:400−03.

110. This was true in the early 1780s, when Burke began his investigation of Hastings. Later, by the time of the trial, some other British leaders were more knowledgeable, notably Henry Dundas, a member of Pitt's government and head of the board of control established by the 1784 legislation.

111. Montesquieu, *Spirit of the Laws*, 11.3−4.

112. John Stuart Mill, "On Liberty," in *Essays on Politics and Society*, ed. J. M. Robson, vol. 18 of *Collected Works of John Stuart Mill* (Toronto: University of Toronto Press, 1977), 224. "On Liberty" appeared shortly after the Indian rebellion or "mutiny" of 1857, which led to a harsher view of Indians in England.

113. Montesquieu, *Spirit of the Laws* 6.3, 5.16.

114. Ibid., 5.15, 13.2.

115. Ibid., 5.14, 14.6.

116. Ibid., 6.21.

117. Ibid., 5.19.

118. Ibid., 3.10.

119. Ibid., 5.14.

120. See C. P. Courtney, *Montesquieu and Burke* (Oxford: Blackwell, 1963). Amazingly, Courtney does not mention the oriental despotism controversy. Burke sometimes praised Montesquieu, even after denouncing his views on Asia—for example, in "Ap-

peal," 198. Elsewhere, he remarked that Montesquieu was "sometimes misled by system" (*Corr.* 6:81).

121. Koebner, "Despot," 285.

122. P. J. Marshall and Glyndwr Williams, *The Great Map of Mankind: Perceptions of New Worlds in the Age of Enlightenment* (Cambridge: Harvard University Press, 1982), 17−20.

123. For example, Franco Venturi, "Oriental Despotism," *Journal of the History of Ideas* 24 (1963): 133−42.

124. Marshall and Williams, *Great Map*, 140.

125. Voltaire, *Essai sur les moeurs et l'esprit des nations*, ed. René Pomeau (Paris: Garnier, 1963), 1:836, 2:322.

126. Richter, "Despotism," 13; Venturi, "Oriental Despotism," 137−38; Marshall and Williams, *Great Map*, 141.

127. On the preparation of Hastings's defense speech of May 1−2, 1786, and Halhed's role in it, see Rocher, *Orientalism, Poetry, and the Millennium*, 132−33; see also chapter 4 of this volume on *The Code of Gentoo Laws* and its favorable reception in Europe. Burke expressed contempt for Halhed personally as merely "one agent in [Hastings's] numerous corps" (*Corr.* 5:323).

128. Montesquieu, *Spirit of the Laws*, 17.5.

129. Voltaire, *Moeurs*, 1:807, 804−05.

130. Edward Gibbon, *The Decline and Fall of the Roman Empire*, vol. 2 (New York: Modern Library, n.d.), chap. 65.

131. Marshall and Williams, *Great Map*, 88, 136. For an earlier example, see David Hume, "Of National Characters," in *Essays*, 208n.

132. Bond, *Speeches*, 2:534.

133. "Conciliation" predates Burke's study of India. In *Reflections*, Burke contrasted Asian despotism with the French monarchy; Janes ("Flying Leap," 510) suggests he deliberately referred to the Turkish situation but not to South Asian cases so as not to spoil the argument he was concurrently making against Hastings.

134. Marshall and Williams, *Great Map*, 159. Curiously, in taking this view, eighteenth-century British officials seem to have overlooked or ignored the large, nonelite Muslim population in eastern Bengal.

135. Hastings, "Minutes," 670.

136. Hastings indeed claimed to have inherited Shuja al-Daula's authority, including a "general, perhaps arbitrary" right to fine a recalcitrant vassal. This was perhaps a "defect" of Indian government, but a legitimate power nonetheless (Hastings, "Minutes," 694).

137. Cf. the absence of attention to the caste system in the selections in P. J. Marshall, ed., *The British Discovery of Hinduism in the Eighteenth Century* (Cambridge: Cambridge University Press, 1970). Eighteenth-century British students of Hinduism seem to have been more interested in its theological and philosophical doctrines. Recall, however, Burke's description (in chapter 3) of loss of caste through humiliating treatment.

Chapter 5. Political Philosophy

1. Michael Freeman, *Edmund Burke and the Critique of Political Radicalism* (Chicago: University of Chicago Press, 1980), 94. I do, however, find two uses of the word "traditionary" in the *Reflections* (102). "Traditionalism" and "conservatism" are nineteenth-century coinages, to be sure, denoting nineteenth-century ideologies, arguably inspired by Burke's writings.

2. Pocock, "Ancient Constitution," 202.

3. George D. Bearce, *British Attitudes Towards India 1784–1858* (Oxford: Oxford University Press, 1961), 14. Other early contributors to such a theory are said to have been the Scottish historian William Robertson and the Calcutta judge and linguist Sir William Jones. See also Embree, *Charles Grant and British Rule,* 198.

4. This view, expressed in conventional formulas, was a commonplace of eighteenth-century politicians, including Hastings as well as Burke. The name of Solon was often invoked, though Montesquieu was no doubt the primary authority. Even Rousseau, however, in so "abstract" a work as the *Social Contract* (II.8–10) makes the familiar point.

5. Burke expresses here a common European view of the extreme conservatism of Asia in general and of the Hindus in particular, including the unchanging nature of their customs. Tradition, always important, was more so in India. Burke omits the usual explanation, though he may be alluding to it: that Asian despotism removed all incentives to improvement. Marshall and Williams, *Great Map of Mankind,* 123, 130. On the developing British view that Hinduism was a source of oppression and should be challenged in the interest of popular welfare, see Embree, *Charles Grant and British Rule,* chap. 7.

6. For a contemporary assessment of the value of social norms, see Jon Elster, *The Cement of Society: A Study of Social Order* (Cambridge: Cambridge University Press, 1989), chap. 3. Elster, however, distinguishes social norms from tradition by invidiously defining "tradition" as "mindlessly repeating or imitating today what one's ancestors did yesteryear" (104). Burke contrasts tradition with rationalism in a way that seems close to Elster's contrast between social norms and rational or strategic calculation as a basis for conduct. Neither distinction implies mindlessness.

7. In older civil or Roman law works, the term "usucaption" denoted the acquisition of rights through usage, while "prescription" denoted the loss of rights through disuse. Hence the assertion of "imprescriptible rights" by some American and French revolutionaries: basic rights to liberty and self-government could not be deemed to have been lost through long nonexercise. "Usucaption" itself, however, went out of use, or was not used in England, and Burkean "prescription" refers to the generation of right.

8. Pocock, "Ancient Constitution." Cf. Dreyer, *Burke's Politics,* 74. Dreyer argues plausibly that Burke is not a legal theorist in any significant way and that the legal concept of prescriptive right constitutes at best a small part of his traditionalism, which rests primarily on sociological and moral considerations.

9. Blackstone, *Commentaries,* book 2, chap. 17.

10. This distinction is noted by Wilkins, *Problem*, 200, and is explored more fully in Paul Lucas, "On Edmund Burke's Doctrine of Prescription; Or, an Appeal from the New to the Old Lawyers," *Historical Journal* 11 (1968): 35–63. Lucas claims that Burke usually intended this noncustomary sense of prescription. Since common lawyers, including Blackstone, did not differentiate between custom and prescription in this way, holding that both had to be immemorial, Burke's use of prescription in this sense was not a borrowing from common law. Lucas also points out that most jurists, but not Burke, required bona fides in the possession leading to a prescriptive title, lest a clearly unjust usurpation eventually become good because it is unnoticed or uncontested.

11. For more on prescription, with special reference to Hume, see Frederick G. Whelan, "Time, Revolution, and Prescriptive Right in Hume's Theory of Government," *Utilitas* 7 (1995): 97–119.

12. Paine accused Burke and other adherents of a prescriptive monarchy of not going back far enough (e.g., to before the conquest), and of trying to hide corrupt origins in the mists of time. This criticism, however, misses the point that avoiding disputes about remote origins was one of the explicit purposes of the standard legal doctrine of prescription. Cf. Steven Blakemore, *Burke and the Fall of Language* (Hanover: University Press of New England, 1988), 19.

13. Lucas, "Burke's Doctrine of Prescription," 53–54. A politically charged legal case in 1769 is said to have given prescription new currency; more important, however, both Lucas and Wilkins (in *Problem*, 60–61), suggest that Burke, like Hume, was attracted to prescription as a result of his antirationalism and his general appreciation for the role of custom in social and moral life.

14. Marshall, *New Cambridge History*, 113; Embree, *Charles Grant and British Rule*, 273.

15. Hutchins, *Illusion of Permanence*, 3. See also Marshall, *Problems*, 61.

16. For example, Hastings spoke three Indian languages and could converse directly with rulers such as Shuja al-Daula (Barnett, *North India*, 87); he dispatched the first European expedition to acquire information about Tibet (Marshall and Williams, *Great Map of Mankind*, 88); he supported Sir William Jones in founding the Asiatic Society of Bengal; and he pursued a "cultural policy" of promoting Orientalist scholarship (Kopf, *British Orientalism*, 5, 17–22).

17. Hastings, quoted in Jones, *Hastings in Bengal*, 337. On other occasions Hastings was less tolerant; for example, he overruled a Muslim law that allowed a murderer to be pardoned by the victim's kin as "barbarous" and "contrary to the first principles of Civil Society" (333).

18. Charles Wilkins, a company employee, published his translation of the *Bhagavad Gita* in 1785, after studying Sanskrit in Benares, which Hastings had added to the empire. Hastings is said to have overcome the usual secretiveness of the Brahmin pandits and their reluctance to share their learning with foreigners. Marshall and Williams, *Great Map of Mankind*, 76–77.

19. Warren Hastings, "Letter to Nathaniel Smith" (preface to Wilkins's *Bhagvat-Geeta*), in Marshall, *British Discovery of Hinduism*, 187, 189. In typical Enlightenment

fashion, Hastings seeks evidence of universal human nature and of common ground between Hindu and Christian theology, rather than emphasizing the distinctiveness of Indian culture.

20. Gleig, *Memoirs*, 2:18. Dr. Johnson was at one stage on friendly terms with Hastings, and with William Jones, and was interested in their Orientalist studies. He appears to have developed misgivings about Hastings's military exploits, however, and declined a request by the governor-general in 1784 to prepare a defense of his actions. Thomas M. Curley, *Samuel Johnson and the Age of Travel* (Athens: University of Georgia Press, 1976), 26–27, 235–37.

21. Fox, echoing Burke, argued for example that both in form and substance Chait Singh's resistance was "according to the custom of princes of that country," a point Hastings must have been aware of, but which he disregarded in his punitive response. Bond, *Speeches*, 1:217.

22. Ernest Barker, "Burke on the French Revolution," in *Essays on Government*, 223.

23. Strauss, *Natural Right and History*, 318–19.

24. See Wilkins, *Problem*, 81. Wilkins warns against reading Burke backwards from the nineteenth century. See also Dreyer, *Burke's Politics*, 54. Dreyer emphasizes the universalist themes in Burke as well as his historical sense.

25. Burke's perception of India casts doubt on Wilkins's claim that he lacked a sense of profoundly different cultures and their uniqueness, though Burke did not theorize generally on this subject, in the manner of Herder or Hegel. Wilkins, *Problem*, 81.

26. Burke used this phrase in complimenting William Robertson on his history of America. *Corr.* 3:351.

27. The Oxford edition gives "rights" instead of "rites" in this passage ("Speech on Opening," 277).

28. Burke entertained several Maratha agents—observant Brahmins—who visited England in 1781 (*Corr.* 4:367–68). These were presumably the only Indians Burke ever actually met.

29. Strauss, *Natural Right and History*, 294–96 ff. Strauss notes that all of Burke's statements on natural right "occur in statements *ad hominem* and are meant to serve immediately a specific practical purpose" (295). But, then again, all Burke's political writings and speeches were occasional pieces, addressing some practical issue.

30. Stanlis, *Burke and the Natural Law*, 43, 58, 67; Canavan, *Political Reason*, 18. References to a higher law and general moral principles are certainly present in *Reflections* as well, though in that work they tend to be overshadowed by Burke's traditionalism and other themes.

31. Dreyer, *Burke's Politics*, 69, 66. In placing Burke in the modern natural law tradition, Dreyer explicitly denies that he is a Thomist, insofar as Thomism is different from Lockeianism (80). Burke's self-characterization occurs in his "Appeal from the New to the Old Whigs."

32. Wilkins, *Problem*, chap. 2.

33. Ibid., 32–34.

34. This is noted by Dreyer, *Burke's Politics*, 12. Dreyer canvasses various explanations,

including Burke's possible belief that bribery, and especially "present" taking, can be defined as an offense only by positive law, and thus cannot be condemned in the name of natural law. It seems more likely that Burke was following Aristotle's advice to litigators: if the "written law" supports your case, rest your case on it; if not, appeal to the "universal law" (*Rhetoric* 1:15). I assume that such a sense of legal strategy need not cast doubt on the sincerity of Burke's appeals to the unwritten law on appropriate occasions.

35. Cf. Cone, *Nature of Politics*, 2:228. The fact that all the managers of the impeachment made natural law the centerpiece of their arguments suggests that doing so was an agreed-upon strategy; for Cone, however, this point does not cast doubt on the sincerity of Burke's utterances on the subject.

36. In *Edmund Burke* (98 and 105), O'Gorman first casually dismisses Burke's references to natural law as rhetorical, but later says, more weakly, that there was only "an element of calculation in his rhetoric," in the midst of a morally serious critique of Hastings and the Indian empire. The point is that Burke embraced moral principles that overrode Hastings's appeal to success, and that it was principle, not partisanship, that determined his position on India.

37. In *Burke and the Natural law* (54–55), Stanlis suggests that protection against arbitrary power was a major practical expression of Burke's belief in natural law.

38. In "Burke and India," Conniff argues that Burke turned to a natural law standard for the Indian empire after becoming convinced that a trusteeship conception of government would not work there, given the absence of both procedural accountability and a sympathetic bond of trust between rulers and ruled. Evidence of Burke's adherence to natural law predates his Indian involvement, however, and he invoked it from the outset of his Indian campaign.

39. This appeal to a universal moral law evokes Cicero's famous description of a law that is eternally the same, in Athens as in Rome (*De republica* 3.22).

40. Burke's characterization of the eternal law in these passages is traditional, that is, Ciceronian (Stoic) or Thomist; the insistence on the impermissibility of arbitrary government as the content of natural law might be a modern (Lockeian or liberal) theme, as might assertions such as: "To name a man a Magistrate is to say that the Subject has a property to be preserved" ("Speech on Opening," 470).

41. The use of the phrase "supreme power" rather than "sovereign" is Lockeian, but Burke draws upon the standard theory that sovereignty in the sense indicated is a necessity in a state.

42. Mansfield shows that Burke appealed to God far more often in his impeachment speeches to the House of Lords (with its bishops) than in his Indian speeches in the Commons (*Statesmanship and Party Government*, 259–60, n. 54). There are difficulties with the implication that Burke was simply making opportune use of Christian rhetoric, however, apart from the point that his having done so need not impugn the reality of his own faith. Only a few bishops attended the proceedings (Ditchfield, "House of Lords and the Impeachment," 289), and most of these were pro-Hastings from the start, as Burke knew (*Corr.* 5:341). It was primarily in the speeches to the House of Lords that Burke made his natural—or divine—law case against Hastings.

43. The best discussion is in Wilkins, *Problem*, part 2. The assumption of an underlying human nature was fairly standard among most eighteenth-century thinkers, though they often differed in their account of it.

44. To illustrate the point that taste and intelligence are similar everywhere, Burke tells the story of an Asian ruler's reaction to a European picture of the head of John the Baptist. Burke, however, omits the sequel, in which the ruler orders a slave to be beheaded in order to check the picture's verisimilitude. Burke, *Sublime and Beautiful*, 20. The full story raises troubling questions not only about human nature but also about Asian governance.

45. O'Brien, *Great Melody*, 505.

46. Whelan, "Vattel's Doctrine." The dominant "naturalist" school of early modern international law extended from the sixteenth-century Spanish Thomists through Grotius to Vattel, the leading authority during Burke's period.

47. Examples of ambiguity in legal translation that figured importantly in the Burke-Hastings dispute were the exact position and property rights of zamindars in Bengal, and the exact status and obligations of a subordinate ruler or vassal such as Chait Singh.

48. See Alexandrowicz, *Law of Nations in the East Indies*. In addition to the Mogul emperor, the major sovereigns in the area were the kings of Persia, Ceylon, Burma, and Siam; lesser independent states included Mysore and the Maratha Confederacy in India and the sultanates of the Malay peninsula and archipelago. In the early nineteenth century, the natural law approach declined and a positivist doctrine of international law developed, based on the actual practices of civilized states. Since "civilized" referred to a European "standard of civilization" which no non-European societies met, and since only a few Asian states were gradually admitted to the European system, this modern international law was more parochial than the earlier law of nations (10). Philosophically, this shift reflected the replacement of natural law by positivism in European social thought; politically, it expressed the growing dominance of Europe and European imperialism in the world.

49. Alexandrowicz agrees that Chait Singh was entitled to more respectful treatment under the law of nations as understood in India. Alexandrowicz, *Law of Nations in the East Indies*, 23, 152, 231.

50. Burke referred to Vattel's *Droit des gens*, book 1, chap. 16, which is entitled "Voluntary Submission of a State to a Foreign Power in Order to Obtain Protection" and emphasizes the contractual nature of such voluntary arrangements and the rights retained by the weaker party in case of nonprotection.

51. One must carefully distinguish the political revolution that established British rule in Bengal, which Burke accepted, from the following social revolution, which he condemned.

52. Marshall expresses this verdict on Burke's intentions, though he believes Burke was often mistaken about the facts. Marshall, *Impeachment*, 186.

53. Burke, however, never expressed support for actual rebellion in Ireland. He disapproved of the Irish Volunteer movement of 1782, which in his view "extorted" legislative independence on terms unfavorable to the Catholic majority (Mahoney, *Burke and*

Ireland, 134), and he deplored the growing disturbances in the 1790s, in which the French were sometimes involved.

54. Cf. Freeman, *Critique of Political Radicalism,* 18, 136–37. Burke's sympathy for the oppressed is the theme of O'Brien, *Great Melody.*

55. Burke defended liberty as the "birthright of our species," but he explained he did not mean "solitary, unconnected, individual, selfish liberty, as if every man was to regulate the whole of his conduct by his own will," but rather "*social* freedom," marked by "equality of restraint" and virtually equivalent to justice ("Letter to Depont," 7).

56. Mahoney, *Burke and Ireland,* 320.

57. Sheridan, speaking as an impeachment manager, praised Burke as a defender of the "rights of man against man's oppression" in India. Bond, *Speeches,* 1:481. This was a contentious characterization, given Burke's concurrent attack on the French "rights of man" and the controversy this provoked with Paine and others. Sometimes, to be sure, Burke clearly ranked "happiness" above rights as a standard for government ("Unitarian Petition," 45).

58. Hence Burke's shifts from duties to rights need not raise doubts about whether he adhered to classical or modern natural right, or be interpreted as rhetorical choices, as Strauss suggested. They are consistent with the logic of the theory.

59. Cf. Strauss, *Natural Right and History,* 298; Canavan, *Political Reason,* 118–19; Wilkins, *Problem,* 230.

60. In *New Cambridge History* (62), Marshall writes that the usual response to excessive tax demands was desertion rather than revolt, since land was abundant in eighteenth-century Bengal and many peasants were migratory. Burke suggested that the more rigorous and efficient British regime suppressed this pattern and its deterrent effects on oppression.

61. Hastings, "Insurrection," 170–71. Hastings openly admits that many of the notables and former officials of Oudh, whom he viewed as largely corrupt, were indeed threatened by company influence over Asaf al-Daula, and hated the English. The problem of distinguishing between spontaneity and organization in explaining the rapid spread of violence was to come up again in the case of the great "Mutiny" or rebellion of 1857, which strongly affected this same region, among others.

62. Again speaking of Ireland, in 1792 Burke more cautiously maintained that disturbances at least sometimes have "just complaints for their origin" (*Letter to Langrishe,* 630).

63. Morley, *Burke, a Historical Study,* 150–52. In *Burke and the Natural Law* (47), Stanlis argues that Burke's "expediency" is better understood as classical prudence than as anything like Benthamite calculation. Consequences matter in either case.

64. The claim that prescription was part of natural law was tenable but debatable in the eighteenth century, according to Lucas; many jurists upheld prescription in terms not of equity but of its social utility in restricting litigation and creating security of property. Thus, there was a triple convergence of the apparently quite distinct standards of prescription, utility, and natural law. Lucas, "Burke's Doctrine of Prescription," 39.

65. Wilkins, *Problem,* 14. Strauss is correct in saying that substantive beneficence is the basis of government legitimacy for Burke, but incorrect in saying that Burkean prescrip-

tion is simply "proved beneficence" (over time). Strauss, *Natural Right and History,* 199. If prescription generates strong rights, it can obstruct beneficent policies, as Strauss later observes (319).

66. On the convergence of different normative criteria in Burke, see Freeman, *Political Radicalism,* 92–96, 101.

67. Stephen, *English Thought,* 187.

68. Strauss, *Natural Right and History,* 295, 321. Cicero's *De republica* is rightly said to be close in spirit to Burke's views on the English constitution. Burke frequently cites Cicero, but he could have known this particular work only in the fragments that were available in the eighteenth century; there was a similarity in theory between the two thinkers, not necessarily direct influence.

69. Hampsher-Monk, "Rhetoric and Opinion," 459.

70. For a clear statement, see David Hume, "Of Refinement in the Arts," *Essays,* 275. As Colley notes (*Britons,* 102), Gibbon began his *Decline and Fall* in the year after the Treaty of Paris. The lesson drawn from the conventional story of Rome's corruption and decline was a reason for many in England to oppose the acquisition of an Asian empire until the end of the eighteenth century. Opponents of the empire admiringly compared Tipu Sultan of Mysore, who resisted the British until his defeat in 1799, to Hannibal resisting Rome. Marshall and Williams, *Great Map of Mankind,* 155–57. Macaulay ("Hastings," 634) cemented this link in the minds of later generations by remarking on the presence of "the historian of the Roman Empire" at the opening of the impeachment.

71. In "The Impeachments of Verres and Hastings: Cicero and Burke," *Classical Journal* 9 (1913–1914): 199–211, H. V. Canter considers similarities of form and style for the most part. Cicero's query, whether one thing is just in Rome, another in Sicily, is echoed in Burke's denunciation of geographical morality (209). Politically, the prosecution of Verres in 69 B.C. was a democratic attack on oligarchical corruption (204); Fox, but not Burke, might have conceived of Hastings's impeachment in similar terms. In "Burke as Modern Cicero," in *The Impeachment of Warren Hastings,* ed. Geoffrey Carnall and Colin Nicholson (Edinburgh: Edinburgh University Press, 1989), Geoffrey Carnall points out that the absence of scandal in Hastings's private life, unlike Verres's, removed a potential line of attack (85); Burke did, however (perhaps unconvincingly), argue that Hastings was personally corrupt.

72. Wilkins, *Problem,* 36, 194–95. Coke and Blackstone, both of whom Burke cites approvingly, held this view. Property, prescription, due process, and other procedural requirements of the rule of law, as well as an extensive set of individual rights or liberties, were indicated by the higher law and spelled out precisely in common law.

73. This orientation is implied by Pocock, "Ancient Constitution."

74. This thesis is suggested by Barker in "Burke and the French Revolution" (226), and is developed in Clark, *English Society,* 247–58. The Anglican view presents itself as a special case of the larger theory of a "Christian commonwealth" in accordance with Christian natural law, but even in the extended version the theory could not embrace a non-Christian society such as India.

75. See Welsh, *Burke and International Relations,* chap. 3.

BIBLIOGRAPHY

1. Works of Burke

I have used two editions of Burke's collected works, giving preference to the new Oxford edition, which promises to become standard, though it remains incomplete and omits some well-attested materials included in older editions of Burke's works. On some problems of editing Burke's speeches, see P. J. Marshall's remarks in the Oxford edition, 6:265–66.

The Writings and Speeches of Edmund Burke. Boston: Little Brown, 1901. 12 volumes. Cited below as *Boston.*

The Writings and Speeches of Edmund Burke. Ed. Paul Langford. Oxford: Clarendon Press, 1981–. Cited below as *Oxford.*

For sake of convenience, I also refer to a paperback edition of Burke's *Reflections* (see below) and to the following collection:

Further Reflections on the Revolution in France. Ed. Daniel E. Ritchie. Indianapolis: Liberty Fund, 1992. Cited below as *Further Reflections.*

Particular works of Burke are cited in the text using the following abbreviated titles:

"Address to the Colonists"	"Address to the British Colonists in North America" (1777). In *Boston,* vol. 6.
"Address to the King"	"Address to the King" (1777). In *Boston,* vol. 6.
"Almas Ali Khan"	"Speech on Almas Ali Khan" (1784). In *Oxford,* vol. 5.
American Taxation	*Speech on American Taxation* (1774). In *Oxford,* vol. 2.
"Appeal"	"An Appeal from the New to the Old Whigs" (1791). In *Further Reflections.*
Arcot's Debts	*Speech on Nabob of Arcot's Debts* (1785). In *Oxford,* vol. 5.
"Articles of Charge"	"Articles of Charge of High Crimes and Misdemeanors Against Warren Hastings, Esquire, Late Governor-General of Bengal" (1786). In *Boston,* vols. 8–9.

347

"Articles of Impeachment"	"Articles of Impeachment" (1787). In *Oxford*, vol. 6.
"Bengal Judicature"	"Speech on Bengal Judicature Bill" (1781). In *Oxford*, vol. 5.
"Bill to Amend"	"Speech on Bill to Amend 1784 India Act" (1786). In *Oxford*, vol. 6.
"Conciliation"	"Speech on Moving Resolutions for Conciliation with America" (1775). In *Boston*, vol. 2.
Conquests	*Policy of Making Conquests for the Mahometans* (1779). In *Oxford*, vol. 5.
Corr.	*The Correspondence of Edmund Burke*. Ed. Thomas W. Copeland. 10 vols. Cambridge and Chicago: Cambridge University Press and University of Chicago Press, 1958–1978.
"East India Select Committee"	"Speech on East India Select Committee" (1772). In *Oxford*, vol. 2.
"East India Settlement"	"Speech on East India Settlement" (1769). In *Oxford*, vol. 2.
"Economical Reform"	"Speech on . . . a Plan for the Better Security of the Independence of Parliament, and the Economical Reformation of the Civil and Other Establishments" (1780). In *Boston*, vol. 2.
"Electors of Bristol"	"Speech to the Electors of Bristol (1774). In *Boston*, vol. 2.
Eleventh Report	*Eleventh Report of Select Committee* (1783). In *Oxford*, vol. 5.
"Evidence"	"Evidence on Begams of Oudh" (1788). In *Oxford*, vol. 6.
First Report	*First Report Select Committee: "Observations"* (1782). In *Oxford*, vol. 5.
Fox's Bill	*Speech on Fox's India Bill* (1783). In *Oxford*, vol. 5.
"French Affairs"	"Thoughts on French Affairs" (1791). In *Further Reflections*.
"Letter to Bingham"	"Letter to Sir Charles Bingham" (1773). In *Oxford*, vol. 9.
"Letter to Depont"	"Letter to Charles-Jean-François Depont" (1789). In *Further Reflections*.
Letter to Langrishe	*Letter to Sir Hercules Langrishe* (1792). In *Oxford*, vol. 9.
Letter to Kenmare	*Letter to Lord Kenmare* (1782). In *Oxford*, vol. 9.
"Motion for Papers"	"Speech on Motion for Papers on Hastings" (1786). In *Oxford*, vol. 6.

"National Assembly"   "A Letter to a Member of the National Assembly" (1791). In *Further Reflections*.

"Negro Code"   "A Letter to the Right Hon. Henry Dundas . . . with the Sketch of a Negro Code" (1792). In *Boston*, vol. 6.

Ninth Report   *Ninth Report of Select Committee* (1783). In *Oxford*, vol. 5.

Noble Lord   *A Letter to a Noble Lord* (1796). In *Further Reflections*.

"North's Resolutions"   "Speech on North's East India Resolutions" (1773). In *Oxford*, vol. 2.

"Notice of Motion"   "Speech on Notice of Motion on Hastings" (1786). In *Oxford*, vol. 6.

Policy of Allies   *Remarks on the Policy of the Allies* (1793). In *Oxford*, vol. 8.

"Popery Laws"   "Tracts Relating to Popery Laws" (1765). In *Oxford*, vol. 9.

Present Discontents   *Thoughts on the Present Discontents* (1770). In *Oxford*, vol. 2.

Reflections   *Reflections on the Revolution in France* (1790). Ed. Conor Cruise O'Brien. Harmondsworth: Penguin, 1968.

Regicide Peace 1   *First Letter on a Regicide Peace* (1796). In *Oxford*, vol. 9.

Regicide Peace 3   *Third Letter on a Regicide Peace*, (1797). In *Oxford*, vol. 9.

"Richard Burke"   "Letter to Richard Burke" (1792). In *Oxford*, vol. 9.

"Rohilla Speech"   "Speech on Rohilla War Charge" (1786). In *Oxford*, vol. 6.

"Scarcity"   "Thoughts and Details on Scarcity" (1795). In *Boston*, vol. 5.

"Second Letter to Langrishe"   "Second Letter to Sir Hercules Langrishe" (1795). In *Oxford*, vol. 9.

Sheriffs of Bristol   *A Letter to John Farr and John Harris, Esqrs., Sheriffs of the City of Bristol, on the Affairs of America* (1777). In *Boston*, vol. 2.

"Sixth Article"   "Speech on the Sixth Article of Charge" (1789). In *Boston*, vol. 10.

"Speech at Arrival"   "Speech at His Arrival at Bristol" (1774). In *Boston*, vol. 2.

"Speech in Opening"   "Speeches in the Impeachment of Warren Hastings, Esquire, Late Governor-General of Bengal. Speech in Opening the Impeachment" (1788). In *Boston*, vols. 9–10.

"Speech in Reply"   "Speech in General Reply" (1794). In *Boston*, vols. 11–12.

"Speech on Opening"   "Speech on Opening of Impeachment" (1788). In *Oxford*, vol. 6.

"Speech on
Representation"

"Speech on a Motion . . . to Inquire into the State of the
Representation of the Commons in Parliament" (1782). In
Boston, vol. 7.

Sublime and Beautiful

*A Philosophical Enquiry into the Origin of Our Ideas of the
Sublime and Beautiful* (1757). Ed. James T. Boulton. Notre
Dame: University of Notre Dame Press, 1958.

"Unitarian Petition"

"Speech on . . . a Petition of the Unitarian Society" (1792). In
Boston, vol. 7.

2. Other Works

Alexandrowicz, C. H. *An Introduction to the History of the Law of Nations in the East Indies*. Oxford: Clarendon Press, 1967.

Aristotle, *Rhetoric* (with *Poetics*). Trans. W. Rhys Roberts. New York: Modern Library, 1954.

Ayling, Stanley. *The Elder Pitt*. New York: David McKay, 1976.

Bacon, Francis. "The Humble Submission and Supplication of the Lord Chancellor." In *The Works of Francis Bacon*. Ed. James Spedding et al. Vol. 14. 1874. Reprint, New York: Garrett, 1968.

———. "Of Plantations." In *Francis Bacon's Essays*. London: Dent, 1968.

Barker, Ernest. *Essays on Government*. 2d ed. Oxford: Clarendon Press, 1951.

Barker, Francis, Peter Hulme, Margaret Iverson, and Diana Loxley, eds. *Literature, Politics, and Theory*. London and New York: Methuen, 1986.

Barnett, Richard B. *North India Between Empires: Awadh, the Mughals, and the British 1720–1801*. Berkeley: University of California Press, 1980.

Bayly, C. A. *Rulers, Townsmen and Bazaars: North Indian Society in the Age of British Expansion 1770–1870*. Cambridge: Cambridge University Press, 1983.

Bearce, George D. *British Attitudes Towards India 1784–1858*. Oxford: Oxford University Press, 1961.

Blackstone, William. *Commentaries on the Laws of England*. Vol. 4. Facsimile of the First Edition of 1765–1769. Chicago: University of Chicago Press, 1979.

Blakemore, Steven. *Burke and the Fall of Language*. Hanover: University Press of New England, 1988.

Bond, E. A., ed. *Speeches of the Managers and Counsel in the Trial of Warren Hastings*. 4 vols. London: Longman, Brown, Green, Longmans, and Roberts, 1859.

Brewer, John. *The Sinews of Power: War, Money and the English State, 1688–1783*. London: Unwin Hyman, 1989.

Browne, Stephen H. *Edmund Burke and the Discourse of Virtue*. Tuscaloosa: University of Alabama Press, 1993.

Bruyn, Frans de. "Edmund Burke's Gothic Romance: The Portrayal of Warren Hastings in Burke's Writings and Speeches on India." *Criticism* 29 (1987): 415–38.

Canavan, Francis P. *The Political Reason of Edmund Burke*. Durham: Duke University Press, 1960.

Cannon, John. *The Fox-North Coalition*. Cambridge: Cambridge University Press, 1969.

Canter, H. V. "The Impeachments of Verres and Hastings: Cicero and Burke." *Classical Journal* 9 (1913–1914): 199–211.

Carnall, Geoffrey. "Burke as Modern Cicero." In Carnall and Nicholson, eds., *Impeachment*.

Carnall, Geoffrey, and Colin Nicholson, eds. *The Impeachment of Warren Hastings*. Edinburgh: Edinburgh University Press, 1989.

Chapman, Gerald W. *Edmund Burke; The Practical Imagination*. Cambridge: Harvard University Press, 1967.

Clark, J. C. D. *English Society 1688–1832*. Cambridge: Cambridge University Press, 1985.

Colley, Linda. *Britons: Forging the Nation 1707–1837*. New Haven: Yale University Press, 1992.

Cone, Carl B. *Burke and the Nature of Politics*. 2 vols. University of Kentucky Press, 1957.

Conniff, James. "Burke and India: The Failure of the Theory of Trusteeship." *Political Research Quarterly* 46 (1993): 291–309.

Constant, Benjamin. *Principles of Politics Applicable to All Representative Governments*. In *Political Writings*. Ed. and trans. Biancamaria Fontana. Cambridge: Cambridge University Press, 1988.

Courtney, C. P. *Montesquieu and Burke*. Oxford: Blackwell, 1963.

Curley, Thomas M. *Samuel Johnson and the Age of Travel*. Athens: University of Georgia Press, 1976.

Dasgupta, A. P. *The Central Authority in British India 1774–1784*. Calcutta: Calcutta University Press, 1931.

Davies, C. Collin. *Warren Hastings and Oudh*. London: Oxford University Press, 1939.

———. "Warren Hastings and the Younger Pitt." *English Historical Review* 70 (1955): 609–22.

Ditchfield, G. M. "The House of Lords and the Impeachment of Warren Hastings." *Parliamentary History* 13 (1994): 277–96.

Dreyer, Frederick A. *Burke's Politics: A Study in Whig Orthodoxy*. Waterloo: Wilfrid Laurier University Press, 1979.

Edwardes, Michael. *Warren Hastings: King of the Nabobs*. London: Hart-Davis, Mac-Gibbon, 1976.

Elster, Jon. *The Cement of Society: A Study of Social Order*. Cambridge: Cambridge University Press, 1989.

Embree, Ainslie Thomas. *Charles Grant and British Rule in India*. New York: Columbia University Press, 1962.

Feiling, Keith. *Warren Hastings*. London: Macmillan, 1954.

Forrest, G. W., ed. *Selections from the State Papers of the Governors-General of India*. Vol. 2, *Warren Hastings: Documents*. Oxford: Blackwell, 1910.

Freeman, Michael. *Edmund Burke and the Critique of Political Radicalism*. Chicago: University of Chicago Press, 1980.

Fry, Michael. *The Dundas Despotism*. Edinburgh: Edinburgh University Press, 1992.

Furber, Holden. "Edmund Burke and India." *Bengal Past and Present* 76 (1957): 11–21.

Gibbon, Edward. *The Decline and Fall of the Roman Empire*. Vol. 2. New York: Modern Library, n.d.

——. *The Letters of Edward Gibbon*. Ed. J. E. Norton. Vol. 2. New York: Macmillan, 1956.

Gleig, G. R. *Memoirs of the Life of the Right Hon. Warren Hastings, First Governor-General of Bengal*. 3 vols. London: Richard Bentley, 1841.

Guha, Ranajit. *A Rule of Property for Bengal*. Paris: Mouton, 1963.

Hampsher-Monk, Iain. "Rhetoric and Opinion in the Politics of Edmund Burke." *History of Political Thought* 9 (1988): 455–84.

Hastings, Warren. "Letter to Nathaniel Smith." Preface to Wilkins's *Bhagvat-Geeta*. In Marshall, *British Discovery of Hinduism*.

——. Letter to Willam Pitt, Dec. 11, 1784. In Davies, "Warren Hastings and the Younger Pitt."

——. *Warren Hastings' Letters to Sir John MacPherson*. Ed. Henry Dodwell. London: Faber and Gwyer, 1927.

——. "Memoirs Relative to the State of India." In Forrest, *Selections*.

——. "Minutes of What Was Offered by Warren Hastings, Esquire, Late Governor General of Bengal at the Bar of the House of Commons . . ." *Journals of the House of Commons* 41 (May 1–2, 1786): 668–733.

——. "A Narrative of the Insurrection Which Happened in the Zemeedary of Banaris in the Month of August, 1781, and of the Transactions of the Governor-General in that District." In Forrest, *Selections*.

See also entries under Bond and Gleig.

Himmelfarb, Gertrude. *The Idea of Poverty: England in the Early Industrial Age*. New York: Knopf, 1984.

——. *Victorian Minds*. New York: Knopf, 1968.

Holzman, James M. *The Nabobs in England: A Study of the Returned Anglo-Indian, 1760–1785*. New York, 1926.

Hume, David. *Essays Moral, Political, and Literary*. Ed. Eugene F. Miller. Rev. ed. Indianapolis: Liberty Classics, 1987.

——. *The History of England*. Boston: Phillips, Sampson, 1849.

Hutchins, Francis G. *The Illusion of Permanence: British Imperialism in India*. Princeton: Princeton University Press, 1967.

Janes, Regina. "At Home Abroad: Edmund Burke in India." *Bulletin of Research in the Humanities* 82 (1979): 160–74.

——. "Edmund Burke's Flying Leap from India to France." *History of European Ideas* 7 (1986): 509–27.

——. "Edmund Burke's Indian Idyll." *Studies in Eighteenth-Century Culture*. Ed. Roseann Ruate. Vol. 9. Madison: University of Wisconsin Press, 1979.

Jones, M. E. Monckton. *Warren Hastings in Bengal 1772–1774*. Oxford: Clarendon Press, 1918.

Kant, Immanuel. *Kant's Political Writings*. Ed. Hans Reiss. Cambridge: Cambridge University Press, 1970.

Koebner, R. "Despot and Despotism: Vicissitudes of a Political Term." *Journal of the Warburg and Courtauld Institutes* 14 (1951): 275–302.

Kopf, David. *British Orientalism and the Bengal Renaissance*. Berkeley: University of California Press, 1969.

Kramnick, Isaac. "The Left and Edmund Burke." *Political Theory* 11:2 (1983): 189–214.

——. *The Rage of Edmund Burke*. New York: Basic Books, 1977.

Langford, Paul. *A Polite and Commercial People: England 1727–1783*. Oxford: Clarendon Press, 1989.

Lock, F. P. *Burke's Reflections on the Revolution in France*. London: George Allen and Unwin, 1985.

Lucas, Paul. "On Edmund Burke's Doctrine of Prescription; Or, An Appeal from the New to the Old Lawyers." *The Historical Journal* 11 (1968): 35–63.

Macaulay, Thomas Babington. "Lord Clive" and "Warren Hastings." In *Critical and Historical Essays*. Vol. 1. London: Dent, 1966.

Machiavelli, Niccolò. *The Prince and the Discourses*. Trans. Luigi Ricci and Christian E. Detmold. New York: Modern Library, 1950.

Macpherson, C. B. *Burke*. New York: Hill and Wang, 1980.

Mahoney, Thomas H. D. *Edmund Burke and Ireland*. Cambridge: Harvard University Press, 1960.

Mansfield, Harvey C., Jr. *Statesmanship and Party Government: A Study of Burke and Bolingbroke*. Chicago: University of Chicago Press, 1965.

——. *Taming the Prince: The Ambivalence of Modern Executive Power*. Baltimore: Johns Hopkins University Press, 1993.

Marshall, P. J. *East Indian Fortunes: The British in Bengal in the Eighteenth Century*. Oxford: Clarendon Press, 1976.

——. *The Impeachment of Warren Hastings*. Oxford: Oxford University Press, 1965.

——. *The New Cambridge History of India*. Vol. 2, *Bengal: The British Bridgehead. Eastern India 1740–1828*. Cambridge: Cambridge University Press, 1987.

——. *Problems of Empire: Britain and India 1757–1813*. London: George Allen and Unwin, 1968.

Marshall, P. J., ed. *The British Discovery of Hinduism in the Eighteenth Century*. Cambridge: Cambridge University Press, 1970.

Marshall, P. J., and Glyndwr Williams. *The Great Map of Mankind: Perceptions of New Worlds in the Age of Enlightenment*. Cambridge: Harvard University Press, 1982.

Meinecke, Friedrich. *Machiavellism: The Doctrine of Raison d'Etat and Its Place in Modern History*. Trans. Douglas Scott. London: Routledge and Kegan Paul, 1957.

Mill, John Stuart. "A Few Words on Non-Intervention." In *Essays on Politics and Culture*. Ed. Gertrude Himmelfarb. Garden City: Anchor, 1963.

——. "On Liberty." In *Essays on Politics and Society*. Ed. J. M. Robson. Vol. 18 of *Collected Works of John Stuart Mill*. Toronto: University of Toronto Press, 1977.

Mitchell, L. G. *Charles James Fox and the Disintegration of the Whig Party 1782–1794*. Oxford: Oxford University Press, 1971.

Montesquieu. *The Spirit of the Laws*. Ed. and trans. Anne M. Cohler, Basia Carolyn Miller, and Harold Samuel Stone. Cambridge: Cambridge University Press, 1989.

Moon, Penderel. *Warren Hastings and British India*. New York: Collier, 1962.

Morley, John. *Burke*. 1888. Reprint, London: Macmillan, 1913.

——. *Edmund Burke, a Historical Study*. 1866. Reprint, New York: Knopf, 1924.

Musselwhite, David. "The Trial of Warren Hastings." In Barker et al., *Literature, Politics, and Theory*.

Namier, Sir Lewis. *England in the Age of the American Revolution*. 2d ed. London: Macmillan, 1961.

Noonan, John T., Jr. *Bribes*. New York: Macmillan, 1984.

O'Brien, Conor Cruise. *The Great Melody: A Thematic Biography and Commented Anthology of Edmund Burke*. Chicago: University of Chicago Press, 1992.

——. Introduction to Burke, *Reflections*.

——. "Warren Hastings in Burke's Great Melody." In Carnall and Nicholson, eds., *Impeachment*.

O'Gorman, Frank. *Edmund Burke: His Political Philosophy*. Bloomington: Indiana University Press, 1973.

——. *Voters, Patrons, and Parties: The Unreformed Electoral System of Hanoverian England 1734–1832*. Oxford: Clarendon Press, 1989.

Paine, Thomas. *Rights of Man*. Harmondsworth: Penguin, 1969.

Parker, Geoffrey. "Europe and the Wider World, 1500–1750: The Military Balance." In *The Political Economy of Merchant Empires*. Ed. James D. Tracy. Cambridge: Cambridge University Press, 1991.

Paulson, Ronald. *Representations of Revolution (1789–1820)*. New Haven: Yale University Press, 1983.

Pitkin, Hanna Fenichel. *The Concept of Representation*. Berkeley: University of California Press, 1972.

Pocock, J. G. A. "Burke and the Ancient Constitution: A Problem in the History of Ideas." In *Politics, Language, and Time*. New York: Atheneum, 1973.

——. Introduction. In *Reflections on the Revolution in France*. By Edmund Burke. Ed. J. G. A. Pocock. Indianapolis: Hackett, 1987.

——. "The Political Economy of Burke's Analysis of the French Revolution." In *Virtue, Commerce, and History*. Cambridge: Cambridge University Press, 1985.

——. "Edmund Burke and the Redefinition of Enthusiasm: The Context as Counter-Revolution." In *The French Revolution and the Creation of Modern Political Culture*. Ed. François Furet and Mona Ozouf. Vol. 3. Oxford: Pergamon Press, 1989.

Pole, J. R. *Political Representation in England and the Origins of the American Republic*. Berkeley: University of California Press, 1966.

Reid, Christopher. *Edmund Burke and the Practice of Political Writing.* Dublin: Gill and Macmillan, 1985.

Richter, Melvin. "Despotism." *Dictionary of the History of Ideas.* Vol. 2. New York: Scribner's, 1973.

Riddy, J. "Warren Hastings: Scotland's Benefactor?" In Carnall and Nicholson, eds., *Impeachment.*

Robertson, John. "Universal Monarchy and the Liberties of Europe: David Hume's Critique of an English Whig Doctrine." In *Political Discourse in Early Modern Britain.* Ed. Nicholas Phillipson and Quentin Skinner. Cambridge: Cambridge University Press, 1993.

Rocher, Rosane. *Orientalism, Poetry, and the Millennium: The Checkered Life of Nathaniel Brassey Halhed 1751–1830.* Columbia, Missouri: South Asia Books, 1983.

Sanyal, Suprakash. *Benares and the English East India Company, 1764–1795.* Calcutta: World Press, 1979.

Schama, Simon. *Citizens: A Chronicle of the French Revolution.* New York: Knopf, 1989.

Schwartz, Bernard. "Edmund Burke and the Law." *Law Quarterly Review* 95 (1979): 355–75.

Shklar, Judith N. *Montesquieu.* Oxford: Oxford University Press, 1987.

——. *Ordinary Vices.* Cambridge: Harvard University Press, 1984.

Smith, Adam. *An Inquiry into the Nature and Causes of the Wealth of Nations.* Ed. Edwin Cannan. New York: Modern Library, 1937.

Speer, Richard. "The Rhetoric of Burke's Select Committee Reports." *Quarterly Journal of Speech* 57 (1971): 306–15.

Stanlis, Peter J. *Edmund Burke and the Natural Law.* Ann Arbor: University of Michigan Press, 1958.

Stephen, Sir James Fitzjames. *The Story of Nuncomar and the Impeachment of Sir Elijah Impey.* 2 vols. London: Macmillan, 1885.

Stephen, Sir Leslie. *History of English Thought in the Eighteenth Century.* Vol. 2. 1876. Reprint, New York: Harcourt, Brace, and World, 1962.

Stokes, Eric. *The English Utilitarians and India.* Oxford: Clarendon Press, 1959.

Strachey, John. *Hastings and the Rohilla War.* Oxford: Clarendon Press, 1892.

Strauss, Leo. *Natural Right and History.* Chicago: University of Chicago Press, 1953.

Suleri, Sara. *The Rhetoric of English India.* Chicago: University of Chicago Press, 1992.

Sutherland, Lucy S. *The East India Company in Eighteenth-Century Politics.* Oxford: Clarendon Press, 1952.

Thomas, Keith. "How Britain Made It." *New York Review of Books,* Nov. 19, 1992, 35–38.

Thomson, Janice E. *Mercenaries, Pirates, and Sovereigns: State-Building and Extraterritorial Violence in Early Modern Europe.* Princeton: Princeton University Press, 1994.

Tuck, Richard. *Philosophy and Government 1572–1651.* Cambridge: Cambridge University Press, 1993.

Venturi, Franco. "Oriental Despotism." *Journal of the History of Ideas* 24 (1963): 133–42.

Viroli, Maurizio. *From Politics to Reason of State*. Cambridge: Cambridge University Press, 1992.

Voltaire. *Essai sur les moeurs et l'esprit des nations*. Ed. René Pomeau. 2 vols. Paris: Garnier, 1963.

Walpole, Horace. *Selected Letters of Horace Walpole*. Ed. W. S. Lewis. New Haven: Yale University Press, 1973.

Weitzman, Sophia. *Warren Hastings and Philip Francis*. Manchester: Manchester University Press, 1929.

Welsh, Jennifer M. *Edmund Burke and International Relations: The Commonwealth of Europe and the Crusade against the French Revolution*. New York: St. Martin's, 1995.

Whelan, Frederick G. "Socrates and the Meddlesomeness of the Athenians." *History of Political Thought* 4 (1983): 1–29.

——. "Time, Revolution, and Prescriptive Right in Hume's Theory of Government." *Utilitas* 7 (1995): 97–119.

——. "Vattel's Doctrine of the State." *History of Political Thought* 9 (1988): 59–90.

White, Stephen K. "Burke on Politics, Aesthetics, and the Dangers of Modernity." *Political Theory* 21 (1993): 507–27.

Wilkins, Burleigh Taylor. *The Problem of Burke's Political Philosophy*. Oxford: Clarendon Press, 1967.

Willis, Kirk. "The Role in Parliament of the Economic Ideas of Adam Smith, 1776–1800." *History of Political Economy* 11 (1979): 505–44.

Winch, Donald. *Classical Political Economy and Colonies*. Cambridge: Harvard University Press, 1965.

Wood, Neal. "The Aesthetic Dimension of Burke's Political Thought." *Journal of British Studies* 4 (1964): 41–64.

INDEX